Understanding Community Colleges

Understanding Community Colleges provides a comprehensive review of the community college landscape—management and governance, finance, student demographics and development, teaching and learning, policy, faculty, and workforce development—and bridges the gap between research and practice. This contributed volume brings together highly respected scholars in the field who rely upon substantial theoretical perspectives—critical theory, social theory, institutional theory, and organizational theory—for a rich and expansive analysis of community colleges. The latest text to publish in the *Core Concepts in Higher Education* series, this exciting new text fills a gap in the higher education literature available for students enrolled in Higher Education and Community College graduate programs.

This text provides students with:
- A review of salient research related to the community college field.
- Critical theoretical perspectives underlying current policies.
- An understanding of how theory links to practice, including focused end-of-chapter discussion questions.
- A fresh examination of emerging issues and insight into contemporary community college practices and policy.

John S. Levin is Bank of America Professor of Education Leadership and Director of the California Community College Collaborative, University of California, Riverside, USA.

Susan T. Kater is Director of Institutional Planning, Research, and Effectiveness at GateWay Community College, Phoenix, Arizona.

Core Concepts in Higher Education
Series Editors: Edward P. St. John and Marybeth Gasman

The History of U.S. Higher Education: Methods for Understanding the Past
Marybeth Gasman, editor

Understanding Community Colleges
John S. Levin and Susan T. Kater, editors

Forthcoming

Reframing Strategies for Preparation, Access, and Success
Edward P. St. John, Natan Daun-Barnett, and Karen Moronski-Chapman

Organizational Theory in Higher Education
Kathleen Manning

Understanding Community Colleges

Edited by

John S. Levin and Susan T. Kater

Routledge
Taylor & Francis Group

NEW YORK AND LONDON

First published 2013
by Routledge
711 Third Avenue, New York, NY 10017

Simultaneously published in the UK
by Routledge
2 Park Square, Milton Park, Abingdon, Oxon OX14 4RN

Routledge is an imprint of the Taylor & Francis Group, an informa business

Library of Congress Cataloging in Publication Data
Understanding community colleges / [edited] by John S. Levin & Susan T. Kater.
    p. cm. — (Core concepts in higher education)
    Includes bibliographical references and index.
     Community colleges—United States. 2. Community college students—
United States—Case studies. I. Levin, John S. II. Kater, Susan.
    LB2328.15.U6U64 2012
    378.1'5430973—dc23
    2011047694

ISBN: 978-0-415-88126-5 (hbk)
ISBN: 978-0-415-88127-2 (pbk)
ISBN: 978-0-203-11893-1 (ebk)

Typeset in Minion
by EvS Communication Networx, Inc.

Printed and bound in the United States of America
by Edwards Brothers, Inc.

CONTENTS

LIST OF ILLUSTRATIONS

FIGURES

TABLES

SERIES EDITOR INTRODUCTION

EDWARD P. ST. JOHN

It is a pleasure to introduce *Understanding Community Colleges*, edited by John S. Levin and Susan T. Kater, as the second book in the *Core Concepts in Higher Education* series with Routledge Press. The series aims to foster a new generation of research in higher education that recognizes the foundational theories now well established in the field, integrates an emphasis on social justice rather than treating concerns about equity as marginal to the core content of the field, and advances critical thinking about research issues in the field. This book achieves a new understanding of community colleges because of the authors' willingness to look beyond the current paradigmatic assumptions about community colleges and to select authors who also have critical concerns about these vital institutions.

When deciding on authors to contribute to a new book on community colleges, Levin and Kater came to mind because of their previous book, *Community College Faculty: At Work in the New Economy* (by Levin, Kater, & Wagoner, 2006, 2011), which provides an excellent critical analysis of the changing role of faculty. More so than other texts on community colleges, Levin et al.'s work both accepts the workforce realities thrust upon community colleges and provides a critique that informs community college educators about how to contend with the new complexities of governing and teaching in this sector of higher education. John Levin is the Bank of America Professor of Educational Leadership at UC Riverside where he directs the California Community College Collaborative. Susan Kater has emerged as an important scholar-practitioner who has wide-ranging administrative responsibilities at the GateWay Campus of Maricopa Community College.

Levin and Kater chose authors who address critical issues in their scholarship on community colleges. The collective contributions take a step beyond the traditional positivist framework for viewing community colleges and the deficit frame frequently used to critique their students, but also raise issues that can help a new generation of scholars define research questions that have the potential of supporting continued efforts in community colleges to respond to the demands of workforce preparation in institutions increasingly viewed by policy-makers as college preparatory institutions with a goal of increasing the percentage of students who transfer to four-year colleges. Individually and collectively the authors dig beneath the surface of contemporary rhetoric about community colleges and their missions to identify questions that merit consideration by a new generation of scholars and practitioners.

REFERENCE

Levin, J. S., Kater, S., & Wagoner, R. L. (2006, 2011). *Community college faculty: At work in the new economy.* New York, NY: Palgrave.

PREFACE

SUSAN T. KATER AND JOHN S. LEVIN

With this volume of the *Core Concepts in Higher Education* series, we introduce for the study of community colleges what series editors Ed St. John and Marybeth Gasman have labeled the "third generation of scholarship" (Gasman, 2010). Community colleges are the most responsive postsecondary education sector of public higher education, enrolling 43% (7.5 million credit students) of the postsecondary education student population, yet they continue to be the most understudied. Community college enrollments increased by 25% in the first decade of the 21st century (U.S. Department of Education, 2011), but the magnitude of their influence within postsecondary education is not matched by a scholarly understanding of their complex functioning, and is not reflected in research and scholarship in the social sciences.

Taking a historical view, we find the community college literature, in the main, since the 1960s has been torn between a social sciences' critical perspective and a form of practitioner literature that praises the progress of the institution (Frye, 1994). This schism has been bridged from time to time with research on students and their educational attainment, noting on the one hand that community college students come from a deficit condition and on the other hand that the institution is making progress in alleviating these deficits (Bailey & Morest, 2004; Bailey, Calcagno, Jenkins, Kienzl, & Leinbach, 2005). This research is highly functional and in the main reliant upon research methods that could be termed "positivistic" in their orientation. During the period of the 1990s and early 2000s, there were a variety of different tales told about community colleges and those tales conveyed the lived experiences of those who work and study within the institution. This discourse, which we term "interpretive," has provided insight into the behaviors of community college participants, yet it has not had the influence upon scholarly research and practice that the more positivistic research has achieved. From this interpretive literature there is illumination of organizational life accompanying personal, political alliances (Cooper & Kempner, 1993), the experiences of students within an institutional context (Shaw, Rhoads, & Valadez, 1999), the plight of non-traditional college students (Herideen, 1998), the work of faculty in the instructional realm (Grubb et al., 1999), and the strategies and behaviors of management (Levin, 2001).

With few exceptions, that pattern, which stretched back to 1978 (London, 1978; Weis, 1985), declined in the face of efforts in the world of policy to boost the profile of the community college and correspondingly in research output to address shortcomings in student attainment, often with the label of "inequity" (Dowd, 2003). This period saw the rise of foundations—Gates and Lumina in particular—in pursuing improvements in the community college, for a variety of purposes, and Lumina's Achieving the Dream project lined up research on community colleges that would address student and institutional shortcomings in moving students to credentials. These improvement initiatives, whether national—*Community College Survey of Student Engagement* (Center for Community College Student Engagement, 2010)—or state focused (Shulock & Moore, 2007), while well-intentioned, have preoccupied practitioners and policy-makers and both reflect and reinforce the pattern of research on community colleges that deflects attention from both a comprehensive view of the institution, in general, and an experiential view, in particular.

It is from this history then that we move forward with a scholarly understanding of community colleges which we expect to inform and motivate future scholars to continue the comprehensive, critical, and empirical study of community colleges—work that combines "research, teaching and practice...into a third generation of scholarship" (Gasman, 2010, p. x) and serves graduate students in the social sciences and education with an advanced understanding of salient community college literature while offering insights into contemporary practice and policy.

ORGANIZATION OF THE VOLUME

In planning the *Core Concepts in Higher Education* volume on community colleges, our intention was that it set a precedent for future scholarship: add to the breadth of comprehensive, critical literature, support St. John and Gasman's third generation of scholarship (Gasman, 2010), and create value for higher education scholars and community college graduate students—those who intend to be academic scholars as well as those who are or will be community college practitioners. As master's and doctoral programs in community college leadership expand to meet the development of community college programs and enrollments, and as other programs in the field of higher education acknowledge the significance of the community college, the importance of relevant literature cannot be understated. *Understanding Community Colleges* creates another view of the community college, from a critical and theoretical perspective, by a diverse cadre of authors, emerging and established, bringing with them a rich and expansive analysis of community colleges.

This edited work is not divided along the typical functional lines of community colleges, or along the literal themes of instruction, student services, governance, funding, and leadership, but rather the framework is a larger organic theoretical structure. Section I of the volume begins with a critical and analytical perspective of the changing mission and the students affected in the teaching and learning process, the dual core of community colleges as an organization. Section II of the book moves to organizational and external issues involved in planning, managing and leading, governing, and funding community colleges. These works are historical reviews which are theoretically grounded and provide a springboard for more third generation scholarship. In Section III, we engage the future in a broad stroke which includes a view of the community college from an international political scientist perspective, the vocational, technical education economic mission, and the increasingly defined entrepreneurial agency role of the community college. We conclude the volume with Section IV, a critical evaluation of the state of knowledge about community colleges as institutions.

Section I opens with Ken Meier's important work which outlines the salient issues of the community college mission over time. "Community College Mission in Historical Perspective" presents an historical analysis of the community college mission debate. Spanning the 20th century and relying on historiography as well as sociological theory, the chapter reviews the literature of the past 30 years that pertains to community college mission and national discussions of that mission. Ken's prose alone is worthy of repetition by future scholars, as it is uniquely theoretical yet approachable; the chapter eloquently and expansively reviews what we know about the changing mission of the community college. Within the chapter, Ken acknowledges the ambiguity regarding the community college's mission and purpose, and conceptualizes the community college mission as an historically contingent social and educational process structured by the needs of communities and students, as well as regional and national imperatives for economic and workforce development. U.S. community colleges are adaptive institutions, with missions expanding as social and economic policies at the local, and now national and global, stages evolve. The work is important as well as appropriate in setting the tone for the rest of the book.

While the mission drives the institution, we are quickly at the heart of the community college, the students. Lindsey Malcom, in Chapter 2, evaluates the demographics of community college students in her chapter "Student Diversity in Community Colleges: Examining Trends and Understanding the Challenges." While a plethora of works accurately describe student diversity in community colleges, Lindsey's work, using national and state-level data, goes beyond descriptive data to provide an integrated examination of community college diversity including an analysis of how community colleges have evolved into a *de facto* minority-serving institutional sector. This inductive reasoning applied to student enrollment data is an example for students and potential scholars in the art and science of critical thinking. The chapter also identifies those factors that have been demonstrated to lead diverse students to enroll in community colleges. Lindsey's analysis includes student choice factors as well as institutional issues, and weaves together an important discourse on the rich diversity of community college students and the co-construction of their educational experiences.

Continuing to develop our understanding of the student literature, Joan Hirt and Tara Frank review the roots of the student services profession from both a student development and a consumerism theoretical framework. In Chapter 3, "Student Development and Consumerism: Student Services on Campus," Joan and Tara provide an overview of the history of the student affairs profession and contextualize the discussion of the influences that shape professional practice at community colleges. Admittedly, student services research is "meager" as the authors note, which made their critical analysis of the literature even more challenging, but as you will read they effectively summarized the historical timeline and issues specific to student services, while providing us with a look into the future of the profession. Joan and Tara pose important questions in their chapter, including "How is development measured over a two-year enrollment period or for students who stop in and out of their academic program over several years?" and they note the dearth of appropriate theories that could address the unique institutional culture of community colleges. Scholars as well as student services leaders would benefit from pursuing their line of reasoning and follow up on the questions they posit.

Linda Hagedorn and Yi (Leaf) Zhang, co-authors of Chapter 4, address another topic ripe for further research, that of the international student population within community colleges. Their chapter, "International Students in U.S. Community Colleges: Status, Opportunities, and Future," concedes that while research on international students at universities is readily available, the community college literature is sparse. Using a theoretical framework that describes how the acceleration of knowledge production has influenced the global demand for a skilled workforce, the authors expand on the particular needs of international students from the institutional as well as the student perspectives. Linda and Leaf help us understand why students outside of the U.S. elect to attend (or not attend) community colleges as an international destination, the demographics of international students, and how colleges benefit academically, socially, economically, and culturally from the enrollment of international students.

Chapter 5, "Adult Student Development: The Agentic Approach and its Relationship to the Community College Context," by Virginia Montero-Hernandez and Christine Cerven, presents a review of the community college student literature with a focus on adult student development. Adult student development is analyzed as an agentic approach to the development of self-confidence, self-understandings, skills, and knowledge among students aged 25 years and older. The authors identify the key issues of an agentic approach which are related to conceptualization and definitions of adult students, adult students' approach to education in concert with other adult roles they carry, such as family member, worker, community citizen, and how these other identity anchors affect their experiences within their education and their goal attainment. The chapter also reviews the work on the effects of the community college as an institution on adult student development. The chapter concludes with a discussion of the gaps and inconsistencies in the literature, as well as underdevelopment in the literature on adult students, suggesting opportunities for further research.

With a title that resonates with community college faculty across the country, both full-time and adjunct, "Teaching Academically Underprepared Students in Community Colleges" by Dolores Perin discusses the challenges faced by academically underprepared community college students and developmental education approaches designed to improve achievement. In Chapter 6, Dolores, a recognized expert in the scholarship of teaching, provides an examination of developmental education in light of the need to prepare students for the full college curriculum, which requires the ability to transfer reading, writing, and math skills to disciplinary classrooms. Over 40% of community college students take at least one developmental education course, and with a national completion agenda pressing in a period of declining resources, empirical research utilized to inform practice and improve student success is warranted. Criticisms raised in the literature about developmental education in its traditional form are discussed. Contextualization, which may improve students' transfer of skill and level of academic motivation, is suggested as an alternative. Dolores concludes her chapter with recommendations regarding the structure of developmental education and interdisciplinary professional development.

In Section II we turn to the operational and environmental issues of program planning, management and leadership, governance, and funding of community colleges. The section leads off with Chapter 7 by David Ayers and Michael Ayers, "Planning

Programs for Community College Education: Theory, Policy, and Practice." An understudied but essential function within community colleges is program planning—the planning, design, implementation, and evaluation of learning experiences of students. In this chapter, David and Michael review the literature on educational programming in the community college, specific to the practice, policy, research, and theory on program planning. Comprehensively, they review classical, naturalistic, and critical programming viewpoints while comparing and contrasting the prescriptive programming literature—how educators should plan programs compared to how educators do plan programs. This discussion is framed within the context of community college program planning within national, state, and local policy contexts, demonstrating how human capital theory informs policy and political rhetoric. The Ayers engage readers in the discussion by reviewing a number of mid-range theories, including human capital, screening and filtering, signaling, cultural capital, institutional, and credentialist. The chapter concludes with a review of the literature on the role of the community college in promoting community college leadership through community-based programming.

Chapter 8, "Managing Today's Community Colleges: A New Era?," by Pam Eddy uses a postmodern lens to provide an historical review of management practice as reflected in research and practice. From early conceptualization of the colleges as bureaucratic institutions due to rapid expansion and unionization to systems of shared governance and collaboration, community colleges reflect larger trends in management. Pam summarizes the eras of management in community colleges, which complement Twombly's (1995) topology of leadership eras. Throughout the chapter, Pam suggests contextual nuances due to the mission, vision, and location of community colleges in the communities they serve. She highlights the important shifts in management eras over time while noting key issues for each era. The significance of organizational structure as it influences management is discussed, and the utilization of a postmodern perspective illuminates the influence of underlying structures on management options.

Moving from management to leadership in Chapter 9, Marilyn Amey reviews contemporary theories of leadership in "Leadership: Community College Transitions." The chapter considers contemporary theories of leadership in the community college context, as the confluence of climate, expectation, and market economy influence how we think about leaders and leadership. Marilyn provides an argument which suggests that traditional forms of leadership are not adequate to lead contemporary community colleges effectively; that the influence of external forces including economic, social, cultural, and global initiatives has created pressures necessitating new theoretical frameworks of leadership. These new theories are driven by forces such as organizational change, adaptive work, and collaboration; they support a "distributed leadership" framework for leadership development, which acknowledges the increasing complexity of community colleges as organizations.

In Chapter 10, we continue our analysis and evaluation of structural issues, moving the discussion from institutional management and leadership to the broader view of governance. Sociopolitical issues, declining funding, and diminished access are all part of the future of community colleges and have implications for governance. In "Deconstructing Governance and Expectations for the Community College," Carrie Kisker and Susan Kater review the historical governance literature related to community colleges. Governance, consistent with other topics, ebbs and flows in terms of interest, but plotting the interest over time, the spikes show a correlation to fiscal declines—hence the current attention paid to governance in the literature. The chapter explores the various internal and external patterns of governance, including state governance patterns for community colleges, shared governance, and expansion of governance issues as community college planning bridges the K-16 boundaries. Utilizing specific examples of cross-sector collaboration, the chapter illustrates how various community college governing structures connect to expectations for community colleges—particularly those where power is concentrated solely within the community college sector. The chapter includes recommendations for leveraging the power and authority within state governance systems to improve community college collaboration with K-12 schools and universities.

Jim Palmer, to whom many in the community colleges turn for integral assessment of fiscal issues, annotates the condition of declining public political support for funding community colleges, which is now jeopardizing the access mission. In Chapter 11, "State Fiscal Support for Community Colleges," Jim provides a review of and update to the literature on state funding, defining the significant lines of inquiry over the years while analyzing each of the lines in terms of the questions that have guided researchers, the theories and research methods they have used, and the insights that have been achieved, as well as unanswered questions. Jim notes that over the years, researchers have pursued three primary lines of inquiry on community college finance—the most prevalent entailing an examination of funding trends and state funding mechanisms via a macroeconomic perspective. Another important line of inquiry examines internal costs and fiscal management. Within this line scholars have taken a microeconomic perspective, examining fiscal problems and challenges within institutions. The third strand of inquiry focuses on equity. Within this frame researchers have examined the link between the funding of community colleges and the goal of equal access and outcomes. The chapter suggests what practitioners understand, that the responsibility for the fiscal health of community colleges will increasingly be determined by policies and initiatives internal to the institutions themselves.

Chapter 12, "Career and Technical Education: Old Debates, Persistent Challenges in Community Colleges" by Debra Bragg, is an historical analysis of the important mission of vocational education in community colleges. Debra, a recognized expert in career and technical education, evaluates the role of public policy as it affects funding for the wide array of programs that fall under the umbrella of career and technical education. In addition, she describes the evolution of vocational education, critical to the economic development mission of the community college, including salient issues of placement of programs outside of the traditional mainstream access mission of the community college. In its current and projected future state, vocational education should be at the forefront of colleges' program planning, but Debra suggests that the lack of rigor in outcomes assessment and program evaluation may threaten federal support at a time when the national agenda is focused on school to work, the core of career and technical education.

From an institutional and organizational view of vocational education, Luciana Dar brings a comparative analysis to the volume in Chapter 13, "The Comparative Political Economy of Vocational Education: Lessons for the Study of Community Colleges in the U.S." As a political scientist, Luciana brings a unique and important perspective to the literature on community colleges through her analysis of vocational education and training. In her chapter, Luciana reviews the social sciences literature and within it integrates the political economy of the welfare state to demonstrate the relationship between workers' investments in skills, the international product market strategies of firms, and electoral politics and social protection. In this, she focuses on how political and economic institutions have led to different training systems across the Organization for Economic Co-operation and Development (OECD) countries. The economic decisions made at a political level in funding postsecondary education may enhance one mission, such as economic development, at the expense of an equally important mission, such as social equity—a key component of the community college mission.

In looking back while providing a framework for future planning, Matthew Mars, in Chapter 14, utilizes academic capitalism and globalization theories as a framework to analyze economic workforce development within community colleges. The chapter, "Community College Economic and Workforce Development Education in the Neoliberal and Academic Capitalist Contexts," dissects the ongoing tension between the academic and access mission of the community college with the important and emerging role colleges play as economic development engines. When we overlay fiscal constraints over the academic versus access pressures, Matt is able to follow up on the theme of internal control suggested by Jim Palmer in Chapter 11 as he discusses the importance of the emerging entrepreneurial mission of community colleges. The chapter also complements the concepts presented by Debra Bragg in her chapter on career and technical education, by integrating new vocationalism, which centers on integrated curricula that are created to reflect broad occupational fields with contemporary social and workforce needs and opportunities. As he concludes the chapter, Matt develops the important and emerging entrepreneurial education mission of the community college as a source of market agency for students, local and regional economic development, and another organizational challenge and opportunity for the community college.

The final chapter, Chapter 15, "Understandings of Community Colleges in Need of Resuscitation: The Case of Community College Faculty" by John Levin, states the case for improvement in community college scholarship. A critical scholar of community college literature, John suggests that the research and contemporary understandings of community colleges are stagnant, obstructed by the institution's own lack of an organizational saga. By utilizing faculty as a case study in understanding the broader organization, John parallels the gaps in comprehending the complex nature of faculty work noting the field's incomplete understanding of the community college, which is marred by competing perspectives and clouded by our lack of deep understanding of organizational behaviors. John closes the volume with a call to current and future scholars to take up the charge of improved understanding of community colleges, not from a functional perspective but rather from a spectrum of theoretical perspectives that also include an international context. It is from this expanded research vision that we will chart the course for the new generation of scholarship.

REFERENCES

Bailey, T. R., Calcagno, J. C., Jenkins, D., Kienzl, G. S., & Leinbach, T. (2005). *The effects of institutional factors on the success of community college students.* New York, NY: Community College Research Center, Teachers College, Columbia University.

Bailey, T., Jenkins, D., & Leinbach, T. (2005). *Is student success labelled institutional failure? Student goals and graduation rates in the accountability debate at community colleges.* New York, NY: Community College Research Center, Teachers College, Columbia University.

Bailey, T. R., & Morest, V. S. (2004). *The organizational efficiency of multiple missions for community colleges.* New York, NY: Teachers College, Columbia University.

Center for Community College Student Engagement. (2010). *Community college survey of student engagement.* The University of Texas at Austin. Retrieved from http://www.ccsse.org/

Cooper, J., & Kempner, K. (1993). Lord of the flies community college: A case study of organizational disintegration. *The Review of Higher Education* (Summer), 419–437.

Dowd, A. C. (2003). From access to outcome equity: Revitalizing the democratic mission of the community college. In K. Shaw & J. Jacobs (Eds.), *Community colleges: New environments, new directions.* Thousand Oaks, CA: Sage Publications.

Frye, J. (1994). Educational paradigms in the professional literature of the community college. In J. Smart (Ed.), *Higher education: Handbook of theory and research* (Vol. X, pp. 181–224). New York, NY: Agathon Press.

Gasman, M. (Ed.). (2010). The history of higher education. In M. Gasman & E. P. St. John (Series Eds.), *Core concepts in higher education.* New York, NY: Routledge Taylor & Francis.

Grubb, W. N., Worthen, H., Byrd, B., Webb, E., Badway, N., Case, C., et al. (1999). *Honored but invisible: An inside look at teaching in community colleges.* New York, NY: Routledge.

Herideen, P. E. (1998). *Policy, pedagogy and social inequality: Community college student realities in postindustrial America.* Westport, CT: Bergin & Garvey.

Levin, J. (2001). *Globalizing the community college: Strategies for change in the twenty-first century.* New York, NY: Palgrave.

London, H. B. (1978). *The culture of a community college.* New York, NY: Praeger.

Shaw, K., Rhoads, R., & Valadez, J. (Eds.). (1999). *Community colleges as cultural texts.* Albany, NY: State University of New York Press.

Shulock, N., & Moore, C. (2007). *Rules of the game: How state policy creates barriers to degree completion and impedes student success in the California community colleges.* Institute for Higher Education Leadership & Policy.

Twombly, S. B. (1995). Gendered images of community college leadership: What messages they send. *New Directions for Community Colleges, 89,* 67–77.

U.S. Department of Education. (2011). *Digest of education statistics.* National Center for Educational Statistics. Retrieved from http://nces.ed.gov/programs/digest/

Weis, L. (1985). Faculty perspectives and practice in an urban community college. *Higher Education, 14*(5), 553–574.

ACKNOWLEDGMENTS

We both want to express our gratitude to the chapter authors who survived this iterative process of writing and thinking through their chapters with us. Everyone behaved in a highly professional manner even though as editors we gave directives that might have seemed capricious. We want to thank Laurencia Walker for her persistence in helping with the details of the reference lists and indexing. John wants to thank Sue, his co-editor, for initiating this project, for working with John with her flexible approach and her humanistic views, and for managing the process to a satisfactory conclusion. John also wants to acknowledge all of those graduate students in community college courses who not only read the work of the community of scholars in this field but also, as practitioners and researchers, have and will in the future shape practice and scholarship. John finally thanks his close family and his colleagues for support in his professional life, all enabling him to devote himself particularly to the community college over the last 40 years. Sue wants to thank Ed St. John, her first doctoral professor, for motivating his students to think broadly and critically about higher education, and John Levin, her last doctoral professor, for continuing to refine that critical thinking and, more importantly, for teaching her the value of each written word while carrying the heavier burden on this volume. She considers it a pleasure and an honor to collaborate with both on this project. And finally, to Bill Butler, for life's advice, "be happy"; to Dee Christopher, a young leader in many ways including on the soccer field, and to Lauren Kennedy, a strong and smart cowgirl, probably the best writer in the family, both of whom Dale and Sue are immensely proud.

Section I

THE CORE: COMMUNITY COLLEGES AND THEIR STUDENTS

1

COMMUNITY COLLEGE MISSION
IN HISTORICAL PERSPECTIVE

KEN MEIER

THE MISSION PROBLEM

Understanding historical context is essential for demystifying the community college mission and the discourses surrounding it. Terms such as "community college mission" or "junior college philosophy" have been undertheorized by scholars. Community college mission discussions often lack precision. In mission debates variant categories and levels of analysis tend to elide differences of meaning or intent, depending on the theoretical stance, rhetorical strategy, or the professional or social interests of the observer or practitioner (Levin, 1998; Meier, 2008).

There is a history of ambiguity, even confusion, regarding the mission and purposes of the colleges (Breneman & Nelson, 1981; Cross, 1985; Levin, 2000). John Frye remarks that the first junior colleges were "accompanied by no clear mission, set of criteria, nor theoretical framework" (Frye, 1992, p. 1). Employing content analysis of the publications of 56 colleges for the year 1920–1921, an early junior college scholar identified at least 21 distinct educational and social purposes for the colleges (Koos, 1925). Later scholars worried that the colleges lacked a "plausible categorical imperative" (Cohen, 1977, p. 74).

The Carnegie Commission on Higher Education notes that the "most striking structural development in higher education has been the phenomenal growth of the community college." The Commission adds, "[t]he roles of the community college are so diverse as to be bewildering" (Olgivie & Raines, 1971, p. v). Multiple roles and shifting institutional identity are reflected in organizational rituals of public community colleges devoted to "reforming," "renewing," "revitalizing," "reassessing," and "revisiting" the mission (Tillery & Deegan, 1985). Burton Clark views uncertainty about the junior-community college mission as a consequence of open-access and weak institutional connection to the organizational field of higher education: "[T]he building of a communicable and socially acceptable identity is *the* problem resulting from the character of the unselective junior college" (Clark, 1960, p. 171, emphasis in original).

The "academic revolution" of the 20th century defined a mission for the research university focused on the troika of research, teaching, and public service (Jencks & Riesman, 1968). There has never been a similar degree of consensus among practitioners, policy-makers, or university scholars in respect to the community college mission (Breneman & Nelson, 1981). A barrier to theoretical consensus is that some scholars evaluate these community-based, open-access organizations by the standards of selective universities (Frye, 1994).

Another challenge to theorizing the mission is the wide diversity of institutions, communities, and state-level governance systems that exists across the community college organizational field. National mission discourses often overlook community contexts that shape the enacted missions of individual colleges. Arizona Eastern College is a small historically Mormon-led college in Safford, Arizona. It defines and enacts the mission for its relatively homogeneous community and students differently compared to La Guardia Community College in Queens with its 50,000 students from over 160 countries speaking more than 110 native languages (Meier, 2008; Mellow & Heelan, 2008). Reconciling the missions of such different institutions requires both historical understanding and theoretical suppleness. Finally, the volatility of the U.S. social and economic context dictates that community colleges tack and wend continually in response to the frequent and sometimes conflicting gales directed at them from the state, business, labor markets, and local communities (Cohen & Brawer, 2008; Levin, 2001).

A common conception among scholars is that the colleges are "non-specialized by design, their mandate is to offer a comprehensive curriculum and to serve a wide range of community needs" (Owen, 1995, p. 145). The rub is what this means in either theory or practice. Openness, access, and responsiveness amount to a stance, perspective, or attitude rather than constituting either a theory or a purposeful program that differentiates a college from, say, a shopping mall or a theme park. The perennial focus on "inputs" by practitioners begs the question of measurable institutional outcomes.

The idea of comprehensiveness tied to open-access emerged in part from California junior college developments during the depression and World War II (Brossman & Roberts, 1973; Witt, Wattenbarger, Gollattscheck, & Suppinger, 1994). The comprehensive mission gained national currency by the 1960s. The conventional definition of the community college mission incorporates those educational functions that comprise "five traditional community college programs" (Cross, 1985, p. 36). These include: (1) collegiate and transfer education; (2) vocational education; (3) developmental or compensatory education; (4) general education; and (5) community education and service. Some practitioners include guidance and student development in the list of functions (Collins & Collins, 1971). By the 1990s, a "new function" was added to the mix—community economic and workforce development (Dougherty & Bakia, 1999).

One group of scholar-practitioners contends that flux, change, and "multi-variance" are defining characteristics of the colleges and their mission (Blocker, Plummer, & Richardson, 1965). Mutability is a frequently observed characteristic of the mission: "[Community colleges] change frequently, seeking new programs and clients" (Cohen & Brawer, 2008, p. 41). Mission opportunism may lead to muddled institutional identity: "[The] definition of the two year college in not much clearer today than it was before 1940" (Frye, 1991, p. 12).

It is not unusual for community colleges to ignore their publicly expressed missions in response to perceived community needs or demands, external policy signals from the state or federal governments, an enticing revenue stream, or social and economic change. In the restless pursuit of new opportunities, the colleges ignore the history and traditions of higher education: "Unlike four-year colleges and universities, community colleges are non-traditional or untraditional: they do not even adhere to their own traditions. They make and remake themselves" (Levin, 1998, p. 2).

Some observers perceive frenetic activity and weak traditions as symptoms of an inadequately realized "institutionalization project" (DiMaggio, 1988). Others explain mission drift and organizational ambiguity as a consequence of: (1) pioneering on the frontiers of community economic development and social responsibility (Vaughan, 1991); (2) self-aggrandizing behaviors of relatively autonomous professional elites (Dougherty, 1994); (3) cutting-edge entrepreneurial enterprise and technological innovation (O'Banion, 1997); (4) tracking and diverting student ambitions (Brint & Karabel, 1989); and (5) cultural dynamics and adaptive behaviors that maintain and reproduce community college identity (Levin, 1998).

CONCEPTUAL FRAMEWORK

Historical and organizational analyses are necessary for assessing the relative merits of competing perspectives on the mission and the community college *qua* institution. This chapter is the result of nearly two decades of investigation into community college history. It conceptualizes the community college mission as an historically contingent social and educational process that is structured by the needs of local communities, student demands, and regional and national imperatives for economic and workforce development (Gleazer, 1994; Ratcliff, 1994). Multiple missions and influences dictate organizational behavior that is often at variance with traditional higher education. Community college leaders equate non-traditional practice with institutional virtue. Loath to seek a lesser place within the higher education hierarchy, community college leaders assert a community college identity that is "neither the penthouse for the high school nor the first two floors of the senior institution" (Gleazer, 1958, p. 486).

The historical junior-community college mission is more intelligible when analyzed across four theoretical domains: the philosophical, functional, empirical, and formative missions. The philosophical mission is expressed or implied in vision and values statements. It communicates the social and educational purposes of the community college in a democratic society. Historically these philosophical values include student-centeredness, community service, lifelong learning, equity, opportunity, social justice, open access, education for citizenship, and even spirituality (Meier, 2008).

The functional or operational mission is generally articulated in formal college mission and purposes statements. It is reflected in the curriculum and "core" programs that characterize the comprehensive community college. The classic functions are transfer general education, career and technical education, developmental education, student development, and community and cultural programming (Bogue, 1950).

The summative or empirical mission is enacted at the level of the academic schedule and daily organizational commitments and activities of the colleges. It constitutes concrete, replicated organizational behavior. It encompasses the educational, fiscal, and political decisions that shape educational practices and outcomes. This is the nexus at which institutional structures connect to the purposeful professional activity of faculty and the educational and social engagement of students and community. This substantive mission is reflected in measurable organizational outcomes.

The formative or social mission is conceptualized as the long-term effects of more than one thousand public colleges on local communities, higher education, and U.S. society in general. This is the domain in which practitioners, stakeholders, policy-makers, critics, and scholars contend over the efficacy of the community college in U.S. society and as an institution of higher education. Perceived gaps between the philosophical mission and the formative mission are a matter of ideological and theoretical contest to validate or invalidate the community college as an educational institution.

Almost by definition, formal community colleges mission statements are influenced by the expectations of external constituencies: "[M]issions exist at the interface between an institution and its environment" (Richardson & Doucette, 1984, p. 12). The publicly stated mission of an organization is one matter, but the enacted or empirical mission may be quite another as the organization is shaped by and responds to its social and economic environment. Organizational theory provides insights regarding the environmental context of mission enactment.

Resource dependency theory (Pfeffer & Salancik, 1978) frames organizations as open systems influenced decisively by the environment. They are "quasi-markets" that struggle for limited organizational autonomy. Threats and opportunities are defined by influences emanating from broader organizational fields: "The key to organizational survival is the ability to acquire and maintain resources" (Pfeffer & Salancik, 1978, p. 2). Transactions within and between organizational fields in pursuit of marginal dollars and increments of political capital tend to structure organizational behavior.

Institutional theory explains organizational activity and outcomes as nested within networked organizational fields. Organizational forms with similar social, political, or economic purposes take on the characteristics of institutions by emulating each other. Institutional environments comprise historical and cultural as well as technical and economic dimensions: "[O]rganizations compete not just for resources and customers, but for political power and institutional legitimacy, for social as well as economic fitness" (DiMaggio & Powell, 1983, p. 150). Insights from organization theory provide nuances and context for explaining the historical development of the community college mission.

HISTORIOGRAPHY OF THE PUBLIC COMMUNITY COLLEGE

Junior-community college historical research is a relatively underdeveloped field. Practitioners take little interest in their history; individual colleges devote little time and few resources to the preservation of institutional memory. Academic researchers who examine the history of the colleges often evidence ideological assumptions that bias their perceptions of the community mission and outcomes (Pedersen, 2000).

John Frye argues that community college historical writing is mostly "descriptive and promotional," and when it "touches on theory or general models ... it tends to vagueness and imprecision" (1992, p. 6).

> [It] is very rare for any writer on the junior college to show a serious historical interest in the origins of the movement. Typically a few generalizations are made as to formative figures, usually prominent personalities in higher education, who

played a role in initiating the movement. This outline information is passed from author to author in those few introductory or survey studies of the junior college. (Frye, 1992, p. 5)

A relative paucity of accurate historical information leads researchers on the colleges to make assumptions about the mission and history of these institutions that will not stand the test of rigorous theoretical interrogation. The following discussion addresses the contributions and limitations of the most important historical works in the field.

America's Community Colleges: The First Century (Witt et al., 1994), published by the American Association of Community Colleges (AACC), attempts to survey the entire history of community colleges. The authors celebrate rather than critically analyze the movement. The book is ebullient about community college growth without paying much attention to the quality of its outcomes. As community college boosters, they ignore critical research on the colleges. Their work provides a useful state-level chronology of the historical development of community college systems. An important contribution is an extended analysis of junior college developments during World War II. The authors also make a significant point that has not been theorized by community college scholars: community colleges constitute the "only sector of higher education to be called a movement" (Witt et al., 1994, p. xviii).

Brick (1964) provides a shrewd history of the American Association of Junior Colleges (AAJC) to 1960. Brick describes the AAJC as "forum and focus" of the movement. He is one of the first community college historians to employ primary material and careful document analysis to explain community college history from a national perspective. This is an important synthesis of AAJC history to 1960.

Utilizing secondary sources, Tillery and Deegan (1985) develop a brief, schematic history of the community college mission from the founding of the first public junior college in 1901 through the "fourth generation" comprehensive community college that reached "maturity" by the 1980s. They provide a useful typology of community college history as experiencing four discrete stages of development. The primary historical purpose is their establishment of a context for understanding the future trajectory of institutional mission. They predict presciently that the emerging "fifth generation" college will be driven increasingly by the imperatives of economic development and competition in the new postindustrial economy, high technology and computer-based information systems, and heightened external demands for institutional accountability.

Ratcliff (1987) makes a persuasive case that the "first" public junior colleges emerged as a result of broad social and economic forces spawned by the second industrial revolution (*circa* 1870–1920) and its aftermath. Interest group politics grounded in local economic aspirations drove early junior college development rather than visionary leaders. In a later article, Ratcliff (1994, p. 4) identifies "seven streams of educational innovation" that influenced the historical development of the comprehensive community college: (1) "local community boosterism"; (2) "rise of the research university"; (3) "restructuring and expansion of the public educational system" in tandem with the second industrial revolution; (4) "professionalization of teacher education"; (5) "the vocational education movement"; (6) "the rise of adult, continuing, and community education"; and, (7) "open public access to higher education." Taken together, Tillery and Deegan and Ratcliff identify the social and intellectual forces that shaped the institutional development of the colleges.

Dougherty (1994) employs historical analysis in conjunction with case-study materials and national university transfer data to develop a "state-relativist" interpretation of leadership ideology and interests. He argues that a community of interest among educational policy-makers and institutional leaders has been the driving force in shaping and even deforming the community college mission. He perceives an unforced choice on the part of community college leadership to shift the institution away from transfer education to vocational programming. The shift in mission negatively affects the life chances of students while marginalizing the colleges as institutions of higher education. Based on his reading of student transfer data, he makes policy arguments for eliminating the community college as an independent higher education sector.

As prelude to a case study of "vocationalization" in the Massachusetts community college system, Brint and Karabel (1989, 1991) offer a critical, historically informed "institutional-conflict analysis" of the origins and "hidden significance" of the vocational mission. Community colleges sort and track students along class lines primarily, diverting students from liberal transfer education into less prestigious vocational programs. By diverting these students from collegiate to vocational education, community colleges acquire a secure market niche and modicum of influence within the organizational field of higher education. Community college leaders practice "anticipatory subordination" to corporations, labor markets, and elite university opinion. These activities further the professional interests of community college leaders who are rewarded by policy-makers and corporations for "managing the ambitions" of students. Though marred by ideological bias in data collection and analysis, this is one of the most important contributions to the historical sociology of the colleges.

Frye (1992) examines the "vision of the public junior college" from 1900 to 1940. He exposes the irony of a national leadership that, while legitimizing and popularizing the junior college ideal among policy-makers and university elites, was frequently ignored in educational aspirations and practice by both local practitioners and students (1991, 1992). Junior college leaders developed a strategy to acquire social legitimacy and stability through the acquisition of new markets outside the purview of traditional higher education. They sought to popularize the concepts of terminal education and paraprofessional training in the junior college. Frye offers a well-informed practitioner's analysis of the vision and early mission of the public junior college.

Gregory Goodwin's dissertation (1971) on the formation and development of community college ideology is a critical history of the movement told from the perspective of the most widely published AAJC leaders prior to the 1960s. Goodwin offers a penetrating analysis validated by immense research in the primary documents of the national movement. He describes a social and educational reform movement that was for many years "more of an idea than institution" (Goodwin, 1971, p. 189). For the junior college founders, according to Goodwin, the road to individual achievement and discipline was through the classroom. This work has been appropriated by a number of subsequent community college historians. It remains one of the most important works in the field.

Collectively these works establish that there were several broad goals for the early national junior college movement: (1) to capture growing educational and training markets within the increasingly complex ecology of the U.S. education system (Brint & Karabel, 1989); (2) to secure professional respect, personal advancement, and institutional support from policy-makers, stakeholders, and the educational community as a whole (Frye, 1992); (3) to advance a moderate social/educational reform agenda that would support both social order and democratic social progress (Goodwin, 1971); and (4) to support open-access to higher education and "short-cycle needs" of diverse clientele (Ratcliff, 1994). For Edmund Gleazer, historical analysis of the community college mission reveals the "search for [community college] institutional freedom to determine its program and to look to the community [and its needs] as the arbiter of the suitability of its programs rather than the universities" (1994, p. 19).

SOCIAL CONTEXT OF PUBLIC JUNIOR COLLEGE DEVELOPMENT

In community college lore, the first public junior college was founded in 1901 at Joliet, Illinois. Six decades later junior colleges had achieved a ubiquitous national presence. Cohen argues, "[t]he foremost impetus for their growth was the pressure for further education occasioned by the rising numbers of high school graduates" (1998, p. 112). The public high school movement (and eventually the junior college) was stimulated by the education and training requirements of a new corporate industrial order.

During the "Second Industrial Revolution" (*circa* 1870–1930), the U.S. witnessed a series of complementary economic, social, and technological innovations so extensive that each has been characterized as a revolution: (1) an economic revolution that shifted most of the nation in less than three generations from a predominantly agrarian and more or less craft-based economy comprised of both market and subsistence sectors to a corporate, globalizing economy; (2) an energy revolution that moved most of the country and eventually the world from animal, human, wind, water, and timber sources of power to more productive carboniferous and petroleum-based technologies; (3) a demographic and urban revolution that grew the U.S. population almost exponentially, concentrating it around more socially complex industrial centers and away from the rural hinterland or from Europe; and (4) a techno-science, engineering revolution that was both stimulus and consequence of the other interrelated movements (Williams, 2002).

These innovations led to the creation of a new mass consumption society and a growing middle class that demanded more educational services and credentials to provide them with relative economic security in the increasingly competitive industrial society. Professionals and white-collar workers required higher levels of literacy, numeracy, and communication skills for occupational success than previous generations. University administrators, scholars, practitioners, and community boosters proposed the junior college as a solution to the education and training requirements of the new order (Frye, 1992; Ratcliff, 1994).

SOCIAL ORIGINS AND IDEOLOGICAL ASSUMPTIONS OF JUNIOR COLLEGE FOUNDERS

Prior to World War II, university leaders and scholars dominated the junior college movement, theoretically and ideologically. The AAJC attracted a strong group of advocates and theorists to articulate the vision and multiple purposes of the junior-community college (Goodwin, 1973). The professors and practitioners who led the movement came from predominantly small-town, Protestant evangelical backgrounds. Some were ordained ministers and a significant number of the most prominent national leaders held doctorates in education from elite universities such as Chicago, Michigan, Berkeley, Stanford, and Harvard. In their minds, Christianity, educational opportunity, and democracy constituted a unified social philosophy. Edmund Gleazer, who dominated the AAJC for two decades, personifies the evangelical subtext of the movement. The former street preacher also possessed a glittering Harvard doctorate. He proclaimed the open door college as Christian revelation: "We have borrowed from John the Revelator a phrase of almost 20 centuries ago, conceived high on the steep slopes of the Island of Patmos: 'Behold, I have set before thee an open door'" (Gleazer, 1970, p. 49).

Movement leaders developed a variety of justifications for the junior college. These included educational opportunity and socialization for democratic citizenship, social adjustment and social solidarity, strengthening secondary education, training middle-level managers and semi-professionals for a rapidly industrializing society, family health and social hygiene, supporting upward mobility for deserving "bright boys" from the lower orders, facilitating university matriculation, providing general education to the masses, and contributing to social stability and economic development by matching students with labor market niches congruent with their intellectual and emotional development (Goodwin, 1971; Koos, 1924). The leaders believed that education informed by spiritual and moderately democratic values was the most efficient method for addressing social and economic problems. In Gregory Goodwin's words, junior college leaders viewed "the basic mission of the community-junior college as a panacea for social ills" (Goodwin, 1973, p. 13).

THE QUEST FOR AN INSTITUTIONAL FRAMEWORK

Scholars often perceive unity of purpose in the early junior college movement. Some contend that the *raison d'être* of the early public junior colleges was the collegiate transfer function. Shaw and London (2001) assert that the first junior colleges were "originally developed to deliver the equivalent of the first two years of a baccalaureate education" (p. 91). Cohen and Brawer counter that all the elements—academic transfer programs, vocational-technical education, continuing education, developmental education, and community service—of the comprehensive mission "have been present in public colleges from the beginning" (2008, p. 22).

The AAJC was established in 1920. The first issue of the *Junior College Journal*, the association's trade publication, appeared in 1930. With the advent of the *Journal* the AAJC presented itself as an energetic national educational movement that attempted to guide local junior college initiatives. The AAJC sought to establish a coherent institutional identity and compelling social purpose for the colleges. This was a major challenge for a small, scattered educational movement that was more of a dream than a national educational reality. Frye notes, "One is hard pressed to establish an unambiguous purpose for the first public junior college at Joliet, Illinois, or elsewhere" (1992, p. 1).

The AAJC convention in 1922 gave the impression of national unity with its masthead resolution: "The junior college is an institution offering two years of instruction of strictly collegiate grade" (AAJC, 1922). Three years later the AAJC expanded the functional mission to include terminal vocational and paraprofessional training (Thornton, 1972). Multiple functions were present in practice and theory from the inception of the movement. Researchers who focus on the transfer function as the master function of the junior colleges overlook institutional nuances at peril of historical accuracy.

Merton Hill's (1938) longitudinal analysis of the curricula of 39 California public junior colleges confirms multiple functions by the 1930s. Most California colleges were engaged in some vocational, developmental, cultural, and adult programming from their inception. Vocational education increased significantly at a number of colleges during the Depression and was the dominant function for several large urban colleges. Generally speaking, close proximity of a college to a university and an expanding industrial labor market pushed it toward vocational education. More isolated rural colleges with weak local labor markets tended to focus on the terminal general education and transfer functions (Hill, 1938).

Institution building and diversification were challenging processes. As late as 1945, the incoming AAJC President Lawrence L. Bethel bemoaned institutional disorder. Lack of consistency among junior colleges was revealed at state meetings: "Institutions that operated within a stone's throw of each other spoke almost a different language" (1945a, p. 393). For a movement that prided itself on being "sanely progressive" and fostering "social intelligence" disunity was disturbingly inefficient (Goodwin, 1971).

SOCIAL ORIGINS OF THE COMPREHENSIVE COMMUNITY COLLEGE CONCEPT

By the mid-1930s, a new perspective on the mission and purposes of the junior college in an increasingly complex, but troubled, industrial society developed in regions such as the Mississippi Valley, Texas, and California. These were areas where populist and progressive sentiments were closely allied with frontier traditions; this political context was tied to a significant degree of insulation from university influence due to the paucity of four-year collegiate institutions compared to the Upper Midwest and the Northeast (Frye, 1992). California practitioners in particular attempted to shift the philosophical mission to lifelong learning, adult education, and community service (Hayden, 1939; Hill, 1938). Clearly there were regional differences in the development of these institutions. Connections to local communities, student academic preferences, and local labor markets, rather than a national movement, were the primary mission drivers (Frye, 1992).

The economic and social crisis of the Great Depression stimulated community alignment nationally. Edmund Gleazer credits Byron Hollinshead's article in the *Journal* (1936) as a path-breaking redefinition of the junior college as a "community college" focused on meeting community needs. Hollinshead would soon become president of the AAJC. Gleazer sees this article as the intellectual genesis of the comprehensive mission, which "anticipated the marketing approach of the present as did his view on close relationships with the high schools and other community institutions" (Gleazer, 1994, p. 18).

These developments widened the purposes of the institution. Young, rising AAJC leaders expanded the definition of collegiate education. They focused on the ideals of lifelong learning and community service as plausible social justification for a community college that moved beyond the restrictions of the extended high school model. Advocates of a new kind of community college argued that "considering education as a lifelong process is the most important function of the junior college as a community institution" (Hayden, 1939, p. 72). Stimulated by economic crisis and galvanized by New Deal idealism, new leaders reframed the junior college as a local consensus social movement dedicated to providing educational and community services that would blunt the impact of the Depression by wedding mission outcomes to community development: "The junior college which attacks vigorously the problems of the social reconstruction must be a part of the community, warmed or chilled by the same breezes which warm or chill a community" (Kelley, 1936, p. 428). The lifelong education and community service perspective reflected and reinforced the drift in the movement from older progressive notions of social engineering to more liberal-democratic models of social mobilization paralleling the politics of New Deal America. The emerging community college ideology advocated for a comprehensive, fungible mission to address the political conflicts and social problems of the 1930s and ultimately mobilization for war (Goodwin, 1973; Meier, 2008).

The new outlook undermined traditional conceptions of the university patriarchs who sought to restrict the junior college to teaching an extended high school curriculum and socializing youth (Koos, 1924). New AAJC leaders argued that educational services should be accessible to all adults who could profit from the community college experience (President's Commission on Higher Education, 1947a). They asserted the legitimacy of vocational education as an integral element of higher education. AAJC President Bethel defended vocational education through a witty observation on one of the long-standing canards in community college curriculum—cosmetology as higher education:

> Perhaps someday we may regard the art of beautifying a lady's face of collegiate importance equal to the science of engineering. I suspect that it is not so much *what* is taught that makes a curriculum collegiate or sub-collegiate, but instead *how* it is taught and to *whom* it is taught. (1945b, p. 103, emphasis in original)

AAJC leaders, who came up through local colleges that thrived in spite of Depression and war, talked excitedly about meeting community needs. As Thornton observed, "The emphasis in the community junior college is on providing legitimate educational services, rather than conforming to preconceived notions of what is or is not collegiate subject matter, or of who is or is not college material" (Thornton, 1972, p. 277).

In 1939 the *Journal* published a polemic in favor of the community-based comprehensive mission, "Junior College as a Community Institution" (Hayden, 1939). Its author was a Santa Monica College faculty member and past president of the Southern California Junior College Association. Hayden re-imagined the junior college movement as an educational reform movement that employed the curriculum and faculty to "mold public sentiment." The two most important mechanisms for changing public perceptions and effecting local social reform were a "planned public education campaign" and "a program for adult education" (Hayden, 1939, p. 73). The philosophical turn to lifelong learning, community service, and democratic, popular higher education positioned the junior college to expand its social reach and market.

LEGITIMATING THE COMPREHENSIVE MISSION

Junior college practitioners, including those most committed to the vocational project, were quite willing to defend the collegiate and transfer functions in the face of any overt threat from their university brethren. John W. Harberson, principal of Pasadena Junior College, is a case in point. Brint and Karabel label him as the most prominent and effective diverter of potential junior college transfer students into vocational tracks (1989, pp. 54–61). Yet, in 1942 Harberson penned a doughty defense of the "Preparatory Objective of the Junior College." In a lead editorial of the *Journal,* Harberson implored his colleagues not to ignore the transfer function as they once did the terminal function, since "25 to 30 percent of the [junior college] student population can and should continue their education in higher institutions and they comprise too important and sizable a group to disregard" (Harberson, 1942, p. 180).

[T]he universities are taking advantage of the present emphasis on terminal education to proclaim to the world, by inference at least, that in its post-high school training of non-university preparatory students the junior college has at last found its true role and the university preparatory function should be surrendered exclusively to the standard college … [The junior college] can and must, if it continues to merit the financial support of all the people, prepare the potential university student for specialization, research or professional study. (Harberson, 1942, pp. 179–180)

Harberson's position was axiomatic to practitioners. The history of the junior-community college movement witnesses the tenacity of its leaders to neither abandon a market nor cede institutional autonomy without a struggle. Community college leaders possess an abiding professional and institutional interest in defending multiple missions and functions.

The historical literature of the community colleges devotes scant attention to the role of the colleges in World War II. The usual compressed narrative slides quickly over the draft and declining enrollments and then to the almost giddy reactions of national and local leaders to the G.I. Bill and the 1947 Truman Commission Report (Brint & Karabel, 1989). The most informative discussion of the wartime junior college focuses on the rapid shift to short-term job training, extended adult education, and development of "patriotic non-credit courses." The new curriculum ranged from aviation to victory gardens, cartography to riveting, nursing to do-it-yourself functions. These observers note that the sudden shift in emphasis from liberal arts transfer courses to vocational and short-cycle occupational training focused on adult part-time students "had a profound effect on the future mission of American junior colleges" (Witt et al., 1994, pp. 119–121).

Early in the war, Leland Medsker, a prominent junior college administrator and scholar, observed that "several factors seem to make [the junior college] position strategic" for anticipating postwar needs.

Probably no type of accredited institution is less hampered by tradition and by orthodox methods … It is or can be a local institution [with the] experience and ability to deal with all types of students regardless of ability, background, or educational and vocational ambitions. (Medsker, 1943, pp. 19, 38)

Throughout the war, the AAJC hyped successful experiments in short-term training with an eye to strengthening postwar junior college vocational programs in the name of meeting the demands and expectations of their communities (Eells, 1944a, 1944b).

POSTWAR COMMUNITY COLLEGE

At the end of World War II, the junior college movement possessed an articulate national leadership and hundreds of vigorous local colleges (Goodwin, 1971). The movement took advantage of postwar prosperity to expand its reach and influence. Widespread liberal optimism about higher education's potential to stimulate economic growth, strengthen democracy, mitigate class and racial conflict, and to provide Cold War ideological munitions to the nation provided a cultural context supportive of junior college expansion (Meier, 2008).

Postwar explosion of the community college was tied closely to Federal public policy. Initiatives such as the G.I. Bill and the Truman Commission permanently altered the educational landscape by creating a social perception that "college attendance was a right not a privilege" (Vaughan, 1984, p. 25). The comprehensive community college ideal extolled in the Commission report and junior colleges' responsiveness to veteran demands for higher education and workforce training helped to shape the growing national perception of higher education as a necessary public good. Much has been made in the literature of the dual impact of the G.I. Bill and Truman Commission on the growth of the national movement (Brint & Karabel, 1989; Vaughan, 1984; Witt et al., 1994). Of the two federal initiatives, the G.I. Bill had the greatest direct impact on the development of the community college mission. Junior college enrollments doubled to more than 500,000 students between 1944 and 1947. By 1946, more than 40% of all junior college students were veterans. At least 58 new public colleges were established during the decade after the war (Witt et al., 1994).

Community college leaders appreciated the symmetry between their liberal consensus politics and the aims of the G.I. Bill. They relished the opportunity to mobilize massive federal and state resources in pursuit of patriotic aims. Even though the AAJC had virtually no influence on shaping veterans' policy at the national level, local junior colleges proved to be adroit opportunists in taking advantage of the windfall. The emphasis on technical-vocational training during the war positioned the colleges to accept and serve "a more diverse group of students, thereby helping to move the public junior college in the direction of open access" (Vaughan, 1984, p. 25). The arrival of hundreds of thousands of non-traditional students reinforced community college commitment to lifelong learning and adult education, presenting a vista of almost limitless educational markets in the future (Martorana, 1946).

The President's Commission on Higher Education (Truman Commission) recommended that a community college be established within commuting distance of nearly all Americans (1947b, pp. 6–7). The comprehensive ideal promised a spectrum of educational services extending from transfer education and vocational training to adult education and community service programs. It addressed the burgeoning public demand for accessible higher education services and credentials.

The Commission Report emphasized skills training and workforce development. The relative privileging of community colleges is explicable as an economic policy initiative. The Commission asserted that junior colleges "must prepare [their] students to live a rich and satisfying life, part of which involves earning a living" (President's Commission on Higher Education, 1947b, pp. 6–7). The Commission promoted the junior college role in university-level transfer education as well.

In 1948, the California Association of Junior Colleges (CAJC) influenced the "Strayer Report" (Deutsch, Aubrey, & Strayer, 1948) to incorporate the outlines of its version of the comprehensive functional mission and the values of its philosophical mission. These became models for the national movement. The Strayer Report anticipated the 1960 California Master Plan for Higher Education. It outlined the comprehensive community college mission in the following terms: "Terminal Education, General Education, Orientation and Guidance, Lower Division Training, Adult Education, Removal of Matriculation Difficulties." Underpinning this functional mission was a broader philosophical and social mission. The CAJC expressed its commitment to this social mission by articulating a set of values intended to rationalize the comprehensive mission.

1. The junior college is committed to the democratic way of life; 2. The junior college recognizes the individual man as the highest value of the world and universe;

3. The junior college is committed to the policy of granting to the individual man the maximum amount of freedom, personal initiative, and adventure consistent with equal opportunities on the part of his fellows; 4. The junior college is committed to the policy of providing for all the children of all the people, a post-high-school education which will meet their needs. (Deutsch et al., 1948, pp. 6–7)

A key AAJC/CAJC postwar goal was to accelerate the junior college organizational transition from extended secondary education while redefining its place in higher education.

Following the CAJC example, Jesse Bogue, executive leader of the AAJC, promulgated a synthesis of the comprehensive, open-access mission in his influential book, *The Community College* (1950). He emphasized the importance of becoming a community-based institution independent of both high schools and direct university influence: "Community colleges must strike out boldly, demonstrate that they are not bound by tradition or the desire to ape senior colleges for the sake of a totally false notion of academic respectability, and do the job" (Bogue, 1950, p. 313). Bogue's synthesis of 50 years of junior-community college development established the model for a comprehensive, community-based, fungible mission that remains dominant in practitioner ideology to this day.

CONCLUSION

By the 1960s the G.I. Bill, U.S. economic growth, and baby boom demographics helped to establish the comprehensive, open-access college as a national postsecondary education institution. The movement took great pride in the spectacle of a new college being created almost every week in this decade (Witt et al., 1994). Community college leadership side-stepped issues of educational quality and institutional outcomes by emphasizing access, innovation, and growth, equating these organizational attributes with the democratizing mission of the "People's Colleges." They assumed the new institutions must be heading in the right direction because the colleges mirrored the U.S. business model of success—more customers, new markets, bigger profits (Meier, 2008).

Leaders in the 1960s shared a tacit consensus that "the community college was philosophically and economically constituted to be all things to all people" (Vaughan, 1984, p. 38). John Lombardi, President of Los Angeles City College, advanced the ideal of a comprehensive mission with permeable boundaries. He endorsed the comments of prominent political leaders calling for expanded college missions.

> A junior college should be, according to Governor Terry Sanford of North Carolina, an institution which undertakes everything not being taken care of elsewhere. Lest there be any doubt, Governor Sanford spelled out activities such as education of the illiterates, uplifting the underprivileged, retraining the unemployed—a truly comprehensive institution. Senator Walter Stierns of California urged the junior college to undertake the task of preparing Americans for recreational and leisure activities. Secretary of Labor Willard Wirtz looks to the junior college for aid in solving unemployment. (Lombardi, 1964, p. 8)

This outline of a "truly comprehensive institution" was enough of an identity for many community college leaders. But knowledgeable practitioners understood that continual mission expansion opened them to charges by academic critics that "the many qualifications to the definition [of identity and mission] may leave the impression that the community junior college is an entirely amorphous institution, so fluid and adaptable as to lack character and defy consistent definition" (Thornton, 1972, p. 279). There was also the perennial challenge of taking on "new missions without the resources to fund new programs or to integrate them with the existing institution" (Rosenbaum, Deil-Amen, & Person, 2006, p. 1). The most important question was posed by Martorana and Kuhns (1988, p. 230): "Can institutions defined only by access and growth continue to maintain themselves?"

The closing theoretical point is that historically community college organizational behavior tends to mirror social and economic change rather than leading it (Levin, 2000). Changes in mission focus are adaptive behaviors structured by rapid alterations in the social and economic logic of both the public and private sectors. Responding to massive changes in postwar U.S., community colleges reacted reflexively by pursuing new initiatives that might give them a competitive advantage in the education and training marketplace. As suggested by both resource dependency theory (Pfeffer & Salancik, 1978) and institutional theory (DiMaggio & Powell, 1983), all organizations compete for economic survival and social fitness. Their history suggests that community colleges will continue to seek presumed advantages within economic trends and changing labor markets, while continuing their embrace of a fungible, comprehensive mission (Meier, 2008). Multiple missions and multiple identities are inherent in the organizational and social design of community colleges.

QUESTIONS FOR DISCUSSION

1. What justifies the view that the community college and its predecessor, the junior college, was a social movement?
2. Are there examples from the present that indicate that the community college continues as a social movement?
3. What are the four domains of community/junior college mission?
4. What are examples of the expression of mission within each domain?

REFERENCES

American Association of Junior Colleges (AAJC). (1922). *Report of the American Association of Junior Colleges in annual session.* Washington, DC: Author.
Bailey, F. (1967). *Santa Rosa junior college, 1918–1957: A personal history.* Santa Rosa, CA: Santa Rosa College.
Bergquist, W. (1998). The postmodern challenge: Changing our community colleges. In J. Levin (Ed.), *Organizational change in the community college: A ripple or a sea change. New Directions for Community Colleges, no. 102* (pp. 87–98). San Francisco, CA: Jossey-Bass.
Bethel, L. (1945a). Power of coordinated effort. *Junior College Journal, 15*(9), 391–394.
Bethel, L. (1945b). What are 'these institutions'? *Junior College Journal, 16*(3), 101–105.
Blocker, C., Plummer, R., & Richardson, R. (1965). *The two-year college: A social synthesis.* Englewood Cliff, NJ: Prentice-Hall.
Bogue, J. (1950). *The community college.* New York, NY: McGraw-Hill.
Breneman, D., & Nelson, S. (1981). *Financing community colleges: An economic perspective.* Washington, DC: Brookings Institute.
Brick, M. (1964). *Forum and focus for the junior college movement: The American Association of Junior Colleges.* New York, NY: Teachers College, Columbia University.
Brint, S., & Karabel, J. (1989). *The diverted dream: Community colleges and the promise of education opportunity in America, 1900–1985.* New York, NY: Oxford University Press.

Brint, S., & Karabel, J. (1991). Institutional origins and transformations: The case of American community colleges. In W. Powell & P. DiMaggio (Eds.), *The new institutionalism in organizational analysis* (pp. 337–360). Chicago, IL: University of Chicago.

Brossman, S., & Roberts, M. (1973). *The California community colleges.* Palo Alto, CA: First Educational Publications.

Brothers, E. (1934). The new deal and the junior college. *Junior College Journal, 5*(1), 5.

Clark, B. (1960). *The open door college: A case study.* New York, NY: McGraw-Hill.

Clowes, D., & Towles, D. (1985). Lessons from fifty years: Analysis of the association's journal provides insight into shifting leadership interests. *Community, Technical, and Junior College Journal, 55*(1), 28–32.

Cohen, A. (1977). The social equalization fantasy. *Community College Review, 5*(2), 74–82.

Cohen, A. (1998). *The shaping of American higher education: Emergence and growth of the contemporary system.* San Francisco, CA: Jossey-Bass.

Cohen, A. M., & Brawer, F. B. (1994). The changing environment: Contexts, concepts, and crises. In A. M. Cohen & F. B. Brawer (Eds.), *Managing community colleges.* San Francisco, CA: Jossey-Bass.

Cohen, A. M., & Brawer, F. B. (2008). *The American community college* (5th ed.). San Francisco, CA: Jossey-Bass.

Cohen, A. M., Lombardi, J., & Brawer, F. B. (1975). *College responses to community demands.* San Francisco, CA: Jossey-Bass.

Collins, C., & Collins, J. (1971). The case for the community college: Basic assumptions. In W. Olgive & M. Raines (Eds.), *Perspectives on the community-junior college* (pp. 139–148). New York, NY: Appleton-Century-Crofts.

Cross, K. (1985). Determining missions and priorities for the fifth generation. In W. Deegan, D. Tilllery, & Associates (Eds.), *Renewing the American community college.* San Francisco, CA: Jossey-Bass.

Deutsch, M., Aubrey, A., & Strayer, D. (1948). *A report of a survey of the needs of California higher education.* Berkeley: University of California Press.

DiMaggio, P. (1988). Interest and agency in institutional theory. In L. Zucker (Ed.), *Institutional patterns and organizations: Culture and environment* (pp. 3–21). Cambridge, MA: Ballinger.

DiMaggio, P., & Powell, W. (1983). The iron cage revisited: Institutional isomorphism and collective rationality in organizational fields. *American Sociological Review, 47*(2), 147–160.

Dougherty, K. (1994). *The contradictory college: Conflict origins, impacts, and futures of the community college.* Albany, NY: State University of New York Press.

Dougherty, K., & Bakia, M. (1999). *The new economic development role of the community college.* New York, NY: Community College Research Center, Teachers College, Columbia University.

Eells, W. (1931). The junior college—What manner of child shall this be? *Junior College Journal, 1*(5), 309–328.

Frye, J. (1991). *Conflicting voices in the definition of the junior/community college.* Los Angeles, CA: ERIC Clearinghouse for Junior Colleges (ERIC Document Reproduction Service No. ED 337228).

Frye, J. (1992). *The vision of the public junior college, 1900–1940.* New York, NY: Greenwood Press.

Frye, J. (1994). Educational paradigms in the professional literature of the community college. In J. Smart (Ed.), *Higher education: Handbook of theory and research* (Vol. X, pp. 181–224). New York, NY: Agathon Press.

Gleazer, E. (1958). The junior college–Bigger! Better? *Junior College Journal, 28*(9), 484–487.

Gleazer, E. (1970). The community college issue of the 1970s. *Educational Record, 51*(1), 47–52.

Gleazer, E. (1980). *The community college. Values, vision, and vitality.* Washington, DC: American Association of Junior Colleges.

Gleazer, E. (1994). Evolution of junior colleges into community colleges. In G. Baker (Ed.), *A handbook on the community college in America.* Westport, CN: Greenwood Press.

Goodwin, G. (1971). *The historical development of the community-junior college ideology: An analysis and interpretation of the writings of selected community-junior college leaders from 1890–1970.* (Unpublished doctoral dissertation.) University of Illinois, Urbana-Champaign, IL.

Goodwin, G. (1973). *A social panacea: A history of community college ideology.* Los Angeles, CA: ERIC Clearinghouse for Junior Colleges (ERIC Document Reproduction Service No. ED093427).

Grubb, W., & Lazerson, M. (2004). *The education gospel: The economic power of schooling.* Cambridge, MA: Harvard University Press.

Harberson, J. (1942). Preparatory objective of the junior college. *Junior College Journal, 13*(4), 179–180.

Hayden, S. (1939). Junior college as a community institution. *Junior College Journal, 10*(2), 70–73.

Hill, M. (Ed.). (1938). *The functioning of the California public junior college: A symposium.* Berkeley: University of California Press, Works Progress Administration.

Hollinshead, B. (1936). The community junior college program. *Junior College Journal, 7*(3), 111–116.

Jencks, C., & Riesman, D. (1968). *The academic revolution.* Garden City, NY: Doubleday.

Kelley, F. (1936). The junior college and social reconstruction. *Junior College Journal, 6*(8), 428.

Koos, L. (1924). *The junior college.* Minneapolis: University of Minnesota.

Koos, L. (1925). *The junior college movement.* New York, NY: AMS.

Koos, L. (1927a). Conditions favor integration of junior colleges with high schools. *School Life, 12*(9), 164.

Koos, L. (1927b). The junior college curriculum. *The School Review, 35*(9), 657–672.

Levin, J. (1998). Organizational change and the community college. In J. Levin (Ed.), *Organizational change in the community college: A ripple or a sea change? New Directions in Community Colleges, no. 102* (pp. 1–4). San Francisco, CA: Jossey-Bass.

Levin, J. (2000). The revised institution: The community college mission at the end of the twentieth century. *Community College Review, 28*(2), 1–24.

Levin, J. (2001). *Globalizing the community college: Strategies for change in the twenty-first century.* New York, NY: Palgrave Macmillan.

Lombardi, J. (1964). Emergent issues in administration. *Junior College Journal, 35*(3), 4–8.

Martorana, S. (1946). Implications of wartime adjustments for junior colleges. *Junior College Journal, 17*(1), 11–17.

Martorana, S., & Khuns, E. (1988). Community colleges, local and regional development, and the drift toward communiversity. In Eaton (Ed.), *Colleges of choice: The enabling impact of the community college* (pp. 230–247). New York, NY: ACE, Macmillan.

Medsker, L. (1943). The wartime role of our junior colleges. *The School Executive, 62*(5), 18–19.

Meier, K. (2008). *The community college mission: History and theory, 1930–2000.* (Unpublished doctoral dissertation.) University of Arizona, Tucson, AZ.

Mellow, G., & Heelan, C. (2008). *Minding the dream: The process and practice of the American community college.* New York, NY: Rowman & Littlefield Publishers, Inc.

Nelson, J., & Cooperman, D. (1998). Out of utopia: The paradox of postindustrialization. *The Sociological Quarterly, 39*(4), 583–596.

O'Banion, T. (1997). *A learning college for the 21st century.* Phoenix, AZ: Oryx Press.

Ogilivie, W., & Raines, M. (1971). *Perspectives on the community-junior college: Selected readings.* New York, NY: Appleton-Century-Crofts.

Owen, S. (1995). Organizational culture and community colleges. In J. Dennison (Ed.), *Educational leadership in community colleges: Canada's community colleges at the crossroads* (pp. 141–168). Vancouver, BC: University of British Columbia Press.

Pedersen, R. (2000). *The origins and development of the early public junior college: 1900–1940.* (Unpublished doctoral dissertation.) Columbia University, New York.

Pfeffer, J., & Salancik, G. (1978). *The external control of organizations: A resource dependence perspective.* New York, NY: Harper and Row.

President's Commission on Higher Education. (1947a). *Higher education for American democracy: Volume I, Establishing the goals.* Washington, DC: Government Printing Office.

President's Commission on Higher Education. (1947b). *Higher education for American democracy: Volume III, Organizing higher education.* Washington, DC: Government Printing Office.

Ratcliff, J. (1987). 'First' public junior colleges in an age of reform. *Journal of Higher Education, 58*(2), 151–180.

Ratcliff, J. (1994). Seven streams in the historical development of the modern American community college. In G. Baker III (Ed.), *A handbook on the community college in America* (pp. 1–16). Westport, CT: Greenwood Press.

Richardson, R., & Doucette, D. (1984). *An empirical model for formulating operational missions of community colleges.* Paper presented at the American Educational Research Association, New Orleans.

Rosenbaum, J., Deil-Amen, R., & Person, A. (2006). *After admission: From college access to college success.* New York, NY: Russell Sage Foundation.

Shaw, K., & London, H. (2001). Culture and ideology in keeping transfer commitment: Three community colleges. *The Review of Higher Education, 25*(1), 91–114.

Thornton, J. (1972). *The community junior college* (2nd ed.). New York, NY: John Wiley & Sons.

Tillery, D., & Deegan, W. (1985). The evolution of two-year colleges through four generations. In D. Tillery & W. Deegan (Eds.), *Renewing the American community college* (pp. 3–33). San Francisco, CA: Jossey-Bass.

Vaughan, G. (1984). Forging the community college mission. *Educational Record, 65*(3), 24–29.

Vaughan, G. (1991). *Institutions on the edge: America's community colleges.* Los Angeles, CA: ERIC Clearinghouse for Junior Colleges (ERIC Document Reproduction Service No. ED 338270).

Vinen, R. (2001). *History in fragments: Europe in the twentieth century.* London: De Capo Press.

Williams, R. (2002). *Retooling: A historian confronts technological change.* Cambridge, MA: MIT Press.

Winter, C. (1964). *History of the junior college movement in California.* Sacramento: Bureau of Junior College Education, California State Department of Education.

Witt, A., Wattenbarger, J., Gollattscheck, J., & Suppiger, J. (1994). *America's community colleges: The first century.* Washington, DC: Community College Press.

2

STUDENT DIVERSITY IN COMMUNITY COLLEGES

Examining Trends and Understanding the Challenges

LINDSEY E. MALCOM

Community colleges play a critical role in providing access to postsecondary education for a wide range of student populations, including large numbers of racial/ethnic
minorities, low-income students, first-generation college students, adult learners, and
recent immigrants (Hagedorn, 2010; Levin, 2007; National Center for Education Statistics [NCES], 2010a; Phillippe & Gonzalez Sullivan, 2005). Students from these groups
continue to be among those most likely to attend community colleges rather than four-
year institutions, as evidenced by historical and recent student enrollment data (NCES,
2010a). The factors that lead diverse groups of students to enroll in community colleges
are both complex and highly nuanced. Certainly, the relatively low costs, close proximity, program flexibility, and breadth of course offerings of community colleges may be
more attractive to students whose economic, academic, and overall life circumstances
require such institutional characteristics (Adelman, 2005; Brint & Karabel, 1989; Cohen
& Brawer, 2008; Dougherty, 1994; Flores, Horn, & Crisp, 2006; Goldrick-Rab, 2006; Kurlaender, 2006; Levin, 2007). Indeed, the expansion of the community college mission to
include vocational education, remedial education, certificate programs, and continuing
education programs, as well as transfer (Bragg, 2001; Brint & Karabel, 1989; Cohen &
Brawer, 2008; Dougherty, 1992; Rendón & Nora, 1994), has broadened the spectrum of
students attending community colleges.

However, there are also a multitude of factors beyond the individual preferences of
community college students and the institutional characteristics of community colleges
that operate to yield the enrollment patterns currently observed. The social and economic contexts of the U.S., national and state-level higher education policy decisions,
and the persistent disparities in wealth and K-12 educational quality experienced by
disadvantaged communities also lead to the high concentrations of diverse students in
the community college sector (McDonough, 1997; Perna, 2006).

These social, economic, and policy factors are important to understand because they
result in an increasingly wide range of community college students' educational goals,
levels of academic preparation, and attendance patterns, which pose considerable challenges to community college leadership, faculty, and staff. One of the primary challenges

faced by community colleges is the lack of achievement of equity in outcomes for diverse populations, which threatens the educational opportunity that these institutions bring to the communities they serve (Bailey & Morest, 2006).

The purpose of this chapter is to characterize the several forms of diversity present within the community college student population, and to discuss the implications of this diversity for these institutions. I begin by presenting national and state-level data to illustrate the evolution of community colleges into a *de facto* minority-serving educational sector since their expansion of mission in the 1970s (Richardson, Fisk, & Okun, 1983). Following the presentation of these data, I present a theoretical framework for the understanding of factors that lead diverse students to enroll in community colleges based on Perna's (2006) hybrid economic-ecological model of college choice, and discuss the contextual factors that result in community colleges' diverse student enrollment. I conclude the chapter by discussing some of the differences in community college outcomes across diverse populations and consider the implications of the patterns of outcomes for community colleges' continued pursuit of equity (Bailey & Morest, 2006).

CHARACTERIZING STUDENT DIVERSITY
IN COMMUNITY COLLEGES

Since the passing of the Higher Education Act in 1965, participation in postsecondary education has increased considerably. In 1965, for example, fewer than 6 million students were enrolled in U.S. higher education institutions; by 2009, however, that figure exceeded 20 million (NCES, 2010a). Much of this expansion was driven by rising enrollment in the nation's community colleges, which increased sevenfold, from just above 1 million in 1965 to 7 million in 2009 (NCES, 2010a).

As enrollments in the community college sector grew over the past several decades, the student population became increasingly diverse. In 1976, the first year for which enrollment data disaggregated by race and ethnicity are available, students of color (i.e., African Americans, Latinas/os, Asian/Pacific Islanders, and Native Americans) comprised 19.6% of all community college students, nationally (NCES, 2010a). Currently this figure stands at just below 40% (NCES, 2010a). In states with high minority populations and large community college systems, such as California, Florida, and Texas, the proportion of community college students that are racial/ethnic minorities exceeds the national average (see Table 2.1). Half of all students enrolled in California's community college system are racial/ethnic minorities (California Postsecondary Education Commission [CPEC], 2010). In Florida, students of color comprise 43% of all community college students (Florida Department of Education, 2010), and in Texas, the figure stands at 53% (Texas Higher Education Data, 2010). In these states, community colleges are either quickly approaching or have already reached "majority-minority" status.

The racial/ethnic diversity present among community college students is noteworthy. However, there are other forms of diversity present among this student population as well. Community colleges display levels of gender diversity similar to those at four-year institutions. In 2009, 57.5% of community college students were women, compared to 56.2% of undergraduates attending four-year institutions (NCES, 2010a). Considering the rich racial and ethnic diversity among community college students and the relatively low cost of attendance, it is not surprising that community college students are more socio-economically diverse than those enrolled in any other sector of higher education.

Table 2.1   Student ethnicity: Geographical comparative analysis, Fall 2009

Race/Ethnicity	U.S.	California	Florida	Illinois	Texas
Total, Racial/Ethnic Minorities	39.8%	49.3%	42.6%	37.2%	53.3%
African American	14.7%	6.6%	17.4%	15.5%	12.3%
Asian/Pacific Islander	6.7%	10.6%	2.9%	4.5%	4.2%
Hispanic/Latino	17.2%	28.5%	21.8%	16.9%	34.5%
American Indian/ Alaskan Native	1.2%	0.7%	0.5%	0.3%	2.3%

Source: National Center for Education Statistics, 2010a; California Postsecondary Education Commission, 2010; Florida Department of Education, 2010; Illinois Board of Higher Education, 2010; Texas Higher Education Coordinating Board, 2010.

Community college students are more likely to be first-generation college students than those who attend four-year institutions. Nearly 38% of community college students had parents who never enrolled in any form of postsecondary education, compared to just below 25% of students in four-year institutions (NCES, 2010a). In 2004, 44% of community college students who enrolled immediately after high school were considered low-income students, compared to 35% of students who enrolled in a public four-year institution and 12% of students who enrolled in a private not-for-profit four-year institution (NCES, 2008). Furthermore, community college students are more likely to be independent than their counterparts in four-year institutions; 57% of community college students were independent compared to just 32% in four-year institutions (NCES, 2010b). Even among dependent students, those enrolled in community colleges were more likely to come from families with an income of less than $36,000 than those enrolled in four-year institutions (31% compared to 20%) (NCES, 2010b).

The prevalence of community college attendance among independent students is indicative of the extent to which this sector of higher education serves adult learners. In 2003–2004, the average age of undergraduates enrolled in community college was 28.5 years, compared to 23.7 and 25.0 years in four-year public and private, not-for-profit institutions, respectively (NCES, 2008). Fifty percent of community college students are considered adult learners (i.e., they are considered to be of non-traditional college age), compared to 27% of undergraduates enrolled in four-year institutions (NCES, 2010b).

The Role of Context in College Decision-Making: A Conceptual Framework

The Evolving Condition of Choice in Higher Education

College decision-making—if and when to go, where to go, and how to pay—has been the subject of considerable research in the higher education literature (e.g., Hossler & Gallagher, 1987; Hossler, Schmit, & Vesper, 1999; McDonough, 1997; Paulsen, 1990; Paulsen & St. John, 2002; Perna, 2006; Teranishi & Briscoe, 2006). As revealed by Perna's (2006) and Teranishi and Briscoe's (2006) reviews of the literature on college choice, our view of college decision-making has widened since the first studies on the subject. Initially, researchers broached the issue from a primarily human capital, rational choice perspective (Kinzie et al., 2004; Manski & Wise, 1983), which is grounded in economic theory. Researchers have attempted to use this economic analytical framework to understand how students make college enrollment decisions (Hossler, Braxton, & Coopersmith, 1989; Hossler & Gallagher, 1987; Hossler et al., 1999); however, many have argued that this narrow economic framing of college choice ignores the socio-historical and socio-cultural factors that shape the inequitable distribution of information, resources, and opportunity by race/ethnicity, socio-economic status, and generational status (Perna, 2006; Teranishi & Briscoe, 2006).

Since this early work on college choice, other researchers (e.g., Hurtado, Inkelas, Briggs, & Rhee, 1997; McDonough, 1997; Nora, 2004; Sewell, Hauser, & Wolf, 1986; Teranishi & Briscoe, 2006) have applied a socio-cultural perspective to the exploration of college choice, focusing on the role of social and cultural capital and status attainment processes in shaping students' educational aspirations and their college decision-making. Researchers using socio-cultural theory aimed to understand the ways in which resources in the form of social networks, availability of information, and knowledge of admissions and financial aid application processes affect college enrollment. These studies also explore how disparate access to these resources within and between school and community contexts might explain educational inequities. This perspective was a valuable addition to the body of work on college choice in that it centered on the critical ways in which race/ethnicity and class intersect to perpetuate inequities in educational opportunity and attainment. In a sense, these studies' socio-cultural perspective revealed that college "choice" is a misnomer, as low-income students and students of color often make constrained choices at best, and are commonly left with no choice.

The evolving conceptualization of college choice from the economic theoretical perspective of rational choice to the focus on the role of socio-cultural constructs and contexts underscores the complexity of how and why certain decisions about college-going are made. Each of these theoretical perspectives facilitates understandings of the factors that influence students' college decision-making; yet none, taken on its own, provides a sufficient explanation of the ways in which individuals and their situated contexts interact to shape and constrain college choice.

An Integrated Model of College Decision-Making

Due to the aforementioned inadequacies of previous models of college choice, Laura Perna (2006) offers a model that bridges rational choice/economic and socio-cultural perspectives so that we may understand the ways in which contextual factors at the community, institutional, higher education policy, and broader societal levels work in concert with individual characteristics to shape students' college enrollment decisions. The model draws upon previous research to create an integrated economic-ecological framework for understanding college choice, in which an individual's perceptions of the costs and benefits of college and the decision-making process based on the weighing of those costs and benefits are shaped by four layers of nested contexts: (1) the individual's habitus; (2) school and community context; (3) higher education context; and (4) social, economic, and policy context (Perna, 2006). The model maintains the importance of individual characteristics and preferences as economic theories of college choice, while incorporating aspects of ecological frameworks by locating the individual student within nested contextual layers, each of which is further removed from, yet affects that student's characteristics and preferences.

The first layer of the model, "individual habitus," includes the social and cultural capital possessed by a student and his or her demographic characteristics (i.e., race/

ethnicity, gender, and socio-economic status) that have been shown to influence college decision-making (McDonough, 1997; McDonough, Antonio, & Trent, 1997; Teranishi & Briscoe, 2006). School and community context corresponds to the type of organizational habitus (McDonough, 1997) available to the student in the form of resources, institutional agents (Stanton-Salazar, 2001), and information about higher education. More specifically, the concept of organizational habitus refers to the college-going culture, or values that the school and community communicate around college attendance and the patterns of college-going that the culture creates (McDonough, 1997). This layer accounts for the ways in which the presence or lack of resources in the school and community setting can act to facilitate or hinder college decision-making (McDonough, 1997; Stanton-Salazar, 2001). The third layer, higher education context, reflects the multiple ways in which the characteristics and policies of postsecondary institutions shape college choice. These could include the institution's location, its mission, academic programs, and institutional reputation and prestige. Additionally, institutional policies, such as tuition levels and composition of financial aid packages offered by that institution, are included in this contextual layer (Perna, 2004). The highest layer in the model contains the social, economic, and policy contexts that act to shape college decision-making, for example, demographic changes, shifts in the labor market, or higher education policy changes at the state or federal level. This integrated model of college choice also allows for the empirically demonstrated notion that within these layers of context, individual characteristics such as educational aspirations and academic preparation, socio-cultural factors captured by the concepts of social and cultural capital, economic factors such as perceived costs and benefits of higher education, and external factors such as higher education policy, institutional characteristics, and broader social and economic considerations interact to directly and indirectly influence college enrollment decisions (Perna, 2006).

In sum, Perna's conceptual model of college choice provides a framework for understanding the role of context in college decision-making. Rather than offering a one-size-fits-all description of the process by which students make decisions regarding higher education, her model allows for, and even demands, complexity based on the unique, nested environments in which a student is located. Furthermore, the model acknowledges that a student's choice of college might be constrained due to his or her context. The model is particularly helpful in understanding the multitude of factors that result in the diverse community college student population as it acknowledges the role of individual students' characteristics and preferences, as well as the ways in which the institutional features and practices of community colleges including various social, economic, and policy factors, lead these populations to enroll in these institutions. In the following section, I use Perna's (2006) integrated model of college choice as an organizing framework to discuss the factors that lead diverse student populations to enroll in community colleges.

FACTORS THAT LEAD DIVERSE STUDENTS TO ENROLL IN COMMUNITY COLLEGES

Over the past three decades, students customarily considered "non-traditional" (i.e., students of color, women, adult learners, low-income students) have seen a marked increase in their access to higher education, with higher proportions enrolling in postsecondary institutions (NCES, 2010a). As discussed in the previous section, a large percentage of these students are served by the nation's community colleges.

Students of color are more heavily concentrated in community colleges than are White students (NCES, 2010a). In Fall 2009, 36% of African Americans, 48% of Latinas/os, 41% of American Indians, and 36% of Asian/Pacific Islanders enrolled in U.S. postsecondary education institutions attended community colleges, compared to 33% of Whites (NCES, 2010a). Previous empirical research points to a multitude of factors that contribute to the prevalence with which students of color attend community colleges. These factors, which operate within four different layers of context, (1) individual; (2) family/community; (3) higher education institutional; and (4) social, economic, and policy, are discussed below (Perna, 2006).

Individual Characteristics Contributing to Community College Enrollment

Researchers have attempted to understand why students of color, and Latinos in particular, are highly concentrated in the community college sector. Some of these studies focus on student-level characteristics, such as academic preparation, educational aspirations, the possession of college knowledge, and access to resources including social, cultural, and economic capital, as the cause of high levels of community college attendance among students of color. Community colleges are open-access institutions, without the battery of admissions requirements such as standardized test scores and high school transcripts common to most four-year institutions. This has led some to posit that racial/ethnic minority high school graduates choose to enroll in community colleges because they lack adequate academic preparation to enter four-year colleges or universities (Adelman, 2005). While this seems to be a plausible explanation for minority students who disproportionately attend lower performing schools (Carter, 2009; Kozol, 2005; Oakes, 2005), researchers have found that among many students of color, academic preparation and high school achievement are not predictors of the type of postsecondary institution in which students enroll (Kurlaender, 2006). In particular, college-prepared Latinos are more likely to enroll in community colleges than students with similar levels of preparation from other racial/ethnic groups (Admon, 2006; Fry, 2004; Kurlaender, 2006).

Some studies have sought to determine whether differences in educational aspirations (Grubb, 1991) lead to the high concentrations of students of color in the community college sector. While Latinos tend to delay entry to postsecondary education (Rendón & Garza, 1996; Swail, Cabrera, & Lee, 2004), this is not necessarily an indication of low aspirations. High proportions of Latino students who enroll in community college express a desire to earn a bachelor's degree (Admon, 2006; Kurlaender, 2006; Swail et al., 2004). Even among Latino students who have taken steps necessary to attend a four-year institution, such as taking the SAT or ACT, community college enrollment is relatively common (Kurlaender, 2006).

Other researchers have focused on issues of class and socio-economic status to understand the factors that lead students of color to enroll in community colleges in such high proportions. Socio-economic status is typically correlated with the possession of college knowledge, including information about the advantages of attending four-year institutions and financial aid information, as well as access to financial resources (McDonough, 1997; Price, 2004; Tierney & Venegas, 2006). For example, transfer rates among all community college students are low (Dougherty & Kienzl, 2006; Goldrick-

Rab, 2006; Grubb, 1991), which poses a potential barrier for students who intend to earn a bachelor's degree. It is possible, however, that first-generation students might not be aware of the potential of being "diverted" from achieving their educational goals while at a community college (Goldrick-Rab, 2006). This has led some to posit that if students of color, who are more likely to be first-generation students than their White counterparts (NCES, 2008), knew that direct entrance to a four-year institution was advantageous to their educational attainment, they might bypass the community college sector altogether.

Concerns over college costs are also factors that lead students of color and low-income students to enroll in community colleges in relatively high proportions. Community colleges are the lowest-priced postsecondary option available, with average tuition and fees of $2,713 compared to an average in-state tuition and fees of $7,605 for public four-year institutions and $27,293 for private, not-for-profit four-year institutions (College Board, 2010). The cost differences between community colleges and four-year colleges and universities have led researchers to explore the influences of price on college enrollment decisions (Paulsen & St. John, 2002; St. John, Paulsen, & Carter, 2005). Although most of these studies focus on all students' enrollment decisions, they have found that price is of considerable concern to students of color, and particularly for Latinos (Immerwahr, 2003; Tomás Rivera Policy Institute, 2004; Zarate & Pachon, 2006). Kurlaender's (2006) study of Latinos who enroll in community colleges revealed that while socio-economic status (SES) was a predictor of community college enrollment, among Latinos, Whites, and Blacks of the same SES, the Latino students were much more likely to enroll in a community college. Furthermore, even Latinos from affluent households enrolled in community colleges more commonly than Whites and Blacks from high SES backgrounds. Thus, it seems that the low tuition levels of community colleges can account for some of the attraction to these institutions.

The influence of price on the decision to attend community colleges ought not to be divorced from a discussion of the well-documented informational barriers to financial aid access among first-generation college students, low-income students, and racial/ethnic minorities (Admon, 2006; McDonough, 2004; McDonough & Calderone, 2006; Tierney & Venegas, 2006; Tomás Rivera Policy Institute, 2004). Such barriers act to limit these students' awareness of and access to financial aid that could defray college costs. Financial aid and perceptions of college costs go hand in hand, and Admon's (2006) extensive study of the factors that lead to such high levels of community college attendance among Latinos illustrated that a low level of awareness of financial aid is associated with community college enrollment.

Factors in the Family and Community Context that Lead Students to Enroll in Community Colleges

In addition to exploring the individual-level characteristics that might lead historically disadvantaged students to enroll in community colleges in such high proportions, researchers have studied factors in the K-12 school and community contexts that influence community college attendance. In particular, secondary school quality (Karabel, 1972) and resources (Morrow & Torres, 1995) have been identified as two high school characteristics that can function to perpetuate and reproduce educational inequities among low-income students and students of color. Racial/ethnic minorities, on average, attend schools within districts that are underfunded and experience wide disparities in terms of instructional resources, college course offerings (e.g., Advanced Placement courses), quality of teachers, and class size. These disparities limit students' opportunities and exposure to college preparatory curricula and may serve to funnel low-income students and students of color into the community college sector (Goldrick-Rab, 2006; Kurlaender, 2006; Morrow & Torres, 1995; Person & Rosenbaum, 2006; Venezia, Kirst, & Antonio, 2003).

Racial/ethnic minority students in lower quality secondary schools may also suffer the consequences of inadequate levels of college counseling, including incomplete or inaccurate information about college (McDonough, 1997; Tierney & Venegas, 2006). In urban high schools, which enroll large numbers of students of color, student-to-counselor ratios are large. Thus, students in these high schools, many of whom would be first-generation college students (Stanton-Salazar, 2001), simply cannot obtain the type of counseling necessary to inform them of the range of available college options and the advantages and disadvantages of each. Even in those school environments within which counseling is available, the danger of the under-utilization of high school counselors remains. This phenomenon is particularly common among first-generation college students, who tend to rely on the advice of parents or other adults in the community to inform their college decision-making (Fuerstenau, 2002). As a result, first-generation students of color are susceptible to making decisions about college based on incomplete information, which might be a contributing factor to their high concentration in the community college sector.

Even those students of color who attend K-12 schools with college preparatory curricula, strong college-going cultures, and higher levels of resources may not always benefit from attendance due to tracking (Hallinan, 2000). Racial/ethnic minorities are disproportionately placed into non-academic tracks in high school and those students in non-academic tracks are more likely to attend community college than those graduating from academic tracks (Lavin & Hyllegard, 1996). Thus, the intersection of socio-economic status and race within the high school context acts to disadvantage students of color, increasing their chances of enrolling in the community college sector.

McDonough's (1997) notion of "organizational habitus" is an important family/community contextual factor that has been shown to affect students' college decision-making. Student aspirations and expectations as they relate to college-going are largely shaped by the history of achievement in the high school and community context, or its organizational habitus (McDonough, 1997; Person & Rosenbaum, 2006). For example, if previous graduates from a particular high school overwhelmingly attend community college, this trend of community college attendance will shape that high school's students' perceptions about their postsecondary options and constrain college decision-making. Students of color, who tend to be concentrated in underperforming urban high schools, are especially vulnerable to the negative effects of organizational habitus. The concept of organizational habitus also extends to the community in which students of color are located. Admon (2006) and Person and Rosenbaum (2006) found that Latinos' high concentration in community colleges could be linked back to the limited information about postsecondary education within their communities due to community members' historical patterns of college-going. Person and Rosenbaum (2006) describe this as "chain enrollment," by which Latino students select their own higher educational pathway based on where other community members have attended school. Although these two studies focused on Latino students in particular, similar theories may pertain to the patterns of participation among all students of color. "Chain enrollment" is much more common among students with strong social ties to their communities, whereas students who lack social capital within their community are more likely to seek out college information from diverse, external sources on their own (Person & Rosenbaum, 2006). Thus, among those with strong community ties, previous patterns of participation in higher education within the school and community contexts serve to constrain minority students' college decision-making, thereby leading to their high concentrations in the community college sector.

Factors in the Higher Education Institutional Context that Lead Students to Enroll in Community Colleges

Researchers have also looked toward the characteristics of community colleges and their environments in an effort to understand the relationship between higher education institutional contextual factors and high rates of community college attendance among students of color. These factors include location (Admon, 2006; Olivas, 2005), costs (Paulsen & St. John, 2002; Perna, 2004; St. John, 2003; St. John et al., 2005), marketing (Person & Rosenbaum, 2006), and program flexibility (Leigh & Gill, 2007).

Several researchers have found a relationship between students' college decision-making and institutional proximity to students' home communities. Among some racial/ethnic minority student groups, living at home, or attending college close to home, is an important factor in a student's postsecondary institutional pathway (Grodsky, 2002, Person & Rosenbaum, 2006; Zarate & Pachon, 2006). This desire to remain in close proximity to home can be connected to students of color's high levels of community college enrollment due to the locations of these institutions. Community colleges have a wide geographical distribution, and they were intended to bring educational opportunity to the communities that they serve (Cohen & Brawer, 2008). In this sense, familiarity might be responsible in part for the heavy concentration of students of color in community colleges. The intersection of place and college opportunity may be critical. As Olivas (2005) explains, "geography affects opportunity" (p. 182), and the relative ease of community college access juxtaposed with the physical and figurative distance of four-year institutions should not be viewed as benign coincidence. Several scholars (Admon, 2006; Brint & Karabel, 1989; Person & Rosenbaum, 2006) have cautioned that the convenience of community colleges has acted to constrain college choice among low-income students, first-generation college students, and racial/ethnic minorities. Such a view sits in direct opposition to the mission and function of community colleges.

In addition to their location, there are other characteristics of community colleges that may make them particularly attractive to students of color. These include program flexibility and breadth of offerings, both of which are often marketed by community colleges to encourage student enrollment (Leigh & Gill, 2007). In program flexibility, community colleges allow for part-time attendance by offering courses that will fit an employed person's schedule. Furthermore, in suburban and urban communities, the concentration of community colleges and the ease of the community college admissions process allow student mobility via lateral transfer (Adelman, 2005)—an attractive feature for working students, who are more likely to be minority and low-income (NCES, 2010b).

Community colleges also have the unique ability to respond to business and "consumer" demands through academic and vocational program offerings (Cohen & Brawer,

2008; Dougherty, 1994; Dougherty & Bakia, 2000; Leigh & Gill, 2007; Levin, 2001). Thus, as a particular occupational or academic area becomes more desirable, community colleges can react quickly to offer related coursework, and even certificates and degree programs (Dougherty, 1994; Leigh & Gill, 2007; Levin, 2001). This ability to offer on-demand programs may attract students of color and immigrant students who are looking to acquire immediate labor market returns to postsecondary education and the resulting upward economic mobility (Kane & Rouse, 1995).

Factors in the Social, Economic, and Policy Context that Lead Students to Enroll in Community Colleges

There are a variety of economic factors and higher education policies that contribute to the prevalence with which students of color and other historically disadvantaged groups attend community college. Although currently there are a record number of bachelor's degree holders in the U.S. (NCES, 2007), there remains a niche or demand in the U.S. labor market for associate degree earners (Kane & Rouse, 1995; Leigh & Gill, 2007). This is evidenced by the fact that associate degree holders see labor market returns that place them at an advantage over individuals with just a high school diploma or equivalent (Kane & Rouse, 1995). This characteristic of the economic context might encourage students of color to attend community colleges as these institutions can facilitate advances in the labor market on shorter time frames than it would take to earn a bachelor's degree. For low-income minority students, the prospect of near-term economic benefits resulting from community college attendance could be enough to lead them to enroll in the community college sector.

Recent state policy trends with regard to basic skills (i.e., remedial and developmental) education also act to affect community college attendance. In several states, basic skills education is increasingly relegated to the community college sector. For example, in California students are given one year to complete basic skills education in the state university system. If a student cannot successfully complete all basic skills requirements in that time frame, they are dis-enrolled from the four-year institution and forced to reverse transfer to a community college (California State University Office of the Chancellor, 1997). New York has taken further steps, opting to phase out all basic skills education from public four-year institutions. These policies disproportionately affect students of color as they more commonly graduate from under performing high schools in urban areas. Furthermore, the advent of high school exit examinations (e.g., California High School Exit Examination [CAHSEE]) has sealed the community college's fate as "remediator" of the failings of underperforming K-12 schools.

In addition to policies regarding the structure of postsecondary education systems and the function of the community college, higher education financial aid policy also contributes to the concentration of Latinos in the community college sector. Rising college tuitions and decreased buying power of federal grants (e.g., Pell Grants) have led to an increase in the amount of debt students incur to finance college (College Board, 2010; Price, 2004; St. John, 2003). The policy decision to allow appropriations for federal grant programs to lag behind the growing number of students enrolled in postsecondary education and increased college costs has caused loans to become a central part of financial aid packages, particularly among low-income and minority students attending four-year institutions (Price, 2004; St. John, 2003). Additionally, cuts in higher education appropriations at the state level and decreased availability in need-based state grant aid (St. John, 2003) have bolstered the reliance on student loans, particularly in the four-year sector. This financial aid policy environment coupled with the relatively low tuition at public community colleges leads to high minority and low-income student enrollment in the community college sector (Admon, 2006; Nora, 1990; Olivas, 1985; Paulsen & St. John, 2002; Person & Rosenbaum, 2006). In spite of the decreased buying power of the Pell Grant, community college tuition rates are such that grant aid from federal and state sources can cover them in large part. This is evidenced by the fact that borrowing among community college students is low compared to that for students in the four-year sector (NCES, 2010b; Santiago & Cunningham, 2005). In this sense, going to community college in lieu of direct entry to a four-year institution may be an attractive option for those students who do not want to borrow, a condition that is increasingly necessary in the current financial aid policy context.

FROM DIVERSITY TO EQUITY: OUTCOMES OF DIVERSE COMMUNITY COLLEGE STUDENTS

With a high proportion of "non-traditional" students enrolled, community colleges have a high degree of responsibility to contribute to the educational attainment and social mobility of historically disadvantaged populations. In addition to facilitating postsecondary access with open admissions policies, higher institutional capacities, and lower tuition levels, community colleges are faced with the challenge of preparing whoever enters their "open doors" for college-level work and for ensuring college success for students. These three functions of the community college have been described as the "equity agenda" by Bailey and Morest (2006), who argue that it is becoming increasingly difficult for community colleges to accomplish this agenda in the current economic and policy environments.

The data presented in this chapter indicate that community colleges are indeed fulfilling the access portion of the "equity agenda" by enrolling large numbers of racial/ethnic minorities, low-income students, adult students, and immigrant students (Bailey & Morest, 2006). However, in spite of the access that community colleges provide to these students, data regarding student success suggest that realizing equity in educational outcomes remains a significant challenge (Bailey & Morest, 2006; Bensimon, 2007). African American and Latino community college students are less likely to attain a certificate or associate's degree than their White and Asian counterparts (Bailey & Morest, 2006; NCES, 2003). Similarly, African American and Latino community college students are less likely to transfer to a four-year institution than White and Asian students (Bailey & Morest, 2006; NCES, 2003). Certainly, some of these racial/ethnic differences are related to factors such as socio-economic status, academic preparation, and other "risk factors." However, some racial/ethnic differences remain even when controlling for these other factors (Dowd, Cheslock, & Melguizo, 2008; NCES, 2003).

For decades, educational researchers have attempted to determine the implications of community college attendance for students of color. However, empirical investigations of the effects of community college attendance on the educational, professional, and economic outcomes of students have resulted in a somewhat hazy picture. Termed the "democratization" versus "diversion" debate (Rouse, 1995), these studies attempt to disentangle the complex effects of beginning postsecondary education in a community college. While there is a consensus that there are significant economic and labor market returns to community college attendance compared to high school graduates (Kane & Rouse, 1995; Marcotte, Bailey, Borkoski, & Kienzl, 2005; Paulsen, 1998; Rouse, 1995), the effect of community college attendance on educational outcomes is unclear. Furthermore, the ways in which college affects community college students (Pascarella & Terenzini, 2005) are far from established and effects upon students of color are muted. Some researchers argue that community colleges democratize higher education by providing low-cost access to students with lower levels of academic preparation and giving them the opportunity to improve their academic records, which in turn increases the chances of their being admitted by more selective institutions (Hilmer, 1997). Community colleges also afford students a more forgiving transition from high school to postsecondary education, which is particularly helpful to first-generation students. Warburton, Burgarin, and Nuñez (2001) demonstrate that community college attendance actually increased the persistence rates of first-generation Latino students compared to their counterparts who enrolled directly in four-year institutions. These differences may be attributable to the transitional period granted to students by community colleges. Choy (1999) similarly finds that first-generation students who began their postsecondary education in a community college were more likely to persist than those who did not first attend the institution. Further strengthening the democratization argument is Rouse's (1995) finding that bachelor's degree attainment rates among those students who transferred to a four-year institution from a community college do not differ from those for direct enrollees. Similarly, when comparing transfer students to those who directly attended a four-year institution in the High School & Beyond (HSB) sample, Lee, Mackie-Lewis, and Marks (1993) found no significant difference in the probability of bachelor's degree attainment between the two groups, in some contrast to Dougherty (1987). Leigh and Gill (2007) demonstrate that the effect of community college on educational attainment is highly sensitive to the educational aspirations of students upon entry to community college, with significant positive effects for those students who, upon entry to the community college, state that they aspire to complete a bachelor's degree. Community college attendance has also been shown to have a positive, direct effect on the educational expectations of community college students; however, these effects were conditioned on race, gender, and pre-college expectations (Pascarella, Wolniak, & Pierson, 2003).

Although these studies provide some empirical evidence of the positive effects of community college attendance on educational outcomes, many of these findings are contradicted by other research that bolsters the 'diversion' argument by illustrating that community college attendance disadvantages students by depressing educational aspirations, decreasing chances of bachelor's degree attainment, and extending the time to degree (Brint & Karabel, 1989), although the more commonly cited studies are dated, and in the case of Brint and Karabel (1989) based upon one state which may not be typical of the nation. Students who aspire to earn a bachelor's degree and initially enroll in community college are less likely to complete a bachelor's degree in the same period of time as similar students who initially enroll in a four-year institution (Pascarella & Terenzini, 2005). These differences in persistence remain when controlling for a variety of factors including academic ability, high school grades, college grades, family social origins, and work responsibilities (Alba & Lavin, 1981; Cabrera, La Nasa, & Burkum, 2001; Dougherty, 1987, 1992; Lavin & Crook, 1990; Lavin & Hyllegard, 1996; Nunley & Breneman, 1988; Pascarella & Terenzini, 2005). The persistence gap between those students who begin at community colleges and those who begin at four-year institutions may be attributable to numerous factors including barriers encountered during the transfer process (Dougherty, 1992, 1994; Grubb, 1991; Nora, 1993; Nora & Rendón, 1990; Rendón & Nora, 1994) and the "cooling-out" phenomenon (Clark, 1960, 1980; Pascarella, Edison, Nora, Hagedorn, & Terenzini, 1998). Furthermore, critics of the usefulness of the pathway to the baccalaureate via the community college point out that the transfer function of community colleges operates differentially for minority and low-income students, as these students are less likely to transfer successfully to four-year institutions than middle-class Whites and Asians (Bailey & Morest, 2006; Dougherty & Kienzl, 2006; Grubb, 1991). These scholars argue that while the community college does in fact provide access to higher education for many students, community colleges ought to continue to work toward creating conditions in which all students can succeed (Bensimon, 2007; Laanan, 2001). Indeed, it seems that the challenge for community colleges is to foster educational equity and success for all students (Hagedorn, 2010) while continuing to embrace and promote their rich student diversity.

SUMMARY AND CONCLUSIONS

Since their inception, community colleges have provided educational opportunities to individuals who have otherwise been unable to attend four-year colleges and universities. As detailed in this chapter, there are a number of highly complex and nuanced reasons that lead diverse students to enroll in community colleges. Oftentimes, these factors pertain to individual students' need for a lower cost option, a more flexible program, or coursework tailored to their specific needs (e.g., career/technical education, basic skills). However, the striking difference between community college student diversity and what is observed in four-year institutions is also related to many contextual factors. Factors in the K-12 school and community environments in which students are located often act to constrain postsecondary options, leading large percentages of low-income and minority students to view community colleges as their most viable, or sole, option. Similarly, community colleges have responded to the needs and demands of the communities in which they are located, making them more attractive and amenable to diverse students, who often have a wide range of educational goals. Finally, the social, economic, and higher education policy contexts, nationally, have acted to increase the likelihood of diverse students enrolling in community colleges.

As the nation has become more diverse, so have college students. Community colleges have led the way in providing access to a wide range of students, including racial/ethnic minorities, low-income and first-generation students, adult learners, and recent immigrants. While four-year institutions have become more costly and increasingly competitive and exclusionary, community colleges have remained as the "open door" to educational advancement. Similarly, as K-12 schools have become increasingly inequitable resulting in large gaps in college preparedness between African Americans, Latinos, and their White and Asian counterparts, community colleges have continued to provide basic skills, career, and technical education necessary to pave a path to economic mobility for historically disadvantaged groups. In spite of their success in these areas, however, community colleges continue to face significant challenges related to producing equity in educational outcomes for the wide range of students that they currently serve.

QUESTIONS FOR DISCUSSION

1. What conditions led to the growth of under-represented populations in community colleges?
2. Why do under-represented minority populations choose to attend community colleges?
3. What are the challenges for community colleges in responding to these populations?
4. What actions for community colleges are needed to improve educational and training prospects for its diverse student body?

REFERENCES

Adelman, C. (2005). *Moving into town—and moving on: The community college in the lives of traditional-age students.* Washington, DC: U.S. Department of Education.

Admon, N. (2006). *Hispanic students and the decision to attend community college.* (Doctoral dissertation.) *Dissertation Abstracts International, 67* (09), 3355A. (UMI 3235692)

Alba, R., & Lavin, D. (1981). Community colleges and tracking in higher education. *Sociology of Education, 54,* 223–237.

Bailey, T., & Morest, V. S. (2006). *Defending the community college equity agenda.* Baltimore, MD: Johns Hopkins University Press.

Bensimon, E. M. (2007). The underestimated significance of practitioner knowledge in the scholarship of student success. *Review of Higher Education, 30*(4), 441–469.

Bragg, D. D. (2001). Community college access, mission, and outcomes: Considering intriguing intersections and challenges. *Peabody Journal of Education, 76*(1), 93–116.

Brint, S., & Karabel, J. (1989). *The diverted dream: Community colleges and the promise of educational opportunity in America, 1900–1985.* New York, NY: Oxford University Press.

Cabrera, A. F., La Nasa, S. M., & Burkum, K. R. (2001). *Pathways to a four-year degree: The higher education story of one generation.* State College, PA: Center for the Study of Higher Education, The Pennsylvania State University.

California Postsecondary Education Commission. (2011). Higher education enrollment data. Retrieved from http://www.cpec.ca.gov/OnLineData/OnLineData.asp

Carter, P. L. (2009). Equity and empathy: Toward racial and educational achievement in the Obama era. *Harvard Educational Review, 79*(2), 287–297.

Choy, S. P. (1999). College access and affordability. *Education Statistics Quarterly, 1*(2), 74–90.

Clark, B. (1960). The "cooling-out" function in higher education. *American Journal of Sociology, 65,* 569–576.

Clark, B. (1980). The "cooling-out" function revisited. In G. Vaughan (Ed.), *Questioning the community college role. New Directions in Community Colleges, no. 32* (pp. 15–31). San Francisco, CA: Jossey-Bass.

Cohen, A. M., & Brawer, F. B. (2008). *The American community college* (5th ed.). San Francisco, CA: Jossey-Bass.

College Board. (2010). *Trends in college pricing, 2010* (Trends in Higher Education Series). Washington, DC: Author.

Dougherty, K. (1987). The effects of community colleges: Aid or hindrance to socioeconomic attainment? *Sociology of Education, 60,* 86–103.

Dougherty, K. (1992). Community colleges and baccalaureate attainment. *Journal of Higher Education, 63,* 188–214.

Dougherty, K. J. (1994). *The contradictory college: Conflicting origins, impacts, and futures of the community college.* Albany, NY: SUNY Press.

Dougherty, K. J., & Bakia, M. (2000). The new economic role of the community college: Origins and prospects. *CCRC Brief.* New York, NY: Teachers College, Community College Research Center.

Dougherty, K. J., & Kienzl, G. S. (2006). It's not enough to get through the open door: Inequalities by social background in transfer from community colleges to four-year colleges. *Teachers College Record, 108*(3), 452–487.

Dowd, A. C., Cheslock, J., & Melguizo, T. (2008). Transfer access from community colleges and the distribution of elite higher education. *The Journal of Higher Education, 79*(4), 442–472.

Flores, S. M., Horn, C. L., & Crisp, G. (2006). Community colleges, public policy, and Latino student opportunity. *New Directions for Community Colleges, no. 133* (pp. 71–80). San Francisco, CA: Jossey-Bass.

Florida Department of Education. (2010). *The fact book: Report for the Florida college system 2010.* Retrieved from http://www.fldoehub.org/CCTCMIS/c/Documents/Fact%20Books/fb2010.pdf

Fry, R. (2004). *Latino youth finishing college: The role of selective pathways*. Washington, DC: Pew Hispanic Center.

Fuerstenau, C. (2002, April). *Valuing context: The impact of social capital on students' college choice*. Paper presented at the annual meeting of the American Educational Research Association, New Orleans, LA.

Goldrick-Rab, S. (2006). Following their every move: An investigation of social-class differences in college pathways. *Sociology of Education, 79*(1), 61–79.

Grodsky, E. S. (2002). *Constrained opportunity and student choice in American higher education*. (Doctoral dissertation.) Retrieved from Dissertation Abstracts International, *63*(08), 3008A. (UMI 3060591)

Grubb, N. (1991). The decline of community college transfer rates: Evidence from national longitudinal surveys. *Journal of Higher Education, 62*, 184–217.

Hagedorn, L. S. (2010). The pursuit of student success: The directions and challenges facing community colleges. In J. C. Smart (Ed.), *Higher education: Handbook of theory and research* (Vol. XXV, pp. 181–218). New York, NY: Agathon Press.

Hallinan, M. T. (2000). On the linkages between sociology of race and ethnicity and sociology of education. In M. T. Hallinan (Ed.), *Handbook of the Sociology of Education* (pp. 65–84). New York, NY: Kluwer Academic/Plenum.

Hilmer, M. J. (1997). Does community college attendance provide a strategic path to a higher quality education? *Economics of Education Review, 16*, 59–68.

Hossler, D., Braxton, J., & Coopersmith, G. (1989). Understanding student college choice. In J. C. Smart (Ed.), *Higher education: Handbook of theory and research* (Vol. V, pp. 231–288). New York, NY: Agathon Press.

Hossler, D., & Gallagher, K. S. (1987). Studying college choice: A three-phase model and the implications for policy-makers. *College and University, 2*, 207–221.

Hossler, D., Schmit, J., & Vesper, N. (1999). *Going to college: How social, economic, and educational factors influence the decisions students make*. Baltimore, MD: Johns Hopkins University Press.

Hurtado, S., Inkelas, S., Briggs, C., & Rhee, B. (1997). Differences in college access and choice among racial/ethnic groups: Identifying continuing barriers. *Research in Higher Education, 38*(1), 43–75.

Illinois Board of Higher Education. (2010). *2010 data book*. Retrieved from http://www.ibhe.state.il.us/Data%20Bank/DataBook/default.asp

Immerwahr, J. (2003). *With diploma in hand: Hispanic high school seniors talk about their future*. (National Center Report #03–2.) San Jose, CA: National Center for Public Policy and Higher Education, and Public Agenda.

Kane, T. J., & Rouse, C. E. (1995). Labor-market returns to two- and four-year colleges. *American Economic Review, 85*(3), 600–614.

Karabel, J. (1972). Community colleges and social stratification. *Harvard Educational Review, 42*, 521–562.

Kinzie, J., Palmer, M., Hayek, J., Hossler, D., Jacob, S., & Cummings, H. (2004). *Fifty years of college choice: Social political and institutional influences on the decision-making process*. Indianapolis, IN: Lumina Foundation for Education.

Kozol, J. (2005). Still separate, still unequal: America's educational apartheid. *Harper's Magazine, 311*(1864), 41–54.

Kurlaender, M. (2006). Choosing community college: Factors affecting Latino college choice. In S. M. Flores, C. L. Horn, & G. Crisp (Eds.), *Latino Educational Opportunity. New Directions for Community Colleges, no.133* (pp. 7–16). San Francisco, CA: Jossey-Bass.

Laanan, F. S. (2001). Accountability in community colleges: Looking toward the 21st century. In B. K. Townsend & S. B. Twombly (Eds.), *Community colleges: Policy in the future context* (pp. 57–76). Westport, CT: Ablex Publishing.

Lavin, D., & Crook, D. (1990). Open admissions and its outcomes: Ethnic differences in long term educational attainment. *American Journal of Education, 98*, 389–425.

Lavin, D. E., & Hyllegard, D. (1996). *Changing the odds: Open admissions and the life changes of the disadvantaged*. New Haven, CT: Yale University Press.

Lee, V. E., Mackie-Lewis, C., & Marks, H. M. (1993). Persistence to the baccalaureate degree for students who transfer from community colleges. *American Journal of Education, 102*(1), 80–114.

Leigh, D. E., & Gill, A. M. (2007). *Do community colleges respond to local needs? Evidence from California*. Kalamazoo, MI: W. E. Upjohn Institute for Employment Research.

Levin, J. S. (2001). *Globalizing the community college: Strategies for change in the twenty-first century*. New York, NY: Palgrave.

Levin, J. S. (2007). *Non-traditional students and community colleges: The conflict of justice and neo-liberalism*. New York, NY: Palgrave Macmillan.

Manski, C. F., & Wise, A. D. (1983). *College choice in America*. Cambridge, MA: Harvard University Press.

Marcotte, D. E., Bailey, T., Borkoski, C., & Kienzl, G. S. (2005). The returns of a community college education: Evidence from the National Education Longitudinal Survey. *Educational Evaluation and Policy Analysis, 27*, 157–175.

McDonough, P. M. (1997). *Choosing colleges: How social class and schools structure opportunity*. Albany, NY: SUNY Press.

McDonough, P. M. (2004, July). The impact of advice on price: Evidence from research. Retrieved from http://www.teri.org/researchstudies/financial-aid-impact.asp

McDonough, P. M., Antonio, A. L., & Trent, J. W. (1997). Black students, Black colleges: An African American college choice model. *Journal for a Just and Caring Education, 3*, 9–36.

McDonough, P. M., & Calderone, S. (2006). The meaning of money: Perceptual differences between college counselors and low-income families about college costs and financial aid. *American Behavioral Scientist, 49*(12), 1703–1718.

Morrow, R., & Torres, C. (1995). *Social theory and education*. Albany, NY: SUNY Press.

National Center for Education Statistics. (2003). *Community college students: Goals, academic preparation, and outcomes* (NCES 2003–164). Washington, DC: Author.

National Center for Education Statistics. (2005). *Digest of education statistics, 2005*. Washington, DC: Author.

National Center for Education Statistics. (2008). *Community colleges: Special supplement to the condition of education 2008*. (NCES 2008–033.) Washington, DC: Author.

National Center for Education Statistics. (2010a). *Digest of education statistics, 2010*. Washington, DC: Author.

National Center for Education Statistics. (2010b). *National Postsecondary Student Aid Survey 2008* (NPSAS:08). Washington, DC: Author.

Nora, A. (1993). Two-year colleges and minority students' educational aspirations: Help or hindrance? In J. C. Smart (Ed.), *Higher education: Handbook of theory and research* (pp. 212–247). New York, NY: Agathon Press.

Nora, A. (2004). The role of habitus and cultural capital in choosing a college, transitioning from high school to higher education, and persisting in college among minority and non-minority students to college. *Journal of Hispanic Higher Education, 3*(2), 180–208.

Nora, A., & Rendón, L. I. (1990). Determinants of predisposition to transfer among community college students: A structural model. *Research in Higher Education, 31*(3), 235–255.

Nunley, C. R., & Breneman, D. W. (1988). Defining and measuring quality in community college education. In J. S. Eaton (Ed.), *Colleges of choice* (pp. 62–92). New York, NY: Macmillan.

Oakes, J. (2005). *Keeping track: How schools structure inequality* (2nd ed.). New Haven, CT: Yale University Press.

Olivas, M. A. (1985). Financial aid packaging policies: Access and ideology. *Journal of Higher Education, 56*(4), 462–475.

Olivas, M. A. (2005). Higher education as "place": Location, race, and college attendance policies. *Review of Higher Education, 28*(2), 169–189.

Pascarella, E., Edison, M., Nora, A., Hagedorn, L., & Terenzini, P. (1998). Does community college versus four-year college attendance influence students' educational plans? *Journal of College Student Development, 32*, 179–193.

Pascarella, E., & Terenzini, P. (2005). *How college affects students: A third decade of research*. San Francisco, CA: Jossey-Bass.

Pascarella, E. T., Wolniak, G. C., & Pierson, C. T. (2003). Influences on community college students' educational plans. *Research in Higher Education, 44*(3), 301–314.

Paulsen, M. B. (1990). *College choice: Understanding student enrollment behavior*. ASHE-ERIC Higher Education Report No. 6. Washington, DC: George Washington University, School of Education and Human Development.

Paulsen, M. B. (1998). Recent research on the economics of attending college: Returns on investment and responsiveness to price. *Research in Higher Education, 39*(4), 471–489.

Paulsen, M. B., & St. John, E. P. (2002). Social class and college costs: Examining the financial nexus between college choice and persistence. *Journal of Higher Education, 73*(2), 189–236.

Perna, L. W. (2004, July). *Impact of student aid program design, operations, and marketing on the formation of family college-going plans and resulting college-going behaviors of potential students*. Boston, MA: The Education Resources Institute, Inc. (TERI).

Perna, L. W. (2006). Studying college access and choice: A proposed conceptual model. In J. C. Smart (Ed.), *Higher education: Handbook of theory and research* (Vol. XXI, pp. 99–157). Dordrecht, The Netherlands: Kluwer Academic Publishers.

Person, A. E., & Rosenbaum, J. E. (2006). Chain enrollment and college enclaves: Benefits and drawbacks of Latino college students' enrollment decisions. In S. M. Flores, C. L. Horn, & G. Crisp (Eds.), *Latino Educational Opportunity. New Directions for Community Colleges, no. 133* (pp. 51–60). San Francisco, CA: Jossey-Bass.

Phillippe, K. A., & Gonzalez Sullivan, L. (2005). *National profile of community colleges: Trends and statistics* (4th ed.). Washington, DC: Community College Press.

Price, D. V. (2004). *Borrowing inequality: Race, class, and student loans.* Boulder, CO: Lynne Rienner.

Rendón, L. I., & Garza, H. (1996). Closing the gap between two- and four-year institutions. In L. I. Rendón & R. O. Hope (Eds.), *Educating a new majority: Transforming America's educational system for diversity* (pp. 289–308). San Francisco, CA: Jossey Bass.

Rendón, L. I., & Nora, A. (1994). Clearing the pathway: Improving opportunities for minority students to transfer. In L. Bjork (Ed.), *Minorities in higher education* (pp. 120–138). Phoenix, AZ: Oryx Press.

Richardson, R., Fisk, E., & Okun, M. (1983). *Literacy in the open-access college.* San Francisco, CA: Jossey-Bass.

Rouse, C. E. (1995). Democratization or diversion? The effect of community colleges on educational attainment. *Journal of Business & Economic Statistics, 13*(2), 217–224.

Santiago, D. A., & Cunningham, A. F. (2005). *How Latino students pay for college: Patterns of financial aid in 2003–2004.* Washington, DC: Excelencia in Education and the Institute for Higher Education Policy.

Sewell, W. H., Hauser, R. M., & Wolf, W. C. (1986). Sex, schooling and occupational status. *American Journal of Sociology, 86,* 551–583.

Stanton-Salazar, R. D. (2001). *Manufacturing hope and despair: The school and kin support networks of U.S. Mexican youth.* New York, NY: Teachers College Press.

St. John, E. P. (2003). *Refinancing the college dream: Access, equal opportunity, and justice for taxpayers.* Baltimore, MD: Johns Hopkins University Press.

St. John, E. P., Paulsen, M. B., & Carter, D. F. (2005). Diversity, college costs, and postsecondary opportunity: An examination of the financial nexus between college choice and persistence. *Journal of Higher Education, 76*(5), 545–569.

Swail, W. S., Cabrera, A. F., & Lee, C. (2004). *Latino youth and the pathway to college.* Washington, DC: Educational Policy Institute, Inc.

Teranishi, R., & Briscoe, K. (2006). Social capital and the racial stratification of college opportunity. In J. C. Smart (Ed.), *Higher education: Handbook of theory and research* (Vol. XXI, pp. 591–614). Dordrecht, The Netherlands: Kluwer Academic Publishers.

Texas Higher Education Coordinating Board. (2010). *Community college performance.* Retrieved from http://www.txhighereddata.org/interactive/accountability/CC_Participation.cfm?fice=445566

Tierney, W. G., & Venegas, K. M. (2006). Fictive kin and social capital: The role of peer groups in applying and paying for college. *American Behavioral Scientist, 49*(12), 1687–1702.

Tomás Rivera Policy Institute. (2004). *Caught in the financial aid information divide: A national survey of Latino perspectives on financial aid.* Los Angeles, CA: Author.

Venezia, A., Kirst, M., & Antonio, A. (2003*). Betraying the college dream: How disconnected K-12 and postsecondary education system undermine student aspirations.* Final Policy Report from Stanford University's Bridge Project. Stanford, CA: The Bridge Project, Stanford University. Retrieved from www.stanford.edu/group/bridgeproject/betrayingthecollegedream.pdf

Warburton, E. C., Bugarin, R., & Nuñez, A. (2001). *Bridging the gap: Academic preparation and postsecondary success of first-generation students.* Washington, DC: National Center for Education Statistics.

Zarate, M. E., & Pachon, H. P. (2006). Perceptions of college financial aid among California Latino youth. Policy brief. Los Angeles: Tomás Rivera Policy Institute. Retrieved from http://www.trpi.org/PDFs/Financial_Aid_Surveyfinal6302006.pdf

3

STUDENT DEVELOPMENT AND CONSUMERISM

Student Services on Campus

JOAN B. HIRT AND TARA E. FRANK

In 2010, 1,920 community colleges served 8,185,725 students, or nearly 42% of all undergraduates in postsecondary education in the U.S. (Carnegie Foundation for the Advancement of Teaching, 2010). More than 5,000,000 learners were enrolled in non-credit-bearing programs. Over 370,600 faculty (Condition of Education, 2008) educated students at these institutions that conferred 555,000 associate's degrees and 295,000 certificates (American Association of Community Colleges, 2008). Clearly, community colleges play a prominent role in the higher education landscape.

Other chapters in this book have described the mission of community colleges, the types of students they serve, and how these colleges are funded. In short, they are about the institutional terrain. Students do not navigate this terrain alone, however. There are a variety of student services at community colleges that support students' educational endeavors. Surprisingly, recent analytical research about these important campus functions is relatively sparse. Creamer (1994) traces the evolution of community college student services and describes standards of practice for professionals (Creamer, 1988) but even his later work is nearly two decades old. Helfgot and Culp (2005) offer the most recent research on student services when discussing the challenges confronting administrators at community colleges and they exhorted scholars to expand the knowledge base. Yet research on the topic remains meager.

This dearth of literature is related to two conceptual frameworks that have dominated the design and delivery of student services for the past 60 years—the student development framework and the consumerism framework. Neither formally addresses or fully captures the fundamentals of professional practice at community colleges. We argue, however, that student services at community colleges inform and are informed by both frames. In this chapter we explore where these boundaries intersect. We start by describing the two frameworks, paying particular attention to the evolutionary changes in the higher education enterprise that coincided with their emergence. Next, we discuss student services at community colleges and analyze how they influence and are influenced by the two frames. We conclude by identifying future directions for student services at community colleges.

DOMINANT CONCEPTIONS OF STUDENT SERVICES:
DEVELOPMENT VERSUS CONSUMERISM

Educators have provided services to students since the founding of Harvard in 1636, as even the elites who enrolled in the colonial colleges needed to be housed and fed (Brubacher & Rudy, 1997). Indeed, for the first 250 years of U.S. higher education, faculty were charged with not only the tutelage of their students but with their moral, ethical, and spiritual development as well. This *in loco parentis* paradigm assigned academics a pseudo-parental role in which they were responsible for students both in and out of the classroom (Nuss, 2003; Rhatigan, 2009).

In the late 19th and early 20th centuries, research and graduate education became more prominent in the academy and faculty members were less willing to spend their time and resources on non-academic student concerns. Consequently, administrators were hired specifically to address student matters outside of the classroom, laying the foundation for the student services profession (Bradshaw, 1994). Early student services administrators were Deans of Men, Deans of Women, and other personnel professionals including admissions directors, social directors, student counselors, psychologists, directors of dormitories, and vocational counselors (Cowley, 1994; Rhatigan, 2009).

By 1937, the population of student service providers was sufficiently large that the American Council on Education (ACE) held a conference to officially acknowledge this new species of academic professional (Nuss, 2003). The result was publication of *The Student Personnel Point of View* (SPPV), a seminal document for the student affairs profession that emphasized the importance of developing services that address both student needs and institutional mission (Nuss, 2003). In 1949, after the Servicemen's Readjustment Act of 1944 (the G.I. Bill) swelled enrollments at colleges and universities across the country (Rentz, 2004), ACE leaders revised the SPPV to address the increasing complexity of student personnel work and to call for formal academic preparation of professionals (Rhatigan, 2009).

The resulting genesis of graduate programs in college student personnel services in the 1950s and early 1960s was accompanied by two other trends germane to this discussion. First, the more mature veterans who matriculated in droves during the 1950s did not need (or want) a parental approach to services and this led to the demise of *in loco parentis* (Nuss, 2003; Rhatigan, 2009). Second, the demand for postsecondary education was marked by explosive growth in U.S. higher education in general, and the community college sector in particular (Urban & Wagoner, 2000). Hundreds of new community colleges opened in the 1960s and 1970s. As we illustrate below, these two trends evolved independently for all practical purposes yet profoundly influenced one another.

The Student Development Model

In loco parentis withered at the same time that graduate preparation programs in student personnel work emerged. Psychologists designed these programs, most often counseling psychologists who had worked as counselors and advisors on college and university campuses (Hirt, 2006). It is not surprising, then, that the paradigm that emerged to direct professional practice in student services was grounded in developmental psychology and came to be known as the student development model (Nuss, 2003; Rhatigan, 2009).

The model emphasized holistic development of students, attending to their psychological, emotional, spiritual, and physical needs as well as their cognitive growth.

Faculty rapidly produced a body of theoretical work to guide professionals. Some focused on psychosocial development. Expanding on the work of Erikson (1959, 1980) and Loevinger (1976), Chickering (1969) studied students at small colleges and devised a framework of psychosocial development for young adults, aged 18–24. Douglas Heath (1968) and James Marcia (1966) are among the other researchers who offered alternative models describing the psychosocial challenges that young adults must master in order to succeed in later stages of life.

Still other scholars expanded on Piaget's (1952) research on cognitive development among children. Perry's model (1968) was based on data from college students, as was Kohlberg's (1969). Each defined stages of cognitive growth. Gilligan (1982) and Belenky, Clinchy, Goldberger, and Tarule (1986) focused exclusively on women's cognitive development, although the former relied on data primarily from college women while the latter team studied non-college women as well.

Two other groups of theory also emerged in this time frame. Typological theories explained permanent or semi-permanent personality types. These types were relevant to vocational and career counseling (Holland, 1973), learning styles (Heath, 1964; Kolb, 1984), and intra- and interpersonal interactions (Myers, 1980). Person-environment theories grounded in the work of Lewin (1951) looked at college student behavior as a social function of person and environment (e.g., Banning & Kaiser, 1974; Harvey, Hunt, & Schroeder, 1961) in an attempt to understand how college environments could be shaped to maximize developmental opportunities for students.

These foundational theories steered professional practice in student affairs throughout the 1980s. In the latter part of the 20th century, research shifted to issues of social identity. Studies on racial identity development (e.g., Helms, 1990; Phinney, 1990) and sexual identity development (e.g., Cass, 1979; D'Augelli, 1994) were useful to practitioners as student populations became more diverse. Integrative theories also emerged to address questions of faith and spirituality (Fowler, 1981; Parks, 1986), transition (Schlossberg, 1981), and self-authorship (Baxter-Magolda, 2001).

The common thread weaving these theories together for student services professionals is the notion of amalgamated development. Student affairs administrators are socialized in graduate preparation programs to view students holistically. Each student is a unique individual with particular needs, interests, and abilities. For professionals, this translates to systematically designing and delivering programs to promote development in all aspects of human growth. In fact, this student development model of student services persists today at most U.S. colleges and universities (Hirt, 2007).

It is also critical to note that nearly all of the guiding student development theories are based on data from students at (or graduates of) four-year colleges and universities. A few (e.g., Belenky et al., 1986; Schlossberg, 1981) included non-college students in their samples, but none of the theorists intentionally included community college students when devising their schemas. This was likely a matter of expediency not malevolence on the part of scholars. The majority (70%) of graduate programs in student affairs and higher education administration are at research universities. The bulk of the remaining 30% are at master's institutions that were formerly teachers' colleges and normal schools where education is a flagship program and research is expected (Hirt, 2006). The samples most readily available to theorists were students at four-year institutions, thus theories were normed on this population. Nonetheless, the lack of data from community college students in the formulation of student development theories has implications for practice at those campuses. To some extent those implications have been mitigated by the second pervasive model of professional practice that has gripped student services administrators and academics alike for the past 25 years, the market or consumer model.

The Student as Consumer

The context for the student consumerism model is tied to the landmark transition that occurred in the mid-1980s *vis à vis* higher education, the corporate sector, and the state. For 40 years after World War II, the military industrial complex, hence funding to higher education, was driven by the perceived menace of the Soviet Union. Research at colleges and universities was closely linked to winning the Cold War. As the threat of communism faded after 1989, a new narrative was needed to sustain public and private investment in higher education. Burgeoning economies in Japan and China provided the impetus for this new narrative: globalization. Colleges and universities turned their attention to increasing the country's international competitiveness (Greenberg, 1993; Levin, 2001; Slaughter & Leslie, 1997; Slaughter & Rhoades, 2004).

Two derivatives of this shift are relevant to any discussion of community colleges. The first is higher education's widespread adoption of economic rationalism, a philosophy that emphasizes decentralization and market mechanisms (Mok & Welch, 2003; Welch, 2001). Put simply, from an economic rationalist perspective, higher education is a commodity that can be produced, marketed, and traded across national boundaries. Evidence of the commodification of higher education can be found in the burgeoning partnerships between U.S. and international universities and branch campuses of U.S. universities that have sprung up in China, India, and the Middle East, in particular (Lane & Kinser, 2008). Perhaps the most striking consequence of economic rationalism is the proliferation of proprietary institutions in the U.S., particularly for-profit, two-year colleges (Kinser, 2005).

Second, this "capitalization of knowledge" (Etzkowitz, Webster, & Healey, 1998) has led to a culture of managerialism (Deem, 1998; Newman, Couturier, & Scurry, 2004; Rhoades, 1998) in postsecondary education. Efficiency, effectiveness, and accountability are the hallmarks of managerialism and the corporate mentality that has permeated the higher education sector (Welch, 2001). To offer a simple illustration, consider the changes in titles that have occurred on campuses. Provosts are now vice presidents for academic affairs, a more corporate title. Vice presidents for finance, administration, and external relations are commonplace on campuses. In the student affairs arena, deans of men and women were first merged to create dean of students positions only to morph into vice presidents for student affairs as the managerial model evolved (Woodard, 2006).

Perhaps most pertinent to this discussion is how students are perceived in a managerial environment. When higher education is a commodity, students become consumers (Miller, 2006). Consumers (applicants) shop for an educational product, often deciding where to enroll based on competing offers (financial aid, program availability). Contractors (instructors, lecturers) teach select classes under specific contractual terms (Shumar, 1997). Student satisfaction levels and placement rates as opposed to quality of education measure academic success. Institutions are like retailers; the primary goal is to serve the student customer (Moore, 2004). Terms such as "benchmarking," "deliverable," and "value added" are part of the vernacular of student services professionals in the managerial culture.

It is important to note that consumerism does not seem to have supplanted student development as the dominant framework of professional practice. Rather, it acts as a scrim for student services administrators. Student development is still the ultimate aim of practitioners but they achieve this aim through the filter of consumerism (Hirt, 2007; Kinser, 2006). For example, professionals now seek corporate sponsors for major campus events, although the events still ostensibly aim to promote development. Outsourcing student services to private sector providers is commonplace (Slaughter & Rhoades, 2004), even services such as health and counseling that are fundamental to student development. Administrators calculate rates of return on investment before implementing new programs or services that are designed to both serve student consumers and promote student development. Thus, the two frameworks coexist in contemporary student services practice. At issue here is how the two frames play out in the context of student services at community colleges.

STUDENT DEVELOPMENT AND CONSUMERISM IN THE COMMUNITY COLLEGE CONTEXT

Any analysis of student services at community colleges must be prefaced by two caveats—one about student services and the other related to community colleges. From an organizational perspective, what constitutes student services is elusive. The boundaries of what is included in the student affairs portfolio are intangible. On some campuses, functions such as career services and advising fall into the student services domain while on other campuses they are considered academic endeavors. On some campuses, athletics and housing are key components of the student affairs division while on other campuses they fall under the purview of administrative or business affairs (Hirt, 2006). The vagaries of professional borders confound attempts to analyze the profession.

This challenge is further exacerbated by the intricacy of the community college genre. For many years, community colleges were discussed monochromatically in the literature. Nothing could be farther from the truth, however. Community colleges vary dramatically in terms of enrollments, extent of course offerings, facilities, and any number of other characteristics. Only in recent years has the leading authority on institutional types, the Carnegie Foundation (2005, 2010), identified 14 discrete classes of community colleges based on location (rural, suburban, urban), size of enrollment (less than 2,500, 2,500–7,500, greater than 7,500), number of sites (single- vs. multi-campus), and sector (not-for-profit, for-profit). The typology also recognizes Special Use associate's colleges that offer a narrowly focused curriculum and those community colleges that offer both B.A. and A.A. degrees or are formally associated with a four-year institution.

In spite of the imprecision of student affairs boundaries and the complexity of the community college typology, most campuses offer services that can be clustered into four functional areas: enrollment management, learning support, student support, and co-curricular services. The challenge in talking about variation in services or by type of community college campus is that no empirical research on the matter has been conducted. Therefore, the following discussion is based on a review of campus websites and resources. We looked at 15–20% of sites in each Carnegie category and supplemented our information through comments from 27 colleagues who work, or have worked, at different types of institutions in the community college sector (Hirt & Frank, 2011). Our analysis should be interpreted in that context.

Additionally, each of the institutions within the 14 Carnegie categories has its own unique history, traditions, and culture. When we talk about differences by type of community college, our analysis paints institutions in any given category with a very broad brush and may not describe all campuses within a group. On a related note, there were five categories of Associate institutions that we did not include in our research, namely those that were either connected with a four-year institution (e.g., a branch campus or division of a four-year institution, N = 48), those that offered both two- and four-year degrees (a total of 162 schools, both public/private, and for-profit/not-for-profit), and Special Use institutions [N = 12] (Carnegie Classification of Institutions, 2010). The missions of colleges in these categories differed in important ways from other college campuses and we wanted to avoid conflating the data. Even given the parameters of our research, however, these four functions (enrollment management, learning support, student support, and co-curricular services) when viewed through the student development and consumerism lenses yield insights into both present practices and future directions for student services at community colleges.

Enrollment Management Services

The term "enrollment management" was coined in the late 1970s and represents an organizational approach that integrates functional areas such as recruiting, admission, orientation, and registration (Coomes, 2000). The purpose of enrollment management is to attract and retain students (Hossler, 2004). Enrollment management services at community colleges often encompass testing, advising, financial aid, and bursar services as well as admissions. Community college administrators view everyone in their service area as a potential student and, therefore, engage in a broad array of tactics designed to recruit these potential learners (Cohen & Brawer, 2008).

Some elements of the enrollment management function seem to reflect a developmental perspective. For example, because the service area is clearly delineated, admission officers can engage in narrowly focused marketing efforts (Hoover, 2011). They have access to solid data about traditional-aged (18–20-year-old) student characteristics from district high schools and local municipal records (e.g., birth rates, average income, unemployment rates). For adult students, college officials look to data from local business and manufacturing interests. Seeking to understand the needs of the applicant pool assumes a developmental approach to the admissions function.

Even more compelling evidence of the developmental approach to student services is found in the testing function. Community colleges routinely test incoming students' aptitudes (e.g., math, writing) to ensure that students are placed in appropriate entry-level classes. Students most often have personal contact with a professional before they matriculate, enabling staff to make connections with students and identify areas of developmental need. While some college administrators lament that community college students are increasingly academically unprepared for college (Carlson, 2011), it is a developmental perspective (their concern for their students' success) that leads to such claims.

Indeed, the multifaceted mission of community colleges speaks to the developmental approach. Campuses offer both transfer and vocational education along with developmental and continuing education. Matching students to programs most suited to their needs and interests is a fundamental premise of person-environment theory (e.g., Holland, 1973) and of Sanford's (1967) guiding principle of providing college students with appropriate levels of challenge and support. Thus, there is evidence of the developmental perspective in the enrollment management arena but it is somewhat dwarfed by the market approach which most community colleges have embraced.

Evidence of the consumerism perspective in enrollment management is abundant. To start, the service district—i.e., the local market—drives curricula. Campuses located in rural areas offer multiple programs in agricultural sciences and land management while those in suburban areas sponsor more programs in arts and communications (e.g., radio, TV, photography) and urban institutions more frequently confer degrees and/or certificates in areas such as criminal justice. In Los Angeles, colleges sponsor programs in theater arts and real estate. In Seattle, home to Microsoft and Boeing, there are offerings in computer software and aviation sciences. In the heart of NASCAR country (Charlotte) automotive programs abound while in Atlanta, site of the world's busiest airport, airplane maintenance curricula are prominent. The market even influences curricula in transfer programs. Colleges acknowledge their role in the supply chain by identifying the four-year institutions their students most frequently transfer to and crafting articulation agreements to ensure the uninterrupted delivery of students to those baccalaureate institutions (Hirt & Frank, 2011). The recruiting function, then, is market savvy.

Testing services can be viewed as a sorting process used to determine which raw materials (students) are appropriate for each production line (transfer, vocational, developmental) at the institution (Hirt & Frank, 2011). In fact, at some campuses this cataloging process is personalized. Administrators are worried that students become caught in a web of developmental classes and experience such a high level of frustration that they drop out without completing their program of study (Bailey, Jeong, & Cho, 2010). Institutions are evaluated on their completion rates, thus it behooves professionals to maximize those rates. Consequently, in at least one state there is a movement afoot to "customize" remedial programs to better serve students (Carlson, 2011). The customer service orientation could not be more pronounced.

Perhaps the most deliberate manifestation of the market model in the enrollment management arena is found at proprietary colleges (Hirt & Frank, 2011). At many such institutions, the same professional recruits, admits, and orients a student (Kinser, 2006). This concierge approach to enrollment management is designed to convert inquiries to applicants and applicants to students. Admission counselors serve as intermediaries for potential enrollees, explaining admission policies, connecting them to financial aid services, contacting applicants frequently (bi-weekly at many for-profit institutions), and generally ensuring customer (student) satisfaction with the product (enrollment process). Students are instructed to contact their counselor if they encounter any obstacles, have questions, or need assistance (Hirt & Frank, 2011). Proprietary institutions epitomize a customer-service approach to enrollment management.

Learning Support Services

Once admitted, students need assistance to succeed academically. Professionals in learning support services that include tutoring, technology support, and English as a Second Language (ESL) programs, among others, address these academic needs. Learning centers that offer an abundance of tutoring support and study skills programs are prevalent across all types of community colleges (e.g., math and writing centers). Many of these centers also provide technology such as software, calculators, computers, and printers in addition to making available study guides and practice tests to registered students. Computer centers usually provide computer and online services but also offer training on software programs and other devices that enhance student learning (Hirt & Frank, 2011).

The developmental paradigm is more evident in learning support services than in the enrollment management arena. At their core, these programs are designed to advance psychosocial and cognitive development. Tutoring services, for instance, are delivered in ways designed to promote multiple forms of psychosocial development. Professionals hire students who have successfully mastered basic courses in different academic programs to tutor other students who are struggling in those subject areas. This approach encourages intellectual competence among the tutors and instrumental independence among learners, both elements of Chickering's (1969) model of psychosocial development. Learning to use new software or forms of technology boosts manual/physical competency, another Chickering vector.

Cognitive development is manifest in what learning centers aim to achieve—helping students to master higher order thinking skills. In some cases, this entails aiding students to improve their memorization skills in order to better retain information. In other instances, staff members work with students to analyze or synthesize course materials, activities that require more complex reasoning skills (Perry, 1968; Piaget, 1952). Efforts to enhance student learning are typically associated with the developmental paradigm.

Two particular groups of community college students merit attention in terms of psychosocial and cognitive development: adults seeking to learn new vocational skills and immigrants. High unemployment rates have prompted countless displaced workers to enroll in community colleges to retool (Katsinas & Friedel, 2010). Many of these learners have not been in a classroom in decades and need remedial classes or assistance with basic skills in order to succeed. Immigrants are among the fastest growing segments of the U.S. population and may be more likely to start their college careers at community colleges where English reading and writing skills can be honed (Teranishi, Suarez-Orozco, & Suarez-Orozco, 2011). The programs and services that learning support professionals have implemented for these two groups of students are predominately developmental in nature. They are designed to enhance students' social and academic transition to the collegiate setting via culturally sensitive programs and services, hallmarks of the developmental model.

Finally, the developmental paradigm reveals the importance of learning theory in the operation of learning support services. In general, learning theories describe the different ways in which people assimilate and process information. Learning center professionals use different techniques to expand students' repertoires of learning styles. They may ask students to reflect on what a particular lecture or reading assignment means or to observe how an experiment is conducted. At other times, they encourage students to actively experiment with new learning techniques or assistive equipment. These varied approaches reflect forms of learning in developmental models (e.g., Kolb, 1984).

Although learning services might seem more innately linked to developmental than market models, there is ample evidence of consumerism in these functional areas. For example, the size of the market for services breeds the span of those services. Smaller campuses tend to consolidate services for learners into a single center—a one-stop-shopping model. At larger and multi-campus institutions, specialization is evident. Distinct math and writing centers, special reading programs, and websites in Spanish,

Polish, German, even Magyar, reflect a boutique approach to learning services (Hirt & Frank, 2011).

Unsurprisingly, learning support at for-profit institutions is markedly different than it is at non-profits. As Kinser (2006) notes, retention and profitability are closely coupled—"students represent revenue" (p. 271) and institutional revenues rest upon helping students succeed academically. At many proprietary colleges, once the student is enrolled the counselor who facilitated the student's admission to the institution becomes the student's academic advisor, providing ongoing academic services. Most of the time this involves continuing contact, ensuring that students know what courses are required for the degree or certificate they aspire to earn, or that they have a plan of study that clearly delineates the path to success. Maximizing customer satisfaction, a quintessential premise of consumerism, is a hallmark of student services at proprietary colleges (Kinser, 2006).

Student Support Services

Learning support services are tied to students' academic success but students have personal, social, and other needs that community college professionals address through more general student support services. These may encompass a variety of programs but counseling (including career services), advising, TRIO programs, and services for students with disabilities are the most commonplace at community colleges (Cohen & Brawer, 2008). Intuitively, it makes sense that student support services would be grounded in a developmental approach and in many respects that is the case. For instance, career counselors work with students to identify their skills and interests and match those abilities with potential careers. Given the varied missions of community colleges, the developmental elements of career counselors' work extend to identifying the type of program best suited for the student. Vocational programs are most suitable for some but transfer programs are appropriate for others.

TRIO programs, in particular, operate through a developmental lens. These programs include Educational Opportunity Centers, the McNair Scholars Program, Student Support Services Program, Talent Search, Upward Bound Math-Science, and Veterans Upward Bound. They provide avenues for students from educationally and economically disadvantaged backgrounds to attend community colleges and other types of institutions (McElroy & Armesto, 1998). For instance, professionals in these programs strive to boost students' confidence in seeking out and applying for their academic program of choice. TRIO professionals work to enhance students' knowledge of financial aid programs and teach them how to secure funding for their education (Hirt & Frank, 2011), efforts aimed at promoting psychosocial and cognitive development.

Services for students with disabilities offer some of the most tangible evidence of the developmental perspective. To start, community colleges are the institutions of choice for many disabled students (Cohen & Brawer, 2008). Disabled students who enroll at local community colleges are able to pursue their academic goals while retaining the local support network they have developed. Community colleges are particularly well positioned to work with learning disabled students (Marchand, 2010) and are the only viable postsecondary options for many severely disabled students. The foundation of developmental theory is the uniqueness of every individual. In working with disabled students, professionals need to know the distinct challenges of each student. Individualized programs are designed to provide each learner with the appropriate support and assistive technology to facilitate academic adjustment and personal success. This is the embodiment of the developmental approach to student services.

There are challenges in the community college sector, however, that militate against a developmental approach to student support services, particularly the burgeoning numbers of students seeking opportunities at these institutions. Between 1998 and 2008, the number of students attending community colleges rose by 38%, with disproportionately greater growth at public (45%) and for-profit (129%) institutions (*Chronicle of Higher Education Almanac, 2010–11*). Future predictions suggest enrollment increases of 9% on average (Katsinas & Friedel, 2010) and possibly double-digit growth in select states. In fact, a third or more of state community college systems have insufficient capacity to accommodate the predicted increases in student enrollments, a problem exacerbated by the fact that many of these are in states that expect the greatest growth in demand such as California, New York, and Illinois (Katsinas & Friedel, 2010). Attending to individual needs (i.e., taking a developmental approach to services) under such circumstances is daunting for institutions and student services units.

The characteristics and enrollment patterns of students further exacerbate the individuation of student support services. Those drawn to community colleges tend to be older adults, who often have jobs, families, and other responsibilities competing for their time and attention. Many are among the 17,000,000 Americans left unemployed or underemployed by the economic recession of 2007–2009 who are increasingly turning to community colleges for vocational education (Katsinas & Friedel, 2010). Their enrollment can be fluid and they are often forced to drop classes mid-term or even stop out entirely for one or more terms when these other responsibilities intervene (Cohen & Brawer, 2008). Attempts to individualize services for students under these circumstances can seem futile.

Market model practices have emerged to address some of the challenges in student support services. For example, community college leaders have become exceptionally adept at identifying employment opportunities in the local market and rapidly responding. It is not unusual for new vocational programs to be introduced in just 10 weeks (Hirt, 2006). Career counselors under such circumstances are sensitive to the market, not the student. Another illustration of the market model relates to how services are offered. The one-stop versus boutique approach evident in learning support services is also relevant to student support services. At smaller campuses, particularly in rural settings, professionals fulfill multiple functions; the same staff members provide career counseling and personal counseling, for example. At larger institutions, these functions are distinct and housed in separate offices (Hirt & Frank, 2011). The one exception to this pattern involves TRIO offices that focus solely on providing TRIO services. This is likely tied to the federal funding that underwrites such programs and delineates what tasks staff can legitimately undertake (Hirt & Frank, 2011).

The for-profit sector of community colleges supplies the clearest examples of consumerism in terms of student support services. Proprietary institutions offer only those support services that improve student (hence institutional) success (Kinser, 2006). For-profit colleges measure their success, to a large extent, on job placement. To that end, most support services revolve around issues of career; proprietary institutions offer extensive internship and career placement services. Success is also measured by profit margin and that drives some student support services. For instance, many proprietary campuses offer child-care centers that their adult learners need and that are attractive because they operate as separate revenue streams for the institution.

Co-curricular Services

Co-curricular services on community college campuses are the most elusive to encapsulate because there are no standard programs included in this realm. Indeed, we designate them "co-curricular" in order to reflect the broad array of services that institutions offer. In general, however, three labels capture the majority of these programs: athletics, student activities, and housing. Intercollegiate athletics is one of the most popular activities at community colleges; over 72,000 full-time students at over 500 community colleges participated in intercollegiate teams during the 2001–2002 academic year (Castaneda, 2004). Those numbers are likely much higher in the present and will continue to climb as enrollments increase. Student activities encompass clubs, organizations, student government, and other programs designed to increase student involvement in campus life. Finally, residence halls on community college campuses are becoming increasingly common. At present, over 300 community colleges offer some form of housing (Biemiller, 2009).

These co-curricular services are grounded in developmental assumptions that education should address the holistic needs of students, including their physical and social needs. Since developmental theories were most often normed on traditional aged (18–22-year-old) students who were disproportionately Caucasian and from upper-middle-class backgrounds (Evans, Forney, Guido, Patton, & Renn, 2010) some of them do not translate readily to the community college setting, however. For example, community college students participate in campus organizations or in campus-sponsored events at relatively low rates (Chang, 2002). As noted above, large percentages of community college students are older and have work and family obligations (Chang, 2002; Cohen & Brawer, 2008): they have little time for, or interest in, campus life.

Consequently, the market model is increasingly driving co-curricular services (Slaughter & Rhoades, 2004). Housing services are a good example. Rural institutions are building housing programs because they seek to increase convenience by reducing commuting time for students; convenience is a hallmark of consumerism. There is also a cadre of campuses, many of which are private, that offer primarily transfer education. These institutions build housing operations as they strive to capture a greater market share of traditional-aged students who plan on transferring to a four-year institution (where on-campus housing is the norm) to earn a baccalaureate degree and want the amenities of a four-year institution while completing lower division requirements at a community college (Biemiller, 2009). Some urban community colleges (e.g., Long Beach, Los Angeles, Honolulu) are also building residence halls in order to capture a greater market share of international students.

Other patterns in co-curricular services can also be interpreted from a market perspective, particularly in regards to customer appeal. In the southwest region of the country, campuses sponsor rodeo teams (both intercollegiate and intramural) while lumberjack sports prevail at institutions in the northwest. Cross-cultural services and programs for international students are more prevalent at suburban and urban campuses (Hirt & Frank, 2011). Tangentially, geography also influences hours of operation; evening hours are common at suburban and urban campuses but not at other types of community colleges. Serving customers is at the heart of such endeavors, a signature element of the market model.

Predictably, co-curricular services at proprietary colleges differ from those at non-profit institutions and are not predicated by location but by business interests and customer need. Most students are drawn to for-profit institutions because job placement is at the forefront of institutional marketing strategies and securing employment is students' highest priority. Consequently, co-curricular offerings at proprietary campuses are typically limited to organizations that relate to career objectives, such as accounting clubs for students in business or nursing clubs for allied health students (Kinser, 2006).

The nexus between the developmental and market approaches to co-curricular services may become more muddled in the future, however. A report on college-going patterns of recent high school graduates suggests that far greater numbers of traditional-aged students are opting to enroll at community colleges. The sector secured 41.7% of traditional-aged students in 2006, but 44.5% in 2009. In the final year under study (2008 to 2009), enrollments of this group increased by 8.3% (Hoover, 2011). It appears that two types of traditional-aged students are driving this trend and that the economic recession is a factor for both groups. The first are those who might have attended other, more costly institutions if economic conditions were different. The second includes those who might have worked after high school if jobs were available (Hoover, 2011). It will be interesting to see if increased numbers of 18–22-year-olds on campus are accompanied by a concomitant shift to a developmental approach to co-curricular services.

Indeed, while we have contrasted developmentalism and marketization throughout this chapter, the two are not mutually exclusive. The interest in individual students evident in the developmental framework can just as easily be interpreted as meeting institutional needs for success, a marketing perspective. Likewise, activities we attributed to promoting customer satisfaction from a consumer frame (e.g., clearly delineating a pathway to success for every student) might also be viewed as developmental (e.g., integrating the student to campus life). Nonetheless, there are several future issues that emerge when the developmental and market models of student services are juxtaposed.

FUTURE DIRECTIONS IN STUDENT SERVICES

Our analysis leads to three general conclusions about student services at community colleges. First, it is clear that both developmental and consumer models have informed professional practice at these institutions. Dedication to student growth and development is most evident in learning support services where individualizing services to meet student needs is essential and services are, by design, aimed at promoting academic success one student at a time. Equally clear, however, is the inadequacy of current developmental theory to address the needs of community college students. Theorists need to define what psychosocial development means in the context of the community college setting. How is development measured over a two-year enrollment period or for students who stop in and out of their academic program over the span of several years? How does interruption in the formal educational process influence learning and cognitive development? There is a need for research on the relevance of identity theories for community college students, and no person-environment theory has addressed the unique cultures of community college campuses. An adage in higher education argues that "theory without practice is empty and practice without theory is blind." No statement could more accurately encapsulate the need for additional theoretical work on student development among college students.

At the same time, the ways in which student services at community colleges inform both the developmental and consumer frames are often unrecognized and underappreciated by professionals. Developmentally, enrollment management professionals can personalize their outreach to many potential students using the data they have about high schoolers and workers in their service district. As for learning services, community colleges are the only type of institution that routinely conducts individual assessments of every student's ability in order to identify the best academic placement for that student. From the consumer perspective, community colleges are models of adapting to local market conditions when it comes to what services and programs they provide. They are also prototypes of design with respect to how they deliver those programs and services, employing either a one-stop or boutique model as appropriate to their size and complexity. Scholars should pay more attention to how student services at community colleges have enacted both the developmental and consumer frames.

Our final conclusion has to do with the future of student services at community colleges. We have already discussed the impact that burgeoning enrollments at these institutions might have. There is another trend that bears mentioning in this regard: shifts in faculty patterns. In 2007, 69% of community college faculty members were employed part-time. Part-timers typically teach a limited number of course sections, are on campus only to meet class obligations, and have little incentive to engage in the life of the campus (Wilson, 2010). Student service professionals, on the other hand, are generally on campus full-time. Simply by virtue of their presence, they are increasingly likely to become the face of their institution, the staff that students most rely on for both academic and non-academic support. Will they sustain support for student development in the face of these two trends? Will the efficiencies of the market model force them to abandon their commitment to student development?

Scholars have not offered any clear answers. Kinser (2006) argues that student services administrators should model their work on the approach that their counterparts at proprietary institutions have taken, where customer service and satisfaction drive professional practice. On the other hand, Warren (2010, p. 2) laments that "[o]nce upon a time, we didn't so completely adapt our rhetoric and our curricula to the marketplace. We had missions and visions of … colleges that didn't hum 'global economy' … Higher education had another purpose." Absent an intentional response to this conundrum, the direction that student services take in the next few years may signal the approach to student learning and growth that will guide community colleges in the foreseeable future.

QUESTIONS FOR DISCUSSION

1. What are some differences between the student development model and the consumerism model in higher education?
2. Is the developmental model practiced effectively so that the needs of the student are met or the needs of the organization are met?
3. What can we learn from the student development (market) models of private institutions, and what impedes public community colleges from implementing some of the best practices of private colleges?
4. What are the emerging trends in student services on campus, and how do we prepare student services professionals to serve an increasingly diverse population of students?

REFERENCES

American Association of Community Colleges, Stats Home. (2008). Retrieved from http://www2.aacc.nche.edu/research/index.htm

Bailey, T. B., Jeong, D. W., & Cho, S. W. (2010). Referral, enrollment and completion in developmental education sequences in community colleges. *Economics of Education Review, 29,* 255–270.

Banning, J. H., & Kaiser, L. (1974). An ecological perspective and model for campus design. *Personnel and Guidance Journal, 52,* 370–375.

Baxter-Magolda, M. B. (2001). *Making their own way: Narratives for transforming higher education to promote self-development.* Sterling, VA: Stylus.

Belenky, M. F., Clinchy, B. M., Goldberger, N. R., & Tarule, J. M. (1986). *Women's ways of knowing: The development of self, voice, and mind.* New York, NY: Basic Books.

Biemiller, L. (2009, April 24). More community colleges building residence halls. *Chronicle of Higher Education.* Retrieved from http://chronicle.com/article/More-Community-Colleges-Build/36049/

Bradshaw, F. F. (1994). The scope and aims of a personnel program. In A. L. Rentz (Ed.), *Student affairs: A profession's heritage* (2nd ed., pp. 43–65). Lantham, MD: University of America Press. (Original work published in 1936.)

Brubacher, J. S., & Rudy, W. (1997). *Higher education in transition: A history of American colleges and universities* (4th ed.). New Brunswick, NJ: Transaction.

Carlson, S. (2011, July 24). Community college officials swap notes on common worries and challenges. *Chronicle of Higher Education.* Retrieved from http://chronicle.com/article/Community-College-Officials/128225/

Carnegie Foundation for the Advancement of Teaching. (2005). *A classification of institutions of higher education.* Princeton, NJ: Carnegie Council for the Advancement of Teaching.

Carnegie Foundation for the Advancement of Teaching. (2010). Retrieved from http://classifications.carnegiefoundation.org/summary/basic.php

Cass, V. C. (1979). Homosexual identity formation: A theoretical model. *Journal of Homosexuality, 4,* 219–235.

Castaneda, C. (2004). *A national overview of intercollegiate athletics in public community colleges.* (Unpublished doctoral dissertation.) University of North Texas, Denton, TX.

Chang, J. (2002). *Student involvement in the community college: A look at diversity and the value of student activities and programs* (Report ED 470 922). Washington, DC: U.S. Department of Education.

Chickering, A. W. (1969). *Education and identity.* San Francisco, CA: Jossey-Bass.

Chronicle of Higher Education Almanac. 2010–11. Washington, DC: Author.

Cohen, A. M., & Brawer, F. B. (2008). *The American community college* (5th ed.). San Francisco, CA: Jossey-Bass.

Condition of Education. (2008). National Center for Education Statistics. Retrieved from http://nces.ed.gov/programs/coe/2008/analysis/sa_table.asp?tableID=1005

Coomes, M. D. (2000). The historical roots of enrollment management. *New Directions for Student Services, 89,* 5–18.

Cowley, W. H. (1994). The nature of student personnel work. In A. L. Rentz (Ed.), *Student affairs: A profession's heritage* (2nd ed., pp. 43–65). Lantham, MD: University of America Press.

Creamer, D. G. (1988). Excellence in the practice of student affairs in the two-year college. *Journal of Staff, Program, & Organization Development, 6*(1), 3–10.

Creamer, D. G. (1994). Synthesis of literature related to historical and current functions of student services. In G. A. Baker (Ed.), *Handbook of community colleges in America* (pp. 439–453). Westport, CT: Greenwood.

D'Augelli, A. R. (1994). Identity development and sexual orientation. Toward a model of lesbian, gay, and bisexual identity development. In E. J. Trickett, R. J. Watts, & D. Birman (Eds.), *Human diversity: Perspectives on people in context* (pp. 312–333). San Francisco, CA: Jossey-Bass.

Deem, R. (1998). 'New managerialism' and higher education: The management of performances and cultures in universities in the United Kingdom. *International Studies in Sociology of Education, 8*(1), 47–70.

Erikson, E. H. (1980). *Identity and the life cycle.* New York, NY: Norton. (Original work published 1959.)

Etzkowitz, H., Webster, A., & Healey, P. (Eds.). (1998). *Capitalizing knowledge: New intersections of industry and academia.* Albany, NY: State University of New York Press.

Evans, N. J., Forney, D. S., Guido, F. M., Patton, L. D., & Renn, K. A. (2010). *Student development in college: Theory, research, and practice.* San Francisco, CA: Jossey-Bass.

Fowler, J. W. (1981). *Stages of faith: The psychology of human development and the quest for meaning.* New York, NY: HarperCollins.

Gilligan, C. (1982). *In a different voice: Psychological theory and women's development.* Cambridge, MA: Harvard University Press.

Greenberg, D. S. (1993). Clinton unveils program for industrial technology. *Science and Government Report, 23,* 1–5.

Harvey, L. J., Hunt, D. E., & Schroeder, H. M. (1961). *Conceptual systems and personality organization*. Hoboken, NJ: Wiley.

Heath, D. (1968). *Growing up in college*. San Francisco, CA: Jossey-Bass.

Heath, R. (1964). *The reasonable adventurer*. Pittsburgh, PA: University of Pittsburgh Press.

Helfgot, S. R., & Culp, M. M. (2005). Community college student affairs: What really matters. *New Directions for Community Colleges, no. 131* (pp. 33–49). San Francisco, CA: Jossey-Bass.

Helms, J. E. (1990). *Black and white racial identity: Theory, research, and practice*. Westport, CT: Greenwood Press.

Hirt, J. B. (2006). *Where you work matters: Student affairs administration at different types of institutions*. Lanham, MD: University Press of America.

Hirt, J. B. (2007). The student affairs profession in the academic marketplace. *NASPA Journal, 44,* 245–264.

Hirt, J. B., & Frank, T. E. (2011). Data retrieved from community college websites and interviews with community college administrators. Unpublished raw data.

Holland, J. L. (1973). *Making vocational choices: A theory of careers*. Upper Saddle River, NJ: Prentice Hall.

Hoover, E. (2011, July 14). Recession reshaped enrollment patterns but the sky didn't fall. *Chronicle of Higher Education*. Retrieved from http://chronicle.com/article/Recession-Reshaped-College/128223/

Hossler, D. (2004). From admissions to enrollment management. In F. J. D. Mackinnon & Associates (Eds.), *Rentz's student affairs practice in higher education* (3rd ed., pp. 58–88). Springfield, IL: Charles C. Thomas Publisher, Ltd.

Katsinas, S. G., & Friedel, J. N. (2010). Uncertain recovery: Access and funding issues in public higher education. A report by the Education Policy Center. Retrieved from http://education.ua.edu/wp-content/uploads/2010/10/2010-Uncertain-Recovery-Final.pdf

Kinser, K. (2005). A profile of regionally accredited for-profit institutions of higher education. In B. Pusser (Ed.), *Arenas of entrepreneurship: Where nonprofit and for-profit institutions compete. New Directions for Higher Education, no. 129* (pp. 69–84). San Francisco, CA: Jossey-Bass.

Kinser, K. (2006). Principles of student affairs in for-profit higher education. *NASPA Journal, 43,* 264–279.

Kohlberg, L. (1969). Stage and sequence: The cognitive development approach to socialization. In D. A. Goslin (Ed.), *Handbook of socialization theory and research* (pp. 82–173). Stanford, CA: Stanford University Press.

Kolb, D. A. (1984). *Experiential learning: Experience as the source of learning and development*. Upper Saddle River, NJ: Prentice Hall.

Lane, J. E., & Kinser, K. (2008) The private nature of cross-border higher education. *International Higher Education, 53,* 11–13.

Levin, J. S. (2001). *Globalizing the community college: Strategies for change in the twenty-first century*. New York, NY: Palgrave Macmillan.

Lewin, K. (1951). *Field theory in the social sciences*. New York, NY: HarperCollins.

Loevinger, J. (1976). *Ego development: Conceptions and theories*. San Francisco, CA: Jossey-Bass.

Marchand, A. (2010, March 7). 2-year colleges help learning disabled students break into math and science. *Chronicle of Higher Education*. Retrieved from http://chronicle.com/article/Community-Colleges-Help-Lea/64531/

Marcia, J. E. (1966). Development and validation of ego-identity status. *Journal of Personality and Social Psychology, 3,* 551–558.

McElroy, E. J., & Armesto, M. (1998). TRIO and Upward Bound: History, programs, and issues —past, present, and future. *Journal of Negro Education, 67,* 373–380.

Miller, M. A. (2006 January–February). Higher education, the market, and the public good. *Change, 38,* 4.

Mok, K. H., & Welch, A. (2003). Globalization, structural adjustment and education reform. In K. H. Mok and A. Welch (Eds.), *Globalization and educational restructuring in the Asia Pacific region* (pp. 1–31). New York, NY: Palgrave Macmillan.

Moore, R. M. (2004, May–June). The rising tide: "Branding" and the academic marketplace. *Change,* 56–61.

Myers, I. B. (1980). *Gifts differing*. Palo Alto, CA: Consulting Psychologists Press.

Newman, T., Couturier, L., & Scurry, J. (2004). *The future of higher education: Rhetoric, reality and risk of markets*. San Francisco, CA: Jossey-Bass.

Nuss, E. M. (2003). The development of student affairs. In S. R. Komives, D. B. Woodley, Jr., & Associates (Eds.), *Student services: A handbook for the profession*, (4th ed., pp. 65–88). San Francisco, CA: John Wiley & Sons, Inc.

Parks, S. D. (1986). *The critical years: Young adults and the search for meaning, faith, and commitment*. New York, NY: HarperCollins.

Perry, W. G., Jr. (1968). *Forms of intellectual and ethical development in the college years: A scheme*. New York, NY: Holt, Rinehart, & Winston.

Phinney, J. S. (1990). Ethnic identity in adolescents and adults: Review of research. *Psychological Bulletin, 108*, 499–514.

Piaget, J. (1952). *The origins of intelligence in children*. New York, NY: International Universities Press.

Rentz, A. L. (2004). Student affairs: A historical perspective. In F. J. D. Mackinnon & Associates (Eds.), *Rentz's student affairs practice in higher education*, (3rd ed., pp. 27–57). Springfield, IL: Charles C. Thomas Publisher, Ltd.

Rhatigan, J. J. (2009). From the people up: A brief history of student affairs administration. In G. McLellan, J. Stringer, & Associations (Eds.), *The handbook of student affairs administration* (3rd ed., pp. 3–18). San Francisco, CA: Jossey-Bass & Sons, Inc.

Rhoades, G. (1998). *Managed professionals: Unionized faculty and restructuring academic labor*. Albany, NY: State University of New York Press.

Sanford, N. (1967). *Where colleges fail: The study of the student as a person*. San Francisco, CA: Jossey-Bass.

Schlossberg, N. K. (1981). A model for analyzing human adaptation to transition. *Counseling Psychologist, 9*(2), 2–18.

Shumar, W. (1997). *College for sale: A critique of the commodification of higher education*. Washington, DC: Falmer Press.

Slaughter, S., & Leslie, L. L. (1997). *Academic capitalism: Politics, policies, and the entrepreneurial university*. Baltimore, MD: The Johns Hopkins University Press.

Slaughter, S., & Rhoades. G. (2004). *Academic capitalism and the new economy*. Baltimore, MD: The Johns Hopkins University Press.

Teranishi, R. T., Suarez-Orozco, C., & Suarez-Orozco, M. (2011). Immigrants in community colleges. *Immigrant Children, 21*, 1. Retrieved from http://futureofchildren.org/publications/journals/article/index.xml?journalid=74&articleid=544&sectionid=3751

Urban, W., & Wagoner, J. (2000). *American education: A history* (2nd ed.). Boston, MA: McGraw-Hill.

Warren, C. (2010, May–June). The conveyor belt to nowhere. *Academe, 96*(3), 2.

Welch, A. (2001). Globalization, post-modernity and the state. Comparative education facing the third millennium. *Comparative Education, 7*(4), 475–492.

Wilson, D. M. (2010, May–June). The casualties of the twenty-first century community college. *Academe, 96*(3), 12–18.

Woodard, D. B. (2006, July). *Learning and development in higher education*. Symposium conducted at the Technologico de Monterrey, Programa Capacitacion y Desarrollo para-Asuntos Estudiantes, Mexico City, Mexico.

4

INTERNATIONAL STUDENTS IN U.S. COMMUNITY COLLEGES

Status, Opportunities, and Future

LINDA SERRA HAGEDORN AND YI (LEAF) ZHANG

INTRODUCTION

The mission of the U.S. community colleges has historically focused on access to local populations and their specific needs (Cohen & Brawer, 2008). It should, therefore, come as no surprise that rather than target international students, community colleges have more often appealed to the underrepresented and non-traditional students dwelling on U.S. soil; more specifically in the geographical area of the college itself. However, the nation's community colleges have built a respected history of providing intercultural and multicultural programs (Raby & Tarrow, 1996) while catering to the needs of a diverse domestic student population due in part to the colleges' relatively low tuition rates, open-access admission policies, and convenient locations (Boggs, 2001). Many individuals who might not have been successful in four-year institutions have found academic success in community colleges because of the smaller class sizes, increased interactions with faculty members, and an environment that focuses more intently on teaching than research (Cohen & Brawer, 2008; Ewing, 1992).

Effects of neoliberal and global economic policies have altered the community college from a focus on the local community to a more expansive mission, requiring institutional attention to the demands of an extended global community (Levin, 2001, 2002). To counteract increasingly aggressive student recruitment efforts at four-year institutions and continually shrinking funding from state and local governments, community colleges have increased their international recruitment. The first decades of the 21st century have brought a new international awareness of the U.S. community college in their relatively new interest in enrolling international students (Phillippe & Sullivan, 2005).

This chapter proposes a newly adapted framework to explain the increased awareness of community colleges throughout the world and the new initiatives utilized by the colleges to market their programs to international students. Our framework builds on work by Parra-Sandoval, Bozo de Carmona, and Gonzalez (2010) that substantiated a global perspective for Latin American universities. We found that the Parra-Sandoval and colleagues' framework, suitably adapted, fits the specific situation for community colleges. The theory (see Figure 4.1) builds on the acceleration of knowledge production that has created a greater worldwide demand for a more skilled workforce. The need for an educated workforce has led to the expansion of adult or continued education, including traditional postsecondary offerings. Just as the community college expanded as an open-access institution for Americans beginning in the early 1960s, community colleges are now recognized for their entrepreneurial activities and open-access globally (Levin, 2002). Students from countries which do not have the infrastructure to create a similar postsecondary educational sector are seeing new possibilities and opportunities in U.S. community colleges, thus a new interest. Indeed, we note that the largest numbers of international community college students are from less developed countries that cannot satisfy their demand for higher education. Our framework also contends that the timing of the shift is during a phase of global unrest, distrust, and social tension (*Telegraph*, 2011). Education, as a neutral entity of peace, is proposed as a response to enhancing international relations.

Due in large measure to an increasingly interdependent and complex world, the word "community" has expanded from "local" to "global" with a new 21st-century "twist" encompassing global awareness and competence (American Association of Community Colleges [AACC] & Association of Community College Trustees [ACCT], 2000). The changes in perspective and outlook have produced a contemporary community college that includes a growing number of international students and a greater awareness of the U.S. community colleges by potential students overseas (Phillippe & Sullivan, 2005). It may be argued that, for some community colleges, efforts at internationalization are not new, but rather build on earlier efforts in the 1980s and 1990s to bolster the number of international students (Levin, 2001); but whereas the "wave of welcome" may have been sincere in past decades, the current motives are much more widespread and are driven by different purposes.

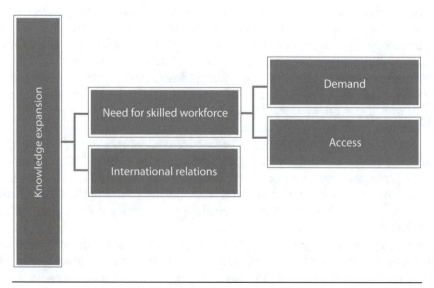

Figure 4.1 International community college student framework.

Applying this framework and theory, we first provide an overview of the trends and current status of international students in U.S. community colleges followed by a discussion of the significance of international students and the challenges of recruitment. This chapter also examines the reasons affecting international student choice of studying at U.S. community colleges and the challenges that these students encounter.

TRENDS AND CURRENT STATUS OF INTERNATIONAL STUDENTS IN THE U.S.

Prior to 1980, students from other countries who studied in the U.S. were typically termed "foreign students." A 1974 National Association of Foreign Student Advisors (NAFSA, formerly the National Association of Foreign Advisers but more currently an association of international educators) study defined foreign students as holders of visas, refugees, and immigrants. Since the 1980s, the more common term is "international students" and is used to define those individuals who temporarily reside in the U.S. to receive an education with a student visa [F-1 or J-1] (Althen, 1980; Montgomery, 2010).

From its early history, U.S. higher education attracted students from around the globe (Hess, 1982). During the colonial period, for example, U.S. institutions were recorded to "have solicited the admission of students from England and the British West Indies, as well as other parts of the world" (Schulken, 1968, p. 13). During the 1800s students from China were brought to the U.S. by the American Board of Commissioners for Foreign Missions to participate in U.S. education. In 1868 a large group of Japanese students were supported by their government to study in the U.S. This was followed four years later (1872) by the Chinese imperial government's first dispatch of 30 teenage students to the U.S. (Chu, 2004).

Christian missionaries participated in the early phase of international student recruitment with the intention of increasing the global Christian population (Mulcahy, 2008). By the early 1920s during the second phase of recruitment, international students were viewed as more than mere recruits for the Christian army; they were looked upon as a source of altruism, international comprehension, and global aid. There was an increasing belief that the only path to world peace resided in the extensive exchange of people and ideas throughout the world (Schulken, 1968). During this period the Carnegie Foundation established the Institute of International Education (IIE), which presently serves as an advocate to promote student study abroad programs for U.S. students as well as to attract international students to the U.S.

The third and current phase of international student recruitment is thematically tied to the enhancement of knowledge and international relations. This phase began at the end of World War II and is focused on increased government involvement in international education, relying upon the belief that cross-cultural and transnational understandings bring about or at least support peace and economic development. Fulbright Commission Scholarships, funded by the income of war supplies to foreign governments, as well as other scholarships sponsored by the U.S. Congress, were aimed at boosting international education (James, 1992).

The result of recruitment and the efforts toward enhanced international relations has resulted in the U.S. becoming a major destination for international students. Figure 4.2 illustrates the dramatic increase in the number of international students coming to the

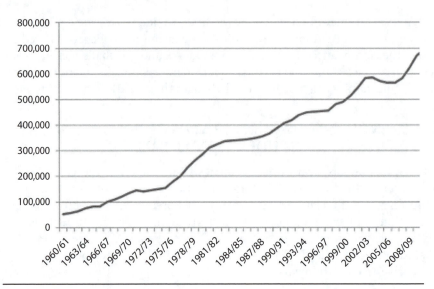

Figure 4.2 Increasing number of international students pursuing higher education in the U.S.
Source: Institute of International Education. (2010). International Student Enrollment Trends, 1949/50–2009/10. *Open Doors Report on International Educational Exchange.*

U.S. for postsecondary instruction (IIE, 2010a). In the 2009–2010 academic year, U.S. colleges and universities attracted a record number of 690,923 international students (IIE, 2010a). The number of student visas issued by the State Department increased almost fivefold from 65,000 in 1971 to 315,000 in 2000 (Borjas, 2002). Mirroring the domestic student population in community colleges, a higher percentage of these international students are female (52%). The majority of students come to the U.S. with an F-1 student visa (84.2%) and enroll full-time (87%) (IIE, 2010c). Almost half of the international students (44%) hail from the top three sending countries: China, India, and South Korea.

In spite of the enhanced international student activity, specifically student enrollments, community colleges are relative newcomers to the international student recruitment arena. A study from the mid-1960s, cited by Scanlon (1990), verifies that community colleges have historically enrolled few foreign students. The U.S. community college is unique and potential students from other countries may not have a clear understanding of how community colleges fit into the global postsecondary structure. The knowledge expansion, demand, and need for access have been increasing globally, but it has taken time for other countries to acknowledge the U.S. community college as an appropriate response (IIE, 2010b; Scanlon, 1990).

The majority of international students enrolled at community colleges come from Asian countries (IIE, 2010c); a geographical sector that has been developing faster than their educational systems can accommodate. Also of note is that this is occurring during a time of heightened steps toward enhanced China–U.S. relations (Dumbaugh, 2006). Consistent with the views of Parra-Sandoval et al. (2010), the U.S. community college can act as a "pressure valve" providing an alternate or auxiliary path to satisfy demand while also being used as a means to improve the relationship between the U.S. and Asia.

SIGNIFICANCE OF INTERNATIONAL STUDENTS IN COMMUNITY COLLEGES

In accordance with the theory of Parra-Sandoval et al. (2010), international students contribute to U.S. higher education in various ways including enhancing international understandings and the global and cultural understanding of U.S. domestic students (Bevis, 2002; Chase, 2009; Chase & Mahoney, 1996; Desruisseaux, 1998; Ewing, 1992; Harrison, 2002). With international students on campus, domestic students have the opportunity to communicate with diverse peers, explore different cultures, and be exposed to multiple points of view. International students may enrich the cultural campus life and make it possible for even small community colleges to experience different cultures. Through international students, U.S. students have opportunities to engage in learning from other cultures and develop an appreciation for and an understanding of cultural diversity and gain sensitivity without going abroad (Dalton, 1999). Scholars have noted that domestic students may improve in their development of cognitive skills and thinking abilities through exposure to diversity and cultural differences (Heyward, 2002). The experiences of international students may also be used to promote international literacy. For example, 60% of the members of the California Colleges for International Education (CCIE) have used international students as guest speakers, culture tutors, study abroad orientation guides, and language teachers (Raby, 2007).

International students make significant contributions to the local, state, and national economy. NAFSA estimated that international students and their dependants contributed approximately $18.8 billion to the U.S. economy through expenditures on tuition, housing, books, fees, and other educational and living expenses during the 2009–2010 academic year (NAFSA, 2010). While these figures reflect the contribution for colleges and universities collectively, in the face of little or no documented evidence on community colleges, it is assumed that the situation is consistent for international students in community colleges. For the nearly 70% of international students who relied on personal and family funds or home government/university as their primary source of funding, on average each contributed almost $30,000 to the U.S. economy (IIE, 2010b). Furthermore, it is important to note that international students, who will pay non-resident tuition rates (in both universities and community colleges), can be a critical source of revenue during times of shrinking state appropriations (Desruisseaux, 1998; Farnsworth, 2005). Institutions have used funding generated from international students to help finance expensive and/or under-enrolled programs (Dunstan, 2001).

INTERNATIONAL STUDENT RECRUITMENT AND CHALLENGES

As discussed earlier, there are numerous reasons why international students are sought by universities and community colleges. Included in the list is the financial benefit for the institution—as international students generally pay a higher tuition level than domestic students. This may be seen as especially attractive for public community colleges during times of lean and decreasing state budgets. We cannot specifically document the marketing of international students for the sole reason of financial return, but we can point to the increase in services and in the number of education agents who provide services for international students who are willing to study in the U.S. (Hagedorn

& Zhang, 2011; Zhang & Hagedorn, 2011). In some cases the agencies are paid by the colleges and universities to bring international students to their doors.

International student recruitment is easily affected by changes in the political environment. A salient example is the terrorist attacks of September 11, 2001. Concerns of national security led to visa restraints and apprehension toward international students, especially those from Muslim-predominated countries, leading the federal government to tighten entry requirements for all foreigners (Kless, 2004). As a result, international student processing has subsequently been handled through the Student Exchange Visitor Information System (SEVIS), a national database that tracks international students and scholars in the U.S. (Rosser, Hermsen, Mamiseishvili, & Wood, 2007). This increased scrutiny adds to the higher cost of the college application process and may have a negative influence on international recruitment. Researchers reported that international students in the U.S. were displeased with visa and SEVIS procedures and noted that these practices may lead to some students changing their international goals to pursue a degree in a country other than the U.S. (Lee & Becskehazy, 2005). In fact, the number of students pursuing education in Australia, New Zealand, Canada, and other countries has been rising since the enhanced U.S. provisions were established (Verbik & Lananowski, 2007). Well aware of benefits that international students could generate, the U.K., Australia, New Zealand, and Canada have taken steps to make their educational programs more attractive to students in the rest of the world. These countries have also improved their services in college application, transition of life, accommodation of learning, and even immigration after graduation (Altbach, 1989, 1998, 2004; Lee & Rice, 2007; Peterson, Briggs, Dreasher, Homer, & Helson, 1999; Verbik & Lasanowski, 2007).

Compared to four-year colleges and universities, community colleges are more likely to encounter difficulties in recruiting international students, since the community college is a relatively new concept outside of the U.S. (Cohen & Brawer, 2008). As a result, potential students from other countries may be concerned about the validity of the academic programs and recognition of the associate degrees in their native country (Raby & Valeau, 2007). Moreover, the concept of "transfer" is not generally understood as most universities outside of the U.S. do not have provisions for any kind of credit transfer or articulation agreements (Redden, 2010). Other factors that may hinder international student recruitment to community colleges include fear of stigmatization as a community college student, low proportion of international students at community colleges, and the perception that community college degrees are less prestigious (*Inside Higher Education*, 2007). An additional reason why international students may not consider community colleges as an educational destination is the stated mission of community colleges to respond to the needs of the local community (Cohen & Brawer, 2008). The colleges themselves may be concerned that international students may be in competition with local domestic students for limited resources (Ng, 2007).

Because international students bring benefits to their community colleges and local communities, it is important not to recognize them as simply "customers" or "consumers," recruited for purposes of revenue to the college (Levin, 2002; Slaughter & Rhoades, 2004). Yet, recruitment activities are not always accompanied by the strong consideration of international students' experiences after enrollment or sufficient attention turned to international student programs (Lee & Rice, 2007). U.S. community colleges are encouraged to pay more attention to the experiences of international students and strategies that facilitate their transition rather than on the numbers of international students on campus (Sewall, 2010).

RATIONALE FOR STUDYING AT COMMUNITY COLLEGES

Although the U.S. community colleges may not be as well understood in foreign countries as they are locally, a number of international students have realized the special features of community colleges and have specifically targeted them for enrollment (Bohman, 2010). The following section explains the rationale and models of international students' choice of studying at U.S. community colleges.

There is limited research on what attracts international students to community colleges and the procedures they follow to make the choice (Doku, 2007; Hagedorn & Lee, 2005; Zeszotarski, 2003). Knowledge expansion and increased demand for education that cannot be fulfilled by local universities, as well as the quest for enhanced international relations (see Figure 4.1), have compelled students to pursue alternate paths that have included the community college. Economic and sociological theoretical frameworks have frequently been used to examine the patterns of four-year college choice and to develop conceptual models that use economic criteria, status-attainment goals, and models that combine both motives (Hearn, 1984; Hossler, Schmit, & Vesper, 1999; Jackson, 1978; Tierney, 1983). All of these models are useful in explaining students' decision-making process in their consideration of college attendance.

The economic model of the college choice process, derived from human capital theory, views students as rational actors who make careful decisions based on an examination of the costs and benefits related to attending college and an understanding of how college is an investment in their future (Hossler et al., 1999). Students make a choice of college, assuming that their actions will accrue personal and professional advantages. According to human capital theory, "expenditure on training and education is costly, and should be considered an investment since it is undertaken with a view to increasing personal incomes" (Becker, 1964, p. 1). Economic choice models assume that students examine the advantages and disadvantages of several colleges and rationally choose the one that can maximize their benefits for the least cost (Hossler, Braxton, & Coopersmith, 1989). The increase in demand and need for access have directed some students to choose community colleges for their lower costs of attendance (Bauer, 2004).

Another perspective comes from status attainment models, originated from sociological theories, and views the decision-making process as utilitarian. The models focus on a wide variety of social and individual factors that affect students' aspirations and choice of institutions. Jackson (1982) indicated that students first develop aspirations based on influences of sociological factors, obtain information about their options, and then evaluate the feasible options, finally making a decision based on their judgments. Numerous studies (e.g., Agarwal & Winkler, 1985; Daily, Farewell, & Kumar, 2010; Lee & Tan, 1984; Mazzarol & Soutar, 2002; McMahon, 1992; Pimpa, 2003) have been conducted on factors that affect international students' choice of educational destination in the four-year sector. There is little extant research on the patterns of college choice among community college students.

The decision-making process by students of oversees study likely occurs in multiple stages. Bohman (2010) identified four steps international students take when they consider studying at a foreign institution. In the first step, students decide to study outside of their home countries. In the second step, termed the destination phase, students decide in which country they would like to study. Step three consists of evaluating different institutional types and deciding upon the most suitable (e.g., community colleges or four-year institutions). Finally, students identify a specific institution that provides the appropriate fit. This was confirmed in research by Mazzarol and Soutar (2002) who studied international students in Australia and found the process to be similar. Mazzarol and Soutar explored "push" and "pull" factors that affect or contribute to students' choice. "Push" factors are those that "operate within the source country and initiate a student's decision to undertake international study," and "pull" factors are those "within a host country to make that country relatively attractive to international students" (p. 82). Other researchers (Bourke, 2000; Srikatanyoo & Gnoth, 2002) found evidence that international students first choose the country in which they wish to study followed by the choice of an institution within that country. Before students can decide to enroll in a community college, they must first understand its premises, its purpose, and how it can be beneficial for their life plan.

We contend that international students attend community colleges for many of the same reasons as their domestic counterparts—that is to say, access and lower cost. But access may be differentially defined. Cohen and Brawer (2008) suggest that domestic students attend community colleges for the lower cost of tuition, smaller class sizes, vocational training programs, personal interests, and transferable credits. Some international community college students may not have access to U.S. universities due to low levels of English competency. Community colleges will often accept students into intense language instruction prior to or in conjunction with degree coursework (Crandall & Shepphard, 2004); not always an option for the four-year sector (Hagedorn & Lee, 2005; Zeszotarski, 2003). International students may also elect to study within the vocational trades, an option that may not be available in postsecondary institutions in their home countries (Blom & Myers, 2003; Blossfeld & Stockmann, 1999; Jachowicz, 2007).

Informed international students may specifically choose a community college because it provides a more desirable learning environment, smaller class sizes, and an emphasis on student learning [rather than on research] (Ewing, 1992). International students who are unfamiliar with the U.S. educational system may be attracted to the community college's low ratio of students to faculty, the smaller campus sizes (Santovec, 2002), or the more flexible course scheduling (Davis, 1997). The lower student–faculty ratio in community colleges encourages a higher level of interaction between students and faculty and fosters a more student-centered learning environment than may be found at four-year colleges and universities (Jenkins, 2003). Another benefit of community college enrollment is the lower cost of tuition that may persuade some potential students to view community colleges as the best first step into higher education in the U.S. (Zeszotarski, 2003).

CHALLENGES OF STUDYING AT COMMUNITY COLLEGES

The adjustment to college life can bring challenges to all students; but for international students the challenges are heightened (Wedding, McCartney, & Currey, 2009). While studying in the U.S. is viewed as an enriching experience, a number of factors have been identified as challenges to international students including English proficiency, differences in communication and interpersonal relationships, lack of social support, financial difficulties, and differences in cultural expectations (Berry, Kim, Minde, & Mok, 1987; Chen, 1996; Cross, 1995; Hayes & Lin, 1994; Jou & Fukuda, 1995; Lin & Yi, 1997; Mallinckrodt & Leong, 1992; Misra, Crist, & Burant, 2003; Mori, 2000; Ye, 2006).

In order to better understand the challenges international students might encounter while studying in the U.S., a theoretical framework utilized to explain adult students' transition is pertinent to the discussion. Such a framework can be found in the transition framework of adults, developed by Nancy Schlossberg in the early 1980s (1981, 1984). A transition was defined broadly as "any event or nonevent that results in changed relationships, routines, assumptions, and roles" (Goodman, Schlossberg, & Anderson, 2006, p. 33). Similar to other adults in transition, international students often experience challenging or confusing conditions when they function in a new culture (Goodman et al., 2006).

A significant challenge that international students often encounter in transition to U.S. community colleges is language. English, with its many idioms, is a difficult language and often presents a steep learning curve to those who intend to study in the U.S. Researchers (Singaravelu & Pope, 2007) reported that a lack of English proficiency has a negative influence on the image that international students project: they may be viewed, erroneously, as less intelligent. Lack of language ability may also require a longer time of study before graduation. It is apparent that there is a gap in the literature specific to the number of international students who come to the U.S. with conditional acceptances that require that they first enroll in intensive English classes (Fischer, 2010).

International students may also find it difficult to adjust to the academic practices and climate of U.S. institutions (Pedersen, 1991; Reynolds & Constantine, 2007; Sodowsky & Lai, 1997). This may be especially germane for Asian students who have been found to experience discomfort in challenging the authority of professors or even in making eye contact during conversations (Hasan, Fouad, & Williams-Nichelson, 2008; Wilton & Constantine, 2003). In addition to typical challenges that may be associated with college life, international students must also deal with difficulties related to the new environment. International students are far away from homes and experience different cultural traditions. They need not only to adjust to a new education system but also, potentially, to new value sets. Although access to the Internet and U.S. media has allowed contemporary international students to have opportunities to become familiar with the U.S. culture, they are not exempt from cultural challenges such as lack of social support, confusion about cultural rituals, homesickness, and discrimination (Reynolds & Constantine, 2007; Wedding et al., 2009). Researchers report that Asian students may be especially uncomfortable using university support services when facing problems, thus informal social networks may take on particular importance (Heggins & Jackson, 2003). International students were also found to be more likely to experience psychological problems than U.S. students (Mori, 2000; Yeh & Inose, 2003) as they may face challenges that can be highly upsetting such as encountering a lack of respect from domestic students, counteracting a lack of respect for their religious practices, and managing family crises from a distance (Mori, 2000; Shen & Herr, 2004; Wedding et al., 2009).

IMPLICATIONS

Community colleges with clear priorities about the role of international educational activities will be more likely to develop effective support services than those that regard international education as peripheral to the core value of the college (Tillman, 1990). However, the survey *Mapping Internationalization on U.S. Campuses* (Siaya & Hayward, 2003) found that the majority of community colleges had not included internationalization in their commitment statements, listed it as a priority in their strategic plan, or assessed their efforts in the past five years. A basic sign of an institution's commitment to international students is the presence of an international student office (O'Connell, 1994). According to the NAFSA guidelines (2002), institutions that enroll culturally diverse international students should provide a central place where students can report concerns and receive assistance. Other support such as orientation, housing assistance, academic tutoring, and counseling should be in place to serve all students (Hayes & Lin, 1994; Tillman, 1990; Zhai, 2004).

It is also important for community colleges to recognize the differences among international students. International students are often viewed as a homogeneous group while in fact there is a wide range of diversity. For this reason, Schram and Lauver (1988) suggest that international programs or activities should be tailored to a specific group of international students, such as students from Africa or Asia. In addition to recognition of differences, institutions should create opportunities for international students to integrate with domestic students and the community at large (Leask, 2009). While Levin (2001) found that many community colleges provide social and/or cultural events aimed at multiculturalism and internationalization, they may not be sufficient or appropriate to bring a true sense of comfort for the students.

CONCLUSIONS

This chapter presented the literature and research on international community college students. Since the extant research is scant, we often had to rely on the literature pertaining to four-year institutions. It is clear, however, that while the number of individuals around the globe aspiring to come to the U.S. to study increases, many will encounter issues that will direct them to a U.S. community college. Also, as the world becomes increasingly educated regarding the benefits of community colleges, more international students will aspire to attend, not as a fallback but as a destination of choice. Be it for reasons of lower cost, broader access, or unique programs, it is clear that the community college will be welcoming a larger proportion of international students. In addition, as budgets and finances remain constrained, colleges will seek to enroll more international students.

We presented a framework to depict current status of international community college students (Parra-Sandoval et al., 2010). This framework explains why the number of international community college students has been growing and will probably continue to grow. We concede that knowledge is expanding and the jobs of today and tomorrow, internationally, require a more trained workforce with education beyond the secondary level (Rojewski, 2002). To alleviate the escalation in demand, an escalation in access must be the response. Just as the community college provided a similar "escape valve" for domestic demand beginning in the 1960s, the institution is again called upon to offer a similar solution with respect to international students, providing both a challenge and an opportunity as this is occurring in a time of necessary and planned improvement of international relations within an environment of strained resources.

QUESTIONS FOR DISCUSSION

1. Is the development of an international student population a result of resource dependency or globalization? Why or why not and what research supports the position?
2. What support programs exist for students in their native countries as part of higher education that we do not offer in the U.S.?
3. What happens to international students after they complete a community college certificate or degree?

REFERENCES

Agarwal, V. B., & Winkler, D. R. (1985). Foreign demand for United States higher education: a study of developing countries in the eastern hemisphere. *Economic Development and Cultural Change, 33*(3), 623–644.

Altbach, P. G. (1989). *Perspectives on comparative higher education: Essays on faculty, students, and reform.* New York, NY: State University of New York at Buffalo.

Altbach, P. G. (1998). *Comparative higher education: Knowledge, the university, and development.* Greenwich, CT: Ablex Publishing Corporation.

Altbach, P. G. (2004). Globalization and the university: Myths and realities in an unequal world. *Tertiary Education and Management, 10,* 3–25.

Althen, G. (1980). *Orientation of foreign student affairs.* Washington, DC: National Association for Foreign Student Affairs. Retrieved from http://eric.ed.gov/PDFS/ED201950.pdf

American Association of Community College (AACC). (2010). *Start your US Education today.* Retrieved from http://communitycollegesusa.com/

American Association of Community Colleges (AACC) & Association of Community College Trustees (ACCT). (2000). *Knowledge net: A report of the new expeditions initiative.* Washington, DC: Community College Press. Retrieved from http://www.aacc.nche.edu/ Resources/aaccprograms/pastprojects/Documents/know-net.pdf

Bauer, C. J. (2004). *The nexus between community college choice and student persistence* (Doctoral dissertation). Available from ProQuest Digital Dissertations database. (AAT 3151924)

Becker, G. (1964). *Human capital and the goal distribution of income: An analytical approach.* New York, NY: Columbia University Press.

Berry, J. W., Kim, U., Minde, T., & Mok, D. (1987). Comparative studies of acculturative stress. *International Migration Review,* 21, 491–511.

Bevis, T. B. (2002). At a glance: International students in the United States. *International Educator, 11*(3), 12–17.

Blom, K., & Myers, D. (2003). *Quality indicators in vocational education and training: International perspectives.* Adelaide, South Australia: NCVER.

Blossfeld, H. P., & Stockmann, R. (1999). Globalization and changes in vocational training systems in developing and advanced industrialized societies (II). *International Journal of Sociology, 29*(1). Armonk, NY: Sharpe, Inc. Retrieved from http://www.jstor.org/ stable/20628548

Boggs, G. R. (2001). The meaning of scholarship in community colleges. *Community College Journal, 72*(1), 23–26.

Bohman, E. (2010). Headed for the heartland: Decision making process of community college bound international students. *Community College Journal of Research and Practice, 34*(1 & 2), 64–77.

Borjas, G. J. (2002, June 17). Rethinking foreign students: A question of the national interest. *National Review.* Retrieved from http://www.hks.harvard.edu/fs/gborjas/publications/popular/NR061702.htm

Bourke, A. (2000). A model of the determinants of international trade in higher education. *The Service Industries Journal, 20*(1), 110–138.

Chase, A. (2009). Community colleges' role in recruiting international students. Retrieved from http://opendoors.iienetwork.org/?p=25127

Chase, A. M., & Mahoney, J. R. (Eds.). (1996). *Global awareness in community colleges: A report of a national survey.* Washington, DC: Community College Press.

Chen, S. F. (1996, April). *Learning multiculturalism from the experience of international students: The experience of international students in a teacher training program.* Paper presented at the Annual Meeting of the American Educational Research Association, New York, NY.

Chu, T. K. (Spring, 2004). 150 years of Chinese students in America. *Harvard China Review.* Retrieved from http://www.cie-gnyc.org/newsletter/150_years_ chinese_students.pdf

Cohen, A. M., & Brawer, F. B. (2008). *The American community college* (5th ed.). San Francisco, CA: Jossey-Bass.

Crandall, J., & Shepphard, K. (2004). *Adult ESL and the community college.* Report by the Council for Advancement of Adult Literacy. Retrieved from http://www.caalusa.org/eslreport.pdf

Cross, S. E. (1995). Self-construals, coping, and stress in cross-cultural adaptation. *Journal of Cross-Cultural Psychology, 26,* 673–697.

Daily, C., Farewell, S., & Kumar, G. (2010). Factors influencing the university selecting of international students: Do students understand and consider AACSB accreditation? *Academy of Educational Leadership Journal, 14*(3), 59–75. Retrieved from http://galenet.galegroup.com.proxy.lib.iastate.edu:2048/servlet/BCRC?vrsn=unknown&locID=iastu_main&ste=5&docNum=A235631639

Dalton, J. C. (1999, Summer). The significance of international issues and responsibilities in the contemporary work of student affairs. *New Directions for Student Services, 86,.* 3–11.

Davis, T. M. (1997, October 9). Open doors 1996–1997: Report on international educational exchange. Retrieved from http://eric.ed.gov/PDFS/ED417651.pdf

Desruisseaux, P. (1998, October 9). Intense competition for foreign students sparks concerns about U.S. standing. *Chronicle of Higher Education.* Retrieved from http://chronicle.com/article/Intense-Competition-for/4612/

Doku, N. S. (2007). *International student experiences at Midwestern community colleges: Voices from within* (Doctoral dissertation). University of Kansas, Lawrence, KS. (AAT 3274492)

Dumbaugh, K. (2006, July). *China–U.S. relations: Current issues and implications for U.S. policy.* Congressional Research Service, The Library of Congress. Retrieved from http://www.fas.org/sgp/crs/row/RL32804.pdf

Dunstan, P. (2001). Internationalizing the student experience. *International Educator, 10*(1), 34–40.

Ewing, R. V. (1992). A supportive environment for international students. In R.W. Franco and J. N. Shimabkuro (Eds.), *Beyond the classroom: International education and the community college* (Vol. 2, pp. 37–44). Honolulu, HI: The Kellogg Foundation.

Farnsworth, K. (2005, Fall). A new model for recruiting international students: The 2 + 2. *International Education, 35*(1), 5–14.

Fischer, K. (2010, August 8). Colleges extend conditional admissions to pull in more international students: Candidates with strong academic backgrounds but weak language skills find more potions in the U.S. *Chronicle of Higher Education.* Retrieved from http://chronicle.com/article/Colleges-Extend-Conditional/123783/

Goodman, J., Schlossberg, N., & Anderson, M. (2006). *Counseling adults in transition: Linking practice with theory* (3rd ed.). New York, NY: Springer Publishing.

Hagedorn, L. S., & Lee, M. C. (2005). *International community college students: The neglected minority?* (ERIC Document Reproduction Service No. 490516.)

Hagedorn, L.S., & Zhang, Y. (2011). The use of agents in recruiting Chinese undergraduates. *Journal of Studies in International Education, 15*(2), 186–202.

Harrison, P. (2002). Educational exchange for international understanding. *International Educator, 11*(4), 2–4.

Hasan, N. T., Fouad, N. A., & Williams-Nichelson, C. (2008). *Studying psychology in the United States: Expert guidance for international students.* New York, NY: Kluwer Academic/Plenum Publishers.

Hayes, R. L., & Lin, H. R. (1994). Coming to America: Developing social support systems for international students. *Journal of Multicultural Counseling & Development, 22,* 7–16.

Hearn, J. (1984). The relative roles of academic ascribed and socioeconomic characteristics in college destinations. *Sociology of Education, 57,* 22–30.

Heggins III, W. J., & Jackson, J. F. L. (2003). Understanding the collegiate experience for Asian international students at a Midwestern research university. *College Student Journal, 37*(3), 379–391. Retrieved from http://www.cobleskill.edu/library/SB354_01.pdf

Hess, G. (1982). *Freshmen and sophomores abroad: Community colleges and overseas academic programs.* New York, NY: Teachers College Press.

Heyward, M. (2002). From international to intercultural. *Journal of Research in International Education, 1*(1), 9–32.

Hossler, D., Braxton, J., & Coopersmith, G. (1989). Understanding student college choice. In J. Smith (Ed.), *Higher education: Handbook of theory and research* (Vol. 4, pp. 231–287). New York, NY: Agathon.

Hossler, D., Schmit, J., & Vesper, N. (1999). *Going to college: How social, economic, and educational factors influence the decisions students make.* Baltimore, MD: Johns Hopkins University Press.

Inside Higher Education. (2007, July 26). "Branding" community colleges abroad. Retrieved from http://www.insidehighered.com/news/2007/07/26/ccabroad

Institute of International Education (IIE). (2010a). *Open doors 2010: International students in the United States.* Washington, DC: Author.

Institute of International Education (IIE). (2010b). International student enrollments rose modestly in 2009/10, led by strong increase in students from China. Retrieved from http://www.iie.org/en/Who-We-Are/News-and-Events/Press-Center/Press-Releases/2010/2010-11-15-Open-Doors-International-Students-In-The-US

Institute of International Education (IIE). (2010c). Open doors data: Special reports: Community college data resources. Retrieved from http://www.iie.org/en/Research-and-Publications/Open-Doors/Data/Special-Reports/Community-College-Data-Resource

Jachowicz, P. L. (2007). *Influences on career decisions of international students attending community colleges in the United States.* (Unpublished doctoral dissertation.) Northern Illinois University, DeKalb, IL.

Jackson, G. A. (1978). Financial aid and student enrollment. *Journal of Higher Education, 49,* 548–574.

Jackson, G. A. (1982). Public efficiency and private choice in higher education. *Educational Evaluation and Policy Analysis, 4*(2), 237–247.

James, G. (1992). Overseas students in the United States: The quest for socio-cultural and linguistic models. *American Studies International, 30*(1), 88–108.

Jenkins, R. (2003, November 10). Not a bad gig. *Chronicle of Higher Education.* Community College News. Retrieved from http://chronicle.com/cc/

Jou, Y. H., & Fukuda, H. (1995). Effects of social support on adjustment of Chinese students in Japan. *Journal of Social Psychology, 135,* 39–47.

Kless, S. H. (2004, October 8). We threaten national security by discouraging the best and brightest students from abroad. *Chronicle of Higher Education.* Retrieved from http://justice.law.stetson.edu/excellence/Highered/archives/2005/DiscouragingBestBrightest.pdf

Leask, B. (2009). Using formal and informal curricula to improve interactions between home and international students. *Journal of Studies of International Education, 13*(2), 205–221.

Lee, J. J., & Becskehazy, P. (2005, April). *Understanding international student attitudes about SEVIS and VISA procedures after 9/11.* Paper presented at the meeting of the American College Personnel Association, Nashville, TN.

Lee, J. J., & Rice, C. (2007). Welcome to America? International student perceptions of discrimination. *Higher Education, 53,* 381–409.

Lee, K. H., & Tan, J. P. (1984). The international flow of third level lesser developed country students to developed countries: Determinants and implications. *Higher Education, 13*(6), 687–707.

Levin, J. S. (2001). *Globalizing the community college: Strategies for change in the twenty-first century.* New York, NY: Palgrave.

Levin, J. S. (2002). Global culture and the community college. *Community College Journal of Research and Practice, 26,* 121–145.

Lin, J. G., & Yi, J. K. (1997). Asian international students' adjustment: Issues and program suggestions. *College Student Journal, 31,* 473–477.

Mallinckrodt, B., & Leong, F. T. L. (1992). International graduate students, stress, and social support. *Journal of College Student Development, 33,* 71–78.

Mazzarol, T., & Soutar, G. (2002). "Push-pull" factors influencing international student destination choice. *The International Journal of Educational Management, 16*(2), 82–90. Retrieved from http://www.emeraldinsight.com/Insight/ viewPDF.jsp?contentType= Article&Filename=html/Output/Published/Emerald FullTextArticle /Pdf/0600160203.pdf

McMahon, M. E. (1992). Higher education in a world market: An historical look at the global context of international study. *Higher Education, 24*(4), 465–482.

Misra, R., Crist, M., & Burant, C. J. (2003). Relationships among life stress, social support, academic stressors, and reactions to stressors of international students in the United States. *International Journal of Stress Management, 10,* 137–157.

Montgomery, C. (2010) *Understanding the international student experience.* Basingstoke: Palgrave Macmillan.

Mori, S. (2000). Addressing the mental health concerns of international students. *Journal of Counseling & Development, 78,* 137–144.

Mulcahy, D. G. (2008). *The educated person: Toward a new paradigm for liberal education.* Lanham, MD: Rowman & Littlefield.

National Association of Foreign Student Advisors (NAFSA). (2002). *NAFSA guidelines and principles*. Washington, DC: Author.

Ng, J. (2007, Summer). Campus politics and the challenges of international education in an urban community college district. *New Directions for Community Colleges, no. 138* (pp. 83–88). San Francisco, CA: Jossey-Bass.

O'Connell, W. (1994). *Foreign student education at 2-year colleges: A handbook for administrators and educators*. Washington, DC: National Association of Foreign Student Advisors.

Parra-Sandoval, M. C., Bozo de Carmona, A. J., & Gonzalez, A. I. (2010). *University: The last call?* Ottawa, Canada: International Development Research Center.

Pedersen, P. B. (1991). Counseling international students. *The Counseling Psychologist, 19,* 10–58.

Peterson, D. M., Briggs, P., Dreasher, L., Homer, D. D., & Nelson, T. (1999). Contributions of international students and programs to campus diversity. *New Directions for Student Services, 86,* 67–77.

Phillippe, K., & Sullivan, L. G. (2005). *National profile of community colleges: Trends and statistics* (4th ed.). Washington, DC: Community College Press.

Pimpa, N. (2003). The influence of family on Thai students' choices of international education. *The International Journal of Educational Management, 17*(5), 211–219.

Raby, R. L. (2007). Internationalizing the curriculum: On- and off-campus strategies. In E. J. Valeau & R. L. Raby (Eds.), *International reform efforts and challenges in community colleges. New Directions for Community Colleges, no. 138* (pp. 5–14). San Francisco, CA: Jossey-Bass.

Raby, R. L., & Tarrow, N. B. (Eds.). (1996). *Dimensions of the community college: International, intercultural, and multicultural perspectives (Vol. 6)*. New York, NY: Garland Publishing Inc.

Raby, R. L., & Valeau, E. J. (2007). Community college international education: Looking back to forecast the future. In E. J. Valeau & R. L. Raby (Eds.), *International reform efforts and challenges in community colleges. New Directions for Community Colleges, no. 138* (pp. 5–14). San Francisco, CA: Jossey-Bass.

Redden, E. (2010, June 16). The 'community college' internationally. *Inside Higher Ed*. Retrieved from http://www.insidehighered.com/news/2010/06/16/intl

Reynolds, A. L., & Constantine, M. G. (2007). Cultural adjustment difficulties and career development of international college students. *Journal of Career Assessment, 15*(3), 338–350. doi: 10.1177/10690727301218. Retrieved from http://jca.sagepub.com. proxy.lib.iastate.edu:2048/content/15/3/338.full.pdf

Rojewski, J. W. (2002). Preparing the workforce of tomorrow: A conceptual framework for career and technical education. *Journal of Vocational Education Research, 27*(1), 7–35.

Rosser, V. J., Hermsen, J. M., Mamiseishvili, K., & Wood, M. S. (2007). A national study examining the impact of SEVIS on international student and scholar advisors. *Higher Education, 54,* 525–542. Retrieved from http://web.ebscohost.com.proxy.lib.iastate.edu: 2048/ehost/pdfviewer/pdfviewer?hid=8&sid=5ce03330-263c-48fb-a3f1-1db79a7a66cd%40sessionmgr11&vid=2

Santovec, M. (2002). Balancing act: Online learning becomes the "third shift" for women. *Distance Education Report, 6*(2), 1–2.

Scanlon, D. G. (1990). Lessons from the past in developing international education in community colleges. In R. K. Greenfield (Ed.), *Developing international education programs. New Directions for Community Colleges, no. 70* (pp. 5–16). San Francisco, CA: Jossey-Bass.

Schlossberg, N. K. (1981). A model for analyzing human adaption to transition. *The Counseling Psychologist, 9*(2), 2–18.

Schlossberg, N. K. (1984). *Counseling adults in transition: Linking theory to practice*. New York, NY: Springer Publishing.

Schram, J. L., & Lauver, P. J. (1988). Alienation in international students. *Journal of College Student Development, 29,* 146–150.

Schulken, E. W. (1968). *A history of foreign students in American higher education from its colonial beginnings to the present: A synthesis of the major forces influencing their presence in American higher education*. (Doctoral dissertation.) Dissertation Abstracts International. (UMI No. 7221329)

Sewall, M. (2010, August 24). U.S. colleges focus on making international students feel at home. *Chronicle of Higher Education*. Retrieved from http://chronicle.com/article/US-Colleges-Focus-On-Making/124108

Shen, Y., & Herr, E. L. (2004). Career placement concerns of international graduate students: A qualitative study. *Journal of Career Development, 31,* 15–29.

Siaya, L., & Hayward, F. (2003). *Mapping internationalization on U.S. campuses: Final report*. Washington, DC: American Council on Education.

Singaravelu, H. D., & Pope, M. (Eds.). (2007). *A handbook for counseling international students in the United States*. Alexandria, VA: American Counseling Association.

Slaughter, S. & Rhoades, G. (2004). *Academic capitalism and the new economy*. Baltimore, MD: Johns Hopkins University Press.

Sodowsky, G. R., & Lai, E. M. W. (1997). Asian immigrant variables and structural models of crosscultural distress. In A. Booth, A. C. Crouter, & N. Landale (Eds.), *Immigration and the family: Research and policy on U.S. immigrants* (pp. 211–234). Mahwah, NJ: Lawrence Erlbaum.

Srikatanyoo, N., & Gnoth, J. (2002). Country image and international tertiary education. *Journal of Brand Management, 10*(2), 139–146.

Telegraph. (2011, July 5). *Global employment crisis will stir social unrest, warns UN agency.* Retrieved from http://www.telegraph.co.uk/finance/economics/8036438/Global-employment-crisis-will-stir-social-unrest-warns-UN-agency.html

Tierney, M. (1983). Student college choice sets: Towards an empirical characterization. *Research in Higher Education, 75*(3), 271–284.

Tillman, M. J. (1990, Summer). Effective support services for international students. In R. K. Greenfield (Ed.), *Developing international education programs. New Directions for Community Colleges, no. 70* (pp. 87–98). San Francisco, CA: Jossey-Bass.

Verbik, L., & Lasanowski, V. (2007, September). *International student mobility: Patterns and trends.* The Observatory on Borderless Higher Education. London. Retrieved from http://www.eua.be/fileadmin/user_upload/files/newsletter/International_Student_Mobility_-_Patterns_and_Trends.pdf

Wedding, D., McCartney, J. L., & Currey, D. E. (2009). Lessons relevant to psychologists who serve as mentors for international students. *Professional Psychology: Research and Practice, 40*(2), 189–193. doi: 10.1037/a0012249. Retrieved from http://psycnet.apa.org/journals/pro/40/2/189.pdf

Wilton, L., & Constantine, M. G. (2003). Length of residence, cultural adjustment difficulties, and psychological distress symptoms in Asian and Latin American international students. *Journal of College Counseling, 6*, 177–186.

Ye, J. (2006). An examination of acculturative stress, interpersonal social support, and use of online ethnic social groups among Chinese international students. *The Howard Journal of Communications, 17*, 1–20.

Yeh, C. J., & Inose, M. (2003). International students' reported English fluency, social support satisfaction, and social connectedness as predictors of acculturative stress. *Counseling Psychology Quarterly, 16*(1), 15–28.

Zeszotarski, P. (2003). *Expectations and experiences of international students in an American community college in the context of globalization.* (Doctoral dissertation.) University of California, Los Angeles. (AAT 3089019).

Zhai, L. (2004). Studying international students: Adjustment issues and social support. *Journal of International Agricultural and Extension Education, 11*(1), 97–104.

Zhang, Y., & Hagedorn, L. S. (2011, Summer). College application with or without assistance of an education agent: Experience of international Chinese undergraduates in the U.S. *Journal of College Admission, 212*, 6–16.

5

ADULT STUDENT DEVELOPMENT

The Agentic Approach and its Relationship to the Community College Context

VIRGINIA MONTERO-HERNANDEZ AND CHRISTINE CERVEN

Since the 1970s, the adult student population in higher education has increased significantly. According to the National Center for Education Statistics (NCES), by 2007 adult student enrollment in postsecondary education reached 36.2% of the total undergraduate enrollment, with community colleges enrolling 43.7% of its population exceeding 24 years of age. Adult students in higher education institutions are typically categorized as being 25 years of age and older (Kasworm, 2003). The additional time adult students have for personal development contributes to their greater level of "maturity and developmental complexity acquired through life responsibilities, perspectives, and financial independence" when compared to their traditionally aged (18–24) counterparts (Kasworm, 2003, p. 3). Adult students in higher education institutions have more obligations to multiple life demands such as work (69% work part-time), marriage (57%), and/or supporting dependants other than their spouse (53%) that compete for the time they devote to their studies (Kasworm, 2003). The multiple role requirements that adults experience on a daily basis influence their academic performance and meaning-making experiences in the undergraduate classroom (Lave & Wenger, 1991; Wenger, 1998).

While scholars have attempted to expand thinking and theorizing about student development to be more holistic (Baxter-Magolda, 2009), there are a limited number of studies that focus on adult student development in higher education and particularly in community colleges (Baxter-Magolda, 2009; Chaves, 2006; Kasworm, 2005). Sissel, Hansman and Kasworm (2001) argue that the lack of understanding about adult students at universities, particularly, leads to the labeling of these students as "nontraditional, commuter, or reentry," a use that simplifies the features of this student population and potentially marginalizes them. Research universities and liberal arts colleges are primarily designed to offer programs and services that target traditional-aged students; thus, these institutions tend to overlook the needs and characteristics of adult learners (Kasworm, Sandmann, & Sissel, 2000; Sissel, Hansman, & Kasworm, 2001; Sissel, Birdsong, & Silaski, 1997). In some distinction to the approach undertaken by universities and four-year colleges, community colleges not only acknowledge the characteristics and needs of adult learners but also design educational structures and services that support this population.

This chapter draws upon the existing scholarship on adult learning, adult development, and adult education to identify and present the ways in which adult students typically engage with their undergraduate educational experiences and the ways in which higher education institutions such as community colleges respond to these students. The literature on the educational experiences of adult learners in community colleges is limited; therefore, our discussion relies on a larger body of literature that includes studies of adult students at universities and liberal arts colleges, and in informal contexts.

Based on our review of existing scholarly literature on adult undergraduates, we introduce the notion of an "agentic approach" to characterize adult learners and their approach to higher education and, particularly, the community college. We define adult students' agentic approach as the series of behaviors and attitudes that adult students exhibit within the academic environment that include self-monitoring, the use of meta cognitive skills, self-directed learning, and educational goal selection—all behaviors that contribute to their own self-advocacy (Donaldson & Graham, 1999; Donaldson & Townsend, 2007; Kasworm, 1990, 1993, 2005, 2010). We emphasize that adults' agentic approach in undergraduate education is based on the development of cognitive, social, and intrapersonal dimensions as well as self-directed behaviors.

Two arguments are central to this chapter. On the one hand, we argue that adult students in community colleges show an agentic approach to their learning experiences as a result of their development into adulthood. On the other hand, we argue that it is at the community college where adult students may encounter the highest concentration of educational programs and student services that resonate with and support adult learners' agentic approach to postsecondary education. We use findings from empirical studies to show that community colleges are responsive to the challenges and multiple roles that adult students experience and their aspirations for self-development and autonomy. At the end of the chapter we discuss the elements of community college educational structures that support and maximize adult students' agentic approach. We emphasize that effective instructional techniques and the construction of caring relationships are central for adult students to navigate their community college experiences successfully.

ADULT STUDENTS' CHALLENGES IN THE PURSUIT OF POSTSECONDARY EDUCATION

The community college student body consists of a majority of adult learners (Carney-Crompton & Tan, 2002; Kasworm, 2005; Levin, 2007). By 2007, adult students (25 years and older) comprised close to 50% of enrollment at community colleges (Pusser & Levin, 2009). Data from the National Center for Education Statistics (NCES) indicate that 38% of the 2007 enrollments in all higher education institutions are adult students (NCES, 2009). The community college student population is also commonly identified and characterized by its disadvantaged economic background and academic preparation (Pusser & Levin, 2009). Community college adult students, who enter programs with academic deficiencies, are often members of ethnic minorities, and/or are recipients of public assistance (Comprehensive Adult Student Assessment System, 2003). The majority of students at community colleges are individuals who undertake the responsibilities of adulthood: they work while studying to be able to pay for their education and to support themselves and/or any dependants.

To be an adult student at either four-year institutions or a community college is associated with three major challenges: role conflicts, lack of confidence/self-doubt, and previous life experiences which lead to fixed belief structures (Belzer, 2004; Crossan, Field, Gallacher, & Merrill, 2003; Giancola, Grawitch, & Borchert, 2009). Adult students' attention is divided between attending college and other activities that are not related to coursework (Ponton, Derrick, & Carr, 2005). It is well documented that adult students in college struggle to meet the multiple demands of family, work, coursework, and community (Kasworm, 1990, 1993, 2010). These multiple demands (often intensified in the case of female, minority, and economically disadvantaged adults) compete for adults' time, create stressful daily conditions, and reduce an adult learner's ability to participate fully in the college environment (Prins, Toso, & Schafft, 2009; Vaccaro & Lovell, 2010).

Another factor threatening adult students' ability to pursue postsecondary education is their self-doubt and lack of confidence or self-esteem. Adult students are apprehensive about enrolling in postsecondary education due to their enrollment in college later in life and their motivations, which are different from those among traditional-aged students (Chen, Kim, Moon, & Merriam, 2008; Donaldson & Townsend, 2007; Kasworm, 1990). Academic structures and services designed to address the needs of traditional-aged students can increase feelings of alienation among adult students who cannot meet institutional norms and standards such as fixed schedules, full-time enrollment, and active involvement in campus life (Chaves, 2006; Kasworm et al., 2000; Sissel et al., 1997; Sissel, Hansman, & Kasworm, 2001). Adults often constitute evening, weekend, and distance learners and, therefore, are not able to fully access postsecondary education institutions that are structured to address traditional-aged students (Sissel et al., 2001). Adult students' failure to meet institutional standards may cause them to question their capacity to achieve academically within an institutional context and to lose their confidence as effective learners (Donaldson & Townsend, 2007; Kasworm, 1990, 2005).

Finally, some of adult students' previous life experiences can lead to more fixed and engrained beliefs and behaviors which affect their ability to change or adapt to a new environment and/or new ideas (Belzer, 2004; Crossan et al., 2003). In a qualitative study that included five adult African American women attending a community-based program for women, Belzer (2004) found that the women resisted taking a more active role in the classroom because of their previous conceptualizations about the traditional role of instructors as authorities and students as passive actors in the learning process. In order to become active learners, students had to speak with counselors repeatedly. The interaction with counselors over a period of time influenced the women students to modify their previous understandings about the role of education in their lives and redefine their own patterns of behavior in the college context.

The everyday life challenges (e.g., family, work, community) that adult students experience as a result of their multiple responsibilities make it necessary for them to receive instrumental and social support in their educational endeavors. With their open-access mission, flexible schedules, small classes, flexible curricular structures, learning communities, and student services (Grubb, Badway, & Bell, 2003; Grubb et al., 1999; Levin, 2007; Levin & Montero-Hernandez, 2009), community colleges serve as environments in which adults can interact with peers and faculty, explore new ideas, gain self-knowledge, overcome their multiple role demands, and, in turn, make productive contributions to work and society (Kasworm, 2005; Ortiz, 1995).

COMMUNITY COLLEGES AS ADULT SERVING INSTITUTIONS

Community colleges play a major role in providing youth and adult students with access to academic and vocational programs in postsecondary education (Bragg, 2001; Bragg & Hamm, 1996; Cohen & Brawer, 2003; Grubb et al., 2003; Levin, 2007; Levin & Montero-Hernandez, 2009). Among their multiple missions (Bailey, 2002; Levin, 2001), community colleges provide adult students with increased access to different educational opportunities including academic transfer preparation, short-term continuing education, vocational-technical training, critical intellectual development, developmental education, community service, and post-baccalaureate credentialing, and, in some cases, baccalaureate credentials (Cohen & Brawer, 2003; Pusser & Levin, 2009).

Legally, the community college is one of the primary educational institutions responsible for providing adult education in the U.S. Based on the Adult Education Act in 1966, the National Literacy Act in 1991, and the Workforce Investment Act of 1998, the U.S. Department of Education authorizes federal grants for the creation of adult education programs to be given to states that qualify (Ziegler & Bingman, 2007). Community colleges are one of the most important local educational organizations that receive federal funds to implement adult education programs. In the 2003 report from the Comprehensive Adult Student Assessment System (CASA) to the Council for Advancement of Adult Literacy (CAAL), within 39 states surveyed, it was found that 27% of adult education providers were community colleges.

Community colleges offer adult educational programs that include adult secondary education (GED or other high school diploma programs), precollege English as a second language (ESL), and adult basic education (ABE) (Boylan, 2004). Adult education programs in community colleges target advancement in three areas of learners' lives: basic skills (i.e., learning to read, write, and speak English and understand basic math), postsecondary degree attainment, and employment (Stasz, Schwartz, & Weeden, 1991; Ziegler & Bingman, 2007). Adult education programs highlight and implement the principles of adult learning such as incorporating students' own language and previous experiences as well as encouraging students to make decisions about their educational experiences (Stasz et al., 1991).

In community colleges, adult education programs, such as ABE, implement methods that resonate with the specific needs of the adult student population. As such, they organize experiential and collaborative learning activities in the classroom and create a caring-relational atmosphere (Perin, Flugman, & Spiegel, 2006; Skinner & Gillespie, 2000). ABE aims to increase the general knowledge of semi-literate and illiterate adults and improve their vocational competence (Kavale & Lindsey, 1977). In the case of Kavale and Lindsey's (1977) work, the goals of the program were to help adult learners become independent, meet their adult responsibilities, and increase their ability to ascertain more productive and profitable employment. Across community colleges, there is diversity in the implementation of ABE programs. However, there are specific instructional methods that these programs use to be effective for adult student engagement (Perin et al., 2006; Skinner & Gillespie, 2000). For example, the ABE program implemented in 1987 in San Diego County was characterized by a curriculum that was systematic, cumulative, and integrated: material was presented in an organized manner; students learned in a stepwise fashion to develop skills in incremental stages; and reading, spelling, and writing were taught as connected entities rather than fragmented modules (Skinner & Gillespie, 2000). Pedagogical techniques in the program included interaction and cooperation between students and faculty in classrooms, individualized attention and work within small, supportive groups, learning by doing, students' reflection and involvement in the discovery process, and the use of technology to reinforce, review, and enrich specific skills (Skinner & Gillespie, 2000).

Student support programs and services (e.g., guidance sessions, remedial studies, learning communities, and centers for service learning) complement adult education programs in community colleges. Community college adult students who receive guidance and support from counselors, tutors, and faculty report greater degree attainment, self-confidence, and improved social and cognitive abilities (Levin & Montero-Hernandez, 2009). Community colleges have implemented mentoring and counseling services that help not only young but also adult students achieve academically and learn how to navigate the college's academic culture and accomplish their goals (Jacobi, 1991; Lee, Olson, Locke, & Michelson, 2009). A study exploring the role of student services in a California community college reported that the guidance that adult students received from institutional agents helped them to understand academic policies and requirements as well as make decisions about what courses to take or procedures in their application for financial aid (Henriksen, 1995).

Learning communities in community colleges represent one college structure that incorporates a constructivist-developmental approach which emphasizes "active and collaborative learning activities that promote student involvement in complementary academic and social activities" (Zhao & Kuh, 2004, p. 116). Learning communities encourage both young and adult students in community colleges to interact with faculty and peers, which leads to their academic and social integration as well as the development of their cognitive skills, such as reading and writing, and a greater sense of self-confidence (Arendale, 1994; Burmeister, 1996; Maxwell, 1998). Supplemental instruction (one of the central features of learning communities in the community college) involves the regular use of workshop sessions designed to promote and enrich student learning while countering any stigma associated with the need for tutoring or any other form of remedial education (Levin, Cox, Habereler, & Cerven, 2011). Maxwell (1998) found that the use of small student groups, individualized feedback, and collaborative-active learning in learning communities resulted in community college students studying together for courses and achieving positive student outcomes (e.g., persistence, academic and social integration).

The academic support, opportunities for interaction with peers and faculty, and significant learning experiences that community colleges offer are factors that promote positive outcomes for adult students such as student retention, persistence, and completion of college degrees and certificates. Carol Kasworm (2005) documents how adult learners in community colleges constructed their student identity via: (1) their other life roles and experiences; (2) their expectations for their studies and ability to learn as adults; (3) their beliefs about access to a particular educational institution; and (4) their interactions with faculty and other students within the classroom. In these interactions, adult students constructed their sense of self (in relation to their understandings of themselves as an adult and the other roles they occupy) and their expectations of how they should act within the classroom. They also derived self-understandings about their role as students by actively comparing themselves to an ideal student image that was, on the whole, defined as being a serious, committed, and successful college attendee. Kasworm (2005) found that adult students' positive and respectful interactions with other students (both younger and older) and faculty within the community college classroom helped ease their initial concerns about attending college, diminished their sense of marginalization, and led to a positive self-image of themselves as adult students.

ADULT STUDENTS: THE AGENTIC LEARNER
IN THE COMMUNITY COLLEGE

Community colleges are adult serving institutions that provide programs and services which are responsive to adult learners' psychosocial development, academic and personal goals, and particular needs for adaptation to academic culture (Levin, 2007; Levin & Montero-Hernandez, 2009). While it is widely noted in the adult education literature that adult students in higher education institutions are agents who exhibit strong motivation and commitment to their education (Chen et al., 2008; Donaldson & Townsend, 2007; Kasworm, 1990), the community college literature demonstrates little effort to conceptualize the characteristics of the adult re-entry student who enrolls in community college programs (Kasworm, 2005).

In this section, we present the notion of adult students' agentic approach as an integrative notion that describes the fundamental characteristics of the adult student population that community colleges serve. We argue that the agentic approach that community college adult students embrace can be defined by explaining five components: (1) adults' cognitive and personal developmental journey; (2) intrinsic motivation; (3) agentic performance; (4) comprehensive involvement; and (5) college goal selection. We acknowledge that the personal background and context of adult students may moderate the degree of development an adult achieves in each one of these dimensions and therefore in their agentic approach. Our conceptualization of adult students' agentic approach to formal education aims to improve the understanding of this student population within the community college.

Adults' Developmental Journey: Predispositions of an Agentic Approach

The agentic approach adult students apply to their undergraduate educational endeavors is linked to their individual socio-cognitive development. Psychosocial and socio-cultural theories on adult development [e.g., Kegan's (1994) constructive-developmental perspective of adulthood and Piaget's (1950) and Erickson's (1968) developmental theories] suggest that the cognitive structure of adults becomes more complex over time due to the multiplicity of experiences and perspectives that they accumulate through their life. The increased cognitive complexity among adults is an important element in the creation of new forms of self-understanding and agency (Drago-Severson, 2004). Adults' cognitive structures include not only the assimilation of multiple types of information but also the development of higher cognitive processes such as meta-cognition or critical thinking (Donaldson & Graham, 1999; Graham & Donaldson, 1999; Justice & Dornan, 2001).

The complexity of adults' cognitive development is related to the fluid and crystallized intellectual abilities adults acquire over their lifespan (Cattell, 1987; Kanfer &

Ackerman, 2004; Schaie, 1996). Individuals' fluid intellectual abilities (i.e., working memory, abstract reasoning, attention, and processing of novel information) typically reach the peak of their development in their early twenties, whereas individuals' crystallized intellectual abilities (i.e., general knowledge, extent of vocabulary, and verbal comprehension) emerge during middle age and beyond (Kanfer & Ackerman, 2004). Adulthood, therefore, is a stage of life in which cognitive structures become increasingly more complex as a result of people's multiple lived experiences and the information they gather over the years.

The evolution of one's cognitive structure throughout adulthood leads to an increased capacity for individual introspection and self-awareness (Graham & Donaldson, 1999). This increased self-reflection leads to the search for greater agency and accomplishment in one's own life (Baxter-Magolda, 2009; Taylor, 2008). Adults act to achieve personal as well as academic goals (Courtney, 1992). This evolving sense of agency is understood in the literature on adult development to occur through cognitive functions such as meta-cognition, critical thinking, and self-reflection (Donaldson & Graham, 1999; Donaldson & Townsend, 2007; Graham & Donaldson, 1999).

Adults' evolving sense of agency is identified in the literature as individuals' efforts to become "authors" of their lives [or otherwise understood to have achieved "self-authorship"] (Baxter-Magolda, 2009; Kegan, 1994). Based on the work of Kegan (1994), Baxter-Magolda (2009) conducted a longitudinal study examining the development and changes of individuals from their years as young adults into mature adulthood and found that they reached a distinct developmental stage in life where they noted that they had greater confidence in their ability to control or "author" their lives. Self-authorship occurs when young adults and adults are capable of sorting through multiple perspectives to choose their own beliefs, identity, goals, and social relationships (Baxter-Magolda & King, 2007; Kegan, 1994; Pizzolato, 2005; Torres & Hernandez, 2007). Self-authorship entails becoming a voice of authority in one's own life, feeling capable of making decisions in one's life, and providing social and instrumental support to other people. Adult students' progression toward authoring their lives bolsters their development and the implementation of their agentic approach throughout their educational endeavors.

Even though adult developmental theories suggest a progression toward increased levels of agency, complex thinking, and information processing, the process of development can be stunted or accelerated by socio-cultural conditions (Roberson & Merriam, 2005). As such, more recent work addresses the ways in which adulthood, development, and participation in formal education are moderated by the diversity in a student's background and social identities [i.e., race, ethnicity, gender, and sexual orientation] (Baxter- Magolda, 2001, 2003; Baxter-Magolda, Abes, & Torres, 2009; Belenky, Clinchy, Goldberger, & Tarule, 1986; Pizzolato, 2005; Torres, Jones, & Renn, 2009). Thus, further research is necessary—both needed and expected—to examine the ways in which the specific contextual factors and unique life circumstances of an individual influence the development of adult learners' agentic approach and their participation in undergraduate education.

Intrinsic Motivation: Education as a Self-Chosen Commitment

In addition to the development of cognitive structures and self-authorship among adults, a second core component of adults' agentic approach encompasses intrinsic motivation (i.e., one's internal driving force to achieve certain goals). When compared to younger students, undergraduate adult learners tend to exhibit higher levels of intrinsic motivation including greater concentration, commitment to learn, and continued engagement with academic tasks (Chen et al., 2008; Donaldson & Townsend, 2007; Kasworm, 1990; Vaccaro & Lovell, 2010).

Adult students have more specific and purposeful reasons for enrolling in college. Rather than entering higher education as a result of parental expectation or with the intention to take advantage of the social aspects a traditional campus has to offer, "adults are more intent on learning, hope to gain something they can apply to their work, approach their college experiences with a clearer purpose in mind, and take the advice of instructors more seriously" (Donaldson & Graham, 1999, p. 27). Additionally, the purpose and clarity with which adult students approach their educational endeavors may be attributed to their motivation to apply their new knowledge and skills immediately in their working worlds where they may witness direct application of their newly gained knowledge (Chaves, 2006; Kasworm, 2010).

Adult students have a variety of reasons why they participate in higher education. General motivations to re-enroll in college include life transitions, aspirations for self-development, desire for success and achievement in life, and family responsibilities. Adults view education as a pathway to social mobility and self-improvement (Courtney, 1992). Adult students also note critical life events such as divorce or the loss of a significant other as a source of motivation to enroll in college (Hensley & Kinser, 2001). As such, life transitions lead adults to reassess their goals and priorities and seek strategies to re-establish their everyday life and routine (Ross, 1988). When adults reflect on their past experiences and the way they expect to live in the future, they usually start looking for autonomy, financial stability, job opportunities, and greater self-awareness and self-understanding; conditions understood to be facilitated by postsecondary education (Courtney, 1992; Hensley & Kinser, 2001; Justice & Dornan, 2001; Prins et al., 2009; Taylor, 2008; Vaccaro & Lovell, 2010). Finally, adults also decide to study while they manage other life responsibilities in order to act as positive role models for their children (Vaccaro & Lovell, 2010).

A concrete example of the agentic approach and its relationship to adult students' intrinsic motivation is the continued commitment and sustained efforts that some adults show over time in spite of frequent interruptions in their patterns of college attendance. In a qualitative study of 28 female adult students attending a small evening and weekend college, Vaccaro and Lovell (2010) found that even though these women had to take time away from college (i.e., formally withdraw for weeks or months) to care for ill relatives or maintain the duties of their employment, they continued their educational pursuits later when their life conditions allowed them to do so. Although these female adult students achieved positive academic outcomes after long periods of time, they viewed themselves as committed and persistent students who could take up their formal education again after temporary periods of absence. In another qualitative study that examined persistence among 63 adult, part-time, female students in a private college, Hensley and Kinser (2001) found that adults worked toward their academic goals tenaciously in spite of their attendance at multiple institutions or their stopping out of college. In the context of fragmented or non-linear patterns of college enrollment, the academic achievement of adults illustrates both their motivation to learn and their commitment to self-improvement—both aspects related to their agentic approach.

Agentic Performance: Self-Directed Learning and Comprehensive Involvement

Adult students in higher education institutions are described in the literature as active and autonomous learners who engage in focused learning activities and interactions with peers, faculty, and members of their larger community. Self-directed learning is one of the central concepts utilized in scholarly work to describe adults' approach to their college activities (Garrison, 1997; Rager, 2003; Roberson & Merriam, 2005). Garrison (1997) explains that self-directed learning occurs when "learners are motivated to assume personal responsibility and collaborative control of the cognitive and contextual processes in constructing and confirming meaningful and worthwhile learning outcomes" (p. 18). Garrison also suggests that an adult who is fully self-directed is a person who can control and organize tasks, learn collaboratively, think critically, and make meaning of specialized and ambiguous information.

Three dimensions comprise self-directed learning: self-management, self-monitoring, and motivation (Garrison, 1997). Self-management refers to the control and implementation of tasks associated with the learning process including study techniques and the use of sources of social support such as peers or family. In self-monitoring, individuals determine which learning strategies are best suited for the task at hand as well as modify their thinking according to the learning goal or task involved. Finally, motivation refers to the driving force that enables individuals to initiate and maintain their efforts and interest to learn and achieve specific assignments. Garrison (1997) posits that self-directed learning "is associated with initiating learning goals, maintaining intention, and striving for quality outcomes" (p. 31).

Strategies that characterize the self-directed learning approach among adult students include reading print materials, using technology to learn about a problem, networking, and seeking support groups (Prins et al., 2009; Rager, 2003). Since adult students have limited opportunities to engage in extra-curricular activities on campus (Chen et al., 2008; Donaldson & Townsend, 2007; Kasworm, 1990), the self-directed learning approach enacted by mature students is linked to an intensive use of the classroom as a place to learn and foster associations with peers and faculty, as well as develop off-campus activities (Graham & Donaldson, 1999). Interactions in classrooms are one of the main opportunities for adult students to garner knowledge, explore questions, ask for academic advice, and become socialized into the academic environment (Tinto, 1997). Adult students' concentrated use of the classroom typifies adult students' greater help-seeking behaviors when compared to younger students (Kasworm, 2010). Older learners construct person-to-person relationships with faculty through asking questions in the classroom, answering faculty queries, and embracing quality class work. In addition, these students report greater use of student services and academic advising (Kasworm, 2005, 2010).

The self-directed learning approach of adult students is not exclusive to learning activities in the classroom. Even though older learners do not participate in extra-curricular activities (e.g., student organizations, college governance, or athletics), they engage in activities that extend beyond the classroom and the college campus. Adults implement their acquired knowledge in their local community, religious groups, family, and work (Crossan et al., 2003). Mature students perceive their off-campus life as a context where they can use their knowledge and refine their abilities (Crossan et al., 2003; Giancola et al., 2009). Adults' distinct cognitive, personal, and social development enables them to engage in multiple learning activities in different contexts, both inside and outside the classroom (Roberson & Merriam, 2005). Through his work on self-directed learning, Tough (1973) found that adults tend to engage in an average of eight learning projects per year. A learning project is a "highly deliberate effort to gain certain knowledge, to improve a skill, or to change one's attitude or emotional reaction" (Tough, 1973, p. 1). Adults' pattern of engagement in learning projects and activities is evidence of adult students' active approach to learning in college programs.

College Goals: Achievement as a Self-Defined Construct

The agentic approach of adult undergraduate learners is also associated with the educational goals they seek to accomplish: adults who choose to attend college make decisions about not only what they want to study, and why, but also what they expect as the result of what they achieve educationally (Courtney, 1992; Donaldson & Graham, 1999; Vaccaro & Lovell, 2010). Although faculty and counselors can advise and guide adult learners through their college education, adults enter college with a more or less refined sense of what they want to achieve (Chaves, 2006; Ponton, Derrick, & Carr, 2005). In their model of college outcomes for adult students, Donaldson and Graham (1999) explain that once enrolled in college, adults choose to pursue specific goals that are meaningful based on their personal trajectories and life conditions such as increased self-confidence and personal growth, networking and social support, and improved skills to make decisions. Donaldson and Graham emphasize the importance of recognizing that adult students' goals may not always correspond to those traditionally defined by the academic community such as degree attainment, social and academic integration, and academic persistence. Adult students' goals often move beyond the scope of the academy and tend to be more personally relevant (e.g., direct application to current work and self-development).

Adults decide on the goals they intend to accomplish in college according to their perception of what constitutes knowledge and how knowledge can be used (Donaldson & Graham, 1999). Adult students differentiate between two types of knowledge. The first type is academic knowledge (i.e., declarative knowledge), which implies learning abstract and theoretical information. The second type of knowledge is experiential knowledge (i.e., procedural knowledge), which includes learning about concrete and relevant problems and solutions (Chen et al., 2008; Donaldson & Townsend, 2007; Kasworm, 1990). Since adults perceive different benefits to the use of either academic or procedural knowledge, they move through their educational endeavors in a judicious manner (Donaldson & Graham, 1999). One conclusion we draw from the assumption that adults pursue specific educational goals according to the kinds of knowledge they seek is that adult students with vocational aspirations may seek experiential learning and the acquisition of procedural knowledge, while those with academic aspirations may show greater interest in the acquisition of declarative knowledge.

CRITICAL ELEMENTS OF A SUPPORTIVE ENVIRONMENT FOR AGENTIC ADULTS

Adult students' agentic approach to learning and education is an asset that enables adult learners to manage competing demands, overcome conflicting roles, and achieve college goals (Giancola et al., 2009). However, the educational structures of higher education institutions play a central role in enhacing the opportunities adults have to become self-directed and productive learners in college. In community colleges, flexible schedules, academic support, and caring instructional techniques are institutional components that help adult students to reduce stress, recover self-confidence, and engage in active learning (Brewer, Klein, & Mann, 2003; Brock, 2010; Chaves, 2006). Both in their design and in their operations, the educational structures and student services that community colleges provide for adult students acknowledge the unique characteristics of this population (Bonk & Kim, 1998; Taylor, 2008).

Additionally, the literature demonstrates two pedagogical approaches that are central to the preservation and encouragement of the adult student's agentic approach in the community college. The first refers to practitioners' design of meaningful learning activities in which adult students can productively engage in classrooms. The second involves the construction of institutional programs that foster interaction between students and faculty or counselors to achieve educational goals and self-improvement. The careful design of learning activities in the classroom is essential considering that adult students cannot invest their time at college undertaking activities other than those strictly related to the classroom, including instructional assignments. A significant number of community college students experience a work–study conflict that presents multiple and competing demands (Levin, Montero-Hernandez, & Cerven, 2010). Adult community college students' multiple responsibilities hinder their ability to participate in extra-curricular activities (e.g., student organizations), thus reducing their opportunities to interact with others and gain knowledge about college life. Because of adult students' limited opportunity to interact with others on campus, the classroom becomes the primary venue where adult students, peers, and faculty interact and share information (Tinto, 1987). Therefore, the careful design of learning experiences within the classroom is central for adult learners to gain the maximum benefit of their education. Learning experiences that are effective for adult learners include the implementation of experiential learning and teaching (Brewer et al., 2003; Kasworm, 2003, 2005; Kolb, 1984). In the community college, the implementation of experiential learning includes the use of adults' experiences as a reservoir of knowledge that may be incorporated with the subject content addressed within the classroom (Chaves, 2006). Experiential teaching and learning methods that incorporate individuals' concrete experiences, reflective observations, and active experimentation help adults understand the connection between what is learned, the skills they adopt, and their problem solving within a specific context (Kolb, 1984).

Adult student development is related to adults' participation in interactions with faculty members, counselors, and peers who show a supportive attitude toward them. Since adults seek mutually respectful relationships in their college experience, there is merit in the creation and establishment of a caring atmosphere in which learners perceive that they are valued and cared for by faculty members and other institutional actors (Belenky, Clinchy, Goldberger, & Tarule, 1986; Lee-Hsieh, Kuo, & Ya-Hsun Tsai, 2004; Noddings, 1984; Smith, 2000; Valenzuela, 1999). Belzer (2004) found that once female adult students in college witnessed frequent and meaningful conversations with counselors and faculty their understanding of themselves and the classroom dynamic shifted to a point where they were able to assume a more active student role. Other studies have shown that adult students in community colleges develop social skills, define goals, and monitor their academic progress when college personnel validate their previous experiential knowledge and provide them with support to achieve their goals (Levin & Montero-Hernandez, 2009). Overall, adult students who witnessed meaningful interactions with peers, faculty, and student service staff in community colleges reported increased self-confidence, academic achievement, sustained motivation, and expanded career aspirations (Chang, 2005; Chaves, 2006; Crisp, 2010; Levin & Montero-Hernandez, 2009; Maxwell, 1998; McConnell, 2000; Thompson, 2001). Collaborative work between adult students and college personnel increases adults' opportunities to learn about academic culture and language, which, in turn, facilitates the development of their cognitive, social, and intrapersonal skills.

It is clear from the literature that support from institutional agents (e.g., faculty, counselors, and mentors) paired with student services (e.g., counseling) and academic structures (e.g., learning communities) is critical in order to produce positive developmental outcomes among adult students in community colleges. College personnel become institutional agents when they provide students with meaningful information and guidance (Stanton-Salazar, 1997, 2010). Faculty members, counselors, or mentors who participate in student support programs and student services can encourage the development of the academic, social, and intrapersonal skills of non-traditional students such as adult learners (Baxter-Magolda, 2009; Baxter-Magolda & King, 2007; Chaves, 2006; Evans, Forney, & Guido-DiBrito, 1998; Lee et al., 2009; Lichtenstein, 2005; Stanton-Salazar, 1997, 2010). Institutional agents who commit to providing support and guidance to college students are central to the creation of a caring atmosphere. Counselors and faculty members in community colleges interact with adult students to help them learn academic language and institutional standards, realize their potential, build skills and abilities, use sources of support, create networks, and define career pathways (Levin & Montero-Hernandez, 2009).

CONCLUDING REMARKS

By the early 21st century, adult student enrollment in postsecondary education reached 36.2% of the total undergraduate enrollment; and 43.7% of community college students were 25 years of age or older (U.S. Department of Education, 2011). Adult undergraduates have characteristics that differ from those among traditional-aged students [18–24 years old] (Kasworm, 2005). Adulthood is a stage of life in which the development of individuals' cognitive, social, and emotional dimensions affects their postsecondary educational experiences (Donaldson & Townsend, 2007; Graham & Donaldson, 1999; Kasworm, 1990). To be a successful adult student in college for large numbers of students requires overcoming one or more significant challenges such as low self-confidence, competing life demands, academic deficiencies, and fixed attitudes and behaviors that are not supportive of an active student role. Adult learners' completion of educational, vocational, and personal goals may be furthered when they operate in educational environments that are sensitive to their unique developmental characteristics of adulthood including their agentic approach to higher education.

In this chapter, we noted the organizational features and instructional techniques used within the community college that are responsive to the needs of the adult student. Community colleges are the premier postsecondary educational institution to provide adult students with educational structures that conform to their multiple life demands and help them to overcome their disadvantaged circumstances. We emphasize that the implementation of adult education programs, student services, and specific instructional mechanisms such as learning communities within the community college are examples of the institutional efforts aimed to address the particular characteristics and needs of adult students and, ultimately, support their educational endeavors.

However, community colleges are not fully effective institutions and need to improve substantial aspects of their structural elements (e.g., approaches to training and credentialing, funding and financial support for students, policies that promote developmental education, infrastructure, and assessment strategies) to be able to fulfill their multipurpose mission (Pusser & Levin, 2009). Among the necessary changes required of community colleges are the preservation and strengthening of the educational structures that address the unique characteristics of adult students. The implementation of a student-centered instructional approach and personalized attention can maximize the agentic approach that adult learners apply to their educational endeavors.

The notion of adult students' agentic approach provides an analytical framework to help both scholars and practitioners improve their understanding of the adult student population in the community college. On the one hand, practitioners can identify principles for the design of organizational and curricular mechanisms to help adult students strengthen their agentic approach to formal education and achieve their personal goals. On the other hand, scholars can take the notion we present in this chapter as a point of departure to examine, on the basis of gender or ethnicity, the ways in which adult students develop and enact their agentic approach to college education.

QUESTIONS FOR DISCUSSION

1. In what ways are adult students different from traditional-aged students?
2. What is "agency" and what are examples from the chapter on adult students' agentic behaviors?
3. What is the role of community college faculty, staff, and administrators in the development of adult students?
4. What are some specific actions that community colleges could take to enhance the education of adult students?

REFERENCES

Arendale, D. R. (1994). Understanding the supplemental instruction model. In D. C. Martin & D. R. Arendale (Eds.), *Supplemental instruction: Increasing achievement and retention* (Vol. 60, pp. 11–21). San Francisco, CA: Jossey-Bass.

Bailey, T. (2002). Community colleges in the 21st century: Challenges and opportunities. In P. A. Graham & N. G. Stacey (Eds.), *The knowledge economy and postsecondary education: Report of a workshop* (pp. 1–10). Washington, DC: National Academy Press.

Baxter-Magolda, M. B. (2001). *Making their own way: Narratives for transforming higher education to promote self-development.* Sterling, VA: Stylus.

Baxter-Magolda, M. B. (2003). Identity and learning: Student affairs' role in transforming higher education. *Journal of College Student Development, 44*(1), 231–247.

Baxter-Magolda, M. B. (2009). The activity of meaning making: A holistic perspective on college student development. *Journal of College Student Development, 50*(6), 621–639.

Baxter-Magolda, M. B., Abes, E., & Torres, V. (2009). Epistemological, interpersonal, and interpersonal development in the college years and young adulthood. In M. Smith & N. Defrates-Densch (Eds.), *Handbook of research on adult learning and development* (pp. 183–219). New York, NY: Routledge.

Baxter-Magolda, M. B., & King, P. M. (2007). Interview strategies for assessing self-authorship: Constructing conversations to assess meaning making. *Journal of College Student Development, 48*(5), 491–508.

Belenky, M. F., Clinchy, B. M., Goldberger, N. R., & Tarule, J. M. (1986). *Women's ways of knowing: Development of self, voice, and mind.* New York, NY: Basic Books.

Belzer, A. (2004). "It's not like normal school": The role of prior learning contexts in adult learning. *Adult Education Quarterly, 55*(1), 41–59.

Berker, A., & Horn, L. (2003). *Work first, study second: Adult undergraduates who combine employment and post-secondary enrollment* (NCES 2003–167). Washington, DC: U.S. Department of Education, National Center for Education Statistics.

Bonk, C. J., & Kim, K. A. (1998). Extending sociocultural theory to adult learning. In M. C. Smith & T. Pourchot (Eds.), *Adult learning and development* (pp. 67–88). Mahwah, NJ: Lawrence Erlbaum Associates.

Boylan, H. (2004). *Forging new partnerships. Adult and developmental education in community colleges.* New York, NY: Council for Advancement of Adult Literacy.

Bragg, D. D. (2001). Community college access, mission, and outcomes: Considering intriguing intersections and challenges. *Peabody Journal of Education, 76*(1), 93–116.

Bragg, D. D., & Hamm, R. E. (1996). *Linking college and work: Exemplary policies and practices of two year college-work based learning programs.* Berkeley, CA: National Center for Research in Vocational Education.

Brewer, S. A., Klein, J. D., & Mann, K. (2003). Using small group learning strategies with adult re-entry students. *College Student Journal, 37*(2), 286–297.

Brock, T. (2010). Young adults and higher education barriers and breakthroughs to success. *The Future of Children, 20*(1), 109–132.

Burmeister, S. (1996). Supplemental instruction: An interview with Deanna Martin. *Journal of Developmental Education, 20,* 22–26.

Carney-Crompton, S., & Tan, J. (2002). Support systems, psychological functioning, and academic performance of nontraditional female students. *Adult Education Quarterly, 52*(2), 140–154.

Cattell, R. B. (1987). *Intelligence: Its structure, growth, and action.* Amsterdam: North-Holland.

Chang, J. C. (2005). Faculty–student interaction at the community college: A focus on students of color. *Research in Higher Education, 46*(7), 769–802.

Chaves, C. (2006). Involvement, development, and retention: Theoretical foundations and potential extensions for adult community college students. *Community College Review, 34*(2), 139–152.

Chen, L.-K., Kim, Y. S., Moon, P., & Merriam, S. B. (2008). A review and critique of the portrayal of older adult learners in adult education journals, 1980–2006. *Adult Education Quarterly, 59*(1), 3–21.

Cohen, A., & Brawer, F. (2003). *The American community college* (4th ed.). San Francisco, CA: Jossey-Bass.

Coker, A. D. (2003). African American female adult learners: Motivations, challenges, and coping strategies. *Journal of Black Studies, 33*(5), 654–674.

Comprehensive Adult Student Assessment System. (2003). *Adult basic education and community colleges in five states.* New York, NY: Council for Advancement of Adult Literacy.

Courtney, S. (1992). *Why adults learn. Toward a theory of participation in adult education.* New York, NY: Routledge.

Crisp, G. (2010). The impact of mentoring on the success of community college students. *The Review of Higher Education, 34*(1), 39–60.

Crossan, B., Field, J., Gallacher, J., & Merrill, B. (2003). Understanding participation in learning for non-traditional adult learners: Learning careers and the construction of learning identities. *British Journal of Sociology of Education, 24*(1), 55–67.

Donaldson, J. F., & Graham, S. (1999). A model of college outcomes for adults. *Adult Education Quarterly, 50*(1), 24–40.

Donaldson, J. F., & Townsend, B. K. (2007). Higher education journals' discourse about adult undergraduate students. *The Journal of Higher Education, 78*(1), 27–50.

Drago-Severson, E. (2004). *Becoming adult learners: Principles and practices for effective development.* New York, NY: Teachers College Press.

Erikson, E. H. (1968). *Identity, youth, and crisis.* New York, NY: W.W. Norton & Company.

Evans, B. C. (2004). Application of the caring curriculum to education of Hispanic/Latino and American Indian nursing students. *Journal of Nursing Education, 43*(5), 219.

Evans, N. J., Forney, D. S., & Guido-DiBrito, F. (1998). *Student development in college: Theory, research and practice.* San Francisco, CA: Jossey-Bass.

Garrison, D. R. (1997). Self-directed learning: Toward a comprehensive model. *Adult Education Quarterly, 48*(1), 18–33.

Giancola, J. K., Grawitch, M. J., & Borchert, D. (2009). Dealing with the stress of college: A model for adult students. *Adult Education Quarterly, 59*(3), 246–263.

Graham, S., & Donaldson, J. F. (1999). Adult students' academic and intellectual development in college. *Adult Education Quarterly, 49*(3), 147–161.

Grubb, W. N., Badway, N., & Bell, D. (2003). Community colleges and the equity agenda: The potential of non-credit education. *Annals of the American Academy of Political and Social Science, 586* (Community colleges: New environments, new directions), 218–240.

Grubb, W. N., Worthen, H., Byrd, B., Webb, E., Badway, N., Case, C., et al. (1999). *Honored but invisible: An inside look at teaching in community colleges.* New York, NY: Routledge.

Henriksen, J. A. S. (1995). Orientation and counseling in a California community college: Surveying the perspectives of a multicultural student population. *Community College Review 23*(2), 59–74.

Hensley, L. G., & Kinser, K. (2001). Rethinking adult learner persistence: Implications for counselors. *Adultspan Journal, 2*(3), 88–100.

Higbee, J. L., Arendale, D. R., & Lundell, D. B. (2005). Using theory and research to improve access and retention in development education. *New Directions for Community Colleges, no. 129* (pp. 5–15). San Francisco, CA: Jossey-Bass.

Jacobi, M. (1991). Mentoring and undergraduate academic success: A literature review. *Review of Educational Research, 61*(4), 505–532.

Justice, E. M., & Dornan, T. M. (2001). Metacognitive differences between traditional-age and nontraditional-age college students. *Adult Education Quarterly, 51*(3), 236–249.

Kanfer, R., & Ackerman, P. L. (2004). Aging, adult development, and work motivation. *The Academy of Management Review, 29*(3), 440–458.

Kasworm, C. (1990). Adult undergraduates in higher education: A review of past research perspectives. *Review of Educational Research, 60*(3), 345–372.

Kasworm, C. (1993). Adult higher education from an international perspective. *Higher Education, 25*(4), 411–423.

Kasworm, C. (2003). Adult meaning making in the undergraduate classroom. *Adult Education Quarterly, 53*(2), 81–98.

Kasworm, C. (2005). Adult student identity in an intergenerational community college classroom. *Adult Education Quarterly, 56*(1), 3–20.

Kasworm, C. (2010). Adult learners in a research university: Negotiating undergraduate student identity. *Adult Education Quarterly, 60*(2), 143–160.

Kasworm, C., Sandmann, L. R., & Sissel, P. A. (2000). Adult learners in higher education. In A. Wilson & E. Hayes (Eds.), *Handbook of adult and continuing education* (pp. 449–463). San Francisco, CA: Jossey-Bass.

Kavale, K. A., & Lindsey, J. D. (1977). Adult basic education: Has it worked? *Journal of Reading, 20*(5), 368–376.

Kegan, R. (1994). *In over our heads: The mental demands of modern life.* Cambridge, MA: Harvard University Press.

Knefelkamp, L., Widick, C., & Parker C. A. (Eds). (1978). *Applying new developmental findings. New directions for student services, 4.* San Francisco, CA: Jossey-Bass.

Kolb, D. A. (1984). *Experiential learning: Experience as the source of learning and development.* Englewood Cliffs, NJ: Prentice Hall.

Lave, J., & Wenger, E. (1991). *Situated learning: Legitimate peripheral participation.* New York, NY: Cambridge University Press.

Lee, D., Olson, E. A., Locke, B., & Michelson, S. T. (2009). The effects of college counseling services on academic performance and retention. *Journal of College Student Development, 50*(3), 305–319.

Lee-Hsieh, J., Kuo, C.-L., & Ya-Hsun Tsai. (2004). An action research on the development of a caring curriculum in Taiwan. *Journal of Nursing Education, 43*(9), 391–400.

Levin, J. S. (2001). *Globalizing the community college. Strategies for change in the twenty-first century.* New York, NY: Palgrave.

Levin, J. S. (2007). *Non-traditional students and community colleges: The conflict of justice and neoliberalism.* New York, NY: Palgrave Macmillan.

Levin, J. S., Cox, E. M., Haberler, Z., & Cerven, C. (2011). The success centers: A case study of basic skills at Chaffey College. *Community College Journal of Research and Practice, 35*(5), 383–409.

Levin, J. S., & Montero-Hernandez, V. (2009). *Community colleges and their students: Co-construction and organizational identity.* New York, NY: Palgrave Macmillan.

Levin, J. S., Montero-Hernandez, V., & Cerven, C. (2010). Overcoming adversity. Community college students and work. In L. W. Perna (Ed.), *Understanding the working college student. New research and its implications for policy and practice* (pp. 43–67). Sterling, VA: Stylus.

Lichtenstein, M. (2005). The importance of classroom environments in the assessment of learning community outcomes. *Journal of College Student Development, 46*(4), 341–356.

Maxwell, W. E. (1998). Supplemental instruction, learning communities, and students studying together. *Community College Review, 26*(2), 1–19.

McConnell, P. J. (2000). What community colleges should do to assist first-generation students. *Community College Review, 28*(3), 75.

National Center for Education Statistics (NCES). (2009). *Digest of Educational Statistics 2009.* Table 192. Total fall enrollment in degree-granting institutions by control and type of institution, age, and attendance status of student: 2007. Retrieved from http://nces.ed.gov/programs/digest/d09/tables/dt09_192.asp?referrer=list

Noddings, N. (1984). *Caring: A feminine approach to ethics and moral education.* Berkeley: University of California Press.

Ortiz, A. M. (1995). Enhancing student development in community colleges. *Community College Review, 22*(4), 63–70.

Perin, D., Flugman, B., & Spiegel, S. (2006). Last chance gulch: Youth participation in urban adult basic education programs. *Adult Basic Education, 16*(3), 171–188.

Piaget, J. (1950). *The psychology of intelligence*, trans, M. Piercy & D. Berlyne. London: Routledge & Kegan Paul.

Pizzolato, J. E. (2005). Creating crossroads for self-authorship: Investigating the provocative moment. *Journal of College Student Development, 46*(6), 624–641.

Pizzolato, J. E., & Ozaki, C. (2007). Moving toward self-authorship: Investigating outcomes of learning partnerships. *Journal of College Student Development, 48*(2), 196–214.

Ponton, M. K., Derrick, M. G., & Carr, P. B. (2005). The relationship between resourcefulness and persistence in adult autonomous learning. *Adult Education Quarterly, 55*(2), 116–128.

Prins, E., Toso, B. W., & Schafft, K. A. (2009). "It feels like a little family to me": Social interaction and support among women in adult education and family literacy. *Adult Education Quarterly, 59*(4), 335–352.

Pusser, B., & Levin, J. (2009). *Re-imagining community colleges in the 21st century.* Washington, DC: Center for American Progress.

Rager, K. B. (2003). The self-directed learning of women with breast cancer. *Adult Education Quarterly, 53*(4), 277–293.

Roberson, D. N., & Merriam, S. B. (2005). The self-directed learning process of older, rural adults. *Adult Education Quarterly, 55*(4), 269–287.

Ross, J. (1988). Transitions, triggers, and the return to college: No simple decision. *Journal of College Student Development, 2*(9), 112–118.

Schaie, K. W. (1996). *Intellectual development in adulthood: The Seattle longitudinal study.* New York, NY: Cambridge University Press.

Sissel, P. A., Birdsong, M. A., & Silaski, B. A. (1997). A room of one's own: A phenomenological investigation of class, age, gender, and politics of institutional change regarding adult students on campus. In R. Nolan (Ed.), *Proceedings of the 38th Annual Adult Education Research Conference.* Stillwater, OK: Oklahoma State University.

Sissel, P. A., Hansman, C. A., & Kasworm, C. E. (2001). The politics of neglect: Adult learners in higher education. In C. A. Hansman & P. A. Sissel (Eds.), *Understanding and negotiating the political landscape of adult education. New Directions for Adult and Continuing Education, no. 91* (pp. 17–27). San Francisco, CA: Jossey-Bass.

Skinner, L., & Gillespie, P. (2000). The challenge of adult literacy: Students with learning disabilities in the ABE classroom. *Adult Basic Education, 10*(3), N/A.

Smith, C. M. (2008). Does service learning promote adult development? Theoretical perspectives and directions for research. *New Directions for Adult and Continuing Education, no. 118* (pp. 5–15). San Francisco, CA: Jossey-Bass.

Smith, M. J. (2000). Caring, community, and transcendence—developing spirit to improve learning. *Community College Review, 28*(3), 57–74.

Stanton-Salazar, R. D. (1997). A social capital framework for understanding the socialization of racial minority children and youth. *Harvard Educational Review, 67,* 1–29.

Stanton-Salazar, R. D. (2001). *Manufacturing hope and despair: The school and kin support networks of U.S. Mexican youth.* New York, NY: Teachers College Press.

Stanton-Salazar, R. D. (2010). A social capital framework for the study of institutional agents and their role in the empowerment of low-status students and youth. *Youth & Society, 20*(10), 1–44.

Stasz, B. B., Schwartz, R. G., & Weeden, J. C. (1991). Writing our lives: An adult basic skills program. *Journal of Reading, 35*(1), 30–33.

Taylor, K. B. (2008). Mapping the intricacies of young adults' developmental journey from socially prescribed to internally defined identities, relationships, and beliefs. *Journal of College Student Development, 49*(3), 215–234.

Thompson, M. D. (2001). Informal student–faculty interaction: Its relationship to educational gains in science and mathematics among community college students. *Community College Review, 29*(1), 35–57.

Tinto, V. (1987). *Leaving college.* Chicago, IL: University of Chicago Press.

Tinto, V. (1997). Classrooms as communities: Exploring the educational character of student persistence. *The Journal of Higher Education, 68*(6), 599–623.

Torres, V., & Hernandez, E. (2007). The influence of ethnic identity on self-authorship: A longitudinal study of Latino/a college students. *Journal of College Student Development, 48*(5), 558–573.

Torres, V., Jones, S. R., & Renn, K. A. (2009). Identity development theories in student affairs: Origins, current status, and new approaches. *Journal of College Student Development, 50*, 577–596.

Tough, A. (1973). *The adult's learning projects: A fresh approach to theory and practice in adult learning* (2nd ed.). Toronto, Canada: Ontario Institute for Studies in Education.

U.S. Bureau of the Census. (2004). *U.S. interim projections by age, sex, race, and Hispanic origin.* Retrieved from http://www.census.gov/ipc/www/usinterimproj

Vaccaro, A., & Lovell, C. D. (2010). Inspiration from home: Understanding family as key to adult women's self-investment. *Adult Education Quarterly, 60*(2), 161–176.

Valenzuela, A. (1999). *Subtractive schooling: U.S.-Mexican youth and the politics of caring.* New York, NY: SUNY Press.

Wenger, E. (1998). *Communities of practice: Learning, meaning, and identity.* New York, NY: Cambridge University Press.

Zhao, C.-M., & Kuh, G. D. (2004). Adding value: Learning communities and student engagement. *Research in Higher Education, 45*(2), 115–138.

Ziegler, M., & Bingman, M. B. (2007). Achieving adult education program quality: A review of systematic approaches to program improvement. In J. Comings, B. Garner, & C. Smith (Eds.), *Review of adult learning and literacy* (Vol. 7, pp. 47–92). Mahwah, NJ: Lawrence Erlbaum Associates.

6

TEACHING ACADEMICALLY UNDERPREPARED STUDENTS IN COMMUNITY COLLEGES

DOLORES PERIN

INTRODUCTION

Higher education in the U.S. is both massive and diverse, with over 1,100 community colleges alone, and over 6 million credit students enrolled in these institutions (Phillippe & Sullivan, 2005). A college education is a conduit to meaningful employment for the mid-level workforce and above, and earning a postsecondary credential is an important way for individuals from families of low socio-economic status to progress beyond menial, low-paid jobs (Mazzeo, Rab, & Alssid, 2003). However, only about 55% of the U.S. population aged 18 and above have college experience. As the highest level of education completed, 27% have attained a bachelor's degree or higher, 9% possess an associate degree, and 19% have accumulated some college credits without graduating (U.S. Census Bureau, 2011, calculated from Table 6.1, civilian, non-institutionalized population). It is possible that difficulties with basic literacy and math skills impede achievement in college, especially among students who have received some college credits but have not completed a degree.

Three-quarters of twelfth graders graduate from high school with low reading skills (Grigg, Donahue, & Dion, 2007), and 42% of community college students take at least one developmental education course. Since skills in reading, writing, and mathematics are the foundation of academic learning, this situation constitutes a major obstacle to both personal and societal progress. Within postsecondary education in the U.S., community colleges, which enroll approximately 44% of the country's undergraduates and 6.5 million degree-credit students (American Association of Community Colleges, 2011), are the primary destination for students who aspire to a college credential but are underprepared for college learning (Jenkins & Boswell, 2002). It is no coincidence that community colleges also enroll disproportionate numbers of low-income, non-Caucasian students, 41% of whom are the first in their families to attend higher education (Achieving the Dream: Community Colleges Count, 2006; Cohen & Brawer, 2008).

Most community colleges direct low-skilled entrants to developmental education, which consists of courses and ancillary services intended to provide preparation for college-level learning (Boylan, 2002). Students must often complete a sequence of developmental courses to meet prerequisites for college-credit courses. Colleges charge tuition for the courses, requiring the use of financial aid, but the courses do not count toward a postsecondary credential. Developmental education is prominent in community colleges but findings on its effectiveness have not been uniformly positive.

A random-assignment trial found that, compared to a control group receiving the typical curriculum, students who participated in a learning community linking developmental English and college-level disciplinary courses, and providing counseling, tutoring, and book vouchers, passed more courses (43% of participants passed all courses, compared to 33% of the control group), earned more credits (11.5 credits for participants versus 10.3 credits for the control group), and showed fewer course withdrawals (26.6% of program participants withdrew from courses compared to 34.5% of the control group). Nevertheless, the positive results disappeared when students were no longer enrolled in the special program (Scrivener & Coghlan, 2011, Tables 4.2 and 4.3). Some studies have found that academic outcomes of students who completed developmental education were comparable to those of non-developmental students (Bahr, 2008; Moss, 2006) but others have reported mixed findings (Boatman & Long, 2010; Calcagno & Long, 2008). Also, developmental education attrition rates are high, and about 50% do not complete the prescribed sequence—they may complete one or two courses but do not return (Bailey, Jeong, & Cho, 2010). Taken together, these studies call into question the considerable investment of students' time and colleges' resources in developmental education in its current form.

Learning is a complex process influenced by a host of cognitive, emotional, cultural, and socio-economic factors. Students need habits of mind conducive to academic learning (Giaquinto, 2009–2010), and community colleges need not only to recognize and value the cultural backgrounds and identities of low-income, non-traditional students (Levin, 2007) but also to provide them with high-quality instruction (Rose, 2005). Although examples of innovative teaching have been found (Perin & Charron, 2006), it has been claimed that, by and large, the type of instruction provided to underprepared community college students is not well suited to their needs (Cox, 2009; Grubb et al., 1999; Rose, 2005).

This chapter examines current instructional practices, and argues for the importance of pedagogy designed to promote the generalization of basic skills from developmental education to college-credit classrooms. The chapter begins by defining academic preparedness, summarizing the characteristics of low-skilled community college students, and outlining the basic academic skills required in postsecondary education. Issues in the transfer of skills from developmental to college-level disciplinary courses and the need to increase the underprepared students' academic motivation are discussed. Following this, current approaches to developmental education instruction are examined, and one approach, contextualization, is discussed as a promising vehicle for transfer and motivation. This approach makes direct and explicit connections between reading, writing, and mathematics skills, and the content that students will study in college credit courses, thereby boosting not only the learning and future application of foundational academic skills but also students' motivation to persist in learning skills that normally are not, in themselves, of great interest to them.

ACADEMIC PREPAREDNESS

Most community colleges assess students on entry in order to determine whether they need to improve their basic academic skills to prepare for the postsecondary curriculum. Assessment methods vary considerably (Hughes & Scott-Clayton, 2011), and there is no commonly agreed-upon measure of college readiness. However, it has been proposed that to be ready for college, competency is required in four overlapping areas: cognitive strategies, content, academic behaviors, and contextual awareness (Conley, 2008). Cognitive strategies include the ability to formulate questions, analyze information, and conduct research; content refers to disciplinary knowledge and foundational reading, writing, and math skills; academic behaviors involve the regulation of one's own learning and the ability to transfer learning from familiar to new settings; and contextual awareness refers to students' understanding of how the college works as an institution, including financial aid procedures. While entering students may be more or less prepared in any of these four areas, the current chapter is primarily concerned with Conley's (2008) content and academic behavior dimensions, and within them, basic skills students need to learn in college-level subject-area classrooms and instructional approaches that may promote transfer of skill to those settings.

When characterizing the academic skills needed for postsecondary learning, it is useful to look to standards that have been identified in several initiatives. Literacy competencies signaling readiness for college-level courses in history, science, and technical subjects include the ability to compile, understand, and summarize written information; interpret the meanings of words and phrases; analyze text structure; evaluate authors' claims; convey complex ideas and information, and one's own arguments in writing; and produce well-organized compositions using appropriate writing style and grammar (National Governors' Association and Council of Chief State School Officers, 2010a). In math, college entrants should possess proficiency in number properties and operations; measurement and geometry; data analysis, statistics, and probability; and algebra. Specific competencies have been stipulated; for example, in statistics and probability, the college entrant should be able to represent and interpret categorical data, make inferences and justify conclusions about data, understand conditional probability and the rules of probability, and use probability to make decisions, e.g., "calculate expected values and use them to solve problems" (National Center for Education Statistics, 2010; National Governors' Association and Council of Chief State School Officers, 2010b).

There is no shortage of standards. In addition to the above-mentioned national efforts, states, college systems, and testing companies have formulated their own sets of standards (e.g., Academic Senate for California Community Colleges, 2010; American College Testing, n.d.; College Board, 2006; Texas Higher Education Coordinating Board, 2009), which tend to include essentially the same competencies although worded or organized differently. Importantly, whatever standards are used to develop curricula and assess students, the math, reading, and writing skills must be tailored and applied by students in specific disciplines as they proceed through the postsecondary curriculum. The challenge in educating academically underprepared community college students is less about prescribing standards than knowing how to teach transferable skills. To place this issue in context, it is useful to consider the characteristics of underprepared students.

CHARACTERISTICS OF ACADEMICALLY
UNDERPREPARED STUDENTS

Between 42% and 58% of community college students take at least one developmental education course (Attewell, Lavin, Domina, & Levey, 2006; Boswell & Wilson, 2004). An often overlooked point is that a large number of underprepared students enroll in college-level courses, and may or may not have participated in developmental education (Lei, Rhinehart, Howard, & Cho, 2010; Perin, 2006). In the literature, discussions of academic preparedness often focus on developmental education, as if this population were sequestered in this unit of the college while all other students were college-ready, but this is not the case. Interviews with instructors of college-credit courses have revealed difficulties in accommodating low-skilled students (Perin & Charron, 2006), and it appears that a good deal of "hidden remediation" occurs (Grubb et al., 1999, p. 104). Furthermore, writing-across-the-curriculum is implemented not only to promote deeper learning of course content but also to improve writing skills (Hampson, Hearron, & Noggle, 2009). Academic needs will vary by program. For example, rigorous screening mechanisms for some programs, such as nursing, increase the likelihood that students will have higher academic skills. However, overall, if it is true that many community college students in college-credit classrooms are academically underprepared, the claim that the demographics of developmental education students are no different from those of the typical college student (Boylan, 1999) is not surprising.

The median age of community college students is 23 years; 58% of students are female, 42% are the first in their families to enter higher education; 59% are full-time students employed part-time; 40% are part-time students employed full-time; 13% are single parents; and 12% have identified themselves as individuals with disabilities (American Association of Community Colleges, 2011). These statistics refer only to students who are earning college credit. However, although developmental education courses do not bear college credit, students in these courses tend to be taking at least one college-credit course concurrent with developmental education enrollment. Community colleges serve disproportionate numbers of Spanish-speaking students: 58% of all Hispanic undergraduates attend these institutions, compared to 42% of White undergraduates (Snyder, Tan, & Hoffman, 2006). It has been reported that many students of Hispanic background are academically underprepared upon entry to college (Crisp & Nora, 2010). Although there are examples of outstanding outcomes (e.g., Alvarez, 2011), the number of students who lack proficiency in English is growing dramatically, and includes "Generation 1.5," individuals with a non-English primary language who have attended school in the U.S. and are fluent in informal but not academic English (Smith, 2010).

Beyond demographic and linguistic variables, it is important to understand the emotional experience of academically underprepared students. Academic motivation is influenced by learners' goals, predispositions, beliefs, attitudes, sense of control, level of interest, preference for challenge, involvement, self-efficacy, competition, recognition, grades received, quality of social interaction, and tendency to approach or avoid work (Taboada, Tonks, Wigfield, & Guthrie, 2009) and personal "cost/benefit estimates" (Hayes, 1996, p. 4). Also necessary for successful learning is self-regulation, or thoughts, feelings, self-efficacy, and behaviors initiated by the learner toward the achievement of academic goals (Kitsantas & Zimmerman, 2009).

Studies of underprepared students have revealed students' high levels of anxiety, memories of academic failure, and perceptions that instructors hold low expectations based on race- or gender-based stereotypical preconceptions (Cox, 2009; Gardenshire-Crooks, Collado, Martin, & Castro, 2010; Goode, 2000; Woodard, 2004). Anecdotal evidence based on conversations the author has had with community college faculty and students suggests that students in developmental education who have recently graduated from high school may be immature or angry about having been placed in a remedial course. All of these factors can serve to inhibit performance or the disposition to engage actively in classroom learning. Teaching underprepared students creates a major challenge for community college faculty. Teacher education programs providing preparation for developmental education instruction are extremely rare: "[f]or many faculty, the knowledge they gained in their graduate programs is significantly different from the knowledge they need to teach developmental classes" (Kozeracki, 2005, p. 42).

COLLEGE-LEVEL ACADEMIC SKILLS

To understand the nature of academic preparedness, it is helpful to reflect on the intricate concepts and processes involved in reading, writing, and math. To comprehend text, the reader gleans information written on the page, and connects it to personal background knowledge in order to understand and think about it (Franzke, Kintsch, Caccamise, Johnson, & Dooley, 2005). This process depends on the ability both to decipher written words on the page and understand oral language (Gough & Tunmer, 1986). Writing involves some of the same processes as reading but also several unique components (Fitzgerald & Shanahan, 2000; Jackson, 2009). The competent writer employs planning, drafting, and revising processes in a simultaneous and recursive manner (Flower & Hayes, 1980). Fluent writing requires the ability to generate ideas mentally, and transcribe them using the spelling system (Berninger & Swanson, 1994). Other important processes are audience awareness (Magnifico, 2010) and reflection on the text one has written so far while moving toward completion of a composition (Hayes, 1996). Also important in the writing process is discourse knowledge, i.e., the writer's understanding of the purposes of writing activity, the characteristics of well-written text, and procedures needed to express ideas in writing (Olinghouse & Graham, 2009).

The learning of mathematics relies on concepts from basic operations to algebra, and includes the depiction of information in graphs and charts (Hodara, 2011; Jitendra et al., 2009; Rittle-Johnson, Siegler, & Alibali, 2001; U.S. Department of Education, 2008; Zawaiza & Gerber, 1993). It is thought that students must be able to understand how a problem can be represented mathematically before they can apply computational procedures to solving it (Brenner et al., 1997). Any one academic skill may be learned as an abstract entity, but must then be applied for a specific purpose in a specific disciplinary context.

DISCIPLINARY READING AND WRITING SKILLS

Because prior knowledge, text structure, and discourse conventions vary across disciplines, different domains may call for different processes. Every subject area has its own distinctive body of knowledge, mode of thought, and way of communicating ideas. Proficiency in generic academic skills may not easily generalize to specific subject areas.

For example, students who are classified as proficient readers based on test scores may have difficulty comprehending biology text if they lack prior knowledge of biological concepts. Furthermore, comprehension of such material may depend on an awareness of how science text is typically structured, and the ability to process text with a density of unfamiliar vocabulary (Cromley, Snyder-Hogan, & Luciw-Dubas, 2010; Snow, 2010). In history courses, a major challenge is to comprehend information in primary and secondary source documents, some of which use dated language. The reading of history involves "corroboration," i.e., the comparison of documents, "sourcing" (i.e., identifying the source of a document before reading it to determine possible bias), and "contextualizing," or considering the time and place of the events described in a text (Reisman & Wineburg, 2008; Stahl & Shanahan, 2004, p. 95). These examples illustrate how different subject areas emphasize different academic skills.

Commonalities also occur across disciplines. For example, persuasive writing is found in both scientific and historical writing. It has been claimed that "the scientific research report is essentially a persuasive argument directed at colleagues working in the researcher's field" (Goldman & Bisanz, 2002, p. 24), and formulating arguments is an important activity in history instruction (Nokes, 2008). However, persuasive essays in history tend to be structured in the form of a statement of a position, a counterargument, a rebuttal, and a conclusion (De La Paz & Felton, 2010) while scientific reports are typically organized in the categories of introduction, experiment, and discussion (Goldman & Bisanz, 2002). One's applying either structure effectively involves an understanding of the content and an ability to use the language typical of the community of interest, so that the writer is communicating "like a historian" or "like a scientist" (Shanahan & Shanahan, 2008; Stahl & Shanahan, 2004).

Another illustration of discipline-specific literacy comes from a comparison of cognitive processes used in reading history in comparison to reading a novel (Voss & Wiley, 1997). For the novel, the reader's task is to construct a mental representation of the plot and characters, and to modify it when proceeding through the text. In contrast, reading history requires the ability to discern and analyze information in the written forms of history, such as primary records, newspaper articles, and artifacts including photographs and paintings. In answering questions based on the reading of novels and historical text, the types of inferences, conclusions, and predictions will be specific to the content (Simmons et al., 2010) so that an all-purpose question-answering strategy may not be helpful for arriving at the answer. Ideally, to accommodate discipline-specific modes of expression, the learner transfers general reading and writing skills to the discipline-specific task at hand.

TRANSFER OF SKILL FROM DEVELOPMENTAL EDUCATION TO COLLEGE-LEVEL DISCIPLINARY CLASSROOMS

Transfer of skill involves the application of skills to new information, settings, and assessment formats. This dimension of learning is critically important for academically underprepared students. There is little point in undergoing the considerable effort needed to teach and learn new skills in developmental education classrooms if students do not apply the skills in the courses they need to complete their programs. Conditions that promote the transfer of skill are instructional procedures, types of text, problems assigned, and students' flexibility, metacognitive skills, and ability to regulate their own learning (Bransford et al., 2000; Nash-Ditzel, 2010; Rittle-Johnson et al., 2009). Instructors can facilitate students' transfer of skill by designing instructions with built-in connections between the environments in which the skill is learned and will later be applied (Stone, Alfeld, Pearson, Lewis, & Jensen, 2006).

Two ways in which transfer occurs are to take the "low road," i.e., practice skills until they are automatic, or the "high road," where the learner abstracts principles that can be applied in other settings (Perkins & Salomon, 1989). Transfer may also be promoted through instructional approaches that focus on either domain-specific material or higher order thinking skills such as making comparison and inferences (Niedelman, 1991). Although historically transfer of skill has been difficult to produce in experimental studies (Detterman & Sternberg, 1993), it may be very much in evidence if it is defined as "transfer of situations rather than transfer *across* situations" (Bereiter, 1995, p. 31, author's italics). This view implies the need for domain-specific instruction in basic skills. Although Neidelman (1991) reported positive results for low road instruction of complex thinking skills with students with learning disabilities, there appear to be no studies that compare this approach to high road or domain-specific teaching for transfer.

Since each subject area has its typical genres and culture of thinking, it is necessary to transfer academic skills for discipline-specific purposes. However, the transfer of basic skills to different domains may be extremely challenging for underprepared students, who may not possess the level of meta-cognitive self-reflection and self-regulation needed to know when and where to use a skill they know (Nash-Ditzel, 2010). Given this situation, questions arise as to what extent developmental education is preparing students for the application of basic skills in college-level content classrooms.

DEVELOPMENTAL EDUCATION INSTRUCTION

Depending on the level, developmental reading courses teach word-decoding and reading comprehension techniques, vocabulary, the nature of paragraph and essay structure, interpretation of charts and graphs, and strategies for studying (McWhorter, 2010). Developmental writing courses focus on the writing process (planning, drafting, revising, and editing); construction of sentence parts, sentences, and paragraphs; supporting arguments; application of the rules of standard written English and recognition of correctly structured sentences and sentence parts (grammar); and word usage (Zachry & Schneider, 2010). The ability to write sentences, paragraphs, and essays is an outcome of successive developmental writing course levels. Levels of developmental math cover basic arithmetic, introduction to algebraic concepts, pre-algebra, elementary algebra, intermediate algebra, and plane geometry (Bahr, 2008). Developmental education courses generally run for a college semester or quarter, with up to four class sessions per week, including regularly scheduled sessions in a computer lab (Perin & Charron, 2006).

To date, there are no comprehensive, nationally representative studies of developmental education instruction that could provide a basis for general statements about approaches to or quality of developmental instruction. However, based on observations in purposive samples of classrooms, a negative note has been sounded. Business as usual in developmental education seems burdened by practices that are "dull and monotonous" (Boylan, 2002, p. 72). Instruction has been criticized for overemphasizing the technical dimensions of grammar, word usage, and math computation, and assigning excessive practice on isolated skills with little exposure to challenging material that might stimulate critical thinking about challenging topics. Skills are separated from content, and as a result there is scarce use of authentic reading, writing, or mathematics (Grubb et al., 1999; Rose, 2005). This type of instruction has been labeled "discrete skills" in a typology of adult literacy instruction (Beder & Medina, 2001). In contrast are approaches Beder and Medina (2001) call "meaning-making," where instructors use real-world materials such as newspaper articles and student writings, but, Grubb et al. (1999) claimed, they "often find that they have to back away from discussions prompted by these readings because the purpose of the class is not to explore such material" (p. 184).

Problems in the instruction of academically underprepared students in college-level composition classrooms have been reported in a study by Cox (2009). In some classrooms, a discrepancy was noted between instructors' plans and students' expectations as to the content and process of instruction. In one class, students indicated that sitting in a circle to discuss a novel, consistent with progressive views of active engagement, reflective inquiry, and collaborative learning, was demeaning and not conducive to learning. In another class, students were not interested in the assigned readings and did not value required peer review activities because no course credit was given for participation. Students did not see teachers who used participatory learning and other student-centered approaches as knowledgable, and attrition rates were high in both of these classrooms.

In contrast, persistence was much better in classrooms where the instructors were perceived by students as authorities in their subject area, and provided explicit instruction, imposed rigorous demands, provided consistent encouragement, and gave constructive feedback on their writing. A striking finding of Cox's (2009) study was students' sensitivity to criticism; teachers' feedback on students' writing or responses to questions asked in class could, unknown to instructors, cause students to feel insecure and demoralized. Feeling this way, the students were unwilling to submit further work, and as a result earned low grades.

Balancing these unfavorable findings are numerous reports of alternate approaches that practitioners articulate to help underprepared students learn. For example, a number of community colleges in the "Achieving the Dream" initiative instituted two changes, creating learning communities linking developmental education and college-credit courses, and modifying the length of developmental math courses, lengthening them for low-skilled students and shortening them for higher achievers (Zachry & Schneider, 2009). As Zachry and Schneider noted, however, these approaches were structural and did not necessarily involve changes in teaching process.

In another initiative, other structural changes are seen in a "modular-emporium model" for math, in which students study only the skills in which they are weak, and receive individualized instruction from instructors and computer-based practice in a learning center; and a "co-requisite model," a type of accelerated learning in which students who test within a few points of the college cut score for developmental placement enroll concurrently in developmental and college-level English or math courses (Education Commission of the States, n.d.). In the National Field Study conducted by the Community College Research Center (Bailey & Morest, 2006), Perin and Charron (2006) identified a number of modifications to developmental education courses, including having students work at their own pace through computerized math exercises, tutoring, intensive courses during the summer, and combining developmental reading and writing instruction. For example, students at one of the colleges in the study chose between a traditional developmental math offering and a self-paced, open-exit, open-entry course in a math lab. Two-thirds of the students selected the latter option (outcome data were not available). At another college, students whose placement scores were within ten points of the cut point for exemption from developmental education were offered group and individualized tutoring. This service became quickly oversubscribed, indicating its popularity among students. At other sites, an accelerated course option was offered for remedial reading whereby instruction was provided in half the time of the traditional course. Accelerated developmental education courses were offered in other colleges in the study, although an interviewee stated that the courses were not effective because students tended to lack the needed self-discipline to work quickly through course material.

The majority of alternatives to standard developmental education seem to be structural, whereas the criticisms of Rose (2005), Grubb et al. (1999), and Cox (2009) suggest the need for changes in the teaching process. One modification found by Perin and Charron (2006) that did involve teaching processes was contextualized developmental education. In one example, developmental writing instruction was customized for students who were interested in entering nursing degree programs, and, in another, academically underprepared students in a criminal justice degree program alternated between basic skills instruction and job-related applications. In both of these examples, the material used as the basis of skills development was personally meaningful to students in its relation to the degrees and, later, careers they intended to pursue. The next section discusses contextualization as a change in teaching process that may benefit students through transfer of skill and increased motivation.

CONTEXTUALIZATION AS AN ALTERNATIVE TO TRADITIONAL DEVELOPMENTAL EDUCATION

Contextualization, an approach to instruction at any educational level that creates direct connections between skills and authentic practices, has been defined as

> a diverse family of instructional strategies designed to more seamlessly link the learning of foundational skills and academic or occupational content by focusing teaching and learning squarely on concrete applications in a specific context that is of interest to the student. (Mazzeo, Rab, & Alssid, 2003, p. 4)

The phrase "of interest" refers to material that students find useful or otherwise compelling. As an instructional practice, contextualization reflects a constructivist assumption that instruction should be student-centered (Dewey, 1966; Dowden, 2007). From a theoretical perspective, the affective and cognitive factors of motivation and transfer of learning may operate simultaneously for contextualization to result in better learning: motivation, and generalization of learning. Regarding motivation, if students know why they are learning a skill, and that the skill will be personally useful to them for a specific purpose, they may be motivated to learn and practice it. Although underprepared students may not tend to enjoy the process of academic learning, most are highly motivated to earn the grades they need to pass courses and earn a college credential. If only for this reason, content drawn directly from college-level courses that count toward a degree may serve as a useful context for basic skills instruction (Baker, Hope, & Karandjeff, 2009; Boroch et al., 2007; Johnson, 2002). Thus, the advantage to underprepared students is "to leverage interdisciplinary skills and help students see connections between vital components of a developmental curriculum" (Boroch et al., 2007, p. 46). At the same time, when skills are taught in a way that directly connects them to the settings in which they will be applied, students are more likely to generalize their learning. As suggested earlier, theories of transfer of skill propose that the extent of similarity between the domains and instruction and application are predictive of the likelihood that students will generalize their learning (Barnett & Ceci, 2002). When teachers create direct connections between basic skills and the content of college-level courses, the probability of transfer of skill to those courses is heightened. Research is needed regarding how much instruction should be contextualized, and how close the contextualization should be to the domain of application, since it has been suggested that teaching can be over-contextualized. The literature on generalization of learning has been discussing this issue for a long time (Bransford, Brown, & Cocking, 2000); conclusive research would have direct implications for the improvement of developmental education.

Pending additional research, contextualization is consistent with recommendations from developmental educators that connections should be made between basic skills and the content of college-level courses (Boylan, 2002; Simpson, Hynd, Nist, & Burrell, 1997). The use of authentic academic text in teaching skills to underprepared students may move them to become more active learners who are subsequently more inclined to use their skills in college-credit courses (Simpson & Nist, 2002).

An example of contextualization is provided in a study of effective "success centers" in which underprepared students received basic skills tutoring to support performance in college-level content courses such as psychology (Levin, Cox, Haberler, & Cerven, 2011). The students may have been particularly motivated to learn the skills in this context because they could see a direct relation to achievement in a content course they wanted to pass.

Traditional developmental instruction rarely relates skills being taught to situations the students find personally useful. However, in real applications, skills are always used for a purpose. For example, Cox (2009) argued that since skills are always used for a specific purpose they should be taught in relation to that purpose.

> [W]riting skills—like any other skill—do not constitute an autonomous or generic tool, ready for application in any writing situation. Instead, writing skills are integrally linked to each activity system in which they are used. A person does not simply write; a person writes something for some purpose. Accordingly, learning how to write according to the conventions of a particular academic discipline is best accomplished while a person is immersed in discipline-specific activities. (Cox, 2009, p. 147)

While most research on the effectiveness of contextualized reading, writing, and math instruction comes from elementary and secondary education populations (Perin, 2011) there is a growing number of examples from postsecondary developmental education Some efforts in this direction are being made in career and technical education, such as a "contextualized instruction model" for low-skilled students in occupational certificate programs (Education Commission of the States, n.d.), but most examples come from academic programs. Allied health students in a developmental math course learned to solve math problems incorporating respiratory therapy, radiology, occupational therapy, medical laboratory, physical therapy, or nursing scenarios from courses they needed to take (Shore, Shore, & Boggs, 2004). Upper-level developmental reading and writing students improved their written summarization skills after ten weeks of practice on reading and writing skills using introductory biology text (Perin, Bork, Peverly, Mason & Vaselewski, 2012). The context of an imagined "publishing company" served as an anchor for a developmental writing course, stimulating students to share their writing with each other (Goode, 2000).

Similar to the "Achieving the Dream" example, above, learning communities in other community colleges linked developmental English, psychology, and student orientation ("success") courses, and service learning experiences (Baker et al., 2009; Cargill & Kalikoff, 2007). Psychology and other social science courses also served as a context for instruction in reading comprehension strategies (Caverly, Nicholson, & Radcliffe, 2004). Baker et al. (2009) reported the use of themes of African American culture, literature, and experience in a community college developmental English course. In a rare contextualized instruction workbook published for developmental reading students, African American themes are also used (Williams, 2010a, 2010b). In this case, the author aimed to motivate inner city students with little prior experience of academic achievement to develop reading comprehension and critical thinking processes they would need at the college level. In another example, positive results on a departmental test were found by a developmental math teacher who presented "engaging exercises and experiences that were relevant to real-life situations" (Galbraith & Jones, 2006, p. 26).

Although contextualization seems promising as a "meaning-making" approach to basic skills instruction, its relation to high-stakes assessment may be problematic. For example, a developmental math instructor who contextualized math instruction in Grubb et al.'s (1999) study by using real-world examples was nonetheless required to prepare students for standardized tests, which were considered a poor means of demonstrating what students had learned through contextualized instruction. In spite of this challenge, however, the potential benefits of contextualization to students in terms of motivation and skills transfer seem high. Also, from an institutional perspective, the interdisciplinary nature of contextualization is consistent with the quality of "cooperation," in which personnel work well with each other and with students. This interaction was identified as an attribute of community colleges producing improved outcomes with underprepared students from under-represented groups (Levin, Cox, Cerven, & Haberler, 2010).

FUTURE DIRECTIONS

This chapter has discussed the nature of academic skill needed at the college level and summarized the difficulties faced by underprepared community college students. Developmental education, both in its "dull and monotonous," and, one hopes, more exciting manifestations, has been described. In particular, contextualized developmental instruction was suggested as an approach that may boost underprepared students' motivation and ability to transfer skill from developmental education to college-level courses. Several implications emerge if this direction is to be taken.

First, contextualized instruction may be easier to accomplish when developmental and content-area faculty have easy access to each other. Community colleges vary in the ways developmental education courses are structured but they are often "isolated in a jigsaw puzzle of developmental reading and writing departments and tutorial programs" (Grubb et al., 1999, p. 172). To prepare low-skilled students effectively for the demands of the full college curriculum, it will be important to integrate developmental education more fully into community college operations (Boylan & Bonham, 2009). Rather than segregating developmental education in separate departments, apart from college-credit offerings (Perin, 2004), it would be beneficial to offer both developmental and college-level courses alongside each other. Bringing developmental education closer to "regular" college courses through contextualization will raise developmental instructors' awareness of the concrete literacy and math requirements of actual courses students must pass toward a degree or certification, and also raise college-credit instructors' awareness of ways they can support academically underprepared students in their courses.

Second, by creating connections to the college curriculum, contextualization may help improve the usefulness and effectiveness of developmental education courses. Norton Grubb et al. (1999) suggested that as long as developmental education offers rigorous courses, it should be "rescued from its second-class status" (p. 174). Contextualization seems to be a promising way simultaneously to bring developmental education closer to the rest of the college and to increase the rigor of preparation of academically underprepared students throughout the college.

Third, contextualization will require carefully planned professional development. Although the skills taught in developmental education may remain the same as in traditional classrooms, to contextualize them will require knowledge of syllabi and course texts used in college-level classrooms. Interdisciplinary collaboration may be an effective and enjoyable way of accomplishing this goal.

A more general implication of this chapter is the need for developmental education instructors to participate in professional development that prepares them to teach low-skilled students. Professional development could focus on standards of proficiency in reading, writing, and math required in college-level disciplinary classrooms, as well as the cognitive and affective patterns of underprepared students. Perhaps the most important implication emerging from this chapter is the need to gather evidence on the outcomes of initiatives such as contextualization and related professional development, in order to plan most effectively to help underprepared students improve their ability to benefit from postsecondary education.

QUESTIONS FOR DISCUSSION

1. Who are developmental community college students and what are the challenges they face in college education?
2. What constitutes good practices for improving persistence of developmental education students?
3. What are some examples of alternatives to standard developmental education practices or approaches?
4. In what ways can developmental education become integrated or more integrated into college operations and offerings?

REFERENCES

Academic Senate for California Community Colleges. (2010). Statement on competencies in mathematics expected of entering college students. Retrieved from http://www.universityofcalifornia.edu/senate/reports/mathcomp.html

Achieving the Dream: Community Colleges Count. (2006). Fact sheet—Community colleges: Challenges and benefits, Retrieved from http://www.lee.edu/atd/pdf/FS-ChallengeBenefit.pdf

Alvarez, L. (2011, April 30). A community college in Florida works to attract the poor and the presidential: National section. Retrieved from http://www.nytimes.com/2011/04/30/us/30dade.html?_r=1&ref=todayspaper

American Association of Community Colleges. (2011). Community college fast facts. Retrieved from http://www2.aacc.nche.edu/research/index.htm

American College Testing. (n.d.). *College readiness standards.* Iowa City, IA: American College Testing, Inc. Retrieved from http://www.act.org/standard/

Attewell, P., Lavin, D., Domina, T., & Levey, T. (2006). New evidence on college remediation. *Journal of Higher Education, 77*(5), 886–924.

Bahr, P. R. (2008). Does mathematics remediation work?: A comparative analysis of academic attainment among community college students. *Research in Higher Education, 49*(5), 420–450.

Bailey, T., Jeong, D. W., & Cho, S. (2010). *Student progression through developmental sequences in community colleges.* CCRC Brief No. 45. New York, NY: Community College Research Center, Teachers College, Columbia University. Retrieved from http://ccrc.tc.columbia.edu/Publication.asp?uid=812

Bailey, T., & Morest, V. S. (Eds.). (2006). *Defending the community college equity agenda.* Baltimore, MD: Johns Hopkins Press.

Baker, E. D., Hope, L., & Karandjeff, K. (2009). *Contextualized teaching and learning: A faculty primer.* Sacramento, CA: Center for Student Success, Research and Planning Group, and Academic Senate, Chancellor's Office of California Community Colleges. Retrieved from http://www.careerladdersproject.org/docs/CTL.pdf

Barnett, S. M., & Ceci, S. J. (2002). When and where do we apply what we learn? A taxonomy for far transfer. *Psychological Bulletin, 128*(4), 612–637. doi: 10.1037//0033-2909.128.4.612

Beder, H., & Medina, P. (2001). *Classroom dynamics in adult literacy education, Report No. NCSALL-R-18, Education Resources Information Center (ERIC) Report ED465026.* Cambridge, MA: National Center for the Study of Adult Learning and Literacy. Retrieved from http://www.eric.ed.gov/ERICWebPortal/custom/portlets/recordDetails/detailmini.jsp?_nfpb=true&_&ERICExtSearch_SearchValue_0=ED465026&ERICExtSearch_SearchType_0=no&accno=ED465026

Bereiter, C. (1995). A dispositional view of transfer. In A. McKeough, J. Lupart, & A. Marini (Eds.), *Teaching for transfer: Fostering generalization in learning* (pp. 21–34). Mahwah, NJ: Lawrence Erlbaum Associates.

Berninger, V. W., & Swanson, J. (1994). Modifying Hayes & Flower's model of skilled writing to explain beginning and developing writing. In E. C. Butterfield (Ed.), *Children's writing: Toward a process theory of the development of skilled writing, Vol. 2 of Advances in cognition and educational practice* (pp. 57–81). Greenwich, CT: JAI Press, Inc.

Boatman, A., & Long, B. T. (2010). *Does remediation work for all students? How the effects of postsecondary remedial and developmental courses vary by level of academic preparation.* Paper prepared for NCPR Developmental Education Conference: What Policies and Practices Work for Students? September 23–24, 2010. New York, NY: Teachers College, Columbia University.

Boroch, D., Fillpot, J., Hope, L., Johnstone, R., Mery, P., Serban, A., et al. (2007). *Basic skills as a foundation for student success in California community colleges.* Sacramento, CA: Center for Student Success, Research and Planning Group, Chancellor's Office, California Community Colleges. Retrieved from http://css.rpgroup.org

Boswell, K., & Wilson, C. D. (2004). *Keeping America's promise: A report on the future of the community college.* Denver, CO: Education Commission of the States, League of Innovation in the Community College.

Boylan, H. R. (1999). Demographics, outcomes, and activities. *Journal of Developmental Education, 23*(2), 2–4, 6, 8, 10.

Boylan, H. R. (2002). *What works: A guide to research-based best practices in developmental education.* Boone, NC: Continuous Quality Improvement Network and the National Center for Developmental Education, Appalachian State University.

Boylan, H. R., & Bonham, B. S. (2009). Program evaluation. In R. F. Flippo & D. C. Caverly (Eds.), *Handbook of college reading and study strategy research* (2nd ed., pp. 379–407). New York, NY: Routledge.

Bransford, J. D., Brown, A. L., & Cocking, R. R. (2000). *How people learn: Brain, mind, experience, and school.* Washington, DC: National Academy Press. Retrieved from http://www.nap.edu/openbook.php?record_id=6160

Brenner, M. E., Mayer, R. E., Moseley, B., Brar, T., Durán, R., Reed, B. S., et al. (1997). Learning by understanding: The role of multiple representations in learning algebra. *American Educational Research Journal, 34*(4), 663–689.

Calcagno, J. C., & Long, B. T. (2008). *The impact of postsecondary remediation using a regression discontinuity approach: Addressing endogenous sorting and noncompliance. An NCPR Working Paper.* New York, NY: Teachers College, Columbia University.

Cargill, K., & Kalikoff, B. (2007). Linked psychology and writing courses across the curriculum. *The Journal of General Education, 56*(2), 83–92.

Caverly, D. C., Nicholson, S. A., & Radcliffe, R. (2004). The effectiveness of strategic instruction for college developmental readers. *Journal of College Reading and Learning, 35*, 25–49.

Cohen, A. M., & Brawer, F. B. (2008). *The American community college* (5th ed.). San Francisco, CA: Jossey-Bass.

College Board. (2006). *College Board standards for college success: Mathematics and statistics.* Retrieved from http://www.collegeboard.com/prod_downloads/about/association/academic/mathematics-statistics_cbscs.pdf

Conley, D. T. (2008). Rethinking college readiness. *New Directions for Higher Education, 144*(Winter), 3–13.

Cox, R. D. (2009). *The college fear factor: How students and professors misunderstand each other.* Cambridge, MA: Harvard University Press.

Crisp, G., & Nora, A. (2010). Hispanic student success: Factors influencing the persistence and transfer decisions of Latino community college students enrolled in developmental education. *Research in Higher Education, 51*(2), 175–194.

Cromley, J. G., Snyder-Hogan, L. E., & Luciw-Dubas, U. A. (2010). Reading comprehension of scientific text: A domain-specific test of the direct and inferential mediation model of reading comprehension. *Journal of Educational Psychology, 102*(3), 687–700.

De La Paz, S., & Felton, M. K. (2010). Reading and writing from multiple source documents in history: Effects of strategy instruction with low to average high school writers. *Contemporary Educational Psychology, 35*(3), 174–192.

Detterman, D. K., & Sternberg, R. J. (Eds.). (1993). *Transfer on trial: Intelligence, cognition, and instruction.* Norwood, NJ: Ablex.

Dewey, J. (1966). *Democracy and education.* New York, NY: The Free Press.

Dowden, T. (2007). Relevant, challenging, integrative and exploratory curriculum design: Perspectives from theory and practice for middle level schooling in Australia. *Australian Educational Researcher, 34*(2), 51–71.

Education Commission of the States. (n.d.). *Getting past go*: Retrieved from http://gettingpastgo.org/

Fitzgerald, J., & Shanahan, T. (2000). Reading and writing relations and their development. *Educational Psychologist, 35*, 39–50.

Flower, L. S., & Hayes, J. R. (1980). A cognitive process theory of writing. *College Composition and Communication, 32*, 365–387.

Franzke, M., Kintsch, E., Caccamise, D., Johnson, N., & Dooley, S. (2005). Summary Street®: Computer support for comprehension and writing. *Journal of Educational Computing Research, 33*(1), 53–80.

Galbraith, M. W., & Jones, M. S. (2006). The art and science of teaching developmental mathematics: Building perspective through dialogue. *Journal of Developmental Education, 30*(2), 20–27.

Gardenshire-Crooks, A., Collado, H., Martin, K., & Castro, A. (2010). *Terms of engagement: Men of color discuss their experiences in community college.* Educational Resources Information Center (ERIC) Document No. ED508982. New York, NY: MDRC.

Giaquinto, R. A. (2009–2010). Instructional issues and retention of first-year students. *Journal of College Student Retention: Research, Theory & Practice, 11*(2), 267–286.

Goldman, S. R., & Bisanz, G. L. (2002). Toward a functional analysis of scientific genres: Implications for understanding and learning processes. In J. Otero, J. A. Leon, & A. C. Graesser (Eds.), *The psychology of science text comprehension.* Mahwah, NJ: Erlbaum.

Goode, D. (2000). Creating a context for developmental English. *Teaching English in the Two-Year College, 27*(3), 270–277.

Gough, P. B., & Tunmer, W. E. (1986). Decoding, reading, and reading disability. *Remedial & Special Education, 7*, 6–10.

Grigg, W., Donahue, P., & Dion, G. (2007). *The nation's report card: 12th grade reading and mathematics.* NCES 2007–468. Washington, DC: Department of Education, National Center for Education Statistics, U.S. Government Printing Office.

Grubb, W. N., Worthen, H., Byrd, B., Webb, E., Badway, N., Case, C., et al. (1999). *Honored but invisible: An inside look at teaching in community colleges.* New York, NY: Routledge.

Hampson, M. P., Hearron, T., & Noggle, M. (2009). Combining emerging technology and writing across the curriculum: Professional development that works! *Community College Journal of Research and Practice, 33*(11), 915–918.

Hayes, J. R. (1996). A new framework for understanding cognition and affect in writing. In C. M. Levy & S. Ransdell (Eds.), *The science of writing: Theories, methods, individual differences, and applications* (pp. 1–27). Mahwah, NJ: Erlbaum.

Hodara, M. (2011). *Reforming mathematics classroom pedagogy: Evidence-based findings and recommendations for the developmental math classroom.* CCRC Working Paper No. 27. *Assessment of Evidence Series.* New York, NY: Community College Research Center, Teachers College, Columbia University.

Hughes, K. L., & Scott-Clayton, J. (2011). Assessing developmental assessment in community colleges. *Community College Review, 39*(4), 327–351. doi:10.1177/0091552111426898

Jackson, J. M. (2009). Reading/writing connection. In R. F. Flippo & D. C. Caverly (Eds.), *Handbook of college reading and study strategy research* (2nd ed., pp. 145–173). New York, NY: Routledge.

Jenkins, D., & Boswell, K. (2002). *State policies on community college remedial education: Findings from a national survey* (Technical Report No. CC–0201). Denver, CO: Education Commission of the States, Center for Community College Policy.

Jitendra, A. K., Star, J. R., Starosta, K., Leh, J. M., Sood, S., Caskie, G., et al. (2009). Improving seventh grade students' learning of ratio and proportion: The role of schema-based instruction. *Contemporary Educational Psychology, 34*(3), 250–264.

Johnson, E. B. (2002). *Contextual teaching and learning: What it is and why it's here to stay.* Thousand Oaks, CA: Corwin Press.

Kitsantas, A., & Zimmerman, B. J. (2009). College students, homework and academic achievement: The mediating role of self-regulatory beliefs. *Metacognition and Learning, 4*(2), 97–110.

Kozeracki, C. (2005). Preparing faculty to meet the needs of developmental students. In C. A. Kozeracki (Ed.), *Responding to the challenges of developmental education. New Directions for Community Colleges, no. 129* (pp. 39–49). San Francisco, CA: Jossey-Bass.

Lei, S., Rhinehart, P., Howard, H., & Cho, J. (2010). Strategies for improving reading comprehension among college students. *Reading Improvement, 47*(1), 30.

Levin, J. S. (2007). *Non-traditional students and community colleges: The conflict of justice and neo-liberalism.* New York, NY: Palgrave Macmillan.

Levin, J. S., Cox, E., Haberler, Z., & Cerven, C. (2011). Basic skills programming at California success centers. *Community College Journal of Research & Practice, 35*(5), 383–409.

Levin, J. S., Cox, E. M., Cerven, C., & Haberler, Z. (2010). The recipe for promising practices in community colleges. *Community College Review, 38*(1), 31–58.

Magnifico, A. M. (2010). Writing for whom? Cognition, motivation, and a writer's audience. *Educational Psychologist, 45*(3), 167–184.

Mazzeo, C., Rab, S. Y., & Alssid, J. L. (2003). *Building bridges to college and careers: Contextualized basic skills programs at community colleges.* Brooklyn, NY, and San Francisco, CA: Workforce Strategy Center.

McWhorter, K. T. (2010). *College reading and study skills* (11th ed.). Boston, MA: Longman.

Moss, B. G. (2006). Shaping policies related to developmental education: An evaluation using the regression-discontinuity design. *Educational Evaluation and Policy Analysis, 28*(3), 215–229.

Nash-Ditzel, S. (2010). Metacognitive reading strategies can improve self-regulation. *Journal of College Reading and Learning, 40*(2), 45–63.

National Center for Education Statistics. (2010). *The nation's report card: Grade 12 reading and mathematics 2009 national and pilot state results.* (NCES 2011–455) Washington, DC: Institute of Education Sciences, U.S. Department of Education.

National Governors' Association and Council of Chief State School Officers. (2010a). *Common core state standards: English language arts and literacy in history/social studies, science, and technical subjects.* Retrieved from http://www.corestandards.org/Files/K12ELAStandards.pdf

National Governors' Association and Council of Chief State School Officers. (2010b). *Common core state standards: Mathematics.* Retrieved from http://www.corestandards.org/assets/CCSSI_Math%20Standards.pdf

Niedelman, M. (1991). Problem solving and transfer. *Journal of Learning Disabilities, 24*(6), 322–329.

Nokes, J. D. (2008). Aligning literacy practices in secondary history classes with research on learning. *Middle Grades Research Journal, 3*(3), 29–55.

Olinghouse, N. G., & Graham, S. (2009). The relationship between the discourse knowledge and the writing performance of elementary-grade students. *Journal of Educational Psychology, 101*(1), 37–50.

Perin, D. (2004). Remediation beyond developmental education community colleges: The use of learning assistance centers to increase academic preparedness in community colleges. *Community College Journal of Research and Practice, 28*, 559–582.

Perin, D. (2006). Can community colleges protect both access and standards? The problem of remediation. *Teachers College Record, 108*(3), 339–373.

Perin, D. (2011). *Facilitating student learning through contextualization*. CCRC Working Paper No. 29, Assessment of Evidence Series. New York, NY: Teachers College, Columbia University. Retrieved from http://ccrc.tc.columbia.edu/

Perin, D., & Charron, K. (2006). "Lights just click on every day:" Academic preparedness and remediation in community colleges. In T. Bailey & V. S. Morest (Eds.), *Defending the community college equity agenda* (pp. 155–194). Baltimore, MD: Johns Hopkins University Press.

Perin, D., Bork, R. H., Peverly, S. T., Mason, L. H., & Waselewski, M. (2012). *A contextualized intervention for community college developmental reading and writing students*. CRC Working Paper No. 38. New York, NY: Community College Research Center, Teachers College, Columbia University.

Perkins, D. H., & Salomon, G. (1989). Are cognitive skills context-bound? *Educational Researcher, 18*(1), 16–25.

Phillippe, K. A., & Sullivan, L. G. (2005). *National profile of community colleges: Trends and statistics* (4th ed.). Washington, DC: Community College Press.

Reisman, A., & Wineburg, S. (2008). Teaching the skill of contextualizing in history. *The Social Studies, 99*(5), 202–207.

Rittle-Johnson, B., Siegler, R. S., & Alibali, M. W. (2001). Developing conceptual understanding and procedural skill in mathematics: An iterative process. *Journal of Educational Psychology, 93*(2), 346–362.

Rittle-Johnson, B., Star, J. R., & Durkin, K. (2009). The importance of prior knowledge when comparing examples: Influences on conceptual and procedural knowledge of equation solving. *Journal of Educational Psychology, 101*(4), 836–852.

Rose, M. (2005). *Lives on the boundary: A moving account of the struggles and achievements of America's educationally underprepared*. New York, NY: Penguin Books.

Scrivener, S., & Coghlan, E. (2011). *Opening doors to student success: A synthesis of findings from an evaluation at six community colleges*. MDRC Policy Brief. New York, NY: MDRC. Retrieved from http://www.mdrc.org/publications/585/overview.html, accessed March 17, 2011.

Shanahan, T., & Shanahan, C. (2008). Teaching disciplinary literacy to adolescents: Rethinking content-area literacy. *Harvard Educational Review, 78*(1), 40–59.

Shore, M., Shore, J., & Boggs, S. (2004). Allied health applications integrated into developmental mathematics using problem based learning. *Mathematics and Computer Education, 38*(2), 183–189.

Simmons, D., Hairrell, A., Edmonds, M., Vaughn, S., Larsen, R., Willson, V., et al. (2010). A comparison of multiple-strategy methods: Effects on fourth-grade students' general and content-specific reading comprehension and vocabulary development. *Journal of Research on Educational Effectiveness, 3*(2), 121–156.

Simpson, M. L., Hynd, C. R., Nist, S. L., & Burrell, K. I. (1997). College academic assistance programs and practices. *Educational Psychology Review, 9*, 39–87.

Smith, R. (2010). Feeling supported: Curricular learning communities for basic skills courses and students who speak English as a second language. *Community College Review, 37*(3), 261–284.

Snow, C. E. (2010). Academic language and the challenge of reading for learning about science. *Science, 328*(5977), 450–452.

Snyder, T. D., Tan, A. G., & Hoffman, C. M. (2006). *Digest of education statistics 2005 (NCES 2006–030)*. Washington, DC: U.S. Government Printing Office: U.S. Department of Education, National Center for Education Statistics.

Stahl, S. A., & Shanahan, C. (2004). Learning to think like a historian: Disciplinary knowledge through critical analysis of multiple documents. In T. L. Jetton & J. A. Dole (Eds.), *Adolescent literacy research and practice* (pp. 94–115). New York, NY: Guilford.

Stone, J. R., III, Alfeld, C., Pearson, D., Lewis, M. V., & Jensen, S. (2006). *Building academic skills in context: Testing the value of enhanced math learning in CTE (Final study)*. St. Paul, MN: National Research Center for Career and Technical Education. Retrieved from http://136.165.122.102/UserFiles/File/Math-in-CTE/MathLearningFinalStudy.pdf

Taboada, A., Tonks, S., Wigfield, A., & Guthrie, J. T. (2009). Effects of motivational and cognitive variables on reading comprehension. *Reading and Writing, 22*, 85–106.

Texas Higher Education Coordinating Board. (2009). *Texas college and career readiness standards*. Austin, TX: Author. Retrieved from http://www.thecb.state.tx.us/collegereadiness/crs.pdf

U.S. Census Bureau. (2011). Educational attainment in the United States: 2010—detailed tables. Retrieved from http://www.census.gov/hhes/socdemo/education/data/cps/2010/tables.html

U.S. Department of Education. (2008). *Foundations for success: The final report of the National Mathematics Advisory Panel*. Washington, DC: Author. Retrieved from http://www2.ed.gov/about/bdscomm/list/math-panel/report/final-report.pdf

Voss, J. F., & Wiley, J. (1997). Developing understanding while writing essays in history. *International Journal of Educational Research, 27*(3), 255–265.

Williams, N. (2010a). Embracing student potential: Creating space for instrinsic motivation in community college developmental reading courses. *Language Arts Journal of Michigan* (Spring–Summer 2010), 36–41.

Williams, N. (2010b). *Engaging literacy! Urban achievement—A supplemental workbook for reading development.* New York, NY: Learning Solutions.

Woodard, T. (2004). The effects of math anxiety on post-secondary developmental students as related to achievement, gender, and age. *Inquiry: The Journal of the Virginia Community Colleges, 9*(1), 1–5. Education Resources Information Center (ERIC) EJ876845.

Zachry, E. M., & Schneider, E. (2009). *Promising instructional reforms in developmental education. A case study of three Achieving the Dream colleges.* New York, NY: MDRC. Retrieved from http://www.mdrc.org/publications/504/full.pdf

Zachry, E. M., & Schneider, E. (2010). *Building foundations for student readiness: A review of rigorous research and promising trends in developmental education.* New York, NY: Teachers College, Columbia University.

Zawaiza, T. R. W., & Gerber, M. M. (1993). Effects of explicit instruction on math word-problem solving by community college students with learning disabilities. *Learning Disability Quarterly, 16*(1), 64–79.

Section II

INSTITUTIONAL ISSUES FOR THE
COMMUNITY COLLEGE

7

PLANNING PROGRAMS FOR COMMUNITY COLLEGE EDUCATION

Theory, Policy, and Practice

DAVID F. AYERS AND MICHAEL V. AYERS

The community college is fundamentally about educational programs. Whether it is basic law enforcement training, a single course toward the associate's degree, or an entire degree curriculum, the comprehensive community college is committed to improving quality of life through a variety of educational programs. In this chapter, we discuss program planning in the community college. Similar to others (e.g., Boone, Safrit, & Jones, 2002; Caffarella, 2002), we define an educational program as an event or series of events developed within an institutional context and intended to promote learning. This definition is intentionally broad, because we plan to address not only formal academic and vocational study but also informal programs (Merriam, Caffarella, & Baumgartner, 2007).

Our aim is to examine the cultural, political, and economic context for program planning in the community college. We argue that a discourse of learner needs both animates planning practice and justifies policy decisions. What is often not discussed, however, are the ideologies underlying the discourse of needs, much less the attendant assumptions about human capital formation. To begin such a conversation, we describe human capital theory; demonstrate how it informs educational policy at global, national, and local scales; and parse assumptions about learner needs that may or may not be warranted. Needs-based programs defined by human capital theory will then be contrasted to those implicit in the Truman Commission Report, "Higher Education for American Democracy"—a foundational document in the history of community colleges in the U.S. (President's Commission on Higher Education, & Zook, 1947).

First, however, we will review the literature related to program planning.

PROGRAM PLANNING MODELS AND VIEWPOINTS

Educational programs do not just happen; they are planned. Most program planning models offer normative theories about what program planners should do, and there is remarkable consistency in these notions of program planning across models. Boone et al. (2002) reviewed 13 prominent program planning models in adult education (Beal, Blount, Powers, & Johnson, 1966; Boone, Dolan, & Shearon, 1970; Boyle, 1981; Brookfield, 1986; Caffarella, 2002; Cervero & Wilson, 1994; Freire, 1970; Houle, 1996; Kidd, 1973; Knowles, 1970; Lippit, Watson, & Westley, 1958; Sork, 2000; Tyler, 1949). From these models, Boone et al. (1970) distilled three subprocesses: (1) planning; (2) design and implementation; and (3) evaluation and accountability. As such, it should be noted that planning is only the first phase of a much more involved programming process.

Scholars have observed five general similarities across the 13 major programming models. First, most of these models build upon Ralph Tyler's (1949) classic book *Basic Principles of Curriculum and Instruction*. Second, most planning models are not context specific and can be adopted within a variety of settings such as degree, certificate, and diploma programs, as well as continuing education, basic education, and literacy programs, among others. Third, planning models are grounded in philosophical assumptions about learners and learning, although these are often implicit. Fourth, most models advocate a deliberate planning process. Fifth, and finally, learner needs are central to all program planning models (Boone et al., 2002).

The literature on programming models in adult education includes three distinct viewpoints: classical, naturalistic, and critical (Cervero & Wilson, 1994). First, classical models began with Tyler's (1949) curriculum model and include Boone (1985), Knowles (1970), and Sork (2000), among others. Program planners ascribing to versions of the classic model typically identify learner needs by answering some permutation of Tyler's four principles:

1. Identification of a problem or assessment of unmet needs;
2. Formulation of objectives, goals, and means;
3. Formal and informal learning strategies; and
4. An implicit or explicit evaluation.

Cervero and Wilson (1994) note that authors of classical models assume that educational programmers exercise considerable discretion in practice. That is, program planners are empowered to make and implement decisions with few organizational or socio-political constraints. Also, organizational needs are considered to be homogeneous in this viewpoint, which implies a certain convergence among the needs of the organization and its members. Specifically, classical models assume that the needs of the organization—for example, the workplace—are commensurate with the needs of employees. Quite often, however, organizations internalize multiple contradictions, precipitating competing and contradictory interests (Benson, 1976). Such contradictions are commonplace in the current political, economic, and cultural milieu (Seo & Creed, 2002), and the failure to recognize an organization's internal tensions marks a limitation of classical models.

The naturalistic viewpoint—for example, Brookfield (1986), Houle (1972), and Knox (1982)—the second of these viewpoints, recognizes the institutional and societal impediments and contradictions that often complicate program planning. In this view, program planners must often reconcile discordant needs among learners, educators, and other stakeholders; thus, this viewpoint accounts for the competing interests that emerge in practice. Similar to the classical viewpoint, the naturalistic viewpoint affords a considerable discretion to programmers, but this viewpoint also recognizes the complicated judgments that accompany planning practice. Scholars of naturalistic models encourage program planners not only to identify learning objectives but also to make judgments on the best way for these objectives to be met which underscores the ethical component of planning theory (Cervero & Wilson, 1994, 2001, 2006). Finally, naturalistic viewpoints avoid linear planning sequences, resorting instead to a more organic collection of planning tasks, which can be completed in any order to accommodate emerging and unpredictable organizational processes.

In contrast to classical and naturalistic viewpoints, the third viewpoint—the critical viewpoint (Freire, 1970; Griffith, 1978; Hart, 1990)—takes into account structural constraints that limit the discretion of programmers. In this view, educational programs are structurally determined, and institutions are seen not only to perpetuate relations of dominance and inequity but also to provide an opportunity for learners to develop critical consciousness. Critical consciousness occurs when adults learn to question assumptions and fundamental beliefs inherited from others and to reflect on the power structures that have produced the *status quo*. Brookfield (2005) identifies seven learning tasks associated with critical theory, and these are often goals of programs grounded in a critical viewpoint. These include challenging ideology, contesting hegemony, unmasking power, overcoming alienation, learning liberation, reclaiming reason, and learning democracy. The critical viewpoint thus emphasizes the political, economic context of program planning.

LEARNER NEEDS

The classical, naturalistic, and critical viewpoints all center around learner needs. The concept of learner needs is, in fact, one of the two most prominent concepts in adult education, the other being learning (Wiltshire, 1973). Educational needs may be psychological, social, cultural, or physiological in nature and are often conceptualized as a gap between a present state and a desired future state (Boone et al., 2002; Queeney, 1995; Tyler, 1971). It is important to understand learner needs because adults are unlikely to participate in educational programs voluntarily in the absence of some compelling need which the program is assumed to ameliorate. In other words, learners may lack motivation to participate in educational programs if they perceive a disconnection between the program outcomes and their immediate interests.

In recognition of the relation between needs and motivation to learn, program planning scholars have encouraged systematic and deliberative strategies for identifying, understanding, and diagnosing learner needs. Such strategies include focus groups, interviews, survey methods, and observation (Gupta, 1999); interfacing with community leaders (Boone et al., 2002); focused study of target publics or communities (McMahon, 1970); and utilization of extant data such as census reports (Boone et al., 2002; McMahon, 1970). Adult educators have also recognized the interpersonal skills of listening and understanding as a means of understanding learners' needs (Boone et al., 1970; McClendon & Cantanese, 1996).

One point of debate among program planning scholars is the relative involvement of the learner compared to the educator in identifying needs. Tyler (1949) recognizes the centrality of learner needs but affords the educator priority in their identification. Cervero and Wilson (1994, 2001, 2006) insist upon having learners at the planning table to negotiate needs, the ways they are identified, their conversion to program objectives, and the assessment of their satisfaction. Boone et al. (2002) privilege the needs of local learners: "Often national, state, and even county-level adult education organizations package and encourage the application of 'canned' programs without investigating the need for tailoring them to meet local needs" (p. 147). Similarly, Boone (1997) insists that community colleges must establish linkage with learners and learner systems. Representing the critical viewpoint, Paulo Freire (1970) encouraged learners to reflect critically both on their needs and the cultural processes that shape them. Monette (1979) recognizes this practice, but suggests that planning practices often fall short of engaging learners in a thorough examination of needs.

Even with systematic analysis, it may be difficult to distinguish among actual needs, esoteric desires, or ideologically manufactured needs. For this reason, a few scholars reject altogether needs assessment as a starting point for planning educational programs. In a poignant critique of the continued dominance of needs assessment in adult education, Lawy and Armstrong (2009) assert that needs are not objective realities but instead are "manufactured political constructions" (p. 3). Along with a small cadre of scholars (Monette, 1977, 1979; Taylor-Gooby & Dale, 1981; Wiltshire, 1973), Lawy and Armstrong (2009) argue that without a critical examination of expressed needs, educators risk succumbing to a customer-service mentality based on pleasing learners instead of challenging learners to achieve "appropriate" goals. Brookfield (1986) wages a strongly worded critique of this approach: "Those who behave in this manner and who equate the sum total of education with reacting to expressed learner needs are technicians, not educators" (p. 222).

In addition to the danger of accommodating ideologically manufactured needs, there is another pitfall related to relying completely on learners to identify needs; that is, unmet needs may go unnoticed if the consequences of their deprivation are delayed. Without an understanding of nutrition, for example, members of many communities may suffer obesity, hypertension, or diabetes. These effects are not immediate, nor are they always understood to be a consequence of eating habits, thus the need for proper nutrition remains undiagnosed by learners themselves.

To address this dilemma, Bradshaw (1972) offers a four-part classification of needs. A normative need, according to Bradshaw (1972), is a desirable standard imposed upon a client by a professional who deems such a standard necessary. A comparative need is similar in that it is subjective, but this type of need is perceived by the client—not the professional. A felt need is a deficiency experienced by the client but which does not compel the client to action. In such a case, an individual may recognize the need for nutrition but may be unwilling to commit to healthy eating habits. An expressed need, on the other hand, does motivate action. Often, an expressed need emerges as a consequence of a life event. A heart attack, for example, may compel an otherwise resistant individual to commit to a healthy diet.

Strategies used to identify needs cannot focus exclusively on what participants need to know, because mere accrual of facts may not lead to improved quality of life or transformative change. Indeed, educational programs are unlikely to effect change unless program planners understand learning in a holistic sense (Keeling, 2004), which involves not only cognitive but also affective and psychomotor domains of learning (Bloom, 1956). "In the transformative educational paradigm, the purpose of educational involvement is the evolution of multidimensional identity, including but not limited to cognitive, affective, behavioral and spiritual development" (Keeling, 2004, p. 9). As one example, acquiring a basic knowledge of nutrition and wellness may not motivate individuals to eat healthily. Appreciating the need for and committing to a healthy diet require learning in the affective domain. As such, attitudes must be considered in understanding learner needs (Bloom, 1956; Keeling, 2004; Wlodkowski, 1999). By the same token, psychomotor skills are also important considerations in the identification of needs. In keeping with the wellness example, good health requires regular exercise, which may require learners to develop the psychomotor skills necessary for participating in physical activity.

The literature on human development provides essential guidance for program planners in this respect. Of particular importance are recent findings on epistemological reflection (Baxter Magolda, 1992) and self-authorship (Baxter Magolda & King, 2004; Kegan, 1994, 2000). This line of research suggests that facilitating learning "requires consideration of what students know, who they are, what their values and behavior patterns are, and how they see themselves contributing to and participating in the world in which they live" (Keeling, 2004, p. 9). Ayers and Carlone (2007) demonstrate how job-training programs potentially inculcate identities of servitude. In one example, they observed programs in which students learned to "accept authority" and were encouraged to defer ethical judgment to employers. As such, Ayers and Carlone (2007) urge educators to reflect carefully on the identities implicitly constructed for students through their participation in educational programs. In a similar example, Ayers, Miller-Dyce, and Carlone (2008) found that study participants had been ordered to perform unethical and immoral tasks in their current or prior employment. They saw the community college as a way to reclaim dignity, develop meaningful relationships with clients and patients, and devote their time to meaningful work that made a difference in the lives of others.

NEEDS IN A CULTURAL-ECONOMIC CONTEXT

The relationships among program planning, identity, and quality of life draw clear ethical implications for community college educators. As stated above, a classical viewpoint tends to conflate the needs of learners and their employing organization. While there may be a certain degree of convergence among needs and interests of employers and employees, it is also possible that there will be tensions between the two. Should the goal of an educational program be to prepare malleable and docile employees, or should it be to prepare critical thinkers who reflect on ethical issues and worker rights? Should such program outcomes differ for community college learners compared to students at elite colleges? When the interests of employers and employees are not congruent, whom does the community college serve? As these questions show, program planning is never a politically neutral act (Freire, 1970), and power relations are always at work—even if covertly (Cervero & Wilson, 1994, 2001, 2006).

Noting the inequities and redistributive effects of neoliberal capitalism, Apple (2004) describes how ideologies manifest as a hidden curriculum. A hidden curriculum of sorts has been identified within the community college (Brint & Karabel, 1989; Pincus, 1980; Zwerling, 1976). In their analysis of a community-college job-training program, Ayers and Carlone (2007) identified three ideologies supportive of neoliberal assumptions.

> First, the interests of the private sector were universalized, or represented as the common good. Second, learning was reduced to the knowledge and dispositions that were valued by capital, educational credentials were mere indicators of productive capacity, and narrow identities of labour were offered to program participants ... Third, employment stability and the social contract between employer and employee were eschewed as out of date and impractical. (p. 477)

These findings demonstrate an unsubstantiated equivalence between learner needs and employer interests (Laclau & Mouffe, 1985). Other scholars have observed similar phenomena (Aronowitz, 2008; Bourdieu & Passeron, 1990; Bowles & Gintis, 2002; Brint & Karabel, 1991; Levin, 2007; Spring, 1998). As this line of scholarship shows, the very meaning of needs may be construed from an economic perspective and defined by neoliberal capitalism. More importantly, perhaps, these studies demonstrate that needs are subjectively construed and dependent on dominant narratives and ideologies. Needs, in other words, are subject to the norms of cultural hegemony. Here, hegemony is defined as "the permeation throughout society of an entire system of values, attitudes, beliefs and morality that has the effect of supporting the status quo in power relations" (Burke, 2005, ¶ 9).

> Hegemony in this sense might be defined as an 'organising principle' that is diffused by the process of socialisation into every area of daily life. To the extent that this prevailing consciousness is internalised by the population it becomes part of what is generally called 'common sense' so that the philosophy, culture and morality of the ruling elite comes to appear as the natural order of things. (Burke, 2005, ¶ 9)

The concept of hegemony is particularly relevant in the present context, because a prevailing common-sense discourse is colored by neoliberal capitalism and its educational counterpart, human capital theory, drawing considerable implications for the community college and its economic development mission (Ayers, 2005; Levin, 2000, 2001, 2006; Levin, Kater, & Wagoner, 2006).

As the discussion above indicates, determining the needs of learners is complicated and fraught with ideologically formed assumptions. Cervero and Wilson (2001) encourage program planners to reflect carefully on whose needs are met by educational programs, but this question may be difficult to answer given the mystifying effects of cultural hegemony. A program intended to prepare learners for work in a low-wage, demeaning environment may defer to employers' interests and thus not truly address learners' needs. On the other hand, such employment may be viewed as an essential first step toward a better way of life. As this discussion suggests, it is important to avoid a simplified notion of needs. Even more importantly, planners must both recognize the ideological basis of needs and acknowledge the interests that may be served by a hidden curriculum.

POLICY AND HUMAN CAPITAL THEORY

As discussed, needs are often defined in economic terms, and this trend originates with human capital theory (Baptiste, 2001; Schultz, 1970; Spring, 1998; Thurow, 1970). Within the hegemony of neoliberal capitalism, interpretations of human capital theory are so ingrained in contemporary culture that they shape the ways in which we reason about educational needs and program goals (Apple, 2004; Baptiste, 2001). A brief narrative of human capital theory provides a backdrop against which current conceptualizations of learner needs can be understood and critiqued.

Economists define human capital as "the stock of knowledge and skills possessed by the labor force that increases its productivity" (Engel, 2000, p. 24). The current version of human capital theory has its origins in classical economics, specifically Adam Smith's (1776) *The Wealth of Nations*. The theory had been contested on a number of accounts such that it remained controversial until the mid-20th century. Specifically, there was an objection to the dehumanization associated with referring to human beings as capital alongside physical capital and finance capital, but this concern eased in the 1960s (Baptiste, 2001).

Human capital theory has undergone three distinct phases since 1960 (Baptiste, 2001). The first phase "stressed public investment in human capital and was dominated by ambitious claims about the positive and vital link between education and economic growth" (Baptiste, 2001, p. 187). Two prominent works represent this early phase of human capital theory: Gary Becker's (1964) *Human Capital* and Edward Denison's (1962) *The Sources of Economic Growth in the United States*. This phase of theory development lacked methodological sophistication and failed to yield the predicted surge in economic productivity, giving rise to the second phase of theory development.

Countering the first conceptualizations of human capital, the screening hypothesis gained popularity in the 1970s (Thurow, 1970). The screening hypothesis describes the value of educational programs not as a result of the knowledge gained by workers but instead through their function as a screening mechanism. Stated bluntly, educational programs "act as a surrogate for qualities that employers want" (Marginson, 1993, p. 44); they select out learners who fail to demonstrate the knowledge, skills, and attitudes that employers value. Although not the intent of the screening hypothesis, this theory reveals a possibility that educational programs may serve as an apparatus of ideological selection in that learners who resist the ideological worldview of employers may opt out of educational programs, fail to earn credentials, and thus lack qualifications for employment.

The third phase of human capital theory development coincided with a series of structural adjustment policies endorsed by the Organization for Economic Co-operation and Development (OECD) during the Reagan and Thatcher administrations (see Baptiste, 2001). In this era, the OECD recognized that skills, knowledge, and attitudes of workers were essential to economic development. As such, the theory of human capital in this phase emerged as a much more sophisticated version of its 1960s predecessor. Counting humans as a form of capital became common practice, but this version of human capital theory also adopted components of the screening hypothesis. More importantly, perhaps, it took into account the role of technology in production. Given the rapid pace of technological advances in the latter half of the 20th century, economic productivity required workers who could adapt to change and think creatively about new technologies (Baptiste, 2001).

Human capital theory remains a dominant influence on postsecondary education policy (Bills, 2003), particularly as it relates to the community college. Perhaps one reason for its dominance is that it appeals to conservative and progressive voters. It appeals to conservatives because of its emphasis on individual accountability, meritocracy, and business-friendly policy. It appeals to progressives because it promotes employment as a means toward an improved quality of life. In fact, education policy at various scales—local, national, regional, global—coheres around central themes of human capital theory.

At a global scale the World Bank, International Monetary Fund, and the OECD issue policy briefs and research reports, which often recommend specific priorities for community colleges (e.g., Bassanini, 2004). The Global Federation of Competitiveness Councils (2010), for example, issued a report on global competitiveness principles, which includes the following statement: "21st century workforce skills should be the baseline for every citizen in order to reach their full potential while fueling wealth creation and profits" (p. 3). Such policy-oriented documents typically establish economic development as a goal, threats to economic growth as a problem, and preparation of a globally competitive workforce as part of the solution (Fairclough, 2006).

Human capital formation is a goal at the national policy level as well. For example, President George W. Bush's education policy was an outgrowth of his economic policy: "When you've got a growing economy in the 21st century, there's a certain skill set that's needed to fill the jobs. And what we're talking about today is how to fill those jobs" (Office of the Press Secretary, 2005). Similarly, President Barack Obama insisted in the 2011 State of the Union Address: "Because people need to be able to train for new jobs and careers in today's fast-changing economy, we're also revitalizing America's community colleges." Both administrations have justified their education policy in terms of economics, specifically human capital theory.

More locally, public policy related to educational programs is influenced by local growth coalitions.

> These growth machines are led by place entrepreneurs who seek to maximize property values and rents from buildings and land in a locale, and they include real estate owners, bankers and financiers, building developers, construction firms, and real estate brokers and attorneys. Within growth coalitions, place entrepreneurs are supported by local elected and appointed officials (e.g., mayors, county commissioners), the local media, and some (but not all) small-business proprietors and professionals. (Holland, 2007, p. 189)

Holland (2007) adds that these local growth coalitions both lobby for conditions believed to attract capital investment and to bring jobs to the community and market the locality as an optimal space for competitive investment. The community college often figures prominently in this marketing campaign. What is emphasized is the community college's agility in providing customized training through consultation with corporate managers and state industry associations. The interests of capital and the needs of students are often collapsed into a single set of needs defined as competitiveness in a global economy (Jessop, Fairclough, & Wodak, 2008). Community college educators thus define learner needs in terms of competitiveness in labor markets, and program goals follow accordingly.

POLICY CRITIQUE AND DEMOCRATIC ALTERNATIVES

Human capital theory may be the *sine qua non* of contemporary education policy, but this has not always been the case. Collegiate learning in the post-war period emphasized democracy, community, and international understanding. These goals reflect national imperatives for domestic growth and the Keynesian welfare state, and are evidenced by one of the community college's principal documents: the Truman Commission Report (President's Commission on Higher Education, & Zook, 1947). This report, officially titled *Higher Education for American Democracy*, endorsed the "community college" as a name for what was previously known as the junior college. This commission also established a key role for the community college in realizing a tripartite vision for higher education in the U.S. The goals included the following: (1) "Education for a fuller realization of democracy in every phase of living"; (2) "Education directly and explicitly for international understanding and cooperation"; and (3) "Education for the application of creative imagination and trained intelligence to the solution of social problems and to the administration of public affairs." The Truman Commission Report (President's Commission on Higher Education, & Zook, 1947) captured a dominant national discourse at this point in history, emphasizing the public role of higher education. Key themes included cooperation, international understanding, and public affairs. Following this report, communities across the nation established hundreds of community colleges. Students with aspirations of achieving a bachelor's degree arrived at the institution's "open doors" by the thousands (Cohen & Brawer, 2008).

There is a vivid contrast between the civic and democratic aims espoused in the Truman Commission Report (President's Commission on Higher Education, & Zook, 1947) and the neoliberal policy objectives of the contemporary community college. This distinction has not been lost on education scholars, and human capital theory has become a target of critique in the academic world. Engel (2000), for example, argues that educational investment based on human capital theory results in a "cost-benefit strait-jacket for curriculum development" (p. 30). Baptiste (2001) asserts that human capital theory neglects potential conflicts among learners, deferring instead to the universalized needs of the capital. Baptiste thus concludes that educational programs based purely on human capital theory ignore ethical considerations.

> [They] would be determined by "market analysis" and by technical considerations commonly referred to as "needs assessments" rather than by any ethical or moral philosophy of the educator or program. Consensus would be assumed a priori, not sought through political struggle. (Baptiste, 2001, p. 196)

Baptiste's (2001) criticism of needs assessment underscores the need for moral and ethical concerns to guide programming practice. At the same time, a democratic program planning process requires not only representation of learners but also meaningful participation of various stakeholders in a thoughtful diagnosis of needs (Cervero & Wilson, 2006).

The point is not that preparing learners for the world of work is wrong. The point is, rather, that the explicit content of programs is only part of the learning experience (Apple, 2004). There is a role for the community college in helping students improve their quality of life, either through liberal arts education or job training. As Ayers (2010) argues, place-bound students are at a disadvantage within today's neoliberal hegemony in which capital is globally mobile. Under these conditions, those individuals who are capable of understanding, navigating, and critiquing the global milieu have a greater capacity to act in their own interests. Program planning, when based in a critical viewpoint, inspires educators, learners, and entire communities to question inequitable relations and to act together in their own interest. Toward this end, the community college can orchestrate local action through community-based programs.

Through case studies of five community colleges, Boone, Pettitt, and Weisman (1998) demonstrate that via community-based, transformative programs, the community college can cultivate democratic leadership, orchestrate local action, and address pressing community issues: Guilford Technical Community College focused on workforce preparedness in a changing economy; James Sprunt Community College took on the challenge of adult literacy in a rural and economically depressed region; Florence-Darlington Technical College addressed the contentious issue of deteriorating water quality resulting at least in part from increased hog and poultry production and processing; The Technical College of the Lowcountry focused on unemployment by developing physical and social infrastructure; and Paul D. Camp Community College took a leadership role in reestablishing safe, healthy, and pleasant neighborhoods. The community colleges in these cases became catalysts and helped individuals and communities author their own futures. While policy-makers, community leaders, and educators often equate corporate profitability with community economic development, the empirical realities of this assumption are not so clear (Harvey, 2005). When the community college takes a leadership role in helping communities address these and other critical issues, it reclaims a democratic role and serves the interests of U.S. communities.

To conclude this chapter, we suggest a particular direction for research on program planning in the community college. The difference among classical, naturalistic, and critical viewpoints shows that there is no consensus on the most technologically proficient—or even the most appropriate—means of planning educational programs. Planning educational programs is messy, political, and fraught with ethical dilemmas. While most program planning models take an assessment of learner needs as a starting point, in practice, political forces tend to afford primacy to the needs and interests of employers. Even when learners are explicitly engaged in needs assessment, the distinction between actual needs and esoteric desires is elusive. What emerges within the hegemony of neoliberal capitalism is a policy compromise grounded in the assumptions of human capital theory. Yet, these assumptions are too infrequently questioned. The result is a dominant policy discourse in which the needs of local communities and their citizens are conflated with the interests of global capital. With such narrowly constrained goals, the community college risks forfeiting its democratic mission. Nonetheless, community college scholars can interrogate the political and ethical ramifications of program planning within the contemporary political economy. Local, ethnographic research can clarify the needs and interests of communities and their citizens, perhaps identifying points of common interest with employers and local growth coalitions. More importantly, community college scholars can identify those needs obscured by human capital theory, amplify the voices of learners who are ill-served by programs tailored to corporate interests, and animate a national discussion about who benefits—and who should benefit—from community college programs (Cervero & Wilson, 2006).

QUESTIONS FOR DISCUSSION

1. What are three frameworks or viewpoints for planning models in adult education?
2. What are learner needs and what strategies do scholars recommend for addressing these?

3. What is human capital theory?
4. Are there ethical considerations in program planning, and, if so, what are they?

REFERENCES

Apple, M. W. (2004). *Ideology and curriculum* (3rd ed.). New York, NY: Routledge Falmer.

Aronowitz, S. (2008). *The last good job in America: Work and education in the new global technoculture*. Lanham, MD: Rowman & Littlefield.

Ayers, D. F. (2005). Neoliberal ideology in community college mission statements: A critical discourse analysis. *The Review of Higher Education, 28,* 527–549.

Ayers, D. F. (2010). Community colleges and the politics of sociospatial scale. *Higher Education*. Retrieved from doi:10.1007/s10734-010-9388-5

Ayers, D. F., & Carlone, D. (2007). Manifestations of neoliberal discourses in a local job-training program. *International Journal of Lifelong Education, 26,* 461–479.

Ayers, D. F., Miller-Dyce, C., & Carlone, D. (2008). Security, dignity, caring relationships, and meaningful work: Needs motivating participation in a job-training program. *Community College Review, 35,* 257–276.

Baptiste, I. (2001). Pedagogical implications of human capital theory. *Adult Education Quarterly,* 51(3), 184–201.

Bassanini, A. (2004). *Improving skills for more and better jobs: Does training make a difference?* Preliminary draft. Retrieved from http://www.oecd.org/home

Baxter Magolda, M. B. (1992). *Knowing and reasoning in college: Gender-related patterns in students' intellectual development* (1st ed.). San Francisco, CA: Jossey-Bass.

Baxter Magolda, M. B., & King, P. M. (Eds.). (2004). *Learning partnerships: Theory and models of practice to educate for self-authorship*. Sterling, VA: Stylus Press.

Beal, G. M., Blount, R. C., Powers, R. C., & Johnson, H. J. (1966). *Social action and interaction in program planning*. Ames, IA: Iowa State University Press.

Becker, G. (1964). *Human capital: A theoretical and empirical analysis, with special reference to education*. New York, NY: Columbia University Press.

Benson, J. K. (1976). Organizations: A dialectic view. *Administrative Science Quarterly,* 22.

Bills, D. B. (2003). Credentials, signals, and screens: Explaining the relationship between schooling and job assignment. *Review of Educational Research, 73,* 441–469.

Bloom, B. S. (1956). *Taxonomy of educational objectives: The classification of educational goals* (1st ed.). New York, NY: D. McKay.

Boone, E. J. (1985). *Developing programs in adult education* (1st ed.). Englewood Cliffs, NJ: Prentice-Hall.

Boone, E. J. (1997). *Community leadership through community-based programming: The role of the community college*. Washington, DC: Community College Press.

Boone, E. J., Dolan, R. J., & Shearon, R. W. (1970). *Programming in the Cooperative Extension Service: A conceptual schema*. Raleigh: North Carolina Agricultural Extension Service.

Boone, E. J., Pettitt, J. M., & Weisman, I. M. (Eds.). (1998). *Community-based programming in action: The experiences of five community colleges*. Washington, DC: Community College Press.

Boone, E. J., Safrit, R. D., & Jones, J. (2002). *Developing programs in adult education: A conceptual programming model* (2nd ed.). Prospect Heights, IL: Waveland Press.

Bourdieu, P., & Passeron, J. C. (1990). *Reproduction in education, society, and culture* (1990 ed.). Newbury Park, CA: Sage.

Bowles, S., & Gintis, H. (2002). Schooling in capitalist America revisited. *Sociology of Education, 75,* 1–18.

Boyle, P. G. (1981). *Planning better programs*. New York, NY: McGraw-Hill.

Bradshaw, J. (1972, March 30). The concept of social need. *New Society,* 640–643.

Brint, S. G., & Karabel, J. (1989). *The diverted dream: Community colleges and the promise of educational opportunity in America, 1900–1985*. New York, NY: Oxford University Press.

Brint, S. G., & Karabel, J. (1991). Institutional origins and transformations: The case of the American community college. In W. W. Powell & P. J. DiMaggio (Eds.), *The new institutionalism in organizational analysis* (pp. 337–360). Chicago, IL: University of Chicago Press.

Brookfield, S. D. (1986). *Understanding and facilitating adult learning*. San Francisco, CA: Jossey-Bass.

Brookfield, S. D. (2005). *The power of critical theory*. San Francisco, CA: Jossey-Bass.

Burke, B. (2005). Antonio Gramsci, schooling and education. *The encyclopedia of informal education*. Retrieved from: http://www.infed.org/thinkers/et-gram.htm

Caffarella, R. S. (2002). *Planning programs for adult learners: A practical guide for educators, trainers, and staff developers* (2nd ed.). San Francisco, CA: Jossey-Bass.

Cervero, R. M., & Wilson, A. L. (1994). *Planning responsibly for adult education: A guide to negotiating power and interests*. San Francisco, CA: Jossey-Bass.

Cervero, R. M., & Wilson, A. L. (2001). *Power in practice: Adult education and the struggle for knowledge and power in society* (1st ed.). San Francisco, CA: Jossey-Bass.

Cervero, R. M., & Wilson, A. L. (2006). *Working the planning table: Negotiating democratically for adult, continuing, and workplace education*. San Francisco, CA: Jossey-Bass.

Cohen, A. M., & Brawer, F. B. (2008). *The American community college* (5th ed.). San Francisco, CA: Jossey-Bass.

Denison, E. F. (1962). *The sources of economic growth in the United States*. New York, NY: Committee for Economic Development.

Engel, M. (2000). *The struggle for control of public education: Market ideology vs. democratic values*. Philadelphia, PA: Temple University Press.

Fairclough, N. (2006). *Language and globalization*. London: Routledge.

Freire, P. (1970). *Pedagogy of the oppressed*. New York, NY: Herder and Herder.

Global Federation of Competitiveness Councils. (2010). *2010 Global competitiveness principles*. Washington, DC.

Griffith, W. S. (1978). Educational needs: Definition, assessment, and utilization. *School Review, 86*, 382–394.

Gupta, K. (1999). *A practical guide to needs assessment*. San Francisco, CA: Jossey-Bass.

Hart, M. U. (1990). Liberation through consciousness raising. In J. Mezirow (Ed.), *Fostering critical reflection in adulthood: A guide to transformative and emancipatory learning* (pp. 47–73). San Francisco, CA: Jossey-Bass.

Harvey, D. (2005). *A brief history of neoliberalism*. New York, NY: Oxford University Press.

Holland, D. C. (2007). *Local democracy under siege: Activism, public interests, and private politics*. New York, NY: New York University Press.

Houle, C. O. (1972). *The design of education* (1st ed.). San Francisco, CA: Jossey-Bass.

Houle, C. O. (1996). *The design of education* (2nd ed.). San Francisco, CA: Jossey-Bass.

Jessop, B., Fairclough, N., & Wodak, R. (2008). *Education and the knowledge-based economy in Europe*. Rotterdam: Sense Publishers.

Keeling, R. P. (Ed.). (2004). *Learning reconsidered, A campus-wide focus on the student experience*. Washington, DC: National Association of Student Personnel Administrators.

Kegan, R. (1994). *In over our heads: The mental demands of modern life*. Cambridge, MA: Harvard University Press.

Kegan, R. (2000). What "form" transforms?: A constructive-developmental perspective on transformational learning. In J. Mezirow (Ed.), *Learning as transformation: Critical perspectives of a theory in progress* (pp.35–52). San Francisco, CA: Jossey-Bass.

Kidd, R. J. (1973). *How adults learn*. New York, NY: Association Press.

Knowles, M. S. (1970). *The modern practice of adult education: Andragogy versus pedagogy*. New York, NY: Association Press.

Knox, A. B. (Ed.). (1982). *Leadership strategies for meeting new challenges*. San Francisco, CA: Jossey-Bass.

Laclau, E., & Mouffe, C. (1985). *Hegemony and socialist strategy*. London: Verso.

Lawy, R., & Armstrong, P. (2009). The myth of meeting needs revisited: The case of educational research. *International Journal of Lifelong Education, 28*, 3–17.

Levin, J. S. (2000). The revised institution: The community college mission at the end of the twentieth century. *Community College Review, 28*, 1–25.

Levin, J. S. (2001). *Globalizing the community college: Strategies for change in the twenty-first century*. New York, NY: Palgrave.

Levin, J. S. (2006). Faculty work: Tensions between educational and economic values. *Journal of Higher Education, 77*, 62–88.

Levin, J. S. (2007). *Nontraditional students and community colleges: The conflict of justice and neoliberalism* (1st ed.). New York, NY: Palgrave Macmillan.

Levin, J. S., Kater, S., & Wagoner, R. L. (2006). *Community college faculty: At work in the new economy*. New York, NY: Palgrave Macmillan.

Lippit, R., Watson, J., & Westley, B. (1958). *The dynamics of planned change*. New York, NY: Harcourt, Brace & World.

Marginson, S. (1993). *Education and public policy in Australia*. New York, NY: Cambridge University Press.

McClendon, A. H., & Cantanese, A. J. (1996). *Planners on planning*. San Francisco, CA: Jossey-Bass.

McMahon, E. E. (1970). *Needs of people and their communities and the adult educator*. Washington, DC: Adult Education Association of the USA.

Merriam, S. B., Caffarella, R. S., & Baumgartner, L. (2007). *Learning in adulthood: A comprehensive guide* (3rd ed.). San Francisco, CA: Jossey-Bass.

Monette, M. L. (1977). The concept of educational need: An analysis of selected literature. *Adult Education, 27*(2), 116–127.

Monette, M. L. (1979). Needs assessment: A critique of philosophical assumptions. *Adult Education, 29*(2), 83–95.

Office of the Press Secretary. (2005, March 2). *President participates in job training and education conversation.* Retrieved from: http://www.whitehouse.gov/news/releases/ 2005/03/20050302-4.html

Pincus, F. L. (1980). The false promises of community colleges: Class conflict and vocational education. *Harvard Educational Review, 50*, 332–361.

President's Commission on Higher Education, & Zook, G. F. (1947). *Higher education for American democracy, a report.* Washington, DC: U.S. Government Printing Office.

Queeney, D. S. (1995). *Assessing needs in continuing education: An essential tool for quality improvement.* San Francisco, CA: Jossey-Bass.

Schultz, T. W. (1970). *Investment in human capital; the role of education and of research.* New York, NY: Free Press.

Seo, M., & Creed, W. (2002). Institutional contradictions, praxis, and institutional change: A dialectical perspective. *Academy of Management Review, 27*, 222–247.

Smith, A. (1776). *An inquiry into the nature and causes of the wealth of nations.* London: Printed for W. Strahan, and T. Cadell.

Sork, T. J. (2000). Planning educational programs. In A. L. Wilson & E. R. Hayes (Eds.), *Handbook of adult and continuing education* (2nd ed., pp. 171–190). San Francisco, CA: Jossey-Bass.

Spring, J. H. (1998). *Education and the rise of the global economy.* Mahwah, NJ: L. Erlbaum Associates.

Taylor-Gooby, P., & Dale, J. (1981). *Social theory and social welfare.* London: Edward Arnold.

Thurow, L. C. (1970). *Investment in human capital.* Belmont, CA: Wadsworth Pub. Co.

Tyler, R. W. (1949). *Basic principles of curriculum and instruction.* Chicago, IL: University of Chicago Press.

Tyler, R. W. (1971). *Basic principles of curriculum and instruction.* Chicago, IL: University of Chicago Press.

Wiltshire, H. (1973). The concepts of learning and need in adult education. *Studies in Adult Education, 5*(1), 1–15.

Wlodkowski, R. J. (1999). *Enhancing adult motivation to learn: A comprehensive guide for teaching all adults* (rev. ed.). San Francisco, CA: Jossey-Bass.

Zwerling, S. (1976). *Second best: The crisis of the community college.* New York, NY: McGraw-Hill.

8

MANAGING TODAY'S COMMUNITY COLLEGES

A New Era?

PAMELA L. EDDY

This chapter provides an historical perspective of the evolution of management within community colleges. The social and financial context of the community college, as well as the educational aims of these institutions, creates a distinct environment that influences both the ways in which individuals manage and what issues are most salient for institutional managers. Moreover, cultures of community colleges maintain fewer of the traditions typical of universities. Programming that covers only two years of postsecondary education results in a shorter time on campus for students, providing students with a limited window to advocate for change and ultimately creates weaker alumni ties. Teaching staff consist predominantly of adjunct or temporary faculty members who have no or limited focus on research and, as a collective, may not have a major influence on campus management, in spite of the espoused practice of shared governance (Kater & Levin, 2005). Campus administrative leaders are typically not scholars, nor do they share a professional identity with faculty: rather they are managers who respond to demands from the local community, boards of trustees, and state legislatures and policy-makers. The context of the community college itself (Cohen & Brawer, 2008; Levin, 2007)—employment status of its principal labor force, community orientation, governed by state legislation, and comprised of diverse students—influences managerial practices that range from bureaucratic operations to organizational effectiveness.

Initial ideals of management in community colleges formed around the concepts of the institution as a bureaucratic organization (Levin, 1998; Twombly, 1995) that mirrored the management forms of public schools from which a large proportion of community colleges emerged (Brick, 1994). Over time, increased complexity of operations due to expanded mission, demands for accountability, and shifts in faculty personnel and unionization resulted in a different perspective of pressing management issues and conceptions of effective processes (Peterson, 1997). By 2012, research on community college management issues moved the focus to the role of unionization (Linville, Antony, & Hayden, 2011), shifting faculty work (Cejda & Murray, 2010), development of mid-level leadership (Ebbers, Conover, & Samuels, 2010), and the effects of state oversight of

121

the colleges (Ewell, 2011), thus altering the traditional conceptions of management and leadership in the community college.

A topology of leadership eras serves as a template to consider for corresponding management eras (Twombly, 1995). The four eras of leadership include: (1) The Early Years of 1900s–1930s—Great Man Theory; (2) Independence 1940s–1950s; (3) Maturation 1960s–1970s; and (4) Resource Retrenchments and Stabilization 1980s–1990s. A fifth era may be considered for the first decades of the 21st century, namely as leadership in transition that requires multidimensional orientations (Eddy, 2010). The concepts of leadership and management are interconnected, with Twombly's (1995) timeframes of leadership eras complementary to eras of higher education management (Eells, 1931; Kater & Levin, 2002; Koos, 1925; Myran, 1983; Ratcliff, 1994; Richardson, 1972; Richardson, Bracco, Callan, & Finney, 1998). Table 8.1 provides a comparison between the focus of leaders during the various eras relative to management issues that have affected the operations of community colleges. As with any summary, the predominant focus of the eras is presented while recognizing that the lines of demarcation between the periods are not hard and fast. Thus, depending on the culture and context of a community college, the type of management employed may not align precisely with the predominant management practices currently in place.

Management does not occur in a vacuum, as there are other institutional conditions that shape management and affect outcomes. For example, there are considerable differences in an organization dominated by a bureaucratic structure than in one where a political arena is prevalent (Baldridge, Curtis, Ecker, & Riley, 1977). Employee–employer relationships take on formal characteristics—rules, regulations, roles—in a bureaucratic environment and illegitimate and conflict behaviors in a political one (Mintzberg, 1989).

Another perspective, a post-modern one, illuminates the influence of underlying structures on management options and can offer new considerations of approaches to management (Hatch & Cunliffe, 2006; Hickman, 2010). In particular, this perspective allows for a critique of the underlying structures of community colleges that shape actions. Central to post-modernism is the role of power (Foucault, 1982). Power becomes manifested in the organizational structures and roles of institutions, as well as in communication and the value placed on expertise and products. By recognizing the sources of power within their institutions, managers can adjust dysfunctional or deleterious operations, particularly those with imbalances in power, which typically are not addressed when power remains unquestioned.

Table 8.1 Leadership eras and management eras in community colleges

Era	Leadership	Management
1900s–1930s	Great Man leadership—charismatic	Bureaucratic operations
1940s–1950s	Independence—hierarchical	Patriarchic
1960s–1970s	Maturation—building capacity, human resources	Unionization—entrenchment of roles
1980s–1990s	Focus of resource constraints—strategic planning	Shared governance
2000–present	Leadership in transition: multi-dimensional leadership—framing change	Collaboration

MANAGEMENT ERAS

Management practices shifted over time in reaction to changes in the community college. During the establishment of the early junior colleges, the precursors of the community college, bureaucratic management was the prominent framework (Ratcliff, 1994). Bureaucratic forms of management rely on a hierarchy, division of labor, and rules and procedures (Weber, 1946). Emerging from this first management era was a shift to paternalistic management (Maslow, 1943). The founding leaders of the community colleges in the mid-20th century followed the pattern of the "great" leaders that built the first junior colleges, exerting a patriarchal form of leadership and hence management of operations (Brick, 1994). Following this timeframe was the explosive growth of community colleges in the 1960s and early 1970s. This management era is noted for the increased presence of unionization on community college campuses (Hutcheson, 2002) that resulted in a shift of management operations (Richardson, 1972). Instead of a single manager dictating practices, unionized faculty began to assert their voice into management decisions (Chandler & Julius, 1985; Mortimer, 1978). In the 1980s and 1990s, the stabilization of the community college sector and the shift to maintenance of programs during times of fiscal exigency altered roles again. Forms of shared governance gained momentum as a mechanism to address external challenges and to leverage the expertise of the faculty and mid-level leadership (Myran, 1983; Wirth, 1991). Finally, the current era marks a shift in management orientation from a strict top-down approach to collaborative operations (Amey, Jessup-Anger, & Jessup-Anger, 2010). Collaborative management creates different roles for managers, faculty, and leaders (Hickman, 2010).

BUREAUCRATIC ERA—1900s–1930s

The establishment of U.S. community colleges occurred to address particular educational needs and respond to social pressures (Harper, 1903; Ratcliff, 1994). Brick (1994) identified four basic social and economic forces leading to the development of the junior college: "(1) equality of opportunity, (2) use of education to achieve social mobility, (3) technological progress, and (4) acceptance of the concept that education is the producer of social capital" (p. 44). On the one hand, the conception and practices of junior colleges helped meet demands of four-year colleges to provide the first two years of a general liberal arts program (The Changing Role, 2002/2003; Rudolf, 1990). What is commonly considered the nation's first junior college, Joliet Community College, southwest of Chicago, developed in 1901 as a fifth- and sixth-year extension to the established high school curriculum (Cohen & Brawer, 2008).

Yet, on the other hand, this frequently cited rationale for the establishment of the junior college sector relies on a simplistic dependence on the prevalent leadership theory of the day that attributes educational changes to "great men" (Frye, 1992). A major contributing factor in the establishment of junior colleges was the cultural context and local community interactions that created the right environment for establishing this type of college (Ratcliff, 1994). It is the confluence of educational reform efforts, local needs, prevalent political trends, and a certain amount of serendipity that propelled the larger movement of establishing junior colleges.

The utility of bureaucratic management rests on assumptions of rational behaviors and predictability (Gergen, 1992). Yet, a constructivist analytical framework (Hatch &

Cunliffe, 2006) suggests that the establishment and management of the junior college occurred through didactic interactions among the press, community members, and educational leaders (Frye, 1992; Ratcliff, 1994) that were not necessarily rational in practice. The influence of the context and culture of each locale in which a college opened underscores unique histories that are lost in generalizations about the era of formation of community colleges.

The concurrent influences of the burgeoning high school organizational structure and that of four-year colleges contributed to the organization and management of the first junior colleges. Management practices during the early decades of the 1900s adopted elements of classical management theory (Morgan, 2006). Defined roles placed decision-making firmly with top-level college leaders. As a result of the emergence of a centralized workforce as a consequence of industrialization, classical theorists explained how to increase operational efficiencies. Early theorists, such as Fayol, Mooney, and Urwick (as cited in Morgan, 2006), viewed management as a linear process in which rational planning would improve efficiencies. Typically, these theories contained a list of best practices that relied on the chain of command, the division of work, and centralization of authority. The relatively small size of the early junior colleges made this form of management easier to employ as low staff numbers meant simpler tracking and control of employees. Rudolf (1990) identified a more distinct role for college presidents that focused on leadership in contrast to the dual roles colonial presidents maintained in which they were also college faculty. The move to a focus on college leadership vested power in the position of the presidency.

The aftermath of World War I and the booming economy in the 1920s created more rapid expansion of the junior college. Eells (1941) reported the opening of 100 junior colleges between 1901 and 1920, whereas 450 were in operation by 1930 (Cohen & Brawer, 2008). Three states, however, captured 51% of enrollments, specifically California, Texas, and Illinois. The roots of centralized management of the systems in these states, which emerged more fully in the next era, led to structures that facilitated the establishment of colleges in each state system (Yarrington, 1969). More colleges and greater population bases accounted for the higher student numbers in colleges in these three states.

PATRIARCHIC ERA—1940s–1950s

A pivotal moment for community colleges occurred with the release of the report of the President's Commission on Higher Education (1947) that suggested education for students up to grade 14. Another key factor influencing community college development in this era was the Servicemen's Readjustment Act of 1944 (commonly referred to as the G.I. Bill). The combination of these two events provided the momentum that expanded access to higher education for previously excluded populations of students. The Commission report also planted the seeds for a name change from junior colleges to community colleges (Vaughan, 1997) and with the open-access mission, symbolically, these colleges became known as "democracy's college" (Diekhoff, 1950). The 1940s and 1950s set the stage and foundation for the growth period of community colleges in the subsequent decades (Deegan, Tillery, & Associates, 1985).

Colleges became more established in communities as a result, with a growth rate of 57% occurring for public community colleges between 1940 and 1960 (Cohen & Brawer, 2008). The roots of bureaucratic operations shifted to a paternalistic management style in this era. Colleges conformed to management theory that focused on the needs of human resources, with recognition of the need to help employees realize their potential (Maslow, 1943). Organizational leaders were viewed as benevolent and protective of employees, yet they did not share power. Instead, they retained control of decision-making and vision-setting for the college (Nevarez & Wood, 2010). The hierarchy maintained its place in the organization, but employees were no longer viewed as mere cogs in the operation.

During this era community colleges shifted in alignment from high school districts to autonomy.

> [I]n states where statutory provisions existed, except in a few states such as New York, Texas, Mississippi, and California, two-year colleges were legally a part of the public school system as an extension of the high school. One-half had enrollments of under 300 headcount students. (Young, 2002, p. 560)

Community college autonomy and alliance with higher education meant that managers were no longer tethered to the forms of operation utilized at public schools. Furthermore, the increasing size of the institutions meant a change in scale for management, ultimately adding layers to the organizational chart and affecting forms of communication within the colleges and more importantly with newly formed state organizations.

Not only did federal legislation support the need for educational opportunities in local communities (President's Commission on Higher Education, 1947) but also state legislation established an organizational structure for community colleges as separate from public school systems. Legislation also provided opportunities for financial support through taxation (Young, 1951) and financing and managing the financing of community colleges became more central institutional issues.

UNIONIZATION—1960s–1970s

The issue of unionization became prominent on community college campuses beginning in the 1960s as campus faculty flexed their organizing strength. Issues driving unionization efforts included "faculty fear of administration policies, the need for recognition, the size and complexity of the school organization, and job security" (Nelson, 1974, p. 1). Unions in academic settings are situated in a markedly different context relative to industry unions due to the overlapping interests of faculty members and college administrators (Chandler & Julius, 1985).

The fast pace of growth in the community college sector during this era meant that leadership operated with more authoritarian style in order to make decisions rapidly (Chandler & Julius, 1985). Management, in turn, was highly reactive to demands made of it by leaders and state administers (Dill, 1984; Richardson, 1972). Yet, a push back against this directive style of management began as unions and faculty started to advocate a participatory form of governance involving representatives from administration, faculty, and students (Richardson, 1972). During this era, the expansion of unions contributed to managerial behaviors. Among the first community college to unionize was Milwaukee Technical Institute (Hutcheson, 2002). By 1974, of the 212 authorized bargaining agents, 150 were located on community college campuses (Nelson, 1974). A decade later, 35% of all community college faculty members across the country were in a union (Chandler & Julius, 1985) and by 2005, 43% of community college full-time faculty worked on unionized campuses (Cohen & Brawer, 2008). The bulk of unionized community college faculty (60%) work in one of five states: California, Illinois, Washington, New York, and Michigan (Cohen & Brawer, 2008). California and Illinois represent states with the longest, most substantive history with community colleges and also represent states with early state systems of community colleges (Bender, 1975).

Unionization did not occur uniformly across the country, and the prominence of faculty unions in particular states underscores the influence of regional influences. Where prevalent, the onset of collective bargaining at community colleges changed management from a format of paternalistic oversight to negotiation among parties (Ernst, 1975; Lombardi, 1979; Marsee, 1981). Power often shifted in these negotiations, with some research noting how power collected in top leadership positions (Moore, 1981); other research concluding that more power was vested with faculty (Chandler & Julius, 1985); and still others pointing to the power of middle management (Marsee, 1981). These different perspectives highlight that organizational complexity and context matter in governance and management. Here, a political model underscores the role of negotiation among coalitions and highlights how power may collect in any number of locations based on the union contract and internal organizational context (Baldridge et al., 1977). Ultimately, both the rhetoric and presence of unionization and discussion and codification of roles and responsibilities opened the way for conversations regarding shared governance.

Against this backdrop of unionizing efforts on community college campuses, two seminal works on management were published: Mintzberg's (1979) research on patterns in managerial work and Peterson's (1974) review of research regarding the organization and management of higher education. Mintzberg's (1979) work, while not focused upon higher education, provided a means for analyzing the type of management in practice, with his five prototypes ranging from a simple bureaucracy to a professional bureaucracy to adhocracy. Peterson's (1974) review of research found that even though there was an increase in research on organizational issues, the theoretical models were limited, much of the research merely reported descriptive statistics or provided exploratory case studies, and there was not a ready conduit regarding scholarship from different disciplines.

Investigation into the nature of administrative behaviors in higher education (Dill, 1984) concluded that managers spend a great deal of time reacting to issues and rely heavily on verbal skills in interactions with others. Interpersonal skills were noted as critical to the motivation of others. Yet, a reliance on hierarchy in making decisions indicated that bureaucratic management practices continued to exert a stronghold over college operations.

A dilemma for academic administrators was the inability to clearly separate profession-related behavior from the activities of teaching and administration. Given that mid-level leaders at community colleges can and sometimes do have teaching duties, this separation is made more difficult. Dill (1984) concluded that: (1) informal influence and use of networks were important parts of academic administration; (2) academic management was highly intuitive, with less use of data to inform decision-making; and (3) the disciplinary background of the individual influenced the approach a manager took to practice. Community college managers of this era arose largely from the teaching ranks, which could mean K-12 experiences as well. An implication of this orientation to management was a reliance on structure and rules in guiding decision-making (Morgan, 2006).

In the 1960s, community colleges expanded rapidly with a new college opening its doors every two weeks. There were 405 public community colleges in 1960, but by 1980 this number had grown to 1,049 (Cohen & Brawer, 2008). This era expanded the practice of more state control over community colleges (Bender, 1975). Wattenbarger and Bender (1972) advocated for more interaction between individual colleges and state agencies to jointly address issues for community college education. The addition of state-controlling structures meant that local management issues had to take into consideration a check and balance from the overarching state-controlling agency. This level of power over local decision-making created sources of conflict when local goals and aspirations did not match state objectives (Bender, 1976; Morgan, 2006; Richardson, 1972).

Federal legislation also led to changes occurring on community college campuses. The Vocational Education Act of 1963 and the Higher Education Act of 1965 helped to expand the occupational mission of community colleges and opened access to a wider swathe of students. Increased size of operations meant that managers were pushed to address employee issues as well as state and federal requirements dictated by the new legislation. Managerial roles became more complex (Bender, 1975; Richardson, 1972).

The high rate of growth and expansion of community colleges in this timeframe also meant that campuses were involved in establishing facilities of operation. Bender (1977) suggested the evolution of three prototypes of community colleges: the traditional campus-oriented college, the community college without walls, and the contract community college. The evolution of multiple models of community college orientation underscores the attempts by community colleges to meet a wide variety of community needs. Yet, each of these models of operations involves a different focus for management.

The sheer growth of the community college enterprise meant that leaders were younger and had less experience than in the past (Vaughan, 2006). Often, public schools provided many of the founding leaders as community colleges continued to separate themselves from their public education roots. Emerging university programs began to focus attention on training needs for management and leadership (Young, 2002). The structures established under union contracts or due to new campus openings created frameworks of operation that often went unquestioned. In some cases, union contracts articulated broad faculty roles and levels of participation (Chandler & Julius, 1985), whereas in other instances leadership retained authority in most decision-making (Moore, 1981). How campus members made sense (Weick, 1995) of roles and the decision-making process and how leaders framed (Fairhurst & Sarr, 1996) the context of campus plans set the stage for who held power and sway on campus (Foucault, 1982).

SHARED GOVERNANCE—1980s–1990s

The environment of higher education in the decades preceding the millennium was marked with resource constraints, shifting needs by employers of graduates, and less mobility of faculty (Twombly, 1995). The stage was set for a shift from top-down management to notions of shared governance. In this era, shared governance underscored the need for managers and faculty to work together to address institutional problems. Central to this conversation, however, is the use of language (Scott, 1992) and meaning ascribed to the concept of shared governance. On the one hand, shared governance involves investment in joint decision-making and representation of voices of staff and faculty in designing direction of the college (Kater & Levin, 2005). On the other hand, sharing in the creation of a vision and strategy for the college allows not only for the participation of campus members, but also for the sharing of authority (Baker & Associates, 1995; Roueche, 1995). According to Alfred and Carter (1993), successful colleges focused leadership on accountability, involvement, and integration over controlling management practices.

Two significant organizational theories became prominent during this period. Institutional theory (DiMaggio & Powell, 1983) points to the ways that institutions compete for resources, prestige, and legitimacy. Underlying this competition are pressures of conformity, referred to as coercive, normative, and mimetic isomorphism (DiMaggio & Powell, 1983). These pressures include institutional rules and regulations as well as cultural expectations leading to norms and aspirational goals to mimic more prestigious institutions. Resource dependency theory (Pfeffer & Salanick, 1978), in some contrast, focuses more narrowly on the power associated with control of resources, given that institutions such as community colleges are highly dependent upon resources, particularly public resources, for their functioning.

Shared governance occurred against a backdrop of unionization on campus, making the type of decision-making bounded by the ways in which the union contracts were implemented (Bender, 1975; Chandler & Julius, 1985). The coercive institutional pressures (DiMaggio & Powell, 1983) created by roles dictated by union contracts influenced shared governance, with individual faculty losing agency in their roles as campus participants. Faculty passivity enabled authority for decision-making to be more firmly vested in chief executive officers, whether presidents or chancellors (Lucey, 2002). As well, external standards such as state control over funding the institutions contributed to a managerial culture (Levin, 2001).

The last decades of the 20th century were marked again with resource constraints in higher education. As a result, strategic planning strategies borrowed from business were now employed in college settings (Keller, 1983; Leslie & Fretwell, 1996). Myron (1983) advocated for a strategic planning approach for community colleges, noting the need to manage relationships within the community and state governance structures. The change here involved building relationships and framing the issues that were challenging community colleges.

The rhetoric of shared governance also bore witness to an increase in attention to faculty and administrator development (Sorcinelli, Austin, Eddy, & Beach, 2006). The development of employees extends the human resource approach to management and aids in group participation in and acceptance of shared governance systems (Bolman & Deal, 2008). Yet, faculty efforts to participate in shared governance was not an assurance that they would be rewarded for their views; as well, the efficiency of the outcomes of shared governance was questioned (Gilmour, 1991).

COLLABORATION: 2000–PRESENT

As with previous eras, the current century finds community colleges facing a restrictive fiscal environment at the same time that demand for services is on the increase (Boggs, 2004). Shifts in student demographics, combined with a focus on access, push the boundaries of what can be accomplished. As a result, community colleges placed caps or restrictions on enrollment numbers (Boggs, 2004; Phillippe & Mullin, 2011); as well, colleges eliminated programs of study. Although these constraints on community colleges are reminiscent of previous periods of exigency (Twombly, 1995), the national pressures on community colleges to produce more graduates were considerable (Obama, 2009) and community colleges were viewed increasingly as inexpensive alternatives to expensive four-year institutions (Phillippe & Sullivan, 2006).

The multiple demands on community colleges required leaders to rely more on mid-level managers for support (Ebbers et al., 2010). Yet, Fugazzotto (2009) argues that middle-level managers are underutilized in helping institutions develop strategies for improvements. Others have noted that faculty have lost authority as a result of the empowering of managers through union contracts (Rhoades, 1998); and others have lamented the loss of control that community college faculty have over the educational direction of their institutions (Levin, 2007).

Discussions of distributed or collaborative leadership are rooted in assumptions of who holds power and controls resources, and thus decision-making processes. The rhetoric and promotion of collaborative forms of leadership (Hickman, 2010) create implications for managers regarding their views of roles and responsibilities within the institution. A central component of this form of leadership includes relationship building (Wood & Gray, 1991) and communication strategies (Kezar & Lester, 2009). The benefit of creating collaboration in institutions ensures that campus members make localized decisions and contribute to overall planning efforts. Sharing leadership requires trust and transparency of information (Harris, 1995). Research on three sites that use collective leadership (Denis, Lamothe, & Langley, 2001) showed that planned change occurred when the various levels of leadership were connected, but also noted that fragile leadership constellations made sustainability questionable.

Currently, issues facing managers include dealing with multiple demands and organizational oversight that require different managerial approaches. The shift to collaborative decision-making requires agreement on decision-making as well as the recrafting of traditional managerial roles to include different institutional responsibilities. However, the traditional reliance on leader-centered organizations impedes progress due to resistance for sharing authority, largely as a result of lack of trust in, and disregard for the capabilities of, followers (Yukl, 2006). Indeed, California's attempt in 1988 to legislate shared governance did not assure the creation of collegiality, rather the mandate highlighted the political nature of the process and showed that institutional location and culture influenced how governance operated (White, 1998).

CONCLUSIONS

As community colleges grew in both number and size over the last century, they became more complex organizations. Management practices, based upon theories-in-use, adapted to the complexity of the organization, as well as to environmental conditions, such as unionization and state coordination. Of particular note, the role of managers changed in line with both contemporary management practices and societal norms. For example, there was diminution of the role of presidents as authoritarian managers.

Currently, there are several significant pressures on the institution that affect the management of community colleges, most prominently due to state financing trends, which include budget constraints. The decline in funding, coupled with the historically low funding levels for community colleges (National Center for Education Statistics, 2007), serves as a context that requires a markedly different approach to management. Compared to previous periods of financial strain there are low levels of state and local support that have not improved or rebounded to previous levels and to the increased student and public demands for community college response.

Resource dependency theory (Pfeffer & Salancik, 1978) points out that power emanates from the control of institutional resources. College tuition and state funding are the core resources for community colleges (Romano, in press). The lack of management control over these sources of funds creates a constrained context for operations and requires new thinking to move beyond traditional modes of managing. There is little evidence to suggest that funding from the state will increase; colleges' willingness or ability to increase tuition is limited; and faculty members are not poised to obtain external funding. Although there are calls for community colleges to become entrepreneurial (Roueche & Jones, 2005), the effects of these recommendations have yet to be investigated, and it is unclear the extent to which colleges have followed this path. There is recognition both among scholars and practitioners that the financial environment for community colleges is considerably different than it was in the 20th century.

Management now requires planning to address numerous external demands, including increasing college completion (*Achieving the Dream,* 2011; Virginia Higher Education Act, 2011), dealing with a changing faculty base (McCormack, 2008), and meeting compliance requirements emanating from state and federal policy-makers. As noted, management occurs within a particular institutional culture, making it critical for managers to have heightened competency to negotiate among competing players (DiMaggio & Powell, 1983) and to communicate goals and objectives clearly (Fairhurst & Sarr, 1996).

A major area of management involves oversight of faculty work. The trend toward considering education as a commodity versus a public good (Marginson, 2007) alters how faculty look at their work on campus (Levin, 2007). This market-driven perspective gives less power and influence in internal decision-making processes to faculty. With this shift in power relationships, there are different demands on managers.

An approach to address the current conditions of fiscal constraint and altered power relationships builds on using more collaboration and focuses on organizational learning, all in a context of adaptive change. In this scenario, those in management take on leadership roles and greater responsibilities, but at the same time encourage collaboration. Thus, relationships become more central to operations (Beatty & Brew, 2004). Hickman (2010) posits that change in times of chaos and complexity requires collective leadership because this form of leadership creates the adaptive space required for change (Heifetz, 1994). Managers are linchpins in collective leadership as they sit at the nexus of positions between staff and leadership and move most freely between multiple levels of the organization.

Successful managers have the potential to become facilitators and relationship builders as organizations move toward more collaborative forms of operation, calling on the talents of the full range of employees within the college (Peterson, 1997). A movement to collaborative leadership (Denis et al., 2001; Hickman, 2010) shifts roles and expectations of managers and conceptions of management in community colleges. This form of adaptive change requires a break from past practice, including the questioning of the power basis behind organizational decision-making. The demands and complexity of community colleges require that practitioners ask different questions and organize institutions in new ways.

This approach of the questioning of underlying assumptions and structures should be employed by scholars as well. Research on community colleges is more limited than four-year colleges and universities and often takes the form of "show-and-tell" types of articles that showcase best practices on campus. Community college scholars need to focus on critiques of underlying causes that contribute to organizational outcomes and recognize the sources of power and control. Practitioners could then address these issues and achieve greater change.

Yet, the historical roots of bureaucratic management in community colleges create a strong legacy and entrenched perspective on operations. In spite of the rhetoric of changes in practice over time toward shared governance and collaboration, the notion of top-down management continues to maintain a strong foothold in community colleges. Change will occur when accepted practice is questioned, assumptions brought to light and deconstructed, and power shared in more levels of the organization. The changing of the guard of many long-serving college presidents and chief academic officers provides an opportunity to recast the management of community colleges (McNair, Duree, & Ebbers, 2011). On the one hand, an optimistic perspective is that new blood in the leadership and management ranks will bring about change. On the other hand, a look through the various management eras indicates that in spite of changes in management practices, power remains firmly rooted in top-level leaders. The current crisis in higher education, however, may provide just the motivation to break away from old management patterns, suggesting that there may indeed be a new era for community colleges.

QUESTIONS FOR DISCUSSION

1. What theories of power and politics apply to community college leadership?
2. What components of power behaviors contribute to organizational outcomes?
3. How is adaptive change related to theories of power?
4. In what ways has unionization affected community college management?

REFERENCES

Achieving the Dream. (2011). Retrieved from http://www.achievingthedream.org

Alfred, R. L., & Carter, P. (1993). Rethinking the business of management. In R. L. Alfred & P. N. Carter (Eds.), *Changing managerial imperatives. New Directions for Community Colleges, no. 84* (pp. 7–19). San Francisco, CA: Jossey-Bass.

Amey, M. J., Jessup-Anger, E., & Jessup-Anger, J. (2010). Community college governance: What matters and why? In R. C. Cloud & S. T. Kater (Eds.), *Community college governance. New Directions for Community Colleges, no. 141* (pp. 5–14). San Francisco, CA: Jossey-Bass.

Baker, G., & Associates. (1995). *Team building for quality: Transitions in the American community college.* Washington, DC: American Association of Community Colleges.

Baldridge, J. V., Curtis, D. V., Ecker, G. P, & Riley, G. L. (1977). Alternative models of governance in higher education. In G. L. Riley & J. V. Baldridge (Eds.), *Governing academic organizations* (pp. 2–25). Berkeley, CA: McCutchan.

Beatty, B. R., & Brew, C. R. (2004). Trusting relationships and emotional epistemologies: A foundational leadership issue. *School Leadership and Management, 24*(3), 329–356.

Bender, L. W. (1975). *The states, communities, and control of the community college: Issues and recommendations.* Alexandria, VA: AACJC Publications.

Bender, L. W. (1976). *Forces which damage constructive relationships from the two-year college system perspective.* Denver, CO: State Higher Education Executive Officers Association.

Bender, L. W. (1977). *A third-version of the community college: The contract college. An analysis for state planners.* Denver, CO: State Higher Education Executive Officers Association.

Boggs, G. (2004). Community colleges in a perfect storm. *Change Magazine, 36*(6), 6–11.

Bolman, L. G., & Deal, T. E. (2008). *Reframing organizations: Artistry, choice, and leadership* (4th ed.). San Francisco, CA: Jossey-Bass.

Brick, M. (1994). From forum and focus for the junior college movement. In J. L. Ratliff, S. Schwarz, & L. H. Ebbers (Eds.), *Community colleges: ASHE reader series* (2nd ed.) (pp. 43–56). Boston, MA: Pearson.

Cejda, B. D., & Murray, J. P. (Eds.). (2010). Hiring the next generation of faculty. *New Directions for Community Colleges, no. 152* (pp. 1–92). San Francisco, CA: Jossey-Bass.

Chandler, M. K., & Julius, D. J. (1985). *A study of governance in the unionized two-year institution.* Eric Document ED266821.

Cohen, A. M., & Brawer, F. B. (2008). *The American community college* (5th ed.). San Francisco, CA: Jossey-Bass.

Deegan, W., Tillery, D., & Associates. (Eds.). (1985). *Renewing the American community college.* San Francisco, CA: Jossey-Bass.

Denis, J., Lamothe, L., & Langley, A. (2001). The dynamics of collective leadership and strategic change in pluralistic organizations. *Academy of Management Journal, 44,* 809–837.

Diekhoff, J. (1950). *Democracy's college: Higher education in the local community.* New York, NY: Harper and Brother Publishers.

Dill, D. D. (1984). The nature of administrative behavior in higher education. *Educational Administrative Quarterly, 20*(3), 69–99.

DiMaggio, P. J., & Powell, W. W. (1983). The iron cage revisited: Institutional isomorphism and collective rationality in organizational fields. *American Sociological Review, 48,* 147–160.

Ebbers, L., Conover, K. S., & Samuels, A. (2010). Leading from the middle: Preparing leaders for new roles. *New Directions for Community Colleges, no. 149* (pp. 59–64). San Francisco, CA: Jossey-Bass.

Eddy, P. L. (2010). *Community college leadership: A multidimensional model for leading change.* Sterling, VA: Stylus Publishing, LLC.

Eells, W. C. (1931). *The junior college.* Boston, MA: Houghton Mifflin.

Eells, W. C. (1941). *Present status of terminal education.* Washington, DC: American Association of Junior Colleges.

Ernst, R. J. (Ed.). (1975). Adjusting to collective bargaining. *New Directions for Community Colleges, no. 11* (pp. 1–105). San Francisco, CA: Jossey-Bass.

Ewell, P. T. (2011), Accountability and institutional effectiveness in the community college. *New Directions for Community Colleges, no. 153* (pp. 23–36). San Francisco, CA: Jossey-Bass.

Fairhurst, G. T., & Sarr, R. A. (1996). *The art of framing: Managing the language of leadership.* San Francisco, CA: Jossey-Bass.

Foucault, M. (1982). The subject and power. In H. Dreyfus & P. Rabinow (Eds.), *Michel Foucault: Beyond structuralism and hermeneutics* (pp. 208–226). Chicago, IL: Chicago University Press.

Frye, J. H. (1992). *The vision of the public junior college, 1900–1940: Professional goals and popular aspirations. Contributions to the study of education, no. 51.* Westport, CT: Greenwood Publishing Group, Inc.

Fugazzotto, S. J. (2009). College and university middle management and institutional strategy. *College & University, 85*(1), 34–39, 41–43.

Gergen, K. (1992). Organizational theory in the postmodern era. In M. Reed & M. Hughes (Eds.), *Rethinking organization: New directions in organization theory and analysis* (pp. 207–226). Newbury Park, CA: Sage.

Gilmour, J., Jr. (1991). Participative governance bodies in higher education: Report of a national study. *New Directions for Higher Education, no. 75* (pp. 27–39). San Francisco, CA: Jossey-Bass.

Harper, W. R. (1903). *President's annual report, University of Chicago, July 1902.* Chicago, IL: University of Chicago Decennial Publications of the University.

Harris, Z. M. (1995, April). *Leadership for creating community within institutions.* Paper presented at the annual convention of the American Association of Community Colleges, Minneapolis, MN.

Hatch, M. J., & Cunliffe, A. (2006). *Organizational theory: Modern, symbolic, and postmodern perspectives.* New York, NY: Oxford Press.

Heifetz, R. A. (1994). *Leadership without easy answers.* Cambridge, MA: Harvard University Press.

Hickman, G. R. (2010). *Leading change in multiple contexts: Concepts and practices in organizational, community, political, social, and global change settings.* Thousand Oaks, CA: Sage Publications.

Higher Education Act. (1965). Pub. L. No. 89–329.

Hutcheson, P. (2002). Faculty unions. In J. J. F. Forest & K. Kinser (Eds.), *Higher education in the United States: An encyclopedia* (pp. 235–237). Santa Barbara, CA: ABC-CLIO, Inc.

Kater, S., & Levin, J. S. (2002, April). *Shared governance in community colleges in a global economy.* Paper presented at the Annual Meeting for the American Educational Research Association, New Orleans.

Kater, S., & Levin, J. S. (2005). Shared governance in the community college. *Community College Journal of Research & Practice, 29,* 1–23.

Keller, G. (1983). *Academic strategy: The management revolution in higher education.* Baltimore, MD: The Johns Hopkins University Press.

Kezar, A. J., & Lester, J. (2009). *Organizing higher education for collaboration: A guide for leaders.* San Francisco, CA: Jossey-Bass.

Koos, L. V. (1925). *The junior-college movement.* New York, NY: Ginn and Company.

Leslie, D. W., & Fretwell, E. K., Jr. (1996). *Wise moves in hard times: Creating and managing resilient colleges and universities.* San Francisco, CA: Jossey-Bass.

Levin, J. S. (1998). Making sense of organizational change. In J. S. Levin (Ed.), *Leadership in an era of change. New Directions for Community Colleges, no. 102* (pp. 43–54). San Francisco, CA: Jossey-Bass.

Levin, J. S. (2001). Public policy, community colleges, and the path to globalization. *Higher Education, 42*(2), 237–262.

Levin, J. S. (2007). Globalizing higher education: Neo-liberal policies and faculty work. In J. Smart & W. Tierney (Eds.), *Handbook of higher education, 22* (pp. 451–496). Norwell, MA: Kluwer Academic Publishers.

Linville, J., Antony, J. S., & Hayden, R. (2011). Unionization and perceived control among community college faculty. *Community College Journal of Research and Practice, 35*(4), 330–351.

Lombardi, J. (1979). *Changing administrative relations under collective bargaining. Junior college resource review.* Los Angeles, CA: ERIC Clearinghouse for Junior Colleges.

Lucey, C. A. (2002). Civic engagement, shared governance, and community colleges. *Academe, 88*(4), 27–31.

Marginson, S. (2007). The public/private divide in higher education: A global revision. *Higher Education: The International Journal of Higher Education and Educational Planning, 53*(3), 307–333.

Marsee, S. E. (1981). Managers have rights, too. *Community and Junior College Journal, 51*(7), 35–17.

Maslow, A. H. (1943). A theory of motivation. *Psychological Review, 50*(4), 370–396.

McCormack, E. (2008). Community colleges hope to keep aging professors in the classroom. *Chronicle of Higher Education, 54*(40), A14.

McNair, D. E., Duree, C. A., & Ebbers, L. (2011). If I knew then what I know now: Using the leadership competencies developed by the American Association of Community Colleges to prepare community college presidents. *Community College Review, 39*(1), 3–25.

Mintzberg, H. (1979). *The structuring of organizations.* New York, NY: Prentice Hall.

Mintzberg, H. (1989). *Mintzberg on management: Inside our strange world of organizations.* New York, NY: The Free Press.

Moore, A. J. (1981, February). *Collective bargaining in higher education: Its impact upon leadership styles, quality faculty and programs.* Paper presented at the Annual Meeting of the American Association of Colleges for Teacher Education, Detroit, MI.

Morgan, G. (2006). *Images of organizations.* Thousand Oaks, CA: Sage.

Mortimer, K. P. (1978, May). *A survey of American experience with faculty collective bargaining.* Paper presented at the International Intervisitational Program in Educational Administration, Vancouver, BC.

Myron, G. A. (Ed.). (1983). Strategic management in the community college. *New Directions for Community Colleges, no. 44* (pp. 7–20). San Francisco, CA: Jossey-Bass.

National Center for Education Statistics. (2007). *Digest of Education Statistics: 2007* (NCES No. 2008–022). Washington, DC: U.S. Department of Education.

Nelson, H. H. (1974). *Faculty collective bargaining.* Unpublished report. Fort Lauderdale, FL: Nova University.

Nevarez, C., & Wood, J. L. (2010). *Community college leadership: Theory, practice, and change.* New York, NY: Peter Lang Publishing, Inc.

Obama, B. (2009). *The American graduation initiative.* Washington, DC: The White House.

Peterson, M. W. (1974). Organization and administration in higher education: Sociological and socio-psychological perspectives. In F. N. Kerlinger & J. B. Carroll (Eds.), *Review of research in education* (pp. 296–347). Itasca, IL: F. E. Peacock.

Peterson, M. W. (1997). Using contextual planning to transform institutions. In M. Peterson, D. Dill, L. A. Mets, & Associates (Eds.), *Planning and management for a changing environment* (pp. 127–157). San Francisco, CA: Jossey-Bass.

Pfeffer, J., & Salancik, G. R. (1978). *The external control of organizations: A resource dependence perspective.* Newbury Park, CA: Sage.

Phillippe, K., & Mullin, C. (2011). *Community college estimated growth: Fall 2010.* Washington, DC: American Association of Community Colleges.

Phillippe, K. A., & Sullivan, L. G. (2006). *National profile of community colleges: Trends & statistics.* Washington, DC: American Association of Community Colleges.

President's Commission on Higher Education. (1947). *Higher education for American democracy.* Washington, DC: U.S. Government Printing Office.

Ratcliff, J. L. (1994). "First" public junior colleges in an age of reform. In J. L. Ratcliff, S. Schwarz, & L. H. Ebbers (Eds.), *Community colleges: ASHE reader series.* Needham Heights, MA: Simon & Schuster Custom Publishing.

Rhoades, G. (1998). *Managed professionals: Unionized faculty and restructuring academic labor.* Albany, NY: State University of New York Press.

Richardson, R. C. (Ed.). (1972). *Governance for the two-year college.* Englewood Cliffs, NJ: Prentice-Hall.

Richardson, R. C., Bracco, K. R., Callan, P. M., & Finney, J. E. (1998). *Higher education governance: Balancing institutional and market influences.* San Jose, CA: National Center for Public Policy and Higher Education.

Romano, R. (in press). Looking behind community college budgets for future policy considerations. *Community College Review.*

Roueche, J. E. (1995). *The company we keep: Collaboration in the community college.* Washington, DC: American Association of Community Colleges.

Roueche, J. E., & Jones, B. R. (Eds.). (2005). *The entrepreneurial community college.* Washington, DC: The American Association of Community Colleges.

Rudolf, F. (1990). *The American college and university: A history.* New York, NY: A. Knopf.

Scott, W. R. (1992). *Organizations: Rational, natural and open systems* (3rd ed.). Englewood Cliffs, NJ: Prentice-Hall.

Servicemen's Readjustment Act of 1944. P.L. 78–346, 58.

Sorcinelli, M. D., Austin, A. E., Eddy, P. L., & Beach, A. L. (2006). *Creating the future of faculty development: Learning from the past, understanding the present.* Bolton, MA: Anker Press.

The changing role of the community college. (2002/2003, Winter). *Occupational Outlook Quarterly, 46*(4), 14–21.

Twombly, S. B. (1995). Gendered images of community college leadership: What messages they send. *New Directions for Community Colleges, no. 89* (pp. 67–77). San Francisco, CA: Jossey-Bass.

Vaughan, G. B. (1997). The community college's mission and milieu: Institutionalizing community-based programming. In E. J. Boone &Associates (Eds.), *Community leadership through community-based programming* (pp. 21–58). Washington, DC: Community College Press.

Vaughan, G. B. (2006). *The community college story* (3rd ed.). Washington, DC: The American Association of Community Colleges.

Virginia Higher Education Act. (2011). §§ 23–38.87:10 (CHAP0869).

Wattenbarger, J. L., & Bender, L. W. (1972). Challenge ahead: State-level control. *Junior College Journal, 42*(9), 17–20.

Weber, M. (1946). *From Max Weber: Essays in sociology.* Edited and translated by H. H. Gerth and C. Wright Mills. London: Oxford University Press.

Weick, K. E. (1995). *Sensemaking in organizations.* Thousand Oaks, CA: Sage.

Weisman, I. M., & Vaughan, G. B. (2007). *The community college presidency 2006.* Washington, DC: Community College Press.

White, K. (1998). Shared governance in California. In J. S. Levin (Ed.), *Organizational changein the community college: A ripple or a sea change? New Directions for Community Colleges, no.102* (pp. 19–29). San Francisco, CA: Jossey-Bass.

Wirth, P. L. (1991). *Shared governance: Promises and perils.* Maryville, CA: Yuba Community College District.

Wood, D. J., & Gray, B. (1991). Toward a comprehensive theory of collaboration. *Journal of Applied Behavioral Science, 27*(2), 139–162.

Yarrington, R. (1969). *Junior colleges: 50 states/50 years.* Washington, DC: American Association of Junior Colleges.

Young, R. J. (1951). *An analysis and evaluation of general legislation pertaining to the public junior college.* (Unpublished doctoral dissertation.) University of Colorado at Boulder, CO.

Young, R. J. (2002). From persuasion to accommodation in public two-year college development. *Community College Journal of Research and Practice, 26*(7–8), 559–572.

Yukl, G. A. (2006). *Leadership in organizations* (6th ed.). Upper Saddle River, NJ: Prentice Hall.

9

LEADERSHIP

Community College Transitions

MARILYN J. AMEY

In recognizing the changing contexts and environments for community college leadership, this chapter interrogates the extent to which contemporary theories and leadership constructions provide effective perspectives on and strategies for leaders of these institutions. This examination necessarily includes discussion of the leadership pipeline, how it has evolved (or not) over the last 30 or more years since the explosion of leadership development programs in the early 1970s that prepared administrators who occupied senior positions, and who shaped the climate of college campuses and leader expectations among campus constituents. These factors have, in part, affected access to senior-level positions and opportunities for leadership for White women, people of color, those with less traditional backgrounds such as occupational and workforce disciplines, college development, and those without college teaching experience.

The confluence of climate, expectations, and labor market sets a context for how we think about leaders and leadership in the present. The chapter evaluates the different strategies for and theoretical understandings of leadership. Into the mix of more traditional management-based leadership practices well documented in the literature are leadership strategies and theories that are grounded in cognitive theory, intuition and sense making, organizational development and chaos, emotional intelligence, change and entrepreneurialism, adaptive work and collaboration, and intercultural competence. These recent leadership understandings may reflect more accurately the gender, race, and ethnic changes in community college leaders, and they offer alternative understandings through which leaders can effectively shape the direction of community colleges.

LEADING UP TO THE PRESENT: THE CONTEXT, ASSUMPTIONS, AND PATHWAYS OF COMMUNITY COLLEGE LEADERS

The Early Decades of Leadership

Early leadership writing in higher education, as in the private sector, was predominantly focused on White men and the imagery and rhetoric of the Great Man theory of

135

leadership. Those who wrote about and studied community college leaders in the mid-20th century, including among others Bogue (1950), Tillery and Deegan (1985), and Brint and Karabel (1989), articulated the same sense of college leadership. Presidents during the early decades of community colleges were described as missionaries and pioneers leading a movement, and often described in military language with imagery such as generals and intellectual commanders who led the battle to establish this sector and intended to uplift those in society previously denied access to higher education (Brint & Karabel, 1989).

In many respects the leaders of the early community college movement and founding presidents were engaged in a form of "battle" to gain acceptance and credibility for a new breed of education, particularly in areas of the country long dominated by highly selective private institutions. Brint and Karabel (1989, p. 35) go so far as to describe it as storming the "New England citadel." These early presidents and college administrators led from their position of formal authority, from the top down; they were autocratic and bureaucratic, which might have been understandable in the context of the creation of new institutions and systems. They were a singular force on their campuses, charismatic, take-charge builders bent on transforming institutions.

Although language may have changed slightly throughout the 1960s–1990s, the underlying premises about leadership remained intact, as did the demographics of leaders (White, male, mid-50s). New colleges continued to be created in the early 1960s while those established previously were maturing and looking for a shift away from the commander orientation of presidents to more inclusion of faculty in decision-making (Richardson, Blocker, & Bender, 1972). Organizational stability and maturity led to a focus on management strategies, reinforcing core missions, defining new enterprises, and developing efficient structures and processes. At the same time as leaders looked to management theories, some community college scholars focused outward and into the future, urging presidents to create something new from their colleges rather than tinkering around the edges of reform and change. Roueche, Baker, and Rose (1989) profiled "Blue chipper," transformational community college presidents whose visions were held up as examples of the next wave of leadership to move the sector toward organizational renewal (Cameron, 1984).

Researchers have cataloged the challenges facing presidents in the 1990s to lead colleges—without having to return to the images of the Great Man that were exclusionary to those in the system aspiring to senior administrative roles—such as a growing number of White women and people of color (Amey & Twombly, 1992). Lester (2008) and Townsend (1995, 2008) are among those scholars who acknowledged that the demographic shifts within the greater society as well as within higher education itself required changes in models and theories of leadership. Throughout the 1990s, business and industry scholars recognized the same trends in demographics as well as the same transitions in organizational development. Senge's (1990) writing on the learning organizations created a shift in how leaders needed to be seen: not sitting in judgment on high with a book of answers to implement, but rather as critical thinkers involved in examining issues more thoroughly and creating environments where everyone would assume, at least in part, a learner identity (O'Banion, 1997). These newer constructions of organizations and, therefore, of leadership invited labels such as shared leadership, webs of leadership, networks, and flattened hierarchies, many of which are in use currently (Alfred, 2008; Amey, 2007; Eddy & Cox, 2008; Kezar, Carducci, & Contreras-

McGavin, 2006). As will be examined later in this chapter, change in rhetoric does not necessarily lead to inclusive beliefs about leadership, but the evolution or the cyclical development of leadership frames in community colleges lays a foundation for what might be adopted in the future.

Leadership Pipeline, the Labor Market, and Succession Planning

The 1990s also saw the onset of a change in the leadership pipeline and the labor market that pushed against the conceptions of leaders heretofore prevalent in community colleges. The founding (male) presidents were aging and retirement forecasts were abundant, leaving questions as to who would assume college presidencies and what kinds of leaders would be sought (Amey & Twombly, 1992; Boggs, 2003; Shults, 2001). White women and people of color were entering the community college labor market in greater numbers (Weisman & Vaughan, 2007) hence diversity in the pool from which future leaders might be selected provided some of the incentive for new leadership models to emerge. White women and people of color did not necessarily see themselves in the leadership images of the founding fathers and looked for alternative ways to be leaders in community colleges (Lester, 2008; Townsend, 1995, 2008).

Although significant turnover in senior leadership has been forecasted for a decade (Amey & VanDerLinden, 2002; Shults, 2001), the tidal wave of retirements has not occurred as predicted for numerous reasons including individual decisions to work longer, economic changes that affect pensions, and lack of succession planning. Yet, the conditions of a multimodal labor market create challenges and opportunities for community colleges to (re-)consider leadership, what it means, how it is enacted, and who will be involved. The labor market might be described as multimodal because there remains a senior tier of administrators—presidents and vice presidents—many of whom have been leading for a long time (Amey & VanDerLinden, 2002). Moore, Martorana, and Twombly's (1985) comprehensive national study of community college leaders in 1984 found that, typically, those who were presidents at that time began their careers in public schools. Upon entering the community college, would-be presidents became faculty, then moved into academic administration and climbed the rungs to the presidency. As the college mission has evolved, so have the paths to the presidency (Moore et al., 1985).

In replicating the Moore et al. study (1985), Amey, VanDerLinden, and Brown (2002) found that the leadership pipeline was confounded by a change in identity and mission. As community colleges moved away from the "junior college" culture in which public school experience was valued as a launching pad for the college presidency, various paths emerged out of many areas of the college including vocational/occupational education, student services, and, even more recently, institutional advancement and fund raising (Amey et al., 2002). Yet, in 2007, 62% of community college presidents were faculty at one time in their careers (American Council on Education, 2007). The traditional leadership succession plan has been eroded by similarities in professional (and chronological) age of presidents and their immediate subordinates such that vice presidents who are often the same age, or quite similar in age to their retiring president counterpart (Amey & VanDerLinden, 2002; Duree, 2008). This alone makes internal promotions into presidencies from senior academic administration more challenging. In fact, Weisman and Vaughan (2007) found that only 35% of sitting presidents were hired from within their current institution.

The number of prospective presidents who have had a previous presidency also creates unique dynamics in the labor market. Boards of trustees, looking for evidence of particular experiences and political and fiscal savvy, are often quite taken with the chance to hire a sitting president. This does not cultivate significant change in the presidential pool or access to opportunities for those within the college to prepare to assume senior positions when the opportunities arise (Amey & VanDerLinden, 2002; Shults, 2001; Weisman & Vaughan, 2007).

In part, because of this practice, community colleges have not reached their potential as inclusive environments for non-traditional academic leaders, including White women and people of color (Amey et al., 2002; Opp & Gosetti, 2002; Townsend, 2008). Even so, the backgrounds and experiences of community college presidents are considerably different from their predecessors, as are the demographics of faculty and administrators within the college from which future senior leaders may come. The next generation of college leaders may have different expectations for their roles and their lives (Phelan, 2005) and as more enter community colleges, leadership models that represent the ideal worker who puts the job first all the time (Williams, 2000) will likely go by the way (Bailey, 2008). At the same time, when boards of trustees, community members, and college citizens expect that the presidency is 24/7, for example, it is possible that fewer will choose to pursue the presidency and those who do may be judged unsuccessful because they are enacting the role differently from the missionary pioneers of their predecessors. Regardless of the route taken, both institutional and scholarly understanding of the learning needs of community college leaders, how they change as they advance through multiple pathways to the presidency (or not), and how leaders' needs are similar to and different from those we have understood in the past are important to providing the support needed for those in place and for preparing those who need to be ready to take on the leadership challenge (Amey et al., 2002).

Leadership Development as a Form of Succession Planning

Changes in the leadership pipeline suggest a need to go beyond the typical routes to generate pools of leader candidates and to place potentially interested persons into the queue, not only for presidencies but also for other leadership roles (Amey et al., 2002; Shults, 2001). More closely linking leadership development to succession planning can be strategic for the institutions (Piland & Wolf, 2003). The American Association of Community Colleges (AACC), the American Council on Education, and other state, regional, and local entities have invested in leadership development and in studying how to support the cultivation of future leaders more effectively (Patton, 2003). Because of labor market issues and the fiscal limitations of state economies for the supporting of external consultants, "grow your own" programs have become more common in the last decade.

These initiatives must be intentional to be effective, and this is especially important for within-college leadership development programs that Wallin (2006) found are typically more haphazard, temporary, and disconnected versions. Unlike earlier community college eras when the career path was linear, currently it is more commonplace for senior leaders to fall into their position by happenstance. They do not identify with or intend to pursue administrative positions, and thus they often do not take part in institution-based opportunities until after they are in positions of authority (Garza-Mitchell & Eddy, 2008). Even with good intent by the college, the context for the individual is typically that they learn on the job (Garza-Mitchell & Eddy, 2008; VanDerLinden, 2004). Given this reality, one new position gaining ground is that colleges would be better off to ensure that everyone is prepared for leadership, rather than institutions relying on a pipeline for future leader preparation. Programs such as the Leadership Institute for a New Century, designed for women and minorities, and the Community College Leadership Initiative Consortium, focused on early career, and mid-level professionals, have been designed with the purpose of grooming future senior leaders, with the currency of information and strategy for use in the present (Iowa State University, n.d.). In this way, colleges identify people not yet in positional authority to ensure they are ready to assume leadership positions when the time and openings come. This form of succession planning supports broader college capacity building.

Thinking Forward in the Changing Context of Community College Leadership

The dynamic internal and external forces that confront community college leaders over-tax outdated structures and processes, outmoded instructional delivery systems, antiquated ways of servicing students, and recalcitrant faculty who do not respond to the increasingly diverse needs of a diverse society of learners (Riggs, 2000). Riggs (2000) argues for a different conception of the fundamental purposes of community colleges and recommends the re-creation of the systems that support these missions. This argument also entails new approaches to leadership including the recruitment, training, and preparation of leaders. The communities and constituents that community colleges serve continue to change, making traditional responses inadequate. Likely, these external community alterations fuel the calls for different understandings of leadership among practitioners (Boggs, 2003). For example, the concept of leader as expert is associated with past and antiquated practices rather than with contemporary conditions where taking risks, learning from errors, acknowledging potentials, and mediating internal tensions—all leading to new understandings of the circumstances and effective strategies—are actions more aligned with needed contemporary leadership (Amey, 2005; Heifetz, 2004).

In the context of increasing diversity of learners, declining state and local resources, mounting competition for service delivery, new and different calls for accountability, and seemingly boundless expansion of constituents, community college leaders are urged by scholars to help institutional members move toward strategic thinking (Alfred, 2008; Cameron, 1984; Peterson, 1997). Strategic thinking requires cultural adaptation of the organization in order to engage employees in mutually beneficial outcomes and processes that are understood and able to be communicated within and outside of the college (Chaffee, 1985). Those leading help others see the importance of thinking complexly in order to deal with complex problems and the need for second-order change (Amey, 2010; Argyris & Schön, 1978) in order to address the challenges posed. Typically, this kind of organizational work is time-consuming and does not result in quick fixes demanded by the circumstances; rather, this kind of work yields more sustainable and strategic changes and decisions (Alfred, 2008; Amey, 2005; Amey & Brown, 2004; Boggs 2003).

LEADERSHIP THEORIES "RECONSIDERED"

The changing contexts that confront community college leaders suggest that they may be well served if both practitioners and scholars consider new theories of leadership. The

origins of these theories vary, but they present different options for leadership orientations and practice that may be more appropriate to the complex contemporary community college rather than relying on the traditional bureaucratic theories of the mid-1900s
and earlier. Within this mix of traditional management-based leadership practices are
those ideas grounded in other disciplines such as cognitive sciences and organizational
development. For the purposes of this discussion, they are grouped in two overarching categories: individually oriented leadership theories that focus on the person first
and organizationally oriented leadership theories that focus on the collective/group or
institution first.

Individually Oriented Leadership Theories

Cognitive Theory

One leadership approach gaining ground in the literature is referred to as cognitive theory. Cognitive theory focuses on the thought processes of individuals. It seeks to understand how individuals attribute actions and outcomes to leaders, and underscores the
importance of perception and cognition to leadership (Kezar et al., 2006). We process
information in particular ways given the frameworks through which we see the world,
for example, bureaucratic or collegial. Leaders benefit from using multiple frames to
understand their organizations, behaviors, and actions (Birnbaum, 1988; Bolman &
Deal, 2008). Cognitive theorists posit that it is important to recognize that everyone and
every area within the college does not see the world in the same way and thus leaders
need to respond accordingly, taking "the other" into account. Amey (1992) and Kuhnert
and Lewis (1989) indicate that the leader needs to be responsive to the cognitive orientations of followers, too, in order to help them understand why decisions are made and
certain events and activities need to occur.

The principles articulated in cognitive leadership theories are important for leaders
of complex organizations, particularly when they address complex problems such as
those facing community colleges. In cognitive theory, emphasis is placed on how leaders
think about the role of leadership, including the role of president, and accounting for the
different ways in which leaders approach problems. For example, Eddy's (2003) study
of community college presidents demonstrated that the same problem (a technology-
based consortium) could be viewed from a visionary frame by one president, which was
characterized by futuristic orientation with potential gains for the campus, or from an
operational frame by another president, where actions entail problem-solving. Cognitive leadership theories respect both difference and importance of difference, regardless
of the origin of the difference.

Those who study leadership from a cognitive perspective emphasize mental maps
(Senge, 1990, 1998) and cognitive schema, which are ways of organizing interpretations
and responses to situations. These maps and schema are often automatic responses that
cause one to filter information based on held beliefs and assumptions and, as a result,
can preclude the recognition of uniqueness as well as difference in the interpretations
of behaviors and conditions. These maps and schema are not gender specific, but they
emanate from the ways in which individuals make meaning of lived experiences, which
may include gendered factors (Amey, 1992). Self-reflection is a critical component of
cognitive leadership theory so that leaders can incorporate new ideas into their cognitive maps (Amey, 1992; Senge, 1998).

As a result of the way one thinks about problems and issues, different strategies come into play, tools are brought to bear, and postures are taken (defensive or offensive). The development of what is referred to in the literature as a learning organization and a learning environment for all members of the college is an organizational priority when behaviors follow from this perspective (Amey, 2005; O'Banion, 1997). One derivative of this approach is the cognitive team (Bensimon & Neumann, 1993), which is different than teams put together based on position and bureaucratic authority. Rather than relying on titles and reporting structures as a basis for selection of future leaders, which has often been the norm in community colleges and other higher education institutions, the leader draws on worldviews, organizational perspectives, and cognitive orientations of potential group members in constituting teams and work groups. The practical goal is that the leader needs to enable the best ideas to surface through a process of informed and rational dialogue and cognitive interpretation (Amey, 2005; Bensimon & Neumann, 1993). The advantages provided through cognitive leadership are considerable. The time investment in cognitive leadership, however, may be counter to the time pressures for rapid decisions and performance measures faced by college presidents (Boggs, 2003). Leading, here, is viewed as an ongoing negotiation between innovative (cognitive challenges) and traditional thinking (intellectual support) (Amey, 2005).

Sense Making

Closely tied to cognitive frames is the idea of sense making. In 1978, Argyris and Schön took leader and member sense making and cognitive mapping into account when proposing how to foster more broadly defined organizational learning. Sense making accounts for how we understand phenomena, and the variations in sense making explain why members of the same organization can view a circumstance or challenge differently (Weick, 1995). Underlying schema and often subconscious core values of leaders are critical to how their leadership will unfold (Eddy, 2010); so too are the underlying schema and core values of college members key to how they will respond to leadership initiatives and college priorities. The cognitive maps of community college members differ from each other, and in effective leadership there is a need for deeply held assumptions and beliefs to be made conscious, interrogated, and unpacked for their meaning. An important characteristic of cognitive theories, then, is making more conscious the ethical and value drivers of leadership and of organizational members. Fairhurst and Sarr (1996) and Kuhnert and Lewis (1998) suggest that leaders have to make sense first for themselves before they can help others make sense of phenomena. Those who espouse sense making affirm that helping to develop understanding is a leadership responsibility, which leads to a focus on activities such as communication, semiotics, and symbolism (Amey, 1992, 2005; Eddy, 2003, 2010).

Knowing how to frame issues and ideas for others is important, but it is not the same as charismatic communication (Eddy, 2003), which was a characteristic advocated in the Great Man leadership models in community colleges (Roueche et al., 1989). Sense making as a leadership perspective suggests that leaders understand how, what, and when to communicate, behaviors that transcend the persona of the speaker. The staying power of sense making and symbolic leadership is increased if the leader taps into deeply held member values rather than playing only to surface rhetoric and faddish preferences. By having these more complete understandings of the value of cognitive and sense-making approaches the leader is able to help others act, take responsibility, and work on behalf of college initiatives because they understand and share in the meaning of the enterprise. Alignment between leader and follower in terms of cognitive frames and sense making leads to stronger organizational outcomes because members throughout the college have similar understandings of issues, directions, and opportunities as the leaders (Amey, Eddy, & Campbell, 2010; Eddy, 2003, 2010; Kezar et al., 2006).

Framing and sense making take place through a variety of tools or cultural artifacts such as traditions, rituals, ceremonies, and jargon, all of which are rich in academic institutions (Morgan, 2006). Leaders need to know what matters to constituents in order to use cultural symbols effectively, but it is also important for leaders themselves to know what these cultural symbols mean. For example, the espoused value of equity might be demonstrated symbolically by leaders doing away with reserved parking spots for senior leaders, thereby redistributing one form of reward more traditionally held by those in authority (Eddy, 2010). Because of the diversity of campus members and the part-time (non-residential) students and part-time faculty, it may be even more of a challenge to cultivate symbols that resonate with constituents and, therefore, help frame messages, initiatives, and core values.

Those who value sense making as a leadership strategy do not suggest that in an era of data-based decision making and accountability community college leaders rely on this kind of cognitive processing and internal intuition solely, or even predominantly. But rather, those who approach leadership through cognition and sense making acknowledge that rationality is limited (Morgan, 2006) as a perspective from which to lead in higher education institutions, including community colleges (Alfred, 2008), and that more nuanced understandings of complexity that draw upon reflective thought, close examinations of embedded assumptions, and "multi-framing" are valuable.

Emotional Intelligence

Another approach to leadership incorporates emotions and affective ways of knowing. Daniel Goleman's (1995, 1998) work is well recognized in the area of emotional intelligence. A simplification of Goleman's theory is that one's emotions factor into how one responds as a leader, or as a person in general (1995, 1998). Behaviors and actions both within society and formal organizations are neither rational nor logical. Emotions need to be managed, cultivated, and negotiated to be effective in relation with others, and that includes how a community college leader chooses to work with various constituents. Emotions are tied to and perhaps emanate from values and goals (Kezar et al., 2006, p. 85). This is an important consideration in a community college where, for many, the mission is a calling (Amey, 1999) as opposed to "just a job" and where retaining the access mission for underserved students overrides other priorities.

Those with more highly developed emotional intelligence are aware of their emotions, which ones they are feeling, and why, as well as how feelings connect to thought, action, voice, and overall performance (Goleman, 1998). As with sense making, before a leader can help others harness emotions on behalf of the college they need to understand their own emotions first. Emotionally intelligent leaders take into account the emotionality of decisions and environments, and they recognize that their efforts to make college processes more transparent may not equate directly to others' logical interpretation or rational understanding of the actions. More typically, members of formal organizations react first from an emotive perspective, and leaders can thus aid them in making more cognitive interpretations of events and circumstances.

Organizational transitions, which are rampant in contemporary community college settings, are often charged with emotional reactions to the extent that the overly rational leader tends to disregard all but those actions that impede overall change processes (Bridges & Bridges, 2000; Levin, 2001). The role of emotional monitor (Bensimon & Neumann, 1993) for the organization may be a different leadership role for presidents to play, and normally delegated to others within the college more attuned to emotionality or more highly developed in this area. Yet, the ability of a leader to be an emotional monitor is a key factor in cultivating group cohesion and commitment, and in moving a college forward. Nevertheless, these leadership behaviors may run counter to the dominant images of strong, decisive leaders.

Intercultural Competence

Another reason why self-awareness and reflection appear with frequency in leadership discourse has to do with parallel discussions of inclusion, diversity, and intercultural competence (Amey, 1999; Eddy, 2010; Eddy & Cox, 2008; Lester, 2011). Even though the percentage of women presidents has increased to 29% over the last two decades (U.S. Department of Education, 2007), the numbers continue to pale in comparison to the numbers of women students present on community college campuses; the situation is also extreme for leaders of color, with only approximately 14% of all chief executives of community colleges being of color. While these institutions continue to serve the most diverse student population across U.S. higher education, leadership remains male dominated and White (Eddy & Cox, 2008; Lester, 2008). If gender runs through the interpretations of organizational perceptions and sense making, constructions of symbols, interactions, and relationships (and by extension, networks and collaborations) as Acker (1990) claims, then intercultural competence, where gender is concerned, is important to consider in leadership. One could posit that the expectations, traditions, and demands of contemporary community colleges have not always aligned with the tenets and principles of the leadership theories presented here and, therefore, that White women and people of color may not aspire to leadership positions in these environments (Amey, 1999; Eddy & Lester, 2008). At the same time, as noted, research reinforces the advantages of adopting these leadership perspectives within community colleges.

In order to foster leadership development for those who may not represent the majority, institutional attention to cultivating environments holistically and promoting the whole person is key. The disembodied worker Acker (1990) discussed, in which one's life is segmented and the job takes precedence, has been criticized over the last 20 years, leading to the creation of institutional policies and programs to support the multiple identities of organizational members. Work–life balance, family-friendly policies, increased on-campus child care, flex time, and telecommuting are some examples of institutional efforts to mediate the tensions inherent for those who do not identify with the traditional definition of a worker. The leadership hierarchy often assumes that one can focus entirely on the job because someone else is present to take care of the home (Eddy & Cox, 2008). This is not only a male or female stereotype but also traditional versus non-traditional employment stereotype, even for women, and does not take into account differences such as backgrounds, discipline, and marital status. The ideas of gendered organizations about which Townsend wrote in 1995 remain largely intact even if crumbling around the edges.

The concept of intercultural competence suggests that leaders think across cultural boundaries and can communicate and listen, develop relationships, construct meaningful experiences, and be effective with and through cultures other than their own (Cooper & Ideta, 1994). While intercultural competence tends to focus on race, ethnicity, and gender, community college leaders need to be interculturally competent across socio-economic status, social identities, organizational types and sectors, technologies, and global settings. Without these skills and understandings, leaders quickly regress to the more imperialist assumptions that the leader knows best for all constituents (Amey, 1999; Cooper & Ideta, 1994). Community colleges and the societies in which they exist have moved far beyond this stereotype (Eddy & Cox, 2008; Lester, 2008).

These more recent leadership perspectives may reflect the gender, race, and ethnic changes in community college leaders as well as offer alternative understandings through which leaders can shape the direction of community colleges in the future. At the same time, more recent scholarship presents portraits of these "new" leaders that could cause scholars to reexamine assumptions about the new wave of leadership theories to see the extent to which they genuinely account for intercultural dynamics and/or whether they marginalize groups of leaders differently even as did the theories that preceded them (Amey, 1999; Lester, 2008; Rendon, 1999). Acker's (1990) claims on the roots of gendered organizations as they exist at community colleges undermine the adoption of the new(er) theories reviewed here: construction of divisions along gender lines; construction of symbols and images that explain, reinforce, or oppose those divisions; and production of gendered components of individual identity, as well as ongoing processes of creating and conceptualizing social structures (Eddy, 2010). Yet, even though these divisions may continue to exist, the challenge for practitioners is to embrace what is of value in these multiple frames and to construct leadership that will respond appropriately to the complex community college environments. Moving in this direction, then, leads to another set of perspectives on leadership—those that are organizationally focused.

Organizationally Oriented Leadership Theories

In addition to individually oriented leadership theories, there are a number of theories that are oriented to the organization, derived from organizational development/psychology research. The theories often mirror or are closely tied to individually oriented theories. By comparison, leaders who adopt the organizational leadership theories likely start from a more collective orientation to their leadership, focusing on organizational functions rather than on the individuals.

Change and Entrepreneurialism

It is cliché to say that community colleges are changing: they have been characterized as responsive and entrepreneurial since their inception. The rhetoric of change and transition is common across the sector (Boggs, 2003). Defining leadership as tied to change and entrepreneurialism is, however, a more recent phenomenon and speaks to more than adjustments made on the fringes of any central goals of the college. Leading for change means doing more than first order change that maintains the *status quo* (Argyris & Schön, 1978; Heifetz & Laurie, 1997); it entails creating opportunities, innovations, and initiatives for the institution (Kezar et al., 2006). Yet, these opportunities, innovations, and initiatives have to be connected to organizational values if deliberate change is to occur and be sustained so that meaning can be ascribed to these actions and become conscious in the minds of college members (Bolman & Deal, 2008; Bugay, 2001). At the same time that leaders create opportunities and space for innovation and help others make meaning, they tap into ideas from local-level leaders and encourage grass-roots leadership rather than rely primarily on top-down leadership (Kezar & Lester, 2011).

The contemporary literature on the preferred new community college leaders, referred to as entrepreneurial (Fisher & Koch, 2004; Roueche & Jones, 2005), is clear: while emphasizing organizational change, entrepreneurial leaders identify and capitalize on opportunities and locate and define new organizational niches. They know how to take risks, find resources, including human capital, which means being able to read the talents of constituents and build teams and networks. Entrepreneurial leaders develop strategies and strategic thinking, are catalysts of change, are not threatened by adversity and competition, and are creative (Eggert, 1998). One challenge of entrepreneurial leadership is the requirement to adopt an external focus. Even though community college presidents have to connect to their external communities, cultivating new markets and niches may be seen as adopting a business persona, particularly when these efforts focus on revenue generation. Leaders are encouraged to find ways to be both external and internal to the college, which likely requires cultivating sufficient "inside" leaders throughout the organization (Alfred, 2008). Another challenge is the increased competition faced by community colleges from multiple service providers, including the growth of for-profit and online educational organizations. The press to do more with less across an ever-increasing portfolio of objectives seems to lead directly to entrepreneurial leadership and business strategies (Boggs, 2003; Eddy, 2010).

Organizational Development and Chaos

Change is one impetus for new leadership theories. Organizational development and adaptive work, while forms of organizational change (Heifetz & Laurie, 1997), present slightly different ways of thinking about leadership. Organizational development assumes that challenging conditions and supportive behaviors affect institutional actions, creating a need for institutions and leaders to examine organizational beliefs, expectations, ways of being, and delivering services (Alfred, 2008; Amey, 2005). Organizational development and chaos theory assume that organizations are not straightforward and rational; therefore, leadership cannot be only top-down and bureaucratic (Weick, 1995; Wheatley, 1999). Organizational leadership theories take into account several of Wheatley's (1999) tenets and apply them to organizational life (e.g., decentralization, boundary spanning and border crossing, collaboration, flexibility, adaptability, participation, and autonomy). Leadership that depends on highly centralized organizational functioning and classic management principles is likely to be problematical in a world defined as chaotic. In this context, scholars argue, community leaders need to have a strong foundation of values and integrity, and the ability to make the difficult decisions needed to keep the college on course (Anderson, Harbour, & Davies, 2007; Wallin, 2007; Wheatley, 2002) because they are not as able to depend on the tight coupling of institutional processes to guard against the inequities of power and privilege (Scott & Davis, 2006). This is one of the conditions for contemporary community colleges that confounds definitions of leadership and how leadership plays out in the college context.

Leadership is problematic in the community college because the institution is loosely coupled, has limited traditions and sagas, continually changes its processes in efforts to respond to external constituents, is highly resource dependent (while trying to maintain low tuition), and endeavors to be a multifunctional institution (Cohen & Brawer, 2008; Levin, 2001). As a result, not only can there be mission and identity confusion but also, in an effort to respond as if internal and external factors could be addressed rationally, there is inefficiency, inequity, and contradiction of purpose and process (Scott & Davis, 2006).

Rather than proposing that leaders operate from a rational perspective, then, chaos theory encourages leaders to take a different organizational view (Wheatley, 1999). Rather than look centrally for administrative responses, leaders, according to chaos theory, should focus on the influences of local and context-specific situations of the larger enterprise. This recommendation reinforces the need for sense makers throughout the college who are able to cross boundaries for information retrieval and dissemination, seizing opportunities and initiating change activities (Weick, 1995). In this vein, the leader needs to be able to gather information effectively and constantly, to see the cumulative effect of decentralized activity, and to find ways of weaving together distinctions into the collective known as the community college.

Almost by definition, this kind of leadership activity suggests a different level of experimentation, innovation, change, and modifications from across the college campus rather than reliance on technical and routine responses (Heifetz, 2004; Heifetz & Laurie, 1997). New thinking, challenging long-held beliefs, and questioning initiatives constitute aspects of the adaptive work of organizational development (Alfred, 2008; Amey & VanDerLinden, 2002). This adaptive work is generative and multidimensional, requiring multiple frames, multilevel understanding and involvement, and is often anxiety producing (Amey, 2007; Heifetz, 2004; Heifetz & Laurie, 1997; Kezar et al., 2006). The ability to lead from an adaptive frame is the leadership test that confronts contemporary community college leaders.

Collaboration

Inherent in adaptive work and organizational development leadership theories is collaboration: leaders and members throughout the college work across boundaries and work and learn together, co-constructing new realities. There are several labels for this kind of leadership stemming from advancing the ideas of organizational change, adaptive work, and collaboration. Harris and Spillane (2008) call this approach "distributed leadership" where multiple leaders share within and across organizations and units. Bensimon and Neumann (1993) discussed team leadership as the presidential practice of bringing together ways of making sense of institutions from across a spectrum of perspectives to form a collective cognition for decision-making. Horner (1997) refers to shared leadership as moving toward communities of practice. Eddy (2010) calls it multidimensional leadership, which provides flexibility and construction based on individuals' core experiences, beliefs, and capabilities, and is likely the result of collective effort and occurs at multiple levels. Nidiffer (2001) labeled it integrated leadership, which brings together collaboration, participation, generative leadership and authenticity, and without which leaders will be ineffective in the changing college environment.

Relationships and relationship building are important aspects of collaborative leadership (Kezar et al., 2006). For leaders, understanding these relationships, building necessary connections, and finding appropriate and willing partners often lead to network analyses and cognizance of how webs of relationships, information, and resources flow within, around, and through the college (Amey, Eddy, Campbell, & Watson, 2008; Helgeson, 1995; Kezar et al., 2006). This form of networked leadership, or collaborative leadership, requires a foundation built on open communication, sharing information, expertise, power, and ideas (Amey et al., 2005; Ferren & Stanton, 2004). Because of the need for trust, however, collaborative leadership takes time and necessitates development in advance of the moments when it is necessary to draw upon the collaboration.

New scholarship promotes the collective and changes the focus of leadership: leaders need to be thinking about what is good for the college now as well as in the future as these decisions are situated locally and beyond the traditional college boundaries; they need to focus attention on relationships within and external to the college, regularly building those networks so that they are sufficiently in place when needed. This approach to leadership also changes the role of followers to make them more connected to each other and to the leader, and to central players in college processes. From a collective leadership perspective, followers are not subservient members of the college or simply subordinates who respond to the mission and edicts of the leader-on-high. Rather, they are positioned as co-leaders, ready and able to lead, shape the future direction, critique, and contribute to the institution.

Change leadership and collaborative leadership are time-consuming. They require considerable facilitating of transitions as people have to abandon old notions, ways of being, and identities (Bridges & Bridges, 2000; Heifetz, 2004). Ideally, these leadership models will involve more people in decision-making and will support authentic attempts to create a culture of inclusion so that when expediency is critical, the trust is there to move forward even if there was not time for consensus (Amey, 2005). However, trust of this kind has to have been built before the crisis. If community colleges are as entrenched and bureaucratic as they have been stereotyped to be (Birnbaum, 1988; Levin, 1998), making a shift toward these forms of collaborative leadership may be challenging especially with organizational members who are rigid.

CONCLUSION

Unlike former theories, the new scholarly constructions of leadership acknowledge the complexity of community colleges (and higher education in general). New leadership perspectives argue that leaders need to think more complexly and in more nuanced ways, scratching beneath surface observations to work from multiple perspectives, with multiple lenses, and questioning embedded assumptions and institutionalized practice to unearth the "why" of the college's practice and not just the outputs that are tied to accountability and accrediting agencies. Both what matters and why demand a deeper understanding. In resource-constrained environments, with colleges committed to access and opportunity for diverse learners, there is no greater organizational need than for leaders to think through the challenges in ways that are effective first and then efficient, rather than efficient first and then perhaps effective, mirroring the more omnipotent leadership approaches of the past (Brint & Karabel, 1985; Roueche et al., 1989). This results in a broader array of tools with which to solve organizational problems and to draw upon leadership strategies that will enable greater connection to followers or constituents and the ability to reflect on the larger context (Heifetz, 2004). Community colleges are at a crossroads in determining their future directions (Alfred, 2008; Boggs, 2003; Eddy, 2010). Part of their ability to be self-determining will rest on leaders throughout the organization who are able to adapt new leadership strategies appropriate to the circumstances of their colleges.

QUESTIONS FOR DISCUSSION

1. What are the similarities and differences among leadership theories?
2. Are there insufficient approaches to community college leadership, and if so why is this the case?
3. After more than a decade of targeted leadership development programs, are we any further ahead in our succession planning and leadership development? Why or why not?
4. What actions can be taken to prepare future community college leaders?

REFERENCES

Acker, J. (1990). Hierarchies, jobs, bodies: A theory of gendered organizations. *Gender and Society, 4*(2), 139–158.

Alfred, R. L. (2008). Governance in strategic context. In R. C. Cloud & S. T. Kater (Eds.). *Governance in the community college. New Directions for Community Colleges, no. 141* (pp. 79–89). San Francisco, CA: Jossey-Bass.

American Council on Education. (2007). *The American college president: 2007 edition.* Washington, DC: Author.

Amey, M. J. (1992, November). *Cognitive constructions of leadership.* Paper presented at the annual meeting of the Association for the Study of Higher Education, Minneapolis, MN.

Amey, M. J. (1999). Navigating the raging river: Reconciling issues of identity, inclusion, and administrative practice. In K. M. Shaw, J. R. Valadez, & R. A. Rhoads (Eds.), *Community colleges as cultural texts: Qualitative explorations of organizational and student culture* (pp. 59–82). Albany, NY: State University of New York Press.

Amey, M. J. (2005). Leadership as learning: Conceptualizing the process. *Community College Journal for Research and Practice, 29*(9–10), 689–704.

Amey, M. J. (2007). Collaborations across education sectors. *New Directions for Community Colleges, no. 139* (pp. 1–3). San Francisco, CA: Jossey-Bass.

Amey, M. J. (2010). Leading partnerships: Competencies for collaboration. In D. L Wallin (Ed.), *Leadership in an era of change. New Directions for Community College, no. 149* (pp. 13–23). San Francisco, CA: Jossey-Bass.

Amey, M. J., & Brown, D. F. (2004). *Breaking out of the box: Interdisciplinary collaboration and faculty work.* Boston, MA: Information Age Publishing.

Amey, M. J., Eddy, P. L., & Campbell, T. G. (2010). Crossing boundaries: Creating community college partnerships to promote educational transitions. *Community College Review, 37*(4), 333–347.

Amey, M. J., Eddy, P. L., Campbell, T. G., & Watson, J. L. (2008, April). *The role of social capital in facilitating partnerships.* Paper presented at the annual conference of the Council for the Study of Community Colleges, Philadelphia, PA.

Amey, M. J., & Twombly, S. B. (1992). Re-visioning leadership in community colleges. *Review of Higher Education, 15*(2), 125–150.

Amey, M. J., & VanDerLinden, K. E. (2002). Career paths for community college leaders. *American Association of Community Colleges (AACC) Research Brief, 2,* 1–16.

Amey, M. J., VanDerLinden, K., & Brown, D. (2002). Perspectives on community college leadership: Twenty years in the making. *Community College Journal of Research and Practice, 26*(7), 573–589.

Anderson, S. A., Harbour, C. P., & Davies, T. G. (2007). Professional ethical identity development and community college leadership. In D. M. Hellmich (Ed.), *Ethical leadership in the community college: Bridging theory and daily practice* (pp. 61–76). Bolton, MA: Anker Publishing.

Argyris, C., & Schön, D. (1978). *Theory in practice: Increasing professional effectiveness.* San Francisco, CA: Jossey-Bass.

Bailey, J. M. (2008). Work and life balance: Community college occupational deans. *Community College Journal of Research and Practice, 32* (10), 778–792.

Bensimon, E. M., & Neumann, A. (1993). *Redesigning collegiate leadership: Teams and teamwork in higher education*. Baltimore, MD: Johns Hopkins University Press.

Birnbaum, R. (1988). *How colleges work: The cybernetics of academic organization and leadership*. San Francisco, CA: Jossey-Bass.

Boggs, G. R. (2003). Leadership context for the twenty-first century. In W. E. Piland & D. B. Wolf. *Help wanted: Preparing community college leaders in a new century. New Directions for Community Colleges, no. 123* (pp. 15–25). San Francisco, CA: Jossey-Bass.

Bogue, Jesse P. (1950). *The community college*. New York, NY: McGraw-Hill, Inc.

Bolman, L. G., & Deal, T. E. (2008). *Reframing organizations: Artistry, choice and leadership*. San Francisco, CA: Jossey-Bass.

Bridges, W., & Bridges, S. M. (2000). Leading transition: A new model for change. *Leader to Leader*, no. 16. New York, NY: The Peter F. Drucker Foundation for Nonprofit Management. Retrieved from http://www.pfdf.org/leaderbooks/L2L/spring2000/bridges.html.

Brint, S., & Karabel, J. (1989). *The diverted dream: Community colleges and the promise of educational opportunity in America, 1900–1985*. New York, NY: Oxford University Press.

Bugay, D. P. (2001). TransformActional leadership: Leaders building on trust. *International Leadership Association Proceedings*. College Park, MD: Academic of Leadership. Retrieved from http://www.academicy.umd.edu/ILA/2001proceedings/David.htm

Cameron, K. S. (1984, April/May). Organizational adaptation and higher education. *The Journal of Higher Education*, 55, 122–144.

Chaffee, E. E. (1985). Three models of strategy. *The Academy of Management Review*, 10(1), 89–98.

Cohen, A. M., & Brawer, F. B. (2008). *The American community college* (5th ed.). San Francisco, CA: Jossey-Bass.

Cooper, J. E., & Ideta, L. M. (1994). *Dealing with difference: Maps and metaphors of leadership in higher education*. Paper presented at the annual meeting of the Association for the Study of Higher Education, Tucson, AZ.

Duree, C. (2008). Iowa State study of community college presidents finds national shortage on horizon. Retrieved from http://www.public.iastate.edu/~nscentral/news/08/jul/ccleadership.shtml

Eddy, P. L. (2003). Sensemaking on campus: How community college presidents frame change. *Community College Journal of Research and Practice*, 27(6), 453–471.

Eddy, P. L. (2010). *Community college leadership: A multidimensional model for leading change*. Sterling, VA: Stylus Publishing.

Eddy, P. L., & Cox, E. (2008). Gendered leadership: An organizational perspective. In J. Lester (Ed.), *Gendered perspectives on community colleges. New Directions for Community Colleges, no. 142* (pp. 69–89). San Francisco, CA: Jossey-Bass.

Eddy, P. L., & Lester, J. (2008). Strategies for the future. In J. Lester (Ed.), *Gendered perspectives on community colleges. New Directions for Community Colleges, no. 142* (pp. 107–116). San Francisco, CA: Jossey-Bass.

Eggert, N. J. (1998). *Contemplative leadership for entrepreneurial organizations: Paradigms, metaphors, and wicked problems*. Westport, CT: Quorum Books.

Fairhurst, G. T., & Sarr, R. A. (1996). *The art of framing: Managing the language of leadership*. San Francisco, CA: Jossey-Bass.

Ferren, A. S., & Stanton, W. W. (2004). *Leadership through collaboration: The role of the chief academic officer*. Westport, CT: Praeger.

Fisher, J. L., & Koch, J. V. (2004). *The entrepreneurial college president*. Westport, CT: ACE/Praeger Series in Higher Education.

Garza Mitchell, R. L., & Eddy, P. L. (2008). In the middle: A gendered view of career pathways of mid-level community college leaders. *Community College Journal of Research and Practice*, 32(10), 793–811.

Goleman, D. (1995). *Emotional intelligence*. New York, NY: Bantam Books.

Goleman, D. (1998). *Working with emotional intelligence*. New York, NY: Bantam Books.

Harris, A., & Spillane, J. (2008). Distributed leadership through the looking glass. *Management in Education*, 22(1), 31–34.

Heifetz, R. A. (2004). *Leadership without easy answers*. Cambridge, MA: Harvard University Press.

Heifetz, R. A., & Laurie, D. L. (1997). The work of leadership. *Harvard Business Review*, 75(1), 124–134.

Helgeson, S. (1995). *The web of inclusion: A new architecture for building great organizations*. New York, NY: Currency/Doubleday.

Horner, M. (1997). Leadership theory: Past, present, and future. *Team Performance Management*, 3(4), 270–287.

Iowa State University. (n.d.). Retrieved from http://www.cclp.hs.iastate.edu/academics/pro_development.html

Kezar, A. J., Carducci, R., & Contreras-McGavin, M. (2006). Rethinking the "L" word in higher education: The revolution of research on leadership. *ASHE-ERIC Higher Education Report*, 31(6). San Francisco, CA: Jossey-Bass.

Kezar, A. J., & J. Lester, J. (2011). *Enhancing campus capacity for leadership: An examination of grassroots leaders in higher education.* Stanford, CA: Stanford University Press.

King, J. E. (2008). *Too many rungs on the ladder? Faculty demographics and the future leadership of higher education.* Washington, DC: American Council on Education.

Kuhnert, K. W., & Lewis, P. (1989). Transactional and transformational leadership: A constructive/developmental analysis. *Academy of Management Review, 12*(4), 648–657.

Lester, J. (Ed.). (2008). *Gendered perspectives on community colleges. New Directions for Community Colleges, no. 142.* San Francisco, CA: Jossey-Bass.

Lester, J. (2011). Regulating gender performance: Power and gender norms in faculty work. *NASPA Journal About Women in Higher Education, 4*(2), 142–169.

Levin, J. S. (1998). Presidential influence, leadership succession, and multiple interpretations of organizational change. *Review of Higher Education, 21*(4), 405–425.

Levin, J. S. (2001). *Globalizing the community college*: Strategies for change in the twenty-first century. New York, NY: Palgrave.

Moore, K. M., Martorana, S. V., & Twombly, S. B. (1985). *Today's academic leaders: A national study of administrators in two-year colleges.* University Park, PA: Center for the Study of Higher Education.

Morgan, G. (2006). *Images of organization.* Thousand Oaks, CA: Sage.

Nidiffer, J. (2001). New leadership for a new century. In J. Nidiffer & C. T. Bashaw (Eds.), *Women administrators in higher education: Historical and contemporary perspectives* (pp. 101–131). Albany, NY: State University of New York Press.

O'Banion, T. (1997). *A learning college for the 21st century.* Phoenix, AZ: Oryx Press.

Opp, R. D., & Gosetti, P. P. (2002). Equity for women administrators of color in 2-year colleges: Progress and prospects. *Community College Journal of Research and Practice, 26* (7–8), 591–608.

Patton, M. (2003). AACC holds first leading forward summit. *Community College Times,* Novemebr 25, 2003 (p. 3). Retrieved from http://ccleadershipsite.com/pdfs/1125p3.pdf

Peterson, M. (1997). Using contextual planning to transform institutions. In M. Peterson, D. Dill, L. A. Mets, & Associates (Eds.), *Planning and management for a changing environment* (pp. 127–157). San Francisco, CA: Jossey-Bass.

Phelan, D. J. (2005). Crossing the generations: Learning to lead across the leadership life cycle. *Community College Journal of Research and Practice, 29,* 783–792.

Piland, W. E., & Wolf, D. B. (Eds.). (2003). *Help wanted: Preparing community college leaders in a new century. New Directions for Community Colleges,* no. 123. San Francisco, CA: Jossey-Bass.

Rendon, L. I. (1999). Toward a new vision of the multicultural community college for the next century. In K. M. Shaw, J. R. Valadez, & R. A. Rhoads (Eds.), *Community colleges as cultural texts: Qualitative explorations of organizational and student culture* (pp. 195–204). Albany, NY: State University of New York Press.

Richardson, R. C., Blocker, C. C., & Bender, L. W. (1972). *Governance for the two-year colleges.* Englewood Cliffs, NJ: Prentice-Hall.

Riggs, J. (2000). Leadership, change and the future of community colleges. *Academic Leadership Live: The Online Journal,* 7(1), Winter 2009. Retrieved from www.academicleadership.org

Rost, J. C. (2001). *Leadership for the twenty-first century.* New York, NY: Praeger Publishers.

Roueche, J. E., Baker, G. A., III, & Rose, R. R. (1989). *Shared vision: Transformational leadership in American community colleges.* Washington, DC: The Community and Junior College Press and the American Association of Community Colleges.

Roueche, J. E., & Jones, B. R. (Eds.) (2005). *The entrepreneurial community college.* Washington, DC: American Association of Community Colleges.

Scott, W. R., & Davis, G. F. (2006). *Organizations and organizing: Rational, natural, and open systems perspectives.* Upper Saddle River, NJ: Prentice Hall.

Senge, P. M. (1990). *The fifth discipline: The art and practice of the learning organization.* New York, NY: Doubleday.

Senge, P. M. (1998). Leading learning organizations. In W. E. Rosenbach & R. I. Taylor (Eds.), *Contemporary issues in leadership* (4th ed.) (pp. 174–178). Boulder, CO: Westview Press.

Shults, C. (2001) The critical impact of impending retirements on community college leadership. *Leadership Series Research Brief,* no. 1. Washington, DC: American Association of Community Colleges.

Tillery, D., & Deegan, W. L. (1985). The evolution of two-year colleges through four generations. In W. L. Deegan & D. Tillery (Eds.), *Renewing the American community college: Priorities and strategies for effective leadership.* (pp. 3–33). San Francisco, CA: Jossey-Bass.

Townsend, B. K. (1995). Women community college faculty: On the margins or in the mainstream? In B. K. Townsend (Ed.), *Gender and power in the community college. New Directions for Community Colleges, no. 89* (pp. 39–46). San Francisco, CA: Jossey-Bass.

Townsend, B. K. (2008). Community colleges as gender-equitable institutions. In J. Lester (Ed.), *Gendered perspectives on community colleges. New Directions for Community Colleges, no. 142* (pp. 7–14). San Francisco, CA: Jossey-Bass.

U.S. Department of Education (2007). *National Center for Education Statistics: Digest of education statistics.* Washington, DC: Author.

VanDerLinden, K. E. (2004). Gender differences in the preparation and promotion of community college administration. *Community College Review, 31*(4), 1–24.

Wallin, D. L. (2006). Short-term leadership development: Meeting a need for emerging community college leaders. *Community College Journal of Research and Practice, 30*, 513–528.

Wallin, D. L. (2007). Ethical leadership: The role of the president. In D. M. Hellmich (Ed.), *Ethical leadership in the community college: Bridging theory and daily practice* (pp. 33–45). Boston, MA: Anker Publishing.

Watts, G. E., & Hammons, J. O. (2002). Professional development: Setting the context. *New Directions for Community Colleges, no. 120* (pp. 5–10). San Francisco, CA: Jossey-Bass.

Weick, K. E. (1995). *Sensemaking in organizations.* Thousand Oaks, CA: Sage Publications.

Weisman, I. M., & Vaughan, G. B. (2007). *The community college presidency 2006.* Washington, DC: Community College Press.

Wheatley, M. J. (1999). *Leadership and the new science.* San Francisco, CA: Jossey-Bass.

Wheatley, M. J. (2002). Spirituality in turbulent times. *School Administrator, 598*, 42–46.

Williams, J. (2000). *Unbending gender: Why family and work conflict and what to do about it.* New York, NY: Oxford University Press.

10

DECONSTRUCTING GOVERNANCE AND EXPECTATIONS FOR THE COMMUNITY COLLEGE

CARRIE B. KISKER AND SUSAN T. KATER

U.S. community colleges, while often analyzed as a group or sector, encompass small institutions serving relatively insulated communities, large, multicampus behemoths that provide education and occupational training for a wide variety of students, and considerable variation in between. Furthermore, community colleges vary widely in relation to their roles and functions within state systems, and, depending on the ways in which power and authority are distributed within community college governance structures, colleges face different expectations from both internal and external constituents.

Numerous issues confound governance in higher education, while at the same time unique governance structures have served as a defining characteristic of U.S. higher education (Birnbaum, 1988). Within community colleges, and higher education generally, a mix of bureaucratic factors and the academic influence of collegial and professional dynamics solidified the empirical challenges in conceptualizing governance (Baldridge, Curtis, Ecker, & Riley, 1977). Furthermore, "governance systems evolve as unique reflections of institutional history, values, and accidental interactions" (Birnbaum, 1991, p. 178). In spite of a resurgence in research related to governance (Alfred, 2008; Ehrenberg, 2004; Hines, 2000; Pusser, Slaughter, & Thomas, 2006; Tierney, 2004), a lack of "basic descriptive data about the present state of governance" persists (Birnbaum, 1991, p. 4; Kaplan, 2004). Governance of community colleges as complex and varied institutions, then, is a topic deserving of further theoretical and empirical analysis and discussion.

This chapter is presented in two parts. The first provides an overview of the historical and theoretical literature related to community college governance, along the way noting gaps in the literature and areas for further research. The second part of the chapter delves further into an important area of analysis: the connection between governance and expectations for community colleges. In particular, this chapter will explore how various organizational patterns of governance affect expectations for community colleges, as well as how they may influence colleges' abilities to accomplish statewide policy objectives such as cross-sector collaboration.

GOVERNANCE IN THE LITERATURE

In its simplest form, governance is "a process for distributing authority, power, and influence in decision making among constituencies" (Alfred & Smydra, 1985, pp. 201–202). In the context of higher education, this can refer to the distributional processes inherent in both organizational and internal patterns of governance. Furthermore, governance encompasses the relationships or networks between a college and the entities with which it interacts, including business, government, and community organizations (Marginson & Considine, 2000). This latter aspect of governance overlaps with a closely related process: the coordination of institutions of higher education. Indeed, practitioners and scholars often discuss the concepts of statewide governance and coordination in tandem, as the two processes are integrally related in most states. Statewide coordination, as defined by Lovell and Trouth (2002), is the formal mechanism that states use to organize institutions of higher education and ensure that they work collectively toward state interests. And while we focus this chapter primarily on internal and statewide governance systems, we acknowledge the multiple layers of the governance lattice, including a new global perspective of community colleges, as opportunities for new research by community college scholars.

Much of scholarly understanding of community college governance and coordination has come from what has been written about the university sector. However, while there are some similarities, university governance practices do not always apply to the community college sector. What follows is a brief overview of the extant literature related to community college governance and coordination, focusing in particular on governance models and patterns (both organizational and internal).

Deconstructing Governance

Governance in higher education can be viewed as a unique and fluid blend of processes, players, positioning, and politics. Governance structures are grounded in concepts of authority and legitimacy and may be formal or informal, as well as reflective of institutional characteristics and cultural perspectives (Hardy, 1990; Levin, 2000; Rhoades, 1992; Tierney, 2004). Models of governance in higher education must account for the distinctive characteristics of colleges and universities, namely goal ambiguity, clientele, problematic technology, professionalism, and environmental vulnerability (Riley & Baldridge, 1977). These unique organizational characteristics have created what Cohen and March (1986) call "organized anarchies," ensuring a challenge to any governance process. Although constituents and structures of governance change over time, the basic models of institutional governance referenced in the higher education literature have remained constant for decades. Indeed, the fact that there are few contemporary models of community college governance not only speaks to a theoretical void that reflects a lack of constructs specific to community colleges but also points to the complexity of governance in general.

In deconstructing governance, it is important to acknowledge the different dimensions in which decision-making authority occurs. The notion that horizontal and vertical layers operate within fluid processes influenced by "multiple claimants to authority" spurred Hines (2000) to develop five themes that help frame understanding of higher education governance. The first theme includes the presence of a variety of stakeholders who represent multiple interests and a mixture of internal and external constituents.

"Traditionally, we imagine governance in higher education as having two dimensions: internal and external" (Marginson, 2004, p. 1). Observers and scholars often consider faculty, management, and boards as the prime players, but students, part-time faculty, legislators at state, regional, and national levels, accountability and compliance agencies, alumni, and local groups play a role in institutional governance as well. Research indicates that colleges and universities have become decreasingly autonomous and increasingly adjudicated and controlled by external constituents who have little or no understanding of the unique nature of higher education's institutional governance (Lee, 1980–1981; Olivas, 2004). "These relatively new forces have intensified issues of governance by inserting nonacademic interests into the heart of education, adding layers of external complexity to institutions" (Burgan, 2004, p. vii).

The second theme identified by Hines (2000) is "that among these multiple claimants to authority, there seems to be a continuum from participatory governance to a corporate style of governance" (p. 105). This perspective focuses the governance literature internally on what is known as shared governance. Unique to higher education, shared governance is at face value distributed responsibility and authority for decision-making but made complex by the professional nature of faculty and the number of stakeholders, both internal and external to the institution. Shared governance in theory "represents the effort to achieve a balance among academic priorities and values, public responsibility and accountability, and financial, management, and political realities" (Duderstadt, 2004, p. 152). In practice it is an ideal involving primarily administrative-faculty roles and responsibilities, but may also involve staff, students, boards of trustees, and alumni (Alfred, 1998; Birnbaum, 1988; Ehrenberg, 2004; Hines, 2000; Kater, 2003; Levin, 2000; Mortimer & McConnell, 1978). We discuss shared governance in greater detail later in the chapter.

Governance is also affected by changing fiscal, social, and political climates. Thus Hines' (2000) third theme describes an emergence of external political actors with significant influence in campus governance. Policy-makers, who often have statewide perspectives that may overlook individual institutions, are able to exert authority through policies, as well as through resource allocations. Due to their market orientation, community colleges have been historically more susceptible to external influence than other higher educational institutional types (Baldridge, 1971; Levin, 2001). More research on state models of governance is thus warranted, as scholars and practitioners would benefit from a greater understanding of the influence of the state on local governance.

The fourth theme derived from Hines' (2000) review of the literature is one of diffusion of authority. The literature confirms what many practitioners observe firsthand: that there are increasingly more constituents who have some form of influence or authority in institutional governance. Miller and Miles (2008) use the analogy of a quilt to describe how this diffusion of authority pertains to shared governance: "the result is more of a quilt-like approach to decision-making, where administrators can call upon different groups when needed to cover different issues and problems" (p. 42).

Hines' (2000) final theme, which provides a framework for the rest of this chapter, is one that views higher education as a mechanism for policy implementation: "Higher education governance has taken a position closer to center stage than it had been at an earlier time simply because higher education has become a major instrument of state policy" (Hines, 2000, p. 106). Furthermore, community colleges are instruments not only of the states but also of regional and national policies that view them as economic engines of workforce development and of the nation's baccalaureate completion agenda (Levin, 2001).

Governance Models

While the scholarly literature on governance in higher education is expanding (Ehrenberg, 2004; Hines, 2000; Keller, 2004; Tierney, 2004), the primary conceptual models of governance have not changed over the past 30 years, and generalizations of community college governance by scholars as bureaucratic or political (Birnbaum, 1988; Cohen & Brawer, 2008) are incomplete. The historical models fail to account for the negotiated relationship between institutional constituents; for the increasing corporatization and marketization of higher education; for system, regional, national issues; for organizational, demographic, and functional differences between institutions; and, most recently, for globalization (Alfred, 2008; Levin, 2000; Marginson, 2004; Tierney, 2004). Within any model there may be multiple sub-models or themes, which further complicate understanding. For example, within a collegial model of governance, shared governance may be described as both a practice and an ideal, but there are multiple models of shared governance (Tierney, 2004), all of which continue to evolve.

The governance models most often ascribed to community colleges are that of the academic bureaucracy, the university collegium, and the political model (Baldridge et al., 1977; Cohen & Brawer, 2008). As organizations with a large number of independent professionals operating within a well-defined hierarchy, community colleges fit the conceptualization of the professional bureaucracy (Mintzberg, 2000). Our understanding of bureaucracies has been primarily influenced by the works of Max Weber (Morgan, 1997), who characterized bureaucracies as networks of social groups organized for efficiency and governed by the principle of legal rationality. Mintzberg (2000) expanded the bureaucratic concept to encompass the professional nature of faculty as experts in the organization, thus creating a "professional bureaucracy" that characterizes both higher education institutions and hospitals, which also employ a number of independent professionals.

Another classical model, the university collegium, is suggestive of full participation in decision-making by the academic community, in particular the faculty (Baldridge et al., 1977). This model was built on the notion of a community of scholars collaborating to manage the institution. The professional nature of faculty work is a key component of the effectiveness of this model. The collegial model has sub-themes of "decision making by consensus" and "professional authority of faculty members" (Baldridge et al., 1977, p. 13). Institutions at the top of the academic hierarchy with the most prestige and autonomy—research universities—would be expected to have the most collegial systems of governance (Baldridge et al., 1977) and community colleges the least. Indeed, "the collegial image of round-table decision making is not an accurate description of the processes in most institutions" (p. 13). Furthermore, this depiction of consensual decision-making does not adequately account for conflict between stakeholders. The collegial and bureaucratic models thus describe the extremes of governance, with actual practice located somewhere between the two.

A third model of governance, the political model, "assumes that complex organizations can be studied as miniature political systems" (Baldridge et al., 1977, p. 14). A political model focuses on the relationships and processes of policy formation and takes into consideration power structures, interest groups, goals, and conflict. The political model of governance describes the negotiations between faculty and administrators in the collective bargaining process and integrates the concepts of power, conflict, and politics to describe the process of academic decision-making (Kater, 2003). The political model has been revised recently from its original concept to include an environmental and structuralist approach and to take into consideration the impact of "routine bureaucratic processes" (Baldridge et al., 1977, p. 18). Thus, the expanded political model accounts for socio-political contexts that are more in line with the complexity of contemporary community colleges (Pusser, 2003).

Nonetheless, these models of governance are now over 30 years old and appear limited in describing contemporary community college governance. Often overlooked in discussions of governance models are national distributions of authority, which exert pressures on institutional governance (Rhoades, 1992). Specifying the manifestation of different forms of authority across six different levels of authority, from the most basic academic unit to the national government, Clark (1987) draws attention to structures outside individual institutions that shape campus governance. If we were to include global and multinational authorities, we would move closer to a contemporary model that can accurately describe community college governance.

Several scholars have stressed the need for a global framework for governance, as community college governance "constitutes a global public good" and establishes "new regulatory structures that function like communication and transport systems by linking higher education around the world" (Marginson, 2004, p. 21). The structural components of such a governance system could be conceptualized at the micro-level by envisioning the system modeled for the community college. Already a global institution, located at the nexus of K-20 educational systems, and with complex accountability and governance structures, community colleges are appropriate research venues for developing a multidimensional model. We look forward to the development of new multidimensional models that respond to cultural, collaborative, and global dynamics and expand to include not only internal processes and relationships but also the increasingly important system-wide and state structures.

Organizational Patterns of Governance and Coordination

Community college governing and coordinating structures vary widely: from single-state governing boards overseeing all of higher education to minimal state involvement and strong local boards of trustees.

> The relative degrees of state and local control of community colleges generally "follow the money," in that accountability to state and local governing boards and state legislatures is generally about proportional to the funds provided by each level of government. (Tollefson, 2009, p. 386)

Pusser and Turner (2004) confirm that "understanding the linkage between change in revenue sources and changes in institutional form is central to understanding contemporary shifts in the structure and process of academic governance" (p. 247). Indeed, historically, the ways in which community colleges were governed mattered little until state and local budgets grew large enough to warrant legislative scrutiny. As Cohen and Brawer (2008) argue, now that community college budgets total more than $21 billion each year, their governance and funding "command serious attention" (p. 157).

Over the years, several taxonomies of community college governance and coordination have been proposed (Bowen et al., 1997; Education Commission of the States, 2011; McGuinness, 2003; Richardson, Baracco, Callan, & Finney, 1998; Richardson & de los Santos, 2001; Tollefson, 2000). While these classification schemes share several characteristics, their differences reflect the historical development of community colleges (both as an extension of the high school and as the first two years of college) and shed light on the complex relationships states have developed with their community colleges (Lovell & Trouth, 2002).

This section focuses on the taxonomy of state structures for the governance of higher education proposed by Bowen et al. (1997), paying particular attention to the ways in which community colleges are governed within state systems. This classification schema not only describes the various ways in which community colleges are overseen and managed, but, unlike most other taxonomies, it also provides a useful explanation for how and why some community colleges are better able than other institutions to respond to public policy objectives articulated by elected officials, such as collaboration with universities and K-12 schools.

Higher education systems are linked to each other and to state government through a transactional environment that is influenced by both the state and its higher education systems (Bowen et al., 1997). As Bowen and his colleagues explain, this transactional environment is dominated by four work processes which involve some actors representing state government and others representing higher education. These include: (1) information management and assessment of system performance, for example, information about the extent to which educational processes and outcomes reflect state priorities; (2) budgeting, including language and/or negotiations about how to finance and achieve state priorities; (3) program planning, determining the availability, quality, and location of educational programs and services; and (4) articulation and collaboration, the extent to which colleges and universities work closely with each other and K-12 schools to improve student movement among them. Based on which agencies are responsible for each of the four work processes, Bowen and his colleagues (1997) identify four distinct categories of higher education governance: federal systems, unified systems, confederated systems, and confederated institutions. To these we add one additional category: P-16 systems.

Federal Systems

Federal systems are those with institutional and multicampus system governing boards, as well as a statewide coordinating board that has responsibility for all of higher education and substantial authority for the four work processes. States classified as federal systems include Illinois, Ohio, Texas, and Washington. In the latter state, for example, all 27 community colleges are governed by the State Board for Community and Technical Colleges, although the Washington Higher Education Coordinating Board plays a significant role in information management, budgeting, program planning, and articulation and collaboration among community colleges and four-year institutions.

Unified Systems

Unified systems are those in which a single governing board is responsible for all degree-granting public institutions of higher education and has authority for all four work processes. Georgia is an example of a unified system. The University System of

Georgia's Board of Regents has statutory responsibility for the leadership, management, and operational control of the state's 34 colleges and universities, although a separate board oversees the state's 34 postsecondary technical institutions.

Confederated Systems

Confederated systems have a higher education planning or coordinating agency with some authority for the work processes, but also have two or more multicampus or system-wide governing boards in which the board or the president/chancellor negotiates budgets directly with elected officials. California is a prime example of a confederated system; the University of California (UC), California State University (CSU), and California Community College (CCC) systems each have their own statewide governing board (the community colleges are also governed by locally elected boards of trustees), and the relatively weak California Postsecondary Education Commission performs some statewide information management duties.

Confederated Institutions

States with confederated institutions are those where colleges and universities are led by institutional or multicampus governing boards and where there is no statewide agency with substantial responsibility for all higher education. Arizona is an example of a state with confederated institutions of higher education. Although its three public universities are led by a statewide Board of Regents, the 10 community college districts are each governed by local boards of trustees. And since the State Board of Directors for Community Colleges was abolished in 2003, there has been no formal body charged with community college coordination. Thus, most of the collaborative programs among community colleges—and between them and the K-12 or university sectors—have been performed voluntarily. New Jersey's colleges and universities can also be classified as confederated; each is governed by its own board of trustees, although the New Jersey Council of County Colleges provides for some coordination among the state's two-year institutions and the Commission on Higher Education performs a statewide planning and advocacy role. Nonetheless, collaboration among the state's community colleges and four-year institutions has been voluntary in nature or, in the case of the recently developed statewide transfer associate degrees, mandated by law (Kisker, Wagoner, & Cohen, 2011).

P-16 Systems

Because Bowen and his colleagues (1997) only examined state structures for the governance of higher education, they did not attempt to classify those states that have created governing or coordinating structures for the entire pre-kindergarten through college spectrum. However, because community colleges face increasing pressure from legislators and others to collaborate with K-12 schools and improve the overall efficiency and cost effectiveness of the public secondary and postsecondary educational pipeline, an additional category of higher education governance is warranted: states where a P-16 (sometimes called a P-20 or K-20) governing or coordinating structure has been put into place in order to improve student flow throughout the pipeline. Florida is a key example of this type of system, as in 2003 it abolished all existing statewide boards and commissions relating to higher education and transferred their duties to the Florida Board of Education.

> Florida's new K-20 governance structure was developed primarily to ensure seamless student transitions through the state's education system ... Because all institutions—secondary and postsecondary—report to the same statewide board, and because the state board of education approaches all policy and funding decisions from a system-wide perspective, significant collaborations between schools and colleges ... are supported and encouraged in state law. (Kisker, 2006, p. 232)

While most states have not integrated their secondary and postsecondary governance structures to the extent Florida has, many—such as Ohio, Maryland, and Georgia—have set up P-16 councils aimed at establishing collaborative reforms (Boswell, 2000). Although it is reasonable to assume that states with P-16 governance systems or councils might be more responsive to public policy objectives articulated by elected officials—especially those pertaining to cross-sector collaboration—further scholarship in this area would be a logical extension of Bowen et al.'s (1997) work.

Internal Patterns of Community
College Governance

Much of the time when scholars discuss patterns of community college governance and coordination they are talking about the organizational structures—such as those described in the preceding pages—that reflect community college decision-making authority and hierarchy within a state (Levin, 2008). However, governance structures do not exist in a vacuum, and thus patterns of internal governance—the ways in which administrators, faculty, staff, students, and others make decisions about an institution's functioning—are also important to consider. This section focuses on a primary pattern of internal governance: shared governance, or faculty participation in academic decision-making. Shared governance is especially important to consider, as "it is one of several factors shaping how community colleges respond to state and local needs" (Alfred, 1998, p. 2). As with other aspects of community college governance, the concept of shared governance is borrowed from the university sector.

> The shared governance tradition in the United States ... flows from the unique mission of the university: to create knowledge and to develop in students the skills of critical inquiry ... There is wide consensus that the faculty ... should have primary authority over core academic issues including standards for admitting students; curriculum; procedures of student instruction; standards of student competence and ethical conduct; maintenance of a suitable environment for learning; the standards of faculty competence and ethical conduct; and the application of those standards in faculty appointments, promotions, tenure, and discipline. (Hamilton, 2004, pp. 94, 96)

Imported from early English models, shared governance in U.S. public institutions has seen a number of stakeholders (faculty, students, external agents) gain and relinquish power in the enduring struggle over who should run the organizations (Corson, 1960; Ehrenberg, 2004; Hines, 2000; Levin, 2000; Morphew, 1999; Rhoades, 1992; Tierney, 2004).

The academic dualism of shared governance has been portrayed as an intra-organizational conflict of interest between faculty and administrators (Gumport, 1993).

Historically, faculty have been afforded the opportunity to make academic decisions regarding instruction due to the nature of their expertise, intellectual prowess, and standing as professionals, while administrators have retained primary responsibility for fiscal policy and regulations (Corson, 1960; Morphew, 1999; Mortimer & McConnell, 1978; Rhoades, 1992). However, as institutions grew in size and complexity, a struggle for who should run the organization began to emerge (Gumport, 1993).

A review of the historical evolution of U.S. higher education (1636 to 1980) suggests that faculty made significant gains in power and position over time, as small colleges with limited curricula gave way to increasingly complex systems offering specialized curricula necessitating professional management skills (Clark, 1987; Cohen & Kisker, 2010). As administrative authority developed, so too did faculty professional power, and this professionalization resulted in more individual bargaining ability for faculty (Clark, 1987).

The term "shared governance" began to appear in the literature following the American Association of University Professors' pivotal "Statement on Government of Colleges and Universities" adopted in 1966 (AAUP, 1966). By the late 1960s, shared governance "had the strength of general tradition" (Duryea, 1973, p. 12) and faculty senates became the core of the academic governance process (Baldridge & Kemerer, 1977). Yet over time, increased intervention by states removed many decisions from the local level; unionism in many cases supplanted faculty senate involvement; and additional actors emerged in the shared governance process (AAUP, 1966; Baldridge, 1971; Baldridge et al., 1977; Corson, 1960; Duryea, 1973; Mortimer & McConnell, 1978).

By the 1990s, with rising costs of higher education, declining resources and resultant resource dependency, increasing enrollments, governmental intervention, globalization, public distrust, and increased calls for accountability, the nature of academic decision-making was being reevaluated (Alfred, 1998; Deas, 1994; Gilmour, 1991; Hardy, 1990; Levin, 2000; Miller, Vacik, & Benton, 1998; Morphew, 1999; Piland & Bublitz, 1998; Rhoades, 1992; Thaxter & Graham, 1999). Criticisms of shared governance appeared, faulting the system of decision-making as "too sluggish, too obstructive, and too predisposed to preserving the existing apportionment of jobs and resources ... of not being equal to the hard, unpleasant tasks of realigning campus priorities in light of emerging demographics, economic and political realities" (Schuster, Smith, Corak, & Yamada, 1994, p. 9).

In spite of the limits of shared governance in community colleges, internal patterns of governance have received more attention in the scholarly literature than many of the topics discussed earlier in this chapter. Indeed, various theoretical orientations have been applied to the concepts of shared governance and collective bargaining, including community college faculty professionalization (Cohen & Brawer, 2008), organizational constructs of professional bureaucracy and political decision-making (Kater, 2003); globalization (Levin, Kater, & Wagoner, 2011); and the notion that faculty and management share in "economizing behaviors" designed to increase productivity and efficiency (Levin, 2001). Little research, however, has attempted to explain if and how internal patterns of governance influence (or are influenced by) organizational patterns of governance and coordination, or how the two processes intersect in ways that make community colleges more or less responsive to public and legislative expectations. As of now, the future of shared governance is unknown. Keller suggests "we must disenthrall ourselves and think anew. We can safeguard the tattered ideal of shared governance only by reinventing it for the new environment" (2004, p. 174).

PATTERNS OF GOVERNANCE AND EXPECTATIONS
FOR INSTITUTIONAL BEHAVIOR

In recent years, several scholars have examined the connections between organizational patterns of governance and coordination and expectations for community college behaviors, arguing that differences in governance structures do indeed influence the ways in which institutions respond to state priorities, particularly those related to cross-sector collaboration (Amey, Eddy, & Ozaki, 2007; Bowen et al., 1997; Callan & Finney, 2003; Kirst, 2007; Kisker, 2006; Venezia, Callan, Finney, Kirst, & Usdan, 2005). However, similar to much of the community college governance literature, these authors have largely approached the issue from an applied or practical point of view, providing examples from various states in order to support their premises. Only recently has a stronger theoretical perspective—Granovetter's (1985) theory of organizational embeddedness—been applied to the issue. This section begins with an overview of the more applied examinations of the connections between governance patterns and institutional behavior, then extends Alfred's (2008) analysis of Granovetter's theory to provide a theoretical explanation for the ways in which governance structures affect expectations for community colleges, as well as their ability to carry out public policy objectives.

Organizational Patterns and Community College Collaborations
with Other Sectors

Bowen et al.'s (1997) categorization of higher education governance structures provides one explanation for how and why some patterns of organizational governance have a greater ability than others to respond to public policy objectives—in particular those related to cross-sector collaboration. According to their schema, federal and unified systems are highly effective in encouraging or mandating collaboration among community colleges and four-year institutions, as they are managed by a statewide coordinating board that has "enough support and delegated authority to compel institutional attention to state priorities" (p. 39). Thus, federal systems—such as those in place in Illinois, Ohio, Texas, and Washington—have significant capacity to link institutions of higher education and stimulate collaborative reforms. A recent example of effective statewide coordination within a federal system can be found in the Ohio Board of Regents' successful leadership of the development of transfer associate degrees in that state. Transfer associate degrees allow students to earn an associate degree at a community college and transfer seamlessly into a four-year institution with junior status (Kisker et al., 2011).

Unified systems are also highly effective in spurring collaborations among community colleges and their four-year counterparts, as all of the institutions are governed by a single statewide board of trustees. As Bowen and his colleagues (1997) argue, unified systems make strong use of strategic planning and rely on the budgeting process to support strategic objectives. In particular, "the inclusion of two- and four-year institutions in the same system promotes effective articulation and transfer" (p. 39).

Confederated systems, on the other hand, "are harder to characterize," as "the use of work processes and links to state government may be different" for each separate multicampus or system-wide governing board (Bowen et al., 1997, p. 39). For example, in California, the University of California, California State University, and California Community College sub-systems each makes its own decisions about which programs to offer (within the guidance of the 1960 Master Plan for Higher Education), and each negotiates its own budget directly with the governor and legislature. And although the California Postsecondary Education Commission is charged with coordinating the state's higher education efforts, the agency has always held little authority over the three systems, and in recent years has been virtually de-funded by the legislature, further reducing its coordinating influence (California Legislative Analyst's Office, 2009).

As a result, in California and other confederated states, the legislature often acts as the *de facto* coordinating agency among community colleges and four-year institutions (Bowen et al., 1997). In practice this has meant that the vast majority of collaborations between community colleges and universities in California have occurred at a local level, via institution-to-institution articulation and transfer agreements. Statewide collaborations, especially those necessitating agreement among inter-segmental faculty groups on curricular matters, have occurred only when required by the legislature. And while legislative mandates can be powerful tools in ensuring cross-sector collaboration (Kisker et al., 2011), as California's experience with legislatively mandated transfer and articulation reforms has shown, these initiatives tend to fade away as legislative scrutiny lapses (Kisker, Cohen, & Wagoner, 2010).

Similarly, states with confederated institutions of higher education are less likely than states with federal or unified systems to encourage or mandate cross-sector collaboration successfully. Indeed,

> confederated institutions lack any capacity for statewide planning except through voluntary consensus on division of the spoils. They determine their own missions and decide which programs they will offer where … Voluntary agreements on articulation are a matter of institutional interpretation and subscription. (Bowen et al., 1997, p. 40)

The key exception to this is when the legislature steps in and mandates some level of cross-sector collaboration, such as Arizona's legislature did in 1996 when it required (through a footnote in the annual appropriations bill) the Arizona Board of Regents and the (then) State Board of Directors for Community Colleges to form a joint committee to develop and implement transfer associate degrees (Kisker et al., 2011).

Thus, Bowen et al.'s (1997) analysis makes clear that differences in governance structures do indeed influence the performance of higher education systems and, perhaps most importantly, system responsiveness to state priorities. Stated more directly, states that have federal or unified systems of higher education governance are better able to encourage or compel community colleges and four-year institutions to work together in a collaborative manner on issues such as transfer and articulation, and are better able to sustain these coordinated initiatives over time. Cross-sector collaboration may continue to occur in states with confederated systems or confederated institutions, but it often develops locally, out of the goodwill and voluntary efforts of individual institution or system leaders. Statewide transfer and articulation reforms in states with confederated systems or institutions are most often products of legislative mandate.

The higher education governance scheme proposed by Bowen and his colleagues (1997) helps clarify how the distribution of authority within state postsecondary governance systems affects expectations for collaboration among community colleges and four-year institutions. But to examine how organizational patterns of community college governance affect collaborations with K-12 schools, such as dual enrollment and early or middle college high schools (programs that allow at-risk high school students to simultaneously earn a high school diploma and up to two years of college credit), we look to those states—such as Florida—that have instituted governing or coordinating structures that span the entire pre-kindergarten through university (P-16) spectrum.

It has been argued that the success or failure of collaborations between community colleges and K-12 and university partners depends in large part upon differences in governance structures, as well as the processes between partnering organizations (Amey et al., 2007). In particular, states with P-16 systems—or, at a minimum, P-16 councils with significant authority to encourage or coordinate secondary and postsecondary collaboration—are more effective in communicating clear expectations for community colleges and K-12 schools and are thus better able to drive institutional behaviors. In states without P-16 governing or coordinating structures, "a profound organizational, political, and cultural chasm persists … between the governance systems of K-12 and higher education" (Kirst, 2007, as cited in Venezia et al., 2005, p. 2).

Several states are working to improve the connections between their secondary and postsecondary systems, and in 2005, Venezia et al. set out to examine whether particular types of governance structures are more effective than others in using policy levers to facilitate and maintain K-16 reforms. Indeed, they found that states with K-16 governing or coordinating bodies may have a greater ability to develop and maintain cross-sector collaboration than states in which the educational sectors are governed by separate boards. However, simply "convening a commission or holding cross-sector discussions"—as some states have done—"is necessary but not sufficient for reform. To be lasting and effective, K-16 deliberations must be anchored in policy and infrastructure reforms" (Venezia et al., 2005, p. 22).

Furthermore, governing or coordinating structures such as P-16 councils will not be effective if they are "instituted by addition—that is, by simply grafting new programs onto existing policies that divide the levels" (p. 22). In other words, effective long-term collaboration among community colleges and K-12 schools depends on states restructuring their education governance systems in ways that provide incentives and reward institutions for working together to meet the needs of students. Venezia and her co-authors (2005) are quick to note that governance structures by themselves will not ensure greater K-16 collaboration. However, joint governance does "have a strong impact on the range of available options" (p. 38), primarily because it can create incentives—both monetary and in the form of accountability requirements (Haycock, 2002)—for the institutions to work together.

Kisker's (2006) work on the relationship between state policy and school–college collaboration supports this thesis. She found that the relatively recent integration of historically separate K-12 and community college governance and funding structures in several states—as well as the legislative enactment of collaborative policies supporting dual enrollment, Advanced Placement, and early college high schools—served to better support efforts to connect or integrate high school and community college education. Callan and Finney (2003) have come to a similar conclusion. They believe that current K-12 and higher education governing bodies are too focused on the policies of single institutions and sectors, and as a result overlook the linkages between the levels, as well as the transitions students must negotiate. The most effective governance structures for promoting cross-sector collaboration, they argue, feature ongoing forums for discussions about the health of the entire education pipeline, not just one specific part of it; utilize cross-institutional initiatives and funding; and have the ability to change policies, especially those that may inhibit the allocation and reallocation of resources among educational sectors. Until these governance features are present, Callan and Finney (2003) argue that "many existing K-12 and higher education partnerships have little long-term viability" (p. 11). Given the value placed on these collaborations in recent years—both by federal and state governments and major philanthropic organizations— we may expect to see more states reconsidering the traditional separation of K-12 and higher education governance (Boswell, 2000; Kisker, 2006).

A Theoretical Approach: Granovetter's Theory of Organizational Embeddedness

Although the above literature provides examples of ways in which organizational patterns of community college governance influence how institutions respond to state priorities such as cross-sector collaboration, much of it does so without incorporating a strong theoretical perspective. Alfred (2008), however, has utilized Granovetter's (1985) theory of organizational embeddedness in order to provide a conceptual framework for governance in complex service organizations such as community colleges. This section builds on Alfred's (2008) work to further our understanding of why governance patterns affect expectations for community colleges, as well as their ability to carry out public policy objectives.

In essence, Granovetter's conceptual framework views all governance or organizational decisions as embedded within networks of personal relationships involving institutional leaders, their staff, and external stakeholders. "[T]he structural nature of embeddedness posits a tension between *ties* that bind people together and thereby encourage cohesiveness and stability and opportunities or *holes* that encourage change and enable new ideas to gain a foothold in the organization" (Alfred, 2008, p. 85, emphasis in original). In complex organizations such as community colleges, governance decisions are made, reinforced, and sometimes challenged as the relationships among institutional actors change, or remain the same, over time.

Understanding governance through the lens of network embeddedness becomes especially important as more community colleges begin collaborating in significant ways with external organizations such as K-12 schools, universities, business and industry employers, and others to control costs and improve educational quality and efficiency. In particular, Granovetter's theory extends the way we think about community college governance beyond consideration of traditional governance models to include the influence of educational networks created by intra-institutional collaborations. When thinking about community college governance, then, one must consider not only the ties and holes that characterize the relationships between community college leaders and their faculty and staff, but also those between community college leaders and their counterparts at schools, universities, and other organizations with which they collaborate. Consideration of external networks thus "radically alter[s] the context for governance by injecting new and influential players into the decision process" (Alfred, 2008, p. 88).

The influence of these external networks—especially those that are codified through joint governing or coordinating structures—adds new players to the governance process, creates a wider distribution of power and authority among governance actors, and leads to expectations that community college leaders, faculty, and staff will act in ways that reinforce the network and the institution's collaborative mission. Granovetter's (1985) theory of organizational embeddedness—especially when considered with the more practical literature described earlier in this section—thus provides a strong theoretical basis for the fact that organizational patterns of community college governance affect expectations for institutional behavior. This theory puts into context the recent shifts from separate K-12 and community college to P-16 governance systems in several states.

CONCLUSION

Given the complexity and diversity of U.S. community colleges, as well as growing expectations for accountability and responsiveness to public and legislative priorities, the relatively thin literature related to governance and coordination would benefit greatly from further analysis. In particular, more scholarship that connects observed phenomena (such as the notion that community colleges in federal and unified systems seem to be more responsive than their confederated counterparts to public policy demands such as cross-sector collaboration) with theoretical explanations (for example, Granovetter's theory of network embeddedness), as well as the addition of new, multidimensional, adaptive models that account for the influence of globalization and multinationalism, would contribute to the understanding of how these important institutions are governed.

QUESTIONS FOR DISCUSSION

1. Is shared governance practiced in community colleges? If so, in what ways?
2. Network embeddedness theory helps us understand how community college governance decisions may be influenced by external actors and agencies. In what ways might this external influence be beneficial for community colleges and their students? In what ways might it be detrimental?
3. This chapter discusses five organizational patterns of community college governance. Do one or more of these models seem more effective than others in serving the needs of the state and its students? Should states be encouraged to adopt new or different patterns of community college governance? Why or why not?

REFERENCES

Alfred, R. L. (1998). *Shared governance in the community colleges.* Denver, CO: Education Commission of the States.
Alfred, R. L. (2008). Governance in strategic context. In R. C. Cloud & S. T. Kater (Eds.), *Governance in the community college. New Directions for Community Colleges, no. 141* (pp. 79–89). San Francisco, CA: Jossey-Bass.
Alfred, R. L., & Smydra, D. F. (1985). Reforming governance: Resolving challenges to institutional authority. In W. Deegan and D. Tillery (Eds.), *Renewing the American community college.* San Francisco, CA: Jossey-Bass.
American Association of University Professors (AAUP). (1966). Statement on government of colleges and universities. Retrieved from http://www.aaup.org
Amey, M. J., Eddy, P., & Ozaki, C. (2007). Demands for partnership and collaboration in higher education: A model. In M. J. Amey (Ed.), *Collaborations across educational sectors. New Directions for Community Colleges, no. 139,* (pp. 5–14). San Francisco, CA: Jossey-Bass.
Baldridge, J. V. (1971). Environmental pressure, professional autonomy, and coping strategies in academic organizations. In J. V. Baldridge (Ed.), *Academic governance* (pp. 507–529). Berkeley, CA: McCutchan Publishing Corporation.
Baldridge, J. V., Curtis, D. V., Ecker, G. P., & Riley, G. L. (1977). Alternative models of governance in higher education. In G. L. Riley & J. V. Baldridge (Eds.), *Governing academic organizations: New problems, new perspectives* (pp. 2–25). Berkeley, CA: McCutchan Publishing Company.

Baldridge, J. V., & Kemerer, F. R. (1977). Academic senates and faculty collective bargaining. In G. L. Riley & J. V. Baldridge (Eds.), *Governing academic organizations* (pp. 327–347).

Birnbaum, R. (1988). *How colleges work*. San Francisco, CA: Jossey-Bass.

Birnbaum, R. (1991). The latent organizational functions of the academic senate: Why senates do not work, but will not go away. In M. W. Peterson (Ed.), *Organization and governance in higher education* (pp. 195–207). Needham Heights, MA: Simon & Schuster.

Boswell, K. (2000). Building bridges or barriers? Public policies that facilitate or impede linkages between community colleges and local school districts. In J. C. Palmer (Ed.), *Leadership in an era of change. New Directions for Community Colleges, no. 111* (pp. 3–15). San Francisco, CA: Jossey-Bass.

Bowen, F. M., Bracco, K. R., Callan, P. M., Finney, J. E., Richardson, R. C., & Twombley, W. (1997). *State structures for the governance of higher education: A comparative study*. San Jose: California Higher Education Policy Center.

Burgan, M. (2004). Why governance? Why now? In W. G. Tierney (Ed.), *Competing conceptions of academic governance: Negotiating the perfect storm* (pp. xii–xiv). Baltimore, MD: Johns Hopkins University Press.

California Legislative Analyst's Office. (2009). *The master plan at 50: Assessing California's vision for higher education*. Sacramento, CA: Author.

Callan, P. M., & Finney, J. E. (2003). *Multiple pathways and state policy: Toward education and training beyond high school*. Boston, MA: Jobs for the Future and the National Center for Public Policy and Higher Education.

Clark, B. R. (1987). *The academic life: Small worlds, different worlds*. Princeton, NJ: Carnegie Foundation for the Advancement of Teaching.

Cohen, A. M., & Brawer, F. B. (2008). *The American community college* (5th ed.). San Francisco, CA: Jossey-Bass.

Cohen, A. M., & Kisker, C. B. (2010). *The shaping of American higher education: Emergence and growth of the contemporary system* (2nd ed.). San Francisco, CA: Jossey-Bass.

Cohen, M. D., & March, J. G. (1986). *Leadership and ambiguity: The American college president* (2nd ed.). Boston, MA: Harvard Business School Press.

Corson, J. J. (1960). *Governance of colleges and universities*. New York, NY: McGraw Hill.

Deas, E. (1994). Board and administration relationships contributing to community college climate: A case study. *Community College Review, 22*(1), 44–52.

Duderstadt, J. J. (2004). Governing the twenty-first century university. In W. G. Tierney (Ed.), *Competing conceptions of academic governance: Negotiating the perfect storm* (pp. 137–157). Baltimore, MD: Johns Hopkins University Press.

Duryea, E. (1973). Evolution of university organization. In M. Peterson (Ed.), *Organization and governance in higher education* (1991, pp. 3–16). Needham Heights, MA: Simon & Schuster.

Education Commission of the States. (2011). *State profiles: Postsecondary governance structures database*. Denver, CO: Author. Retrieved from http://mb2.ecs.org/reports/Report.aspx?id=221

Ehrenberg, R. G. (Ed.). (2004). *Governing academia*. Ithaca, NY: Cornell University Press.

Gilmour Jr., J. (1991). Participative governance bodies in higher education: Report of a national study. *New Directions for Higher Education, 75*, 27–39.

Granovetter, M. S. (1985). Economic action and social structure: The problem of embeddedness. *American Journal of Sociology, 91*(3), 481–510.

Gumport, P. (1993). The contested terrain of academic program reduction. *The Journal of Higher Education, 64*(3), 283–311.

Hamilton, N. W. (2004). Faculty involvement in system-wide governance. In W. G. Tierney (Ed.), *Competing conceptions of academic governance: Negotiating the perfect storm* (pp. 77–103). Baltimore, MD: Johns Hopkins University Press.

Hardy, C. (1990). Putting power into university governance. In J. Smart (Ed.), *Higher education: Handbook of theory and research* Vol. VI, (pp. 393–426). New York, NY: Agathon Press.

Haycock, K. (2002). Why is K-16 collaboration essential to educational equity? In *Gathering momentum: Building the learning connection between schools and colleges*. New York, NY: The Hechinger Institute on Education and the Media, the Institute for Educational Leadership, and the National Center for Public Policy and Higher Education.

Hines, E. R. (2000). The governance of higher education. In J. C. Smart & W. G. Tierney (Eds.), *Higher education: Handbook of theory and research* (Vol. XV, pp. 105–155). New York, NY: Agathon Press.

Kaplan, G. E. (2004). How academic ships actually navigate. In R. G. Ehrenberg (Ed.), *Governing academia* (pp. 165–208). Ithaca, NY: Cornell University Press.

Kater, S. T. (2003). *Shared governance in the community college: The rights, roles, and responsibilities of unionized community college faculty*. (Doctoral dissertation.) University of Arizona, Tucson, AZ. (UMI No. 5778862)

Keller, G. (2004). A growing quaintness: Traditional governance in the markedly new realm of U.S. higher education. In W. G. Tierney (Ed.), *Competing conceptions of academic governance: Negotiating the perfect storm* (pp. 158–176). Baltimore, MD: Johns Hopkins University Press.

Kirst, M. (2007). Separation of K-12 and postsecondary education: Impact, policy implications, and research needs. In S. Fuhrman. D. Cohen, & F. Mosher (Eds.), *The state of education policy research* (pp. 203–223). New York, NY: Routledge.

Kisker, C. B. (2006). *Integrating high school and community college: A historical policy analysis.* (Doctoral dissertation.) University of California, Los Angeles, CA. (UMI No. 3247442)

Kisker, C. B., Cohen, A. M., & Wagoner, R. L. (2010). *Reforming transfer and articulation in California: Four statewide solutions for creating a more successful and seamless transfer path to the baccalaureate.* Los Angeles, CA: Center for the Study of Community Colleges.

Kisker, C. B., Wagoner, R. L., & Cohen, A. M. (2011). *Implementing statewide transfer and articulation reform: An analysis of transfer associate degrees in four states.* Los Angeles, CA: Center for the Study of Community Colleges.

Lee, B. A. (1980–1981). Faculty role in academic governance and the managerial exclusion: Impact of the Yeshiva University decision. *Journal of College and University Law, 7*(3–4), 222–266.

Levin, J. S. (2000). What's the impediment? Structural and legal constraints to shared governance in the community college. *The Canadian Journal of Higher Education, 30*(2), 87–122.

Levin, J. S. (2001). *Globalizing the community college: Strategies for change in the twenty-first century.* New York, NY: Palgrave.

Levin, J. S. (2008). Yanks, Canucks, and Aussies: Governance as liberation. In R. C. Cloud & S. T. Kater (Eds.), *Governance in the community college. New Directions for Community Colleges, no. 141* (pp. 67–78). San Francisco, CA: Jossey-Bass.

Levin, J. S., Kater, S., & Wagoner, R. (2011). *Community college faculty: At work in the new economy* (2nd ed.). New York, NY: Palgrave Macmillan.

Lovell, C. D., & Trouth, C. (2002). State governance patterns for community colleges. In T. H. Bers & H. D. Calhoun (Eds.), *Next steps for the community college. New Directions for Community Colleges, no. 117* (pp. 91–100). San Francisco, CA: Jossey-Bass.

Marginson, S. (2004). Governance implications of cross-border traffic in higher education. In W. G. Tierney (Ed.), *Competing conceptions of academic governance: Negotiating the perfect storm* (pp. 1–32). Baltimore, MD: Johns Hopkin University Press.

Marginson, S., & Considine, M. (2000). *The enterprise university: Power, governance, and reinvention in Australia.* New York, NY: Cambridge University Press.

McGuinness, A. C. (2003). *Models of postsecondary education coordination and governance in the states.* Denver, CO: Education Commission of the States.

Miller, M. T., & Miles, J. M. (2008). Internal governance in the community college: Models and quilts. In R. C. Cloud & S. T. Kater (Eds.), *Governance in the community college. New Directions for Community Colleges, no 141* (pp. 35–44). San Francisco, CA: Jossey-Bass.

Miller, M. T., Vacik, S. M., & Benton, C. (1998). Community college faculty involvement in institutional governance. *Community College Journal of Research and Practice, 22*(7), 645–654.

Mintzberg, H. (2000). The professional bureaucracy. In C. Brown II (Ed.), *Organization and governance in higher education* (5th ed.) (pp. 50–82). Needham Heights, MA: Simon & Schuster.

Morgan, G. (1997). *Images of organization.* Beverly Hills, CA: Sage Publications.

Morphew, C. C. (1999, Spring). Challenges facing shared governance within the college. *New Directions for Higher Education, 105,* 71–79.

Mortimer, K. P., & McConnell, T. R. (1978). *Sharing authority effectively.* San Francisco, CA: Jossey-Bass.

Olivas, M. A. (2004). The rise of nonlegal legal influences on higher education. In R. G. Ehrenberg (Ed.), *Governing academia* (pp. 258–275). Ithaca, NY: Cornell University Press.

Piland, W., & Bublitz, R. (1998). Faculty perceptions of shared governance in California community colleges. *Community College Journal of Research and Practice, 22,* 99–110.

Pusser, B. (2003). Beyond Baldridge: Extending the political model of higher education organization and governance. *Educational Policy, 17*(1), 121–140.

Pusser, B., Slaughter, S., & Thomas, S. L. (2006). Playing the board game: An empirical analysis of university trustee and board interlocks. *The Journal of Higher Education, 77*(5), 1–29.

Pusser, B., & Turner, S. E. (2004). Nonprofit and for-profit governance in higher education. In R. G. Ehrenberg (Ed.), *Governing academia* (pp. 235–257). Ithaca, NY: Cornell University Press.

Rhoades, G. (1992). Governance models. In B. L. Clark & G. Neave (Eds.), *The encyclopedia of higher education* (pp. 1376–1384). New York, NY: Pergamon Press.

Richardson, R. C., Baracco, K. R., Callan, P. M., & Finney, J. E. (1998). *Designing state higher education systems for a new century.* Westport, CT: Oryx Press.

Richardson, R. C., & de los Santos, G. E. (2001). Statewide governance structures and two-year colleges. In B. K. Townsend & S. B. Twombly (Eds.), *Community colleges: Policy in the future context* (pp. 39–55). Westport, CT: Ablex.

Riley, G. L., & Baldridge, J. V. (Eds.). (1977). *Governing academic organizations: New problems, new perspectives.* Berkeley, CA: McCutchan Publishing.

Schuster, J. H., Smith, D. G., Corak, K.A., & Yamada, M. M. (1994). *Strategic governance: How to make big decisions better.* Phoenix, AZ: Oryx Press.

Thaxter, L., & Graham, S. (1999). Community college faculty involvement in decision-making. *Community College Journal of Research and Practice, 23*, 655–674.

Tierney, W. G. (Ed.). (2004). *Competing conceptions of academic governance.* Baltimore, MD: Johns Hopkins University Press.

Tollefson, T. A. (2000, April). *Martorana's legacy: Research on state systems of community colleges.* Paper presented at the 42nd Annual Meeting of the Council for the Study of Community Colleges, Washington, DC.

Tollefson, T. A. (2009). Community college governance, funding, and accountability: A century of issues and trends. *Community College Journal of Research and Practice, 33*(3), 386–402.

Venezia, A., Callan, P. M., Finney, J. E., Kirst, M. W., & Usdan, M. D. (2005). *The governance divide: A report on a four-state study on improving college readiness and success.* San Jose, CA: The National Center for Public Policy and Higher Education, the Institute for Educational Leadership, and the Stanford Institute for Higher Education Research.

11

STATE FISCAL SUPPORT FOR COMMUNITY COLLEGES

JIM PALMER

INTRODUCTION

The funding mechanisms that support community colleges grew out of the post-World War II transition of the public junior colleges from relatively low-cost extensions of secondary schools to self-standing institutions within state higher education systems. As Wattenbarger (1994) explained, fiscal support for the colleges, once a low-profile matter of local negotiation for in-district funds, became a visible part of state budgeting, and "the emphasis changed from local competition for ... needed tax resources to the state legislature where resource allocation was focused upon many new concerns: Universities, welfare, state health services, state highways, and prisons" (p. 336). Each state went its own way as policy-makers developed strategies for meeting this new fiscal obligation. The result today is an array of state fiscal support structures, most resting on formulas that relate—with varying degrees of complexity—funding to enrollment (Mullin & Honeyman, 2007). During the 2008–2009 fiscal year, the state appropriations derived through these varying approaches to funding constituted 30% of total fiscal support for public community colleges nationwide and were augmented by monies from local, state, and federal contracts (24% of total operating support); local tax appropriations (19% of total support); tuition (17% of total support); and monies from a variety of other sources, including gifts, investment income, and the sales and services of auxiliary enterprises (9% of total support) (Snyder & Dillow, 2011, pp. 513–514).

The result of these efforts across the states—along with the development of federal support, predominantly for student financial aid and career education—can be seen in an unprecedented system of open-access colleges enrolling 53% of all undergraduates at public higher education institutions nationwide in the fall of 2009 (Snyder & Dillow, 2011, p. 296). Yet trends over the past three decades suggest that the levels of state funding assumed in approaches to financing community colleges have been unsustainable and that current educators and policy-makers may, similar to their predecessors in the 1950s and 1960s, need to rethink the ways fiscal support for community colleges can be maintained. This chapter examines these trends, describes theories that have been advanced as explanations for the attenuated state support evident in those trends, and suggests lines of future research that might inform policy-makers and educators as they tackle ongoing funding challenges.

TRENDS IN FISCAL SUPPORT

Any analysis of community college funding must proceed cautiously. Trends in fiscal support over time can be difficult to pin down because of changes in the way college revenue data have been reported and because the population of public two-year colleges often shifts over time as vocational schools become accredited to award the associate's degree and as community colleges become baccalaureate-granting institutions. In addition, overall national averages mask considerable differences between states in terms of the mix of revenues used to support the colleges (Table 11.1). For example, in 2006–2007 (the most recent year for which state-by-state data on community college revenues are available), local tax monies supported community colleges in only 28 of the 50 states, and the proportion of total revenue derived from local taxes in those 28 states ranged from 1% to 50%. The picture becomes all the more complicated with the acknowledgment of within-state variations across institutions. Illinois is a case in point: Among its 39 community college districts, the proportion of revenue derived from tuition in 2008–2009 ranged from 7% to 40%, the proportion derived from local tax monies ranged from 10% to 52%, and the proportion derived from tuition and fees ranged from 18% to 38% (Illinois Board of Higher Education, 2011).

Nonetheless, the literature on state funding—although limited to one of many important revenue streams—points to several indicators of anemic government support. One lies in the vulnerability of state higher education funding to recurrent economic recessions (Delaney & Doyle, 2011; Lingenfelter, 2008; Palmer, 2009), a vulnerability that stems in part from the discretionary character of higher education in state budgets, the availability of tuition as a fallback source of revenue, and the subsequent tendency of legislators to balance state budgets during economic downturns with cuts in higher

Table 11.1 Revenue sources of community colleges, 2007

Revenue source	Number of states in which community colleges receive funding from this source	Proportion of aggregate state support for community colleges that derives from this source		
		Range across the states		
		Minimum	Maximum	Median
Tuition and fees	50	6%	43%	20%
State appropriations	50	3%	60%	32%
State grants and contracts	49	1%	17%	5%
Local appropriations	28	1%	50%	18%
Local grants and contracts	40	1%	8%	1%
Federal grants and contracts	50	7%	39%	14%
Sales and services of auxiliary enterprises	48	1%	12%	5%
Other	48	2%	42%	7%

Source: Data are from the 2007 Integrated Postsecondary Education Data System (U.S. Department of Education, n.d.).

education appropriations (Delaney & Doyle, 2011; Lingenfelter, 2008). As a result, colleges and universities have been subject to unsettling up-and-down swings in state fiscal support that have been characterized as cycles of "recession, retrenchment, and recovery" (Hodel, Laffey, & Lingenfelter, 2006, p. 1). This can be seen in Figures 11.1 and 11.2, which track trends in state tax appropriations per capita for the community colleges in two groups of states: Those in which local tax monies constituted less than 10% of total community college revenue from all government sources (state and federal) in fiscal year 2006–2007 (state community colleges) and those in which local tax monies accounted for 10% or more of all government funding (state-aided community colleges). The figures draw on data from the Grapevine project at Illinois State University (http:// grapevine.illinoisstate.edu) and represent only those states (10 in the state community college category and 20 in the state-aided category) for which revenue data on file with Grapevine are reasonably consistent over time; that is, there were no significant changes in the mix of institutions under the "community college" umbrella since 1979 or in the ways the states reported community college appropriations data to the Grapevine project. Trend lines in both charts show that periods of economic recession have in most cases been followed by downturns in the amount of state tax monies appropriated per capita. Appropriations have subsequently increased after the economy improves.

A second indicator is the apparent inability of state funding over time to keep up with college and university operating costs (Archibald & Feldman, 2006; Cheslock & Hughes, 2011). This is evident in the differing trend lines that emerge when state funding per capita is indexed against the Consumer Price Index (CPI) and when, on the other hand, per-capita funding is indexed against the Higher Education Price Index (HEPI). The CPI trend lines in both Figures 11.1 and 11.2 suggest that state funding since 1979 has kept pace with inflation—at least during peak economic periods—with changes in the prices consumers pay for goods and services tracked by the CPI program; between 1979 and 2009, appropriations per capita indexed against the CPI rose by 29% and 26% in state and state-aided community colleges respectively. But the HEPI trend lines suggest that this funding has not kept pace with changes in the goods and services—predominantly personnel—that are purchased by colleges and universities as they carry out their educational missions; appropriations per capita indexed against the HEPI declined by 1% and 3% in state and state-aided community colleges respectively. This difference in what the State Higher Education Executive Officers (2011, pp. 49–51) have called the "consumer perspective" of funding and the "provider perspective" is in line with the results of previous analyses employing both the CPI and the HEPI to compare trends in state support for higher education generally (e.g., Lingenfelter, 2008; Palmer, 2009). Beyond the obvious strain that this may place on institutional budgets, this difference in the CPI and HEPI trend lines suggests a potentially troubling disconnection between the perspective of citizens for whom taxes represent forgone income that could be devoted to consumer goods and the perspective of college leaders for whom taxes are essential fiscal resources. From the taxpayer's perspective, "state support for higher education since 1980 may appear quite adequate, even generous" (Palmer, 2009, p. 9). But from the academy's perspective, trends in tax support may seem inadequate.

Another sign of attenuated state support lies in the downward trend in state tax appropriations per $1,000 of personal income as calculated by the Bureau of Economic Analysis. This trend, noted by several analysts (e.g., Archibald & Feldman, 2006; McLendon, Hearn, & Mokher, 2009; Mumper, 2003; Palmer, 2009), suggests that smaller

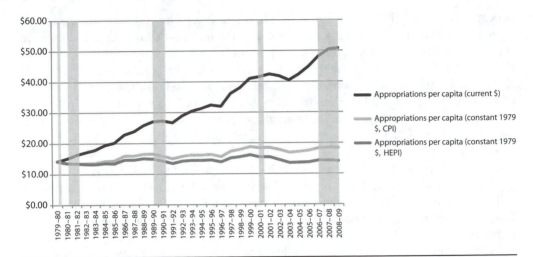

Figure 11.1 Trends in state tax appropriations per capita for "state community colleges," fiscal years 1979–1980 through 2008–2009.

Note: State community colleges are those located in states in which local tax monies constituted less than 10% of total community college revenue from all government sources (state and federal) in the fiscal year 2006–2007, as determined by an analysis of the Integrated Postsecondary Education Data System (U.S. Department of Education, n.d.). The trend lines reflect tax appropriations data recorded in annual historical reports archived by the Grapevine project (http://grapevine. illinoisstate.edu/historical/index.htm) for 10 of these states: Connecticut, Delaware, Indiana, Massachusetts, New Hampshire, Rhode Island, Tennessee, Utah, Virginia, and Washington. CPI = Consumer Price Index; HEPI = Higher Education Price Index. Historical index values for both the CPI and the HEPI were derived from the Commonfund Institute (2011, p. 3). Vertical shaded areas represent approximate periods of economic recession as noted by the National Bureau of Economic Research (2011). State population data used in the per capita calculations are from the U.S. Bureau of the Census (1995, 1996, 1999, 2009).

proportions of available wealth are devoted to higher education, at least through state tax mechanisms. The trend lines in Figure 11.3 illustrate this downward slant for community colleges. Between fiscal years 1979 and 2009, state tax appropriations per $1,000 of personal income declined by 26% for the sample of state community colleges and 22% for the sample of state-aided community colleges. State tax streams now transfer a smaller proportion of state economic wealth to community colleges than they did in the past. Much of the burden has shifted, instead, to individual students through tuition and fees, revenue streams that have increased at a higher rate than state tax appropriations. Between 1979 and 2010, average in-state tuition and fees at community colleges rose by 544% in current dollars, by 106% when indexed against the CPI, and by 63% when indexed against the HEPI (Figure 11.4).

WHAT EXPLAINS THE TREND LINES?

What is striking about the trends described above is how longstanding they are: Attenuated state funding has been a feature of the fiscal environment since at least the early 1980s (Archibald & Feldman, 2006; Mumper, 2003). The underlying causes, therefore, likely represent deeply rooted features of contemporary U.S. society. Writers have offered three possible explanations: (1) an ideological explanation focusing on changing perceptions of who benefits from education; (2) a structural explanation focusing on the

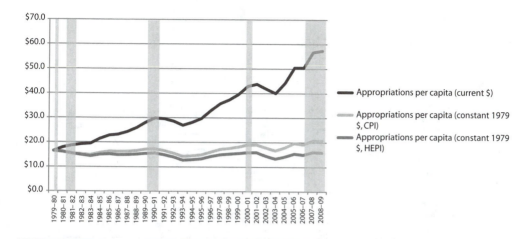

Figure 11.2 Trends in state tax appropriations per capita for "state-aided community colleges," fiscal years 1979–80 through 2008–2009.

Note: State-aided community colleges are those located in states in which local tax monies constituted 10% or more of total community college revenue from all government sources (state and federal) in the fiscal year 2006–2007, as determined by an analysis of the Integrated Postsecondary Education Data System. The trend lines reflect tax appropriations data recorded in annual historical reports archived by the Grapevine project (http://grapevine.illinoisstate.edu/historical/index.htm) for 20 of these states: Arizona, California, Idaho, Illinois, Iowa, Kansas, Maryland, Michigan, Mississippi, Missouri, Nebraska, New Jersey, New York, North Carolina, Ohio, Oklahoma, Pennsylvania, South Carolina, Texas, and Wyoming. CPI = Consumer Price Index; HEPI = Higher Education Price Index. Historical index values for both the CPI and the HEPI were derived from the Commonfund Institute (2011, p. 3). Vertical shaded areas represent approximate periods of economic recession as noted by the National Bureau of Economic Research (2011).

Source: Trends in state tax appropriations are from the Integrated Postsecondary Education Data System (U.S. Department of Education, n.d.). State population data used in the per capita calculations are from the U.S. Bureau of the Census (1995, 1996, 1999, 2009).

inability of the economy to generate the requisite wealth needed to provide year-to-year increases in funding for education; and (3) a socio-political explanation focusing on the unwillingness of the public to increase tax support for community colleges (or other public entities). Each posits a fundamental societal shift as the root cause of attenuated state fiscal support.

The Ideological Explanation

Some have traced the underlying fiscal problems of higher education, and community colleges specifically, to an emergent view of postsecondary education as a private good that channels benefits primarily to individuals and that therefore has only a limited claim on public subsidies. Those taking this view argue that the prevalence of this perspective represents a change in the social contract that undergirds higher education policy, weakening a consensus after World War II that society's interest is best served by maintaining a highly subsidized system of higher education charging only minimal levels of tuition. Kallison and Cohen (2010), for example, maintained that post-war "policies and programs designed to fund and encourage access, affordability, and participation in higher education" gave way after the 1960s to a "much narrower conception of higher education as primarily if not exclusively a private good" (p. 38). Speaking of community colleges specifically and pointing to data suggesting that financial aid

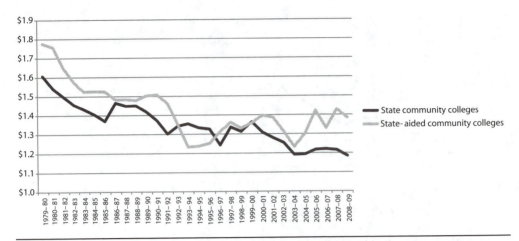

Figure 11.3 Trends in state tax appropriations per $1,000 in personal income for state community colleges and state-aided community colleges, fiscal year 1979–1980 through fiscal year 2008–2009. (See the notes to Figures 11.1 and 11.2 for definitions of both community college categories.)
Source: Appropriations data are from annual historical reports archived by the Grapevine project (http://grapevine.illinois-state.edu/historical/index.htm). State personal income data used are from the Bureau of Economic Analysis (2011).

available to students has not kept up with tuition increases, Mellow and Heelan (2008) also posited a fundamental change in societal views toward education.

As access to higher education becomes more significant to the country's ability to be effective, a lesser percentage of public dollars supports students, who now increasingly rely on their own resources. The clear implication is that education in the eyes of the public funder is turning into a private benefit as opposed to

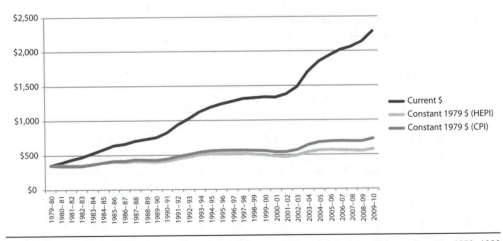

Figure 11.4 Trends in the average annual tuition and fees charged by public two-year colleges nationwide, 1979–1980 through 2009–2010.
Note: CPI = Consumer Price Index; HEPI = Higher Education Price Index.
Source: Trends in tuition and fees are from Snyder and Dillow (2011, p. 494). Historical index values for both the CPI and the HEPI are from the Commonfund Institute (2011, p. 3).

a public good. There are many underdeveloped countries in Africa and South America where private education is the only place to receive a college education. Unfortunately, it looks as if the United States may be moving in that direction. (p. 37)

The unspoken assumption of this view is that decisions about tax allocations to higher education are ideologically driven, tied to the belief—a false belief in the minds of higher education advocates—that funding policy should correct an imbalance between the vastly overstated externalities yielded by public investment in higher education and proportionately understated private benefits that accrue to individual students. But the up-and-down trends of state funding are not consistent with this assumption; the fact that legislators have increased funding after economic upturns (as illustrated in Figures 11.1 and 11.2) does not square with the notion that they are bent on funding reductions that privatize the academy. In addition, the perception of postsecondary education as a private good, to the extent that it exists, is at least as much a product of the changing fiscal environment as it is a driver of policy-making. As Smith (2005) pointed out, diminished public funding of the academy over time "will lead to higher education being perceived less as the public good it once was, and increasingly as a private good, which students must sacrifice to afford" (para. 8). Arguments against the narrow view of education as a private good, although necessary, will therefore be insufficient in ongoing efforts to rethink the ways we fund community colleges.

The Structural Explanation

A second line of discourse explaining attenuated support for higher education focuses on the limits of the economy and its effects on state fiscal capacity—the availability of sufficient tax revenues from which this support must ultimately be drawn. Throughout the 1960s and early 1970s—when contemporary community college systems took their current form—that capacity seemed assured. State funding for higher education continually rose and did not begin the up-and-down pattern discussed above until the early 1980s (Archibald & Feldman, 2006; Mumper, 2003) in the wake of what economist Tyler Cowen (2010) has called the "great stagnation," a decades-long period of attenuated economic growth that persists to the present and stands in stark contrast to the post-World War II era of economic expansion. Examining the "abrupt change in direction around 1980," Mumper (2003) observed that the policy goal of maintaining low tuition through increased state subsidies became a casualty of mounting economic pressures.

Reduced levels of state support were driven by difficult economic conditions in many states. High unemployment produced revenue shortfalls. Those same conditions were leading to increased demands for social and health services as well as for law enforcement and prison construction. This combination led many states to simply abandon their long-standing low-tuition policies. (p. 47)

Since then, the capacity of states to provide annual funding increases that might ease the pressure to increase tuition has become even more precarious. As the trend lines in Figure 11.5 indicate, revenue streams to the states have become less predictable than their expenditures. This suggests a troublesome imbalance between state fiscal obligations and the resources needed to meet those obligations, an imbalance that may become more pronounced and intractable over time as steadily increasing expenditures

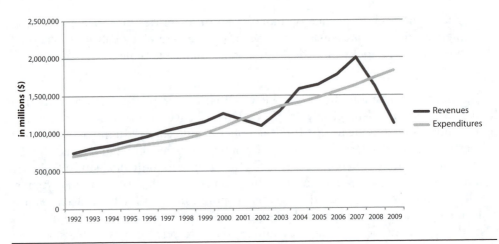

Figure 11.5 Trends in total state revenues and expenditures (in millions of dollars), 1991–1992 through 2008–2009. *Source:* U.S. Bureau of the Census (2011).

(especially in health care and employee pensions) outpace economic growth and state tax revenues (Ward & Dadayan, 2009).

Any redesign of the funding mechanisms used to support community colleges must therefore factor in the uneven year-to-year capacity of states to increase higher education appropriations—a phenomenon that those who originally designed community college funding systems did not often face. Arguing that the pattern of up-and-down funding has become a permanent and predictable feature of the fiscal environment for higher education, Delaney and Doyle (2011) urged "education leaders [to] discuss not only funding levels with their state legislatures, but also volatility in funding patterns" as well as mechanisms that might "reduce the uncertainty that institutions face as a result of [this] volatility" (p. 364). They suggested two potentially helpful approaches: allowing institutions to build and control "rainy day funds" that would be "used in bad budget years to smooth drops in appropriations from the state" and "creating a national insurance program" that, with support of payments from the institutions themselves, would oversee a "national risk pool to insure against bad budget years in their states" (p. 364). Further exploration of these and other creative adaptations to up-and-down patterns of state funding could, as Delaney and Doyle (2011) noted, bring a badly needed degree of stability to higher education funding.

The Socio-Political Explanation

Although limited fiscal capacity caused by economic downturns and growing demands made on state budgets undoubtedly factored into attenuated state support for higher education over the past three decades, that capacity was itself affected by an emergent public reluctance to raise and appropriate ever larger sums to government entities. This diminished political willingness to increase public funding took its most visible form in California's Proposition 13, a tax limitation measure approved by the state's voters in 1978 toward the beginning of the great stagnation. Similar measures were passed thereafter in several states, making it all the more difficult to provide colleges and universities with annual funding increases. In an analysis covering the years 1960 to 2000,

Archibald and Feldman (2006) found that the presence of both tax limitation measures and super-majority requirements for the passage of tax increases "explained over half the observed decline" (p. 634) in state funding for higher education per $1,000 in personal income. This was the case even when controls were introduced for political factors (e.g., the political party of the governor and of the majorities in both the upper and lower legislative houses), the state's spending on corrections as well as on health and hospitals, and the age distribution of the state's population. They concluded that, similar to the up-and-down volatility of state tax support itself, diminished taxpayer willingness had become a feature of the fiscal landscape that the academy would have to get used to. "Attacking the tax and expenditure limitations or the supermajority requirements would require a pro-tax coalition that is stronger than the anti-tax forces that implemented them. But there is no evidence that support for these explicit limitations is waning" (p. 640).

Some of the reluctance to strengthen state capacity by raising taxes is likely the product of fiscal conservatism. Studies have yielded evidence supporting the hypothesis that Republican control of state offices or legislatures is negatively associated with state appropriations for higher education (e.g., McLendon et al., 2009). But the roots of the problem are deeper and can be traced at least partially to the fragile nature of public confidence and trust in the education enterprise. Canvassing the state of community college funding in the early 1970s, Lombardi (1973) observed a growing public wariness that manifested itself in the defeat of local tax levy measures for community college districts. He attributed this in part to an inevitable turnaround in public attitudes as the initial post-war enthusiasm for the expansion of higher education gave way to skepticism and questioning when that very expansion "absorbed an increasingly large proportion of public funds" (p. 1). The nature of that skepticism, which applied to all levels of education, was fundamental, reflecting a perception on the part of many that schools generally were "not accomplishing what they claim" (p. 2). In the case of community colleges, questions emerged about the success of transfer and vocational students, the efficacy of remediation, and "the lack of formal evaluations of courses or programs" (p. 3)—issues that have been the focus of attention by policy-makers and community college educators ever since.

The socio-political analyses of diminished public willingness to increase funding for education highlight the critical role of accountability in securing fiscal support. The result has been a decades-long movement to strengthen public understanding of and confidence in the community college enterprise. This can be seen in the ongoing efforts by some states to report indicators of student outcomes (e.g., California Community Colleges Chancellor's Office, 2011), in the continuing, albeit checkered, attempts of states to experiment with performance budget mechanisms that tie portions of state funding to specific student outcomes (Dougherty, Natow, Hare, Jones, & Vega, 2011), and in the work of the U.S. Department of Education's Committee on Measures of Student Success (2009), which has been charged with the task of developing "recommendations ... regarding the accurate calculation and reporting of completion or graduation rates of entering certificate- or degree-seeking, full-time" students at community colleges, as well as "additional or alternative measures of student success that" reflect "the mission and role of two-year degree-granting higher education institutions" (p. 1). All are a response to a perceived public skepticism of education that has characterized the fiscal environment for decades and that has left community colleges (and other higher education institutions) struggling with the task of explaining and justifying their work.

CONCLUSION

The deeply rooted and longstanding history of tenuous state support for higher education suggests that the fiscal health of community colleges will depend more on state and institutional adaptations to the fiscal environment than on advocacy for incremental subsidies—subsidies that, absent tax increases, can only come at the expense of other equally important public agencies seeking their own share of limited state resources (Archibald & Feldman, 2006). Those adaptations must ultimately be guided by a clear sense of institutional purpose, moving beyond the question of how funding can be increased to the questions of what the community colleges are funded for and how colleges employ those funds. The alternative is to let matters take their own course, perhaps increasing the fiscal burden borne by the many low-income students served by these institutions or otherwise damaging the goals of access and equitable opportunity that are at the core of the institution's mission. This is a challenge faced by all states and state-funded organizations. As Ward and Dadayan (2009) concluded in their examination of long-term fiscal problems in the public sector, "The real question may be *how* states and localities will bring revenues and expenditures into alignment. Failure to [do so] … will mean more spending cuts made with little planning, likely exacerbating damage to services" (p. 472).

At the state level, efforts to align funding formulas with clearly identified priorities may do much to enhance efficiencies in the use of scarce resources available while at the same time clarifying what community colleges are accountable for as educational ends. Harbour and Jaquette (2007), for example, have proposed a framework for state funding that adjusts appropriations with "an equity funding factor" that provides a proportionately greater per-student allotment for the enrollment and retention of "disadvantaged students," including low-income and minority students, as well as "students enrolled in basic literacy and numeracy courses, homeless students, and students with disabilities" (p. 204). Under this framework, the funding formula intentionally highlights and prioritizes the community college's role in serving under-represented populations. The work of Harbour and Jaquette (2007) is in line with the earlier, pioneering analyses of Garms (1977), who suggested several criteria against which funding mechanisms might be judged, including the extent to which they "enhance, rather than impede" the capacity of community colleges to carry out key functions that are unique to these institutions, including serving "those who find access to traditional institutions difficult," providing "courses and programs not provided or provided inefficiently, by the four-year institutions," and responding to local community needs (p. 38). Mindful of the fact that public willingness to support the colleges is not limitless, Garms also emphasized that "the finance program should help keep the expansion of the community colleges within the bounds of public willingness to support them" and simultaneously "take into account the financial health of state and local governments and the competing demands upon them for money" (1977, pp. 38–39).

At the institutional level, research could focus on how funding trends affect decision-making within colleges and, by extension, the institutional mission. In the case of community colleges, it will be critical to examine how decisions made (or not made) affect open-access. An example can be seen in the possibility that as institutions become increasingly tuition driven in the wake of attenuated state support, low-income students may be sidelined for the more affluent, especially if enrollment caps push up registration deadlines. Writing in the wake of the recession experienced earlier in 2001, Vaughan (2004) argued that college leaders would need to factor in the tendency of low-income students to register for classes late in the game, thus raising the likelihood that they would be left behind by a first-come-first-served approach to course registration procedures for courses with enrollment caps. He urged proactive steps that might prevent or minimize this possibility, such as setting aside a certain number of seats for students who have not yet completed the admissions process by a certain time and providing workshops or other forms of support for students who will need additional help in negotiating the admissions and financial aid processes.

Beyond this one example, Vaughan had an important, overarching message: that the expansive understanding of open-access as it emerged in the post-World War II era would of necessity give way to a more consolidated view, trimmed back to reflect the view that "community colleges cannot serve all of the students who want to attend" or "continue to enroll large numbers of students for whom they receive no state financing" (2004, para. 5). Bluntly warning that open-access as it was practiced in the past "is a failure" (2004, para. 5), Vaughan noted that "priorities must be set" and that presidents must take proactive steps with key stakeholders to "define the meaning of access" (2004, para. 9). This is an admonition to sharpen and more clearly define the institution's purpose, in line with the observations of Breneman and Nelson (1981), who noted that amorphous representations of an all-encompassing community college mission devoted to lifelong learning and community development provided state policy-makers with little "help in setting operating policies" (p. 163). Research that examines how college leaders have gone about the process of defining the mission and setting funding priorities will add important insights about the ongoing development of community colleges in the contemporary fiscal climate.

Finally, these studies of leadership initiatives could be augmented by analyses of promising campus initiatives undertaken to cut costs without degrading educational quality. These analyses would, in effect, be case studies of pilot projects or experiments in cost control, similar to the pilot projects advocated by those seeking to reign in health care costs (e.g., Gawande, 2009). Grass-roots experiments in cost control should be encouraged, and their results should be summarized and published. Just as the nation's ambitions for increased access to health care cannot be met without attention to costs, so too will success in attempts to increase educational attainment rest on attention to costs as well as revenue. The newly emerging data sets developed by the Delta Project on Postsecondary Education Costs, Productivity, and Accountability (http://www.deltacostproject.org), as well as the Kansas Study of Community College Instructional Costs and Productivity (http://www.kansasstudy.org), represent an implicit recognition of the need to add cost studies (e.g., Romano, Losinger, & Millard, 2011; Seybert & Rossol, 2010) to the body of research on higher education finance, a body of research that to date has focused much more on revenue streams than on how revenues are ultimately used.

QUESTIONS FOR DISCUSSION

1. How can community colleges adapt to up-and-down swings in state capacity to increase funding?
2. Are community colleges obliged to raise tuition and let the revenue burden fall upon students?
3. As a result of both state funding diminution and the prospects of limited future revenue streams, do community colleges have to curtail access?

REFERENCES

Archibald, R. B., & Feldman, D. H. (2006). State higher education spending and the tax revolt. *The Journal of Higher Education, 77*, 618–644. doi 10.1353/jhe.2006.0029

Breneman, D. W., & Nelson, S. C. (1981). *Financing community colleges: An economic perspective.* Washington, DC: Brookings Institution.

Bureau of Economic Analysis. (2011). *State quarterly personal income.* Retrieved from http://www.bea.gov/regional/sqpi/default.cfm?selTable=SQ1

California Community Colleges Chancellor's Office. (2011, March). *Focus on results: Accountability reporting for the California community colleges.* Sacramento, CA: Author. Retrieved from http://www.cccco.edu/Portals/4/TRIS/research/ARCC/March%20ARCC%202011.pdf

Cheslock, J. J., & Hughes, R. P. (2011). Differences across states in higher education finance policy. *Journal of Education Finance, 36*, 369–393.

Commonfund Institute. (2011). *2011 HEPI.* Retrieved from http://www.commonfund.org/CommonfundInstitute/HEPI/HEPI%20Documents/2011/2011%20HEPI%20Report.pdf

Cowen, T. (2010). *The great stagnation. How America ate all the low-hanging fruit of modern history, got sick, and will (eventually) feel better.* New York, NY: Penguin Group. Available from http://us.penguingroup.com/nf/Book/BookDisplay/0,,9781101502259,00.html

Delaney, J. A., & Doyle, W. R. (2011). State spending on higher education: Testing the balance wheel over time. *Journal of Education Finance, 36*, 343–368.

Dougherty, K. J., Natow, R. S, Hare, R. J., Jones, S. M., & Vega, B. A. (2011). *The politics of performance funding in eight states: Origins, demise, and change. Final report to the Lumina Foundation for Education.* New York, NY: Teachers College, Columbia University. (ERIC Document Reproduction Service No. ED517751)

Garms, W. I. (1977). *Financing community colleges.* New York, NY: Teachers College Press.

Gawande, A. (2009, December 14). Testing, testing: The health-care bill has no master plan for curbing costs. Is that a bad thing? *New Yorker.* Retrieved from http://www.newyorker.com/reporting/2009/12/14/091214fa_fact_gawande

Harbour, C. P., & Jaquette, O. (2007). Advancing an equity agenda at the community college in an age of privatization, performance accountability, and marketization. *Equity & Excellence in Education, 40*, 197–207. doi: 10.1080/10665680701434650

Hodel, R., Laffey, M., & Lingenfelter, P. (2006). *Recession, retrenchment, and recovery: State higher education funding & student financial aid.* Boulder, CO: State Higher Education Executive Officers. (ERIC Document Reproduction Service No. ED502180)

Illinois Board of Higher Education. (2011). *Current fund revenues by source at Illinois public community colleges, FY2009* (Table VI). Retrieved from http://www.ibhe.state.il.us/Data%20Bank/DataBook/2010/Table%20VI-11.pdf

Kallison, J. M., Jr., & Cohen, P. (2010). A new compact for higher education: Funding and autonomy for reform and accountability. *Innovative Higher Education, 35*, 37–49.

Lingenfelter, P. L. (2008). The financing of public colleges and universities in the United States. In H. F. Ladd & E. B. Fiske (Eds.), *Handbook of research in education finance and policy* (pp. 651–670). New York, NY: Routledge.

Lombardi, J. (1973). *Managing finances in community colleges.* San Francisco, CA: Jossey-Bass.

McLendon, M. K., Hearn, J. C., & Mokher, C. G. (2009). Partisans, professionals, and power: The role of political factors in state higher education funding. *The Journal of Higher Education, 80*, 686–713. doi: 10.1353/jhe.0.0075

Mellow, G. O., & Heelan, C. (2008). *Minding the dream: The process and practice of the American community college.* Lanham, MD: Rowman & Littlefield.

Mullin, C. M., & Honeyman, D. S. (2007). The funding of community colleges: A typology of state funding formulas. *Community College Review, 35,* 113–127. doi: 10.1177/0091552107306409

Mumper, M. (2003). Does policy design matter? Comparing universal and targeted approaches to encouraging college participation. *Educational Policy, 17,* 38–59. doi: 10.1177/0895904802239285

National Bureau of Economic Research. (2011). *US business cycle expansions and contractions.* Retrieved from http://www.nber.org/cycles.html

Palmer, J. C. (2009). Trends in state tax support for higher education: Prospects for an entrepreneurial response. In J. C. Knapp & D. J. Siegel (Eds.), *The business of higher education: Vol. 2. Management and fiscal strategies* (pp. 1–16). Santa Barbara, CA: Praeger/ABC-CLIO.

Romano, R. M., Losinger, R., & Millard, T. (2011). Measuring the cost of a college degree: A case study of a SUNY community college. *Community College Review.* Advance online publication, doi: 10.1177/0091552111416226

Seybert, J. A., & Rossol, P. M. (2010). What drives instructional costs in two-year colleges?: Data from the Kansas Study of Community College Instructional Costs and Productivity. *Planning for Higher Education, 38*(3), 38–44.

Smith, M. F. (2005). Government relations: More, please. *Academe Online, 91*(5). Retrieved from http://www.aaup.org/AAUP/pubsres/academe/2005/SO

Snyder, T. D., & Dillow, S. A. (2011). *The digest of education statistics, 2010* (NCES 2011015). Washington, DC: National Center for Education Statistics.

State Higher Education Executive Officers. (2011). *State higher education finance FY 2010.* Boulder, CO: Author. (ERIC Document Reproduction Service No. ED517206)

U.S. Bureau of the Census. (1995). *Intercensal estimates of the total resident population of states: 1970–1980.* Retrieved from http://www.census.gov/popest/archives/1980s/st7080ts

U.S. Bureau of the Census. (1996). *Intercensal estimates of the total resident population of states: 1980 to 1990.* Retrieved from http://www.census.gov/popest/archives/1980s/st8090ts.txt

U.S. Bureau of the Census. (1999). State Population Estimates: Annual Time Series, July 1, 1990 to July 1, 1999. Retrieved from http://www.census.gov/popest/archives/1990s/ST-99-03.txt

U.S. Bureau of the Census. (2009). *Table 1. Annual Estimates of the Resident Population for the United States, Regions, States, and Puerto Rico: April 1, 2000 to July 1, 2009* (NST-EST2009-01). Retrieved from http://hawaii.gov/dbedt/info/census/popestimate/09state_pop_hawaii/NST-EST2009-01.pdf

U.S. Bureau of the Census. (2011). *State government finances. Historical data.* Retrieved from http://www.census.gov/govs/state/historical_data.html

U.S. Department of Education. (n.d.). *Integrated Postsecondary Education Data System (IPEDS), 2007* [Data analysis system online]. Retrieved from http://nces.ed.gov/dasolv2/tables/mainPage.asp?mode=NEW&filenumber=380

U.S. Department of Education's Committee on Measures of Student Success. (2009). *Charter.* Retrieved from http://www2.ed.gov/about/bdscomm/list/acmss-charter

Vaughan, G. B. (2004, December 5). Redefining "open access." *Chronicle of Higher Education.* Retrieved from http://chronicle.com/article/Redefining-Open-Access-/28792

Ward, R. B., & Dadayan, L. (2009). State and local finance: Increasing focus on fiscal sustainability. *Publius: The Journal of Federalism, 39,* 455–475. doi:10.1093/publius/pjp014

Wattenbarger, J. W. (1994). Resource development in the community college: The evolution of resource policy development for community colleges as related to support from local, state, and federal governments. In G. A. Baker, P. Tyler, & J. Dudziak (Eds.), *A handbook on the community college in America: Its history, mission, and management* (pp. 333-339). Westport, CT: Greenwood Press.

Section III

ECONOMIC AND WORKFORCE DEVELOPMENT

12

CAREER AND TECHNICAL EDUCATION

Old Debates, Persistent Challenges in Community Colleges

DEBRA D. BRAGG

INTRODUCTION

Career and technical education is rooted in federal legislation first passed in 1917 to fund secondary vocational education. In spite of staunch support from early junior college advocates, the federal government did not fund career and technical education (then labeled vocational education) beyond high school until the 1960s, and even then appropriations were modest. However, vocational education has expanded and diversified considerably since the mid-20th century, leading scholars to question whether the access agenda of community colleges is threatened by an increasing preoccupation with economic development (Levin, 2001). Critics have claimed the vocational mission of community colleges overshadows individual benefits (Brint & Karabel, 1989), but politicians, business representatives, and college leaders continue to seek an intensified connection to the labor market (Harmon & MacAllum, 2003). Situated in the middle of this long-standing debate is the student who seeks a college education for many reasons, one of which is to secure a good job.

Since 1963, federal legislation has authorized funding for postsecondary vocational education to increase enrollments through strengthened connections to business and industry, with community and technical colleges at the heart of this workforce development strategy (Bragg, 2001a). Integral to implementation of vocational education at the postsecondary level were articulation agreements with high schools to create academic pathways that enable traditional-age students to transition to college. Skill-specific training programs were offered to assist unemployed and incumbent adult workers to obtain credentials and re-enter or advance in the labor market. These diverse trajectories represent the outer boundaries for what has become a broad set of curricular offerings that represent contemporary career and technical education (CTE).

This chapter begins with an analysis of federal support for secondary vocational education that began in 1917. It continues by examining vocational education at the mid-20th century when dramatic social and economic change occurred nationwide, prompting federal funding for vocational education by community, junior, and technical colleges. At the end of the 20th century and beginning of the new millennium postsecondary vocational education evolved into an even more complex, multidimensional enterprise, and the terminology shifted from vocational education to CTE, which was codified in the Carl D. Perkins Career and Technical Education Improvement Act in 2006. Increasingly, CTE has been positioned as an instrumental tool to prepare workers for the global economy, extending the long-standing debate about whether vocational education should be integrated into the general curriculum or kept distinct to facilitate economic development.

FROM VOCATIONAL EDUCATION TO CAREER AND TECHNICAL EDUCATION

Since the early 20th century, the nation has debated the fundamental role of public education. At one extreme, the core purpose of public education is to provide liberal education to develop the whole person and, at the other extreme, the key goal is to develop specific skills for work. This intention to distinguish education for employment from education for life's fuller endeavors represents one of the most important yet contentious debates over public education in the U.S. (see, for example, Labaree, 2010). Over much of the 20th century, this debate played out in public high schools where students prepared to attend college or enter the workplace.

The comprehensive high school took shape at about the turn of the 20th century when educators, politicians, and business leaders actively debated how best to educate the nation's growing and increasingly diverse student population. The nation was seeing an increasing number of young people leave the farms for urban areas, and immigration was bringing non-native speakers into the population (Wirth, 1992). To address these trends, high schools were thought most efficient if they replicated the social and economic order of the day, helping students find a place in the school curriculum that would prepare them to matriculate to college or prepare them for employment. This focus on efficiency contributed to the replication of structural inequalities that separated students by income, ethnicity and race, gender, and other defining characteristics. Hence, high school education for the wealthy and elite class focused on preparation for college, and preparation for the rest, especially the working class, concentrated on preparation for employment. Males were the primary recipients of high school technical instruction, with domestic life as the focus for the education of females (Wirth, 1992).

The Smith Hughes Act

Vocational education began to be offered as part of public schooling when the federal Smith Hughes Act was passed in 1917, through vocational agriculture and manual training programs for males and domestic science (or home economics) for females. Vocational curriculum was especially useful to educate students who were likely to drop out (Lazerson & Grubb, 1974), and was therefore heralded as a democratizing mission of public education, according to the U.S. government (Benavot, 1983; Lazerson & Grubb, 1974). Simultaneously, employers praised the benefits that vocational education provided by offering specific skill training to students who would otherwise fail to find work that would sustain a living wage. Similar to policy-makers, employers foresaw benefits of vocational education for both the economy and students by motivating students to stay in school and enter employment (Wirth, 1992).

Championing vocational education as a democratizing form of public education, Prosser (1913) observed, "The American school will truly become democratic when we learn to train all kinds of men [sic], in all kinds of ways, for all kinds of things" (p. 406). Through vocational education, students were expected to experience a more practical form of education that was presumed to be directly applicable to their future as laborers and line workers in factories that were needed to grow the U.S. industrial economy. Vocational education would heighten students' abilities to secure skilled jobs (rather than fill unskilled jobs that predominated in the labor market at that time). For the working class, education for citizenship and for life was presumed to be fulfilled if they were prepared for work (Wonacott, 2003).

Separate and Unequal

The Smith Hughes Act established vocational education as a separate system of education administered by state boards to perpetuate distinct curricula. Because the administration of federal funds required an independent administrative system, state boards that propagated separate curricula (what eventually became known as tracks) were also perpetuated through separate teacher preparation programs and reinforced by professional and student organizations that complemented practical classroom instruction (Rojewski, 2002). However, critics of the separate system for vocational education, such as John Dewey, claimed that vocational education missed opportunities to connect pedagogical approaches to broader aspects of education, work, and the community that were necessary to move marginalized populations into the mainstream of society (Wirth, 1992). Dewey and others argued that a separate system of vocational education weakened the entire educational system, and these perspectives laid the groundwork for debates about the goals of public education that have lasted for decades (Wirth, 1992).

In an historical account prepared for the U.S. Department of Education, Hayward and Benson (1993) described the "isolation of vocational education from other parts of the comprehensive high school curriculum" as "a division between practical and theoretical instruction" (p. 3) that would have detrimental effects on U.S. public schools. Educating students to perform job-specific skills to the exclusion of academic education limited students' options to transition to college and advance into professional employment. Isolation was not only evident between vocational and academic education but within vocational education because fields of study associated with agriculture, manual training (eventually industrial arts and then technology education), home economics, business, and other areas were funded and delivered separately (Rojewski, 2002). Even within vocational education, different fields of study were separate and unequal, depending on their alignment with larger social and economic strata. This separation of curriculum between vocational and academic education, as well as further differentiation within vocational education, prevailed into the mid-20th century when federal legislation expanded to the postsecondary education level.

At the time the Smith Hughes Act was passed, Charles Prosser and David Snedden, prominent spokespersons, advocated for "an *essentialist* approach toward vocational education—firmly grounded in meeting the needs of business and industry" (Rojewski, 2002, p. 7, emphasis in original). Citing historical accounts authored by Sarkees-Wircenski and Scott (1995), Rojewski observed that essentialism emphasizes instruction in basic academics (reading, writing, and arithmetic), respect for the prevailing power structure, and appreciation of middle-class values. As noted previously, this philosophy was countered by John Dewey, who warned that "too specific a mode of efficiency defeats its own purpose," and he called for education that would be neither too labor-market specific nor too distinct from the rest of schooling so that there was not a diminution of its benefits to the individual or to the community (Dewey, 1916, p. 119). The perspectives of Prosser and Snedden, in contrast to Dewey, which continued to be associated with vocational education to the present, contribute to an uneven playing field for historically marginalized populations who seek opportunities to benefit from public education directed at college and career preparation.

EXTENSION OF VOCATIONAL EDUCATION TO THE POSTSECONDARY LEVEL

Expansion of vocational education to the postsecondary level occurred in the 1960s, launching vocational programs that would continue to evolve throughout the rest of the 20th century. However, the increase in vocational education programs was not without controversy due to the continued delivery of programming that was accessed by and accessible to some but not all student groups. Efforts to diversify the student population that participated in vocational education were acknowledged by new federal legislation in the 1970s, but limitations of these laws contributed to inequities for ethnic and racial student groups.

The Vocational Education Act of 1963

Until the 1960s, federal monies for vocational education were devoted entirely to secondary education. Numerous leaders of junior colleges advanced the idea of terminal vocational education for several decades, including national commissions advocating for applied associate degree programs in the health sciences, manufacturing, and other fields. However, none of these efforts produced support for dedicated federal funding for vocational education beyond high school until the mid-1960s when the nation launched a comprehensive higher education agenda. Intellectual leaders of the junior college were adamant supporters of an alternative curriculum to transfer education for working-class students, and they articulated widely the importance of a strong vocational function in junior colleges (Meier, 2008). Walter Crosby Eells, Leonard V. Koos, and other early scholars of the community college considered vocational education to be a proper alternative to transfer for students who were unlikely to be successful pursuing baccalaureate degrees. They advocated for a diversified curriculum that paralleled the stratified labor market, believing that vocational education was essential to the long-term survival of junior colleges. State higher education systems lent their support, creating separate institutional types to support the administration of two-year college and four-year university education to address a range of student abilities (Brint & Karabel, 1989; Dougherty, 2004). This argument, including the rhetoric of democratizing education, is hauntingly similar to the perspectives of early vocational education advocates who believed a vocational curriculum that replicated the social and economic hierarchy was necessary to sustain high schools.

With the passage of the Vocational Education Act of 1963, the door opened to federal funding for vocational education in junior, community, and technical colleges (Calhoun

& Finch, 1976), resulting in a more visible and integral role for vocational education at the postsecondary level. Federal policy-makers recognized that occupations required higher levels of technical instruction, using the label of "semi-professional" to describe the preferred tier of employment for junior college graduates. Whereas federal funds had been non-existent for vocational education beyond high school prior to the 1960s, the 1963 legislation recommended 20% of federal funding be awarded to programs enrolling students between 20 and 25 years old, 15% to programs enrolling students between 25 and 65, and 5% to programs enrolling students of any age, and the remaining funds appropriated to secondary education (Calhoun & Finch, 1976). To this day, the U.S. Department of Education, Office of Vocational and Adult Education does not prescribe the precise allocation to the secondary and postsecondary level (Bragg, 2001a). Although there are some exceptions, it is common for states to allocate a higher proportion of funds to the secondary than postsecondary level, in spite of strong rationale for most occupational instruction to be delivered by community colleges due to workforce requirements necessary in the modern labor market (Carnevale, Smith, & Strohl, 2010). Looking at funding from all levels of government, Silverberg, Warner, Fong, and Goodwin (2004) estimated federal Perkins funds made up approximately 2% of local community college budgets that support vocational education.

Expanding Access

The 1963 Vocational Education Act also signaled the importance of preparing college-age citizens and adults for employment. Technological advancements prompted by the Kennedy presidency and social commitments supported by the Johnson administration encouraged community colleges to develop vocational programs to prepare students for technical and semi-professional occupations (Rojewski, 2002). Also important during this period, the civil rights movement raised the nation's awareness of discrimination in the workplace, in education, and in public life by expanding voting rights, abolishing national-origin quotas in immigration laws, and banning discrimination in housing. These larger social forces provided an important context for expanding vocational education at the same time that many community colleges were first opening their doors (Cohen & Brawer, 2008). Although there is no evidence to point to the expansion of vocational education as a direct response to the civil rights movement, there is no doubt that the nation's efforts to rectify historical discrimination laid the foundation for scrutiny of all forms of education, including vocational education. The timing was right to encourage community colleges to adopt a comprehensive and inclusive mission, as foreshadowed by the Truman Commission immediately after World War II.

It is not surprising, then, that community colleges established in the late 1960s and 1970s articulated vocational education as integral to their core mission. In an important book defining the emergence of vocational education as a legitimate component of compulsory education, Grubb and Lazerson (1974, p. 1) introduced the notion of "vocationalism" that had swept public education in the 20th century (and before). This book showed how the vocational purpose of schooling had expanded significantly, noting that vocational education had not strayed far from the vision of federal policy-makers in the early 1900s. Over 30 years later, Grubb and Lazerson (2005) projected this same observation onto community colleges and eventually to all of higher education, arguing that vocationalism is at the heart of the entire educational enterprise in the U.S.

The notion of extending vocational education beyond high school to include two years of college, culminating in an associate's degree, was solidified in policy in the 1960s, but in fact not executed fully until the 1970s (Evans & Herr, 1978). Articulation processes were important to the growth of postsecondary vocational education because community colleges needed a way to help students who had participated in high school-level vocational classes to matriculate to college to participate in more advanced vocational training. An action discouraged for vocational education students at the beginning of the early 20th century, transition from secondary to postsecondary education was encouraged by the late 1960s and thereafter. Articulation agreements between local high schools and community colleges began to be forged in the late 1960s in some states, with support from state administrative agencies that authorized vocational course sequences thought appropriate to articulate with advanced vocational training (Bragg, Layton, & Hammons, 1994). Articulated curriculum offered the potential for students to access college, but it also had the disadvantage of extending tracking, with many tracks ending with a two-year applied and terminal degree, primarily the associate of applied science (AAS). These developments created the potential to extend the essentialist approach (Rojewski, 2002) begun in K-12 curriculum to the postsecondary level.

Who's In and Who's Out?

An important factor in the evolution of vocational education was the targeting of programs to special populations, which began to take place in the late 1960s and 1970s. Associated with the enrollment of students thought unable to attend or disinterested in attending college, the Vocational Education Act of 1963 recognized students with special needs as learner populations that could benefit from vocational education (Rojewski, 2002). However, federal legislation passed in 1968 and 1976 established categorical funding for students with disabilities and students identified as economically disadvantaged, along with students with limited English proficiency, teen parents, displaced homemakers, and students in programs considered non-traditional for their gender. The Education of All Handicapped Children Act of 1975 reinforced the importance of vocational education serving special population students, and it aligned vocational education with special education in ways supportive of the enrollment of students with intellectual, emotional, and physical disabilities (Meers, 1987; Sarkees-Wircenski & Scott, 1995).

Racial and ethnic minorities were not identified as a special population group for vocational education. According to LaFollette (2011), the omission of persons of color from the federal vocational education legislation was no mistake. The late Senator Carl Perkins, long-time congressional leader of the federal vocational education agenda, believed strongly that vocational education was necessary to address the poverty he saw in his home state of Kentucky, and he advanced a federal agenda for the nation that was favorable to his constituency. Why other Congressional leaders did not push for equitable access to federally funded vocational education is uncertain. The lack of explicit identification of ethnic and racial minority students as beneficiaries of vocational education raised questions about the commitment of vocational education to enroll racial and ethnic minority students (Oakes & Saunders, 2008) and address historic inequities made evident in the passage of the Civil Rights Act of 1964.

Lauded for democratizing K-12 schools by helping at-risk students graduate from high school and find employment, advocates for aligning vocational education with special education did not anticipate the extent to which this decision would stigmatize vocational programs and their students (Rojewski, 2002). Although well intended, linking vocational education to special education deepened schisms between the curricular tracks: college prep, general education, and vocational education. Although not completely duplicative, students enrolling in vocational programs were many of the same students who were marginalized from mainstream curriculum, especially the college-bound track (Lucas, 1999; Oakes, 1985). Tracking reinforced that college prep was for the most academically and economically privileged; general education was for the middle-ability, middle-income student; and vocational education was for those having inadequate academic preparation, low income status, or other characteristics making them unqualified for or unworthy of a college education. Inequitable curriculum structure created by tracking diverse groups constrained students' abilities to access the academic curriculum and prepare for college (Oakes, 1985). Later, in a national study of vocational education mandated by Congress, Boesel and McFarland (1994), it was suggested that, due to years of implementation in secondary schools, vocational education had become "a backwater, a dumping ground" (p. 11) for economically disadvantaged and disabled students. This research reinforced claims made by Oakes (1985) and others about the ways vocational education contributed to inequitable outcomes. Although this critique was directed at K-12 education, the push for articulation of secondary vocational education with postsecondary curriculum created the potential to replicate patterns of inequitable outcomes at the collegiate level unless drastic changes were made.

THE NEW VOCATIONALISM

Recognizing the inherent problems in tracking that limits students' educational options, a dialogue about a new form of vocationalism emerged among educators and scholars in the latter part of the 20th century. Reflecting on changes to federal legislation associated with reauthorization of the federal vocational education law in 1990, Benson (1997) provided an argument for "new vocationalism" (p. 201) that encouraged the movement of vocational education from the margins to the mainstream of the U.S. curriculum. According to Benson, new vocationalism had three distinct components that distinguished it from vocational education of the past. First, it integrated academic and vocational education by blending theory with practical skills. Second, it aligned secondary with postsecondary education to provide opportunities for more high school students to matriculate to college. Third, it established a "closer relationship between education and work, such that these two main components of human activity should each enhance and elevate the other" (Benson, 1997, p. 201). Various policies governing vocational education from the early 1990s to the present have advanced these tenets of reform, echoing ideas advanced by early 20th-century philosophers such as John Dewey (1916). However, in spite of the promise to revisit the progressive education philosophy of education and the excitement that these reform tenets created (Wirth, 1992), implementation of vocational education reforms has been uneven across the nation, creating a mixed picture of program quality and student outcomes (Lewis, 2008).

Vocational Education Reform

Numerous models emerged in the 1990s that attempted to strengthen the relationship between academic education and vocational education, including tech prep, career academies, youth apprenticeships (Lewis, 2008), and other school reforms of which High Schools that Work (HSTW) is most widely recognized and researched (see, for example, Kaufman, Bradby, & Teitelbaum, 2000). These reforms emphasized better integration between academic education and vocational education. Concerns about tracking were on the minds of educators at all levels by this time; thus reformers associated with new vocationalism were cognizant of the need to increase academic education participation as part of an integrated academic and CTE program of study (Lynch, 2000). Technical preparation (or tech prep) conceived by Parnell (1985) is an example of a model that attempted to execute the tenets of reform associated with new vocationalism as proposed by Benson (1997).

In *The Neglected Majority,* Parnell (1985) criticized the compulsory education system for failing to recognize that individual differences should be attributed to students' unique learning styles and not just to their intellectual abilities. He remarked that "despite our rhetoric about the uniqueness of each individual, many people still advocate that 'academic' means advanced and is for the 'smart' students and that career education is for the 'dumb' students" (p. 55). Building on this image of students locked into distinct tracks that stigmatize them according to their innate intelligence, Parnell advanced the notion of careers education that is both "information-rich and experience-rich" (1985, p. 69), and he advocated for a plurality of pedagogical strategies leading to career opportunities that students could pursue over their lifetimes. The specific proposal that emerged from Parnell's vision was for technical preparation (tech prep) designed to provide the programmatic structure and substance to transition students in the middle two quartiles of the high school student body to a community college where they would study the "mid-range of occupations requiring some beyond-high-school education and training but not necessarily a baccalaureate degree" (1985, p. 140). Enthusiastically adopted by federal policy-makers, the Carl D. Perkins vocational education legislation of 1990 and 1998 provided states and local entities with the authority and funding to implement tech prep as part of the federal Tech Prep Education Act. Accordingly, these programs were expected to offer an integrated academic and CTE curriculum that started by at least the junior year of high school and continued through two years of postsecondary education to the associate degree, a two-year certification or a formal apprenticeship. Articulation agreements providing high school students with college credit (referred to as articulated credit and later dual credit) and applied pedagogical instruction formed the backbone of the tech prep model (Hull, 2005).

In tech prep and other models that emerged as part of new vocationalism, CTE lessened its focus on specific occupations associated with historical federal policy and paid more attention to career development and preparation at the high school level, recognizing that job-specific training may yield immediate pay-offs but limit long-term economic benefits to students (Lewis & Cheng, 2006). Thus, while agriculture, consumer and family studies (formerly home economics), business and marketing, and industrial/technology education continued to exist, CTE began to be conceptualized as part of a progression of educational experiences for students, beginning at the middle school or high school level, extending through the postsecondary level, and into the labor market (Meeder, 2008). Collaborative efforts between the U.S. Department of Education and the U.S. Department of Labor to map the nation's labor force resulted in the States Career Cluster Framework in 1999, which encouraged rethinking of the way students prepare for employment, recognizing that more than one career trajectory had become commonplace in the labor market (Ruffing, n.d.). This framework had a dual purpose: It intended to create more coherency in education for employment for learners at all levels of the lifespan, youth to adults; and it intended to show students how they could progress through the education and training systems, moving in and out of school and college enrollment as they advanced in a career or moved from one career to another.

The States Career Cluster Framework identified 16 clusters of occupations and broad industries, with each cluster further delineated into career pathways and programs of study. This framework has been applied broadly to the nation's entire labor market, and it has guided the development of curriculum and instruction intended to prepare students for the lifelong learning associated with college and career preparation. Curriculum developed to accompany this framework necessitated an integrated approach to academic and CTE, as envisioned by Benson (1997), particularly to nullify the separation of CTE from academic education. The ultimate goal was to provide students with an interdisciplinary approach to education that connects and reinforces theory and practice in ways that enable students to pursue their academic goals and simultaneously prepare for employment. Although the States Career Cluster Framework has not paid substantial attention to citizenship education, this framework has attempted to engage a broad constituency in conversations about the fundamental purpose of schooling. Scholars such as Oakes and Saunders (2008) have pointed out that civic education is a natural ally to CTE in that students need "multiple pathways" that include civic education to prepare them to better serve their communities, the nation, and global interests (p. 6).

Reforms associated with new vocationalism have expected secondary and postsecondary educators to work together collaboratively to develop and align curriculum that prepares students to pursue their college and career goals and aspirations (Taylor et al., 2009). This approach has asked stakeholders to rethink educational goals that have impeded access to and success in college and career preparation (Bragg & Bennett, 2011). Curriculum that helps students pursue a wide range of goals and outcomes, including ensuring that students have access to associate and baccalaureate degrees, represents a pathway unthinkable for vocational education programs in earlier times. Programs of study that extend to the baccalaureate represent an expansion of new vocationalism to the rest of higher education (Grubb & Lazerson, 2005), and a vivid commitment to rectifying social inequities associated with tracking in K-12 (Bragg & Ruud, 2011).

Mixed Results

Research on the new vocationalism is limited, but a few empirical studies address the question of whether CTE programs are working. For example, results of a study of eight tech prep consortia in four states that attempted to implement comprehensive reforms consistent with new vocationalism showed that academic course requirements mattered to students' choices of high school courses (academic and CTE). Students who were encouraged to take more academic courses as part of their tech prep programs did so, and this action was positively associated with matriculation to college (Bragg et al., 2003). When student participation in core academic courses was linked to rigorous course requirements, the students took a greater number of academic courses and they advanced to higher levels in the academic curriculum, which offered them better preparation for college. In a secondary analysis of this same dataset, Bragg, Zamani, Yoo, Jung-sup, and Hill (2001) found that tech prep participants took at least as many advanced academic courses as the comparison group of students who graduated with similar academic performance, and in some cases more. These tech prep students were less likely to need remediation when they entered the community college relative to the comparison group.

Albeit promising, Bragg et al.'s (2001) work also showed results on student outcomes that raised questions about whether tech prep had ameliorated inequities associated with historical tracking policies in high schools. Bragg et al. showed that students' preparation for college differed by ethnic and racial group membership, favoring White students. Although not evident in all eight sites, in the two sites offering some of the most intensive academic course requirements, there was a significant difference between White and African American students on college readiness, controlling for other student characteristics. In both sites, African American students were more likely to require remediation at the community college than White students. Based on their increased likelihood of having to enter college taking remedial courses, African American students were also disadvantaged on other transition outcomes such as progress to degree and college completion relative to White students. This pattern of secondary education that is linked to differential preparation for college by ethnic and racial group and income status represents a troubling pattern of inequity that continues to persist (Schmid, 2010).

In a study of CTE transition programs similar to tech prep, Lekes et al. (2007) studied students in two regions of the country. Findings revealed that CTE transition students in both sites scored significantly higher than their matched non-CTE transition student counterparts on the Reading for Information subtest items of ACT WorkKeys. A significant difference was noted between the two groups on dual credit course-taking, with CTE transition students taking more dual credit than non-CTE students. Such positive findings would be encouraging of new vocationalism were it not for the troubling pattern of differential benefits that emerged, similar to the Bragg et al. (2007) study. Lewis (2008) concluded that various new vocationalism reforms had revealed mixed results due to the questions they raised about equitable outcomes for minority students. His synthesis revealed modest evidence of the advantage of tech prep, career academies, and youth apprenticeships over traditional education, speculating that new vocationalism reforms had not been implemented thoroughly enough to test their effects. He suggested, "POS [Programs of Study] are unlikely to produce marked improvements in achievement and transition to postsecondary education" (p. 180) unless they are implemented sufficiently to overcome patterns associated with the past. He concluded that incremental change, admittedly less complex to implement, had resulted in partial reform and, as a consequence, new vocationalism had not achieved the major effects it had hoped to realize.

THE COMMUNITY COLLEGE ROLE

Much of the conversation about new vocationalism has been directed at the K-12 level, particularly at high schools, except to the extent community colleges have been seen as partners to receive CTE students who are advancing to the postsecondary level (Grubb & Lazerson, 2005). For some community colleges, tech prep, career pathways, and programs of study represented useful avenues to student recruitment to maintain or grow postsecondary CTE program enrollments. However, since many students who enroll in postsecondary CTE classes are beyond traditional college age, community college practitioners have not always embraced models and approaches that transition high school students to college as eagerly as they have adopted workforce development strategies for adults (Alssid & Goldberg, 2011; Grubb, Badway, Bell, Bragg, & Russman, 1997). Whereas concern about access to postsecondary CTE programs for matriculating high school graduates is recognized as important to keeping enrollments healthy, postsecondary CTE programs often enroll substantial numbers of adults who already have labor market experience (with some also having prior college enrollment) and who seek to retrain or upgrade their skills to attain a better job. For many students, the postsecondary CTE curriculum provides a way to fulfill their employment goals, with college and industry-related credentials being the reward for program completion (Alssid & Goldberg, 2011).

In an extensive report on CTE for the National Center for Education Statistics (NCES), Levesque et al. (2008) reported that over 5,000 public, not-for-profit, and for-profit postsecondary institutions offered CTE (called "career education" in the report), suggesting that over 90% of Title IV eligible postsecondary institutions offered these courses. Over 1,100 public community colleges offered CTE courses, accounting for almost 20% of all two-, four-year, and less-than-two year, and public, not-for-profit, or for-profit postsecondary education providers. This summary report claimed that U.S. postsecondary institutions had approximately 4.4 million associate degree seekers and 1 million certificate seekers among all CTE students, with business and marketing, health care, education, and computer science majors as the predominant fields of study among associate degree-seeking students. Personal and consumer services and trade and industry were common CTE majors among students seeking certificates.

Students who enroll in postsecondary CTE programs are more diverse than the overall community college postsecondary student population. Compared to their counterparts enrolled in the general or transfer curriculum, a higher proportion of CTE students represent ethnic and racial minority groups, non-traditional college-age students, individuals who are financially independent from their families and married with financial dependants, students who attend college while also working part- or full-time, and low-income students. Hence, at this level, the diversity of student enrollment is extensive (Bragg, 2001b). This demographic diversity is especially evident among postsecondary CTE students who pursue college credentials at less-than-degree level (Levesque et al., 2008). Thus, whereas students enrolled in postsecondary CTE are demographically diverse relative to the rest of the college enrollment, stratification within CTE is apparent in that more minority and low-income students are present in the student group that pursues certificates rather than degrees. Specific skill training that prepares students for immediate employment is an important goal of many of these students—albeit an "en route" goal to the associate degree (Bragg, Cullen, Bennett, & Ruud, 2011, p. 9), which explains why a career pathway and program of study approach is important to achieving greater equity in student access and completion among underserved student populations (Foster, Strawn, & Duke-Benefield, 2011).

Predominant theories undergirding the skills-training agenda reinforce the essentialist approach (Rojewski, 2002) mentioned earlier in this chapter, along with human capital, globalization, signaling theory, and sheepskin theory, all prevalent in the CTE and higher education literature (see, for example, Levin, 2001). Gray and Herr (1995) pointed to the importance of CTE curriculum to build a competent workforce, arguing that skill-related training is predicated on human capital investment. Human capital theory (Becker, 1993) suggests that individuals and, by extension, the firms that employ them are most productive when high-quality goods and services are produced at a relatively low cost because individuals can apply the knowledge and skills they have acquired through education. Related to human capital theory is signaling theory (Spence, 2002), which suggests that an individual's ability to perform in the workplace is largely obscured from employers who need cues or signals to inform them when a person possesses the ability to perform productively in a job. Signaling theory provides rationale for why employers advocate for credentials and stridently encourage the education system to adopt them. Sheepskin effects extend from signaling theory, suggesting individuals who receive credentials experience benefits over and above students with comparable education but no credentials (Bailey, Kienzl, & Marcotte, 2004). In an age where credentialing has assumed a top priority on the nation's higher education agenda (Matthew, 2011), an examination of CTE's role in awarding credentials to all students, especially underserved populations, is important.

Furthermore, arguments concerning globalization of the economy suggest that CTE reflects the influence of technology and increased commodification of the curriculum, resulting in increased centering of CTE as the primary mission of community colleges (Levin, 2000, 2001). Jacobs (2001) and Jacobs and Dougherty (2006) pointed to the importance of CTE programs that are tightly coupled to the economy to prepare students for technology-rich, globalized work environments. They argued that postsecondary CTE is not only critical to employment in the first job, but to ensuring that students and graduates keep pace with evolving technologies so that they are prepared for career advancement. In this respect, the form of CTE envisioned by Dougherty and Jacobs is consistent with the career pathways and programs of study that award a series of increasingly valuable credentials in the marketplace. Indeed, multiple pathways (Oakes & Saunders, 2008) that provide options for students, including certificates and degrees, represent a potentially democratizing form of curriculum. Questions remain, however, about whether these career pathways and programs of study are fulfilling this democratization goal and whether the credentials and other benefits associated with them are distributed equitably to all.

Promising Results

Research conducted for the national assessment of vocational education (Bailey et al., 2004; Silverberg, Warner, Fong, & Goodwin, 2004) using three national longitudinal datasets showed, overall, that students who completed postsecondary CTE programs did at least as well as, and in some cases significantly better, than students who enrolled in academic programs at comparable levels of postsecondary education. In a comprehensive synthesis of over 20 studies of the benefits of attending and completing a community college education, Belfield and Bailey (2011) reported "strong positive earnings from community college attendance and completion, as well as from progression to a 4-year college" (p. 60), and they reported that these gains increase over time. Certificate and associate degree holders had higher returns than individuals with similar years of postsecondary education but no credential, giving credence to the presence of the sheepskin effect, particularly for female students. Inadequate evidence of effects was available for ethnic, minority, and low-income groups, leaving the question of equity in student outcomes unanswered and suggesting the importance of research that disaggregates results by subgroups to understand the role postsecondary CTE plays in addressing historic inequities faced by underserved populations.

Referencing again the democratization function of community colleges, recent experimentation with new vocationalism at the postsecondary level includes the offering of bridge programs, career pathways, and programs of study that are extended to underserved populations, including ethnic minority and low-income students, particularly adult learners. Prince and Jenkins (2005) observed that adult students are less likely to be retained in college and receive any type of certificate or degree than younger students. Evaluating the effects of bridge and career pathway programs for adults in Washington state, Prince and Jenkins applied the notion of a "tipping point" to the college enrollment and credentialing phenomenon, suggesting the importance of low-income adult learners attending at least one year of college, typically CTE, and earning a credential to boost their labor market outcomes in terms of employment and earnings. Taking remedial courses concurrently with CTE produced significant average rates of employment and quarterly earnings, and these results held true for adults and low-income learners. Again, drawing on data from Washington state, Jenkins and Weiss (2011) recommended that younger learners would benefit from programs of study that link academic and CTE course work systematically with support services that encourage persistence. These results offer modest support for new vocationalism reforms that engage diverse learners and support their completion of certificates and degrees.

OLD DEBATES, PERSISTENT CHALLENGES

Philosophical and theoretical debates have been used to support vocational education policy and practice since its beginning nearly a century ago. As vocational education evolved into CTE, the debate over essentialism versus pragmatism has provided a useful frame for understanding the evolution of differentiated instruction and tracking, including detrimental effects, and the potential for new vocationalism reforms that have emerged slowly over the past two decades and continue to struggle to find a viable place in curriculum. Whereas the human capital rationale looms large as a rationale for CTE on several levels, Rojewski (2002) observed that some educators have consistently argued for CTE to be a response to economic and social issues, having a democratizing effect on the educational system because of its ability to reach and serve underrepresented learners. From this perspective, CTE programs recognize that students are complex, malleable, and receptive to learning when the teaching and learning process is reflective of the multiple dimensions of life (Sarkees-Wircenski & Scott, 1995). This aim suggests that CTE is not so much about preparing people for work as about whetting their appetite for learning and providing them with relevant options and opportunities to help them navigate through education, into the labor market, and, most importantly, on with all of the facets of their lives (Oakes & Saunders, 2008).

In spite of the century-long experience with CTE, there remains relatively limited knowledge of educational and economic benefits, particularly for ethnic and racial minorities, low-income students, and other underrepresented learners. Limitations to research designs that attempt to examine outcomes for students who participate in CTE relative to students with comparable characteristics who have not participated have been a perennial problem, going so far as to threaten future federal support for CTE (Duncan,

2011). Calls for improvements to CTE and better research to report empirical evidence of program quality and student outcomes are frequent (see, for example, Lewis, 2008), but mostly addressed insufficiently to satisfy the critics. Similar to the debate that gave birth to vocational education in the U.S. in 1917, the merits of CTE continue to be contested. Although CTE is unlikely to go away entirely, given the rise of new vocationalism, more scrutiny and better research are needed to understand how CTE benefits the increasingly diverse student populations that seek to access and complete community college credentials and degrees. The promise of a more democratic form of education and a better future for all the nation's learners may be at stake.

QUESTIONS FOR DISCUSSION

1. In what ways does the concept of "new vocationalism" pertain to the community college?
2. How do we address questions of CTE program quality in a period of declining resources combined with increased interest in CTE programs?
3. When education is increasingly looked upon as a private good, and the community college's access mission threatened by an economic development agenda, is CTE appropriately placed within the community college? Why or why not?

REFERENCES

Alssid, J., & Goldberg, M. (2011). Workforce strategies for America's future: Community college contributions. In American Association of Community Colleges, *21st-Century Commission on the Future Community Colleges, Working Briefs* (pp. 72–81). Washington, DC: Author.

Bailey, T., Kienzl, G., & Marcotte, D. (2004, August). Who benefits from postsecondary occupational education? Findings from the 1980s and 1990s, No. 23. New York, NY: Teachers College, Columbia University.

Becker, G. (1993). *Human capital: A theoretical and empirical analysis, with special reference to education* (3rd ed.). Chicago, IL: University of Chicago Press.

Belfield, C., & Bailey, T. (2011). The benefits of attending community college: A review of the evidence. *Community College Review, 39*(1), 46–68.

Benavot, A. (1983). The rise and decline of vocational education. *Sociology of Education, 56*, 63–76.

Benson, C. S. (1997). New vocationalism in the United States: Potential problems and outlook. *Economics of Education Review, 16*(3), 201–212.

Boesel, D., & McFarland, L. (1994, July). *National assessment of vocational education: Final report to Congress* (Vol. I). Washington, DC: U.S. Department of Education, Office of Educational Research and Improvement.

Bragg, D. (2001a). Community college access, mission, and outcomes: Considering intriguing intersections and opportunities. *Peabody Journal of Education, 76*(1), 93–116.

Bragg, D. (2001b). The past, present and future role of federal vocational legislation in the United States. *Journal of Applied Research in Community Colleges, 9*(1), 57–67.

Bragg, D., & Bennett, S. (2011). *Introduction to pathways to results.* Champaign, IL: Office of Community College Research and Leadership, University of Illinois at Urbana-Champaign. Retrieved from http://occrl.illinois.edu/files/Projects/ptr/Modules/PTR%20Intro%20Module.pdf

Bragg, D., Cullen, D., Bennett, S., & Ruud, C. (2011). *All or nothing? Midpoint credentials for college students who stop short of credential requirements* (Working paper). Champaign, IL: Office of Community College Research and Leadership, University of Illinois at Urbana-Champaign.

Bragg, D., Layton, J., & Hammons, F. (1994, September). *Tech prep implementation in the United States: Promising trends and lingering challenges.* Berkeley, CA: National Center for Research in Vocational Education, University of California at Berkeley.

Bragg, D., Loeb, J., Gong, Y., Deng, P., Hill, J., & Yoo, J. (2003). *Transition from high school to college and work for tech prep participants in eight local consortia.* St. Paul, MN: National Research Center for Career and Technical Education, University of Minnesota.

Bragg, D., & Ruud, C. (2011). *The adult learner and the applied baccalaureate: Lessons from six states*. Champaign, IL: Office of Community College Research and Leadership, University of Illinois at Urbana-Champaign. Retrieved from http://occrl.illinois.edu/files/Projects/lumina/Report/LuminaABFinalReport.pdf

Bragg, D., Zamani, E., Yoo, Jung-sup, & Hill, J. (2001, April). *The impact of tech prep on college readiness and retention in two disparate consortia*. Paper presentation at the annual meeting of the American Educational Research Association, Division, J, Seattle, WA.

Brint, S., & Karabel, J. (1989). *Diverted dream: Community colleges and the promise of educational opportunity in America 1900–1985*. London: Oxford University Press.

Calhoun, C., & Finch, A. (1976). *Vocational education: Concepts and operations* (2nd ed.). Belmont, CA: Wadsworth Publishing Company.

Carnevale, A. P., Smith, N., & Strohl, J. (2010). *Help wanted: Projections of jobs and education requirements through 2018*. Washington, DC: Georgetown University, Center on Education and the Workforce. Retrieved from http://cew.georgetown.edu/jobs2018/

Cohen, A. M., & Brawer, F. B. (2008). *The American community college* (5th ed.). San Francisco, CA: Jossey-Bass.

Dewey, J. (1916, March 11). Vocational education. *New Republic, 6*, 159–160.

Dougherty, K. (2004). *The contradictory college: The conflicting origins, impacts, and futures of the community college*. Albany, NY: State University of New York Press.

Duncan, A. (2011, February 2). The new CTE: Secretary Duncan's remarks on career and technical education. (Press release.) Retrieved from http://www.ed.gov/news/speeches/new-cte-secretary-duncans-remarks-career-and-technical-education

Evans, R., & Herr, E. (1978). *Foundations of vocational education* (2nd ed). Columbus, OH: Charles E. Merrill Publishing Company.

Foster, M., Strawn, J., & Duke-Benefield, A. (2011). *Beyond basic skills: State strategies to connect low-skilled adults to an employer-valued postsecondary education*. Center for Law and Social Policy (2010). Retrieved from http://www.clasp.org/admin/site/publications/files/Beyond-Basic-Skills-March-2011.pdf

Gray, K., & Herr, E. (1995). *Other ways to win: Creating alternatives for high school graduates*. Thousand Oaks, CA: Corwin Press, Inc.

Grubb, N., Badway, N., Bell, D., Bragg, D., & Russman, M. (1997, October). *Workforce, economic, and community development: The changing landscape of the entrepreneurial community college*. Mission Viejo, CA: League for Innovation in the Community College, National Center for Research in Vocational Education.

Grubb, W. N., & Lazerson, M. (1974). *American education and vocationalism: A documentary history, 1870–1970*. New York, NY: Teachers College Press.

Grubb, W. N., & Lazerson, M. (2005). *The education gospel: The economic power of schooling*. Cambridge, MA: Harvard University Press, and National Council for Occupational Education.

Harmon, R., & MacAllum, K. (2003). *Documented characteristics of labor market-responsive community colleges and a review of supporting literature*. Washington, DC: Academy for Educational Development. (ED 479 041)

Hayward, G. C., & Benson, C. S. (1993). *Vocational-technical education: Major reforms and debates 1917–present*. Washington, DC: Office of Vocational and Adult Education, U.S. Department of Education. (ERIC Document Reproduction Service No. ED 369 959)

Hull, D. (Ed.). (2005). *Career pathways: Education with a purpose*. Waco, TX: Center for Occupational Research and Development.

Jacobs, J. (2001). What is the future of post-secondary occupational education? *Journal of Vocational Education Research, 26*(2), 172–205.

Jacobs, J., & Dougherty, K. (2006). The uncertain future of the community college workforce development mission. *New Directions for Community Colleges, no. 136* (pp. 53–62). San Francisco, CA: Jossey-Bass.

Jenkins, D., & Weiss, M. (2011, September). *Charting pathways to completion for low-income community college students*. CCR Working Paper No. 34. New York, NY: Teachers College, Columbia University.

Kaufman, P., Bradby, D., & Teitelbaum, P. (2000). *High Schools That Work and whole school reform: Raising academic achievement of vocational completers through the reform of school practice*. Columbus, OH: National Center for Dissemination of Career and Technical Education, The Ohio State University. (ERIC Document Reproduction Service No. ED 438498)

Labaree, D. (2010). *The thinning mission of public mission of the American public school*. Paper presentation for the Educational Theory Summer Institute, College of Education, University of Illinois at Urbana-Champaign.

LaFollette, A. (2011). *An historical policy analysis of the Carl D. Perkins legislation: Examining the history, creation, implementation and reauthorization of the law*. (Doctoral dissertation.) Retrieved from IDEALS http://hdl.handle.net/2142/26060

Lazerson, M., & Grubb, W. N. (1974). *American education and vocationalism: A documentary history 1870–1970*. New York, NY: Teachers College Press.

Lekes, N., Bragg, D., Loeb, J., Oleksew, C., Mazsalek, J., Laraviere, M., & Hood, L. (2007). *The impact of career-technical education transition program practices on student outcomes.* St. Paul, MN: National Research Center for Career and Technical Education, University of Minnesota.

Levesque, K., Laird, J., Hensley, E., Choy, S. P., Cataldi, E. F., & Hudson, L. (2008). *Career and technical education in the United States: 1990 to 2005* (NCES 2008–035). Washington, DC: National Center for Education Statistics, Institute of Education Sciences, U.S. Department of Education.

Levin, J. (2000). The revised institution: The community college mission at the end of the twentieth century. *Community College Review, 28*(2), 1–25.

Levin, J. (2001). *Globalizing the community college: Strategies for change in the twenty-first century.* New York, NY: Palgrave.

Lewis, M. (2008). Effectiveness of previous initiatives similar to programs of study: Tech prep, career pathways, and youth apprenticeships. *Career and Technical Education Research, 33*(3), 165–188.

Lewis, T., & Cheng, S. (2006). Tracking, expectations, and the transformation of vocational education. *American Journal of Education, 113*(1), 67–99.

Lucas, S. (1999). *Tracking inequality: Stratification and mobility in the American high school.* New York, NY: Teachers College Press.

Lynch, R. L. (2000). *New directions for high school career and technical education in the 21st century* (Information Series No. 384). Columbus, OH: The Ohio State University, ERIC Clearinghouse on Adult, Career, and Vocational Education. (ERIC Document Reproduction Service No. ED 444 037)

Matthew, D. (2011). The case for college completion. In American Association of Community Colleges, *21st-Century Commission on the Future Community Colleges, Working Briefs* (pp. 22–30). Washington, DC: Author.

Meeder, H. (2008). *The Perkins Act of 2006: Connection career and technical education with the college and career readiness agenda.* Washington, DC: Achieve, Inc. Retrieved from http://www.achieve.org/files/Achieve-CTEPolicyBrief-02-07-08.pdf

Meers, G. D. (1987). *Handbook for vocational special needs education* (2nd ed.). Rockville, MD: Aspen.

Meier, K. (2008). *The community college mission: History and theory, 1930–2000.* (Unpublished doctoral dissertation.) University of Arizona, Tucson, AZ.

Oakes, J. (1985). *Keeping track: How schools structure inequality.* New Haven, CT: Yale University Press.

Oakes, J., & Saunders, M. (2008). *Beyond tracking: Multiple pathways to college, career, and civic participation.* Cambridge, MA: Harvard University Press.

Parnell, D. (1985). *The neglected majority.* Washington, DC: Community College Press. (ERIC Document Reproduction Service No. ED 262 843)

Prince, D., & Jenkins, D. (2005, April). Building pathways to success for low-skill adult students: Lessons for community college policy and practice from a statewide longitudinal tracking study. *Community College Research Center Brief, no. 25.* New York, NY: Teachers College, Columbia University.

Prosser, C. A. (1913, May). The meaning of industrial education. *Vocational Education, 406,* 401–410.

Rojewski, J. (2002). *Preparing the workforce of tomorrow: A conceptual framework for career and technical education.* Columbus, OH: National Dissemination Center for Career and Technical Education, The Ohio State University.

Ruffing, K. (n.d.). *The history of career clusters.* Retrieved from http://www.google.com/search?q=Ruffing%2C+Career+Clusters%2C+history&ie=utf-8&oe=utf-8&aq=t&rls=org.mozilla:en-US:official&client=firefox-a

Sarkees-Wircenski, M., & Scott, J. L. (1995). *Vocational special needs* (3rd ed.). Homewood, IL: American Technical.

Schmid, C. (2010). Challenges and opportunities of community colleges. In F. Lazin, M. Evans, & N. Jayaram (Eds.), *Higher education and equality of opportunities: Cross-national perspectives* (pp. 25–40). Lanham, MD: Lexington Books.

Silverberg, M., Warner, E., Fong, M., & Goodwin, D. (2004). *National assessment of vocational education.* Washington, DC: United States Department of Education.

Spence, M. (2002, June). Signaling in retrospect and the informational structure of markets. *The American Economic Review, 92*(3), 434–459.

Taylor, J., Kirby, C., Bragg, D., Oertle, K., Jankowski, N., & Khan, S. (2009, July). *Illinois program of study guide.* Champaign, IL: Office of Community College Research and Leadership, University of Illinois at Urbana-Champaign.

Wirth, A. (1992). *Education and work for the year 2000: Choices we face.* San Francisco, CA: Jossey-Bass.

Wonacott, M. (2003). *History and evolution of vocational and career and technical education.* Columbus, OH: Center for Education and Training for Employment, Ohio State University.

13

THE COMPARATIVE POLITICAL ECONOMY
OF VOCATIONAL EDUCATION

Lessons for the Study of Community Colleges in the U.S.

LUCIANA DAR

Although the study of community colleges in the U.S. has a long history, only recently has the institution secured broader attention and legitimacy in the field of higher education (Harper & Jackson, 2011). The same is true for community colleges' standing in U.S. education policy and political discourses, for which the institution has become the focus of the federal government's efforts to increase postsecondary attainment, access by low-income and underrepresented students to higher education, and the efficiency of public investments in the tertiary sector (Biden, 2010). This shift in attention by scholars and policy-makers, albeit delayed, is welcome, given that community colleges enrolled 44% of all undergraduate students in 2008 (American Association of Community Colleges, 2011). Nevertheless, scholarship on community colleges remains segmented and often disconnected from developments that are taking place in the social science disciplines and educational sciences, is based on a limited range of theoretical/conceptual frameworks and methodological approaches, and focuses mainly on issues of access and completion (Dougherty, 2006; Melguizo, 2011).

Conversely, the study of vocational education and training (VET), or career and technical education (CTE), as the U.S.'s legislated term, has been at the center of scholarship in the fields of comparative education sciences, educational sociology, and the economics of education for more than three decades (Brown, Green, & Lauder, 2001; Powell & Solga, 2008; Stevens, Armstrong, & Arum, 2008). By recognizing that one cannot explain the evolution, or ascertain the socio-economic value, of vocational education by analyzing educational systems in isolation, the large and diverse scholarly literature on VET has also addressed a larger set of questions than those tackled by scholarship on community colleges (Mayer & Solga, 2008). Most importantly, this scholarship shows that the design and implementation of VET policies must take into consideration political-economic institutions, relevant actors (i.e., unions, employers, and private education providers), and path-dependent characteristics of VET systems (i.e., school versus employer-based and general versus occupational focus, as well as connections to the labor market).

Since the 1980s, the importance of skills training in industrialized nations has increased substantially in keeping with the growing competitive pressures brought on by economic globalization; accordingly, so has the public demand for better coordination between VET systems and labor markets (Brown et al., 2001; Levin, 2001). Scholars have followed suit with a renewed interest in examining: (1) the institutional settings involved in skills training; (2) issues related to the provision, access, and return to skills training over the working life of an individual; and (3) policy coordination in terms of when, where, and how training should take place (Mayer & Solga, 2008). In particular, political scientists and political economists have begun to contribute to our understanding of the comparative political economy of skill formation, highlighting the importance of vocational training institutions for socio-political and distributive outcomes (Busemeyer & Trampusch, 2011; Culpepper & Thelen, 2008).

Within this scholarly and policy context, this chapter presents an overview of key insights from the VET literature that can help advance scholarship and practice for community colleges. First, I review key theoretical arguments and empirical findings from the more recent literature on the comparative political economy of vocational education. I argue that the main insight from this work for the study of U.S. community colleges is the need for more attention to the policy coordination challenges involved in aligning vocational training, labor market, and social policy goals in liberal market economies such as those of the U.S. (Bosch & Charest, 2010).

Second, I present examples of questions explored in the comparative vocational education literature that are of particular relevance to U.S. community college scholars, policy-makers, and practitioners who seek responses to increasing global competitive pressures and government budgetary challenges. I maintain that to answer these questions, we must move beyond the current fragmentary approach to the study of community colleges in favor of a mix of disciplinary and interdisciplinary strategies, conditional on the problem or problems at hand (Strober, 2010).

Indeed, as highlighted by Busemeyer and Trampusch (2011), Burton Clark's (1983) initial complaint that social scientists do not pay enough attention to educational issues remains pertinent in the present, albeit much less so than in the 1980s. Disciplinary perspectives in the study of skill formation have led to segmentation and isolation, which result in redundancy and a lack of theoretical and empirical foundations and, hence, limited applicability of findings to education policy challenges (Hess, 2008; Mayer & Solga, 2008). I conclude the chapter by reiterating how comparative analyses of states in the U.S. can inform policy and practice on some of the main current issues that face community colleges.

POLITICAL ECONOMY OF VOCATIONAL EDUCATION

Note on the Philosophy of Science and Social Science

Scholarship on the community college in the U.S. embodies the continuing debate over community colleges' mission, evolution, and relevance to society (Bailey & Morest, 2006). Contributors to this debate can usually be divided into two camps, defenders or critics, which is also the most common division observed in political and policy discourses on the community college (Goldrick-Rab, Harris, Mazzeo, & Kienzl, 2009). This body of scholarship reflects the diversity of perspectives and political interests in the field, with contributions by advocates, practitioners, and independent specialists based at research universities or think tanks (Frye, 1994).

A large segment of scholars in this field adopt a functionalist perspective in their work; that is, they focus on the positive social function of the community college, while others advance more critical arguments, using theoretical approaches that highlight the competitive, conflict-driven, and/or oppressive nature of human institutions and interactions (Dougherty, 2006). Nonetheless, in spite of the recent growth in the number and quality of scholarly contributions to our understanding of community colleges and their students, the literature remains limited in scope, methodological rigor, and theoretical foundations (Frye, 1994; Goldrick-Rab, 2010).

The many theoretical and substantive debates that are taking place in the scholarship on community colleges are, in part, simply a reflection of what takes place across the larger research community in social sciences and educational sciences. There are profound disagreements among social scientists over the nature of reality (ontology), the nature of knowledge (epistemology), and which tools to use in our attempt to understand and improve our social world. These disagreements are manifested in divergences about the mission and other relevant aspects of community college policy and practice in the U.S. In this regard, Linchbach (2003) identifies three types of social scientists who are often at odds.

> Each community of scholars deepens Tilly's (1999) [classification] in a particular way: rationalists focus on the complex consequences of individual action; culturalists study the meaning and significance of intersubjective values and beliefs; and structuralists seek the deep structures of power and causation that drive superficial appearances and observable outcomes. (p. 13)

Additional differences within and between these ideal types emerge along four dimensions: ontology (reasons, rules, and interactions); explanatory strategy (positivism, interpretivism, and realism); general laws (universal, social structures, and individual); and internally generated problems (materialism, idealism, and determinism).

There is considerable contentiousness in many of these methodological debates in the higher education field, especially between those espousing competing explanatory strategies, that is, either through description, control, and prediction or through interpretation and self-reflection, and those having different perspectives on the extent and even possibility of the generalizability of findings. I subscribe to Linchbach's (2003) perspective that social science is a multiple-paradigm science, wherein a division of labor must take place. Linchbach recognizes the perils of defending pluralism in social science: "My experience confirms the old adage, 'the person who stands in the middle of the road gets hit by cars going both ways'" (p. xix). Most importantly, Linchbach argues that social science and related fields need all types of contributors, that is, "rationalist generalizers, structuralist typologizers, and culturalist particularizers" (p. 168).

There is a rich theoretical and applied literature in the field of higher education (e.g., Marginson & Rhoades, 2002) that criticizes the theoretical underpinnings of the literature reviewed in this chapter. Here, I provide an overview of the main theoretical and methodological foundations of positive political economy, one theoretical framework widely used in the political economy of vocational education literature.

Political Economy: Theory and Methodology

Positive political economy can be best summarized as a "family" of approaches that applies the methodology of economics to the analysis of political behavior and institutions (Weingast & Wittman, 2006). Political economists are interested in uncovering the micro-foundations of macro-processes as well as both the intended and unintended consequences of individuals' rational actions. As articulated by Bates (as cited in Linchbach, 2003), political economists focus on the "impact of economic interests upon politics and the impact of institutions upon economic interests" (p. 14).

Mainstream economists subscribe to the assumption of one universal human nature and rationality, independent of the context, making possible consistent predictions about human decision-making processes across all social settings (Shepsle, 2006). Conversely, large numbers of scholars in the comparative political economy field do not subscribe to this one universal rationality assumption. They favor a more comprehensive approach wherein culture, norms, and preferences vary, depending on formal and informal constraints, time, and resources (Thelen, 2004). Nevertheless, both groups of scholars agree that only individual-level theories can explain larger macro-level phenomena, such as institutional change or human capital accumulation.

Another important characteristic of this family of approaches to social science research is the preference for more parsimonious, mid-level theoretical frameworks. That is, concrete problems can be explained only by focusing on their relevant parts, such as specific institutions or individual behaviors (Linchbach, 2003). For example, instead of examining broad concepts such as the democratizing function of the community college, a researcher would investigate how the availability of social insurance programs affects individuals' likelihood of investing in vocational education or how different funding strategies affect the percentage of low-income students able to obtain a postsecondary credential.

Underlying the contributions made by political scientists to the comparative political economy of vocational education literature are the most commonly used theoretical approaches of rational choice institutionalism and historical institutionalism (Shepsle, 2006; Thelen, 1999). The former focuses on the role of institutions in constraining human behavior and as a solution to collective action problems (Shepsle, 2006). The latter combines the comparative historical method with a focus on determining the causal mechanisms behind observed empirical patterns. Thelen (1999) presents an overview of the similarities and differences between these two analytical approaches, emphasizing historical institutionalists' view that institutions are themselves changing as a result of socio-political processes.

> Although historical institutionalists are just as interested as "other" institutionalists in the regularities of politics over time, they tend to emphasize historical process over equilibrium order. Whereas alternative conceptions view institutions in terms of their coordinating functions, historical institutionalists see them as the product of concrete temporal processes. Thus, rather than conceiving of institutions as "holding together" a particular pattern of politics, historical institutionalists are more likely to reverse the causal arrows and argue that institutions emerge from and are sustained by features of the broader political and social context. In this approach to institutions, path dependency involves elements of both continuity and [structured] change. (p. 395)

There has been a growing cross-fertilization of ideas between rational choice institutionalism and historical institutionalism, leading to important contributions such as the notion that different institutions may facilitate or hinder the relationship between employers, educational institutions, governments, and individuals (Thelen, 2004). This interaction between these two traditions has led to some of the better answers to questions such as, "Why do firms invest in human capital?", "Why do skill formation systems vary so much across countries?", or "Why is it difficult to produce the amount of human capital needed in a particular country or region?" (Busemeyer & Trampusch, in press).

Varieties of Capitalism

Within the aforementioned positive political economy analytical tradition, political scientists have made significant contributions to the study of education, including developing an understanding of skill formation processes and their effects (Busemeyer & Trampusch, 2011). Alongside this research effort in the social sciences, a few comparative education scholars have demonstrated interest in exploring the connections between vocational education, industrial relations, and labor market institutions (Bosch & Charest, 2010). These two groups—political scientists and comparative education researchers—hold in common the view that understanding the linkages between education and welfare policies is fundamental to explaining the design, implementation, and outcomes of policies such as those affecting skill formation.

The main insight from the political economy literature on VET systems and institutions is that the responsibilities for collective skill formation are shared among the state, the market, and individual firms (Busemeyer & Trampusch, in press). Moreover, these shared responsibilities are created, shaped, and changed depending on the institutional context in which stakeholders are embedded. In brief, skill formation systems directly affect national and subnational socio-economic development paths but are also affected by the progression and growth of other socio-economic institutions. In the case of socio-economic institutions' affecting vocational education systems, for example, empirical evidence shows that firms are more likely to invest in skills when there are socio-economic institutions that minimize the risk (e.g., employment insurance, compressed wages) and that countries with highly competitive and mobile labor markets tend to favor "high end" skills investments over mid-level vocational education programs (Culpepper & Thelen, 2008).

Scholars have sought to identify key mechanisms and explain the effects of the interactions between political and economic institutions and the stakeholders involved in the production of skills. The varieties of capitalism (VOC) literature has provided the strongest explanation so far for the role of these interactions in shaping the amount and kind of human capital observed in developed economies. This literature criticizes other bodies of literature for overly simplifying the role of institutions as well as failing to consider the interplay between the many institutions and actors involved. In response to these criticisms, Hall and Soskice (2001) put firms at the center of the analysis as key actors. These scholars explore "complementarities" between institutions (i.e., firm strategies in production markets, systems of industrial relations, and the nature of institutions providing social protection). They also examine and compare types of institutional advantages that emerge in advanced industrialized economies.

Scholars in the VOC tradition identify two main types of market economies: liberal market economies (LMEs) and coordinated market economies (CMEs). LMEs use market mechanisms to coordinate economic activity, making it riskier for employers to invest in human capital and, hence, increase the responsibility of governments and individuals. In CMEs, there are strong coordination mechanisms in place, making the partnership between firms, governments, and individuals more stable as compared to LMEs. Firms have incentives to invest in skill formation due to lower labor turnover and compressed wages (Acemoglu & Pischke, 1998). LMEs have VET systems that favor general education that is then complemented with on-the-job training. Conversely, CMEs place greater emphasis on vocational education combined with training in the workplace (Hall & Soskice, 2001). In sum, the way that countries organize and coordinate the formation of skills is inextricably tied to other areas of the political economy, and this relationship determines the characteristics of the workforce, alignment with labor market needs, and broader economic and social development trends (Bosch & Charest, 2010; Korpi, 2006).

Drawing from Thelen's (2004) insight that collective skill formation systems can endure only if there is continued support by main political stakeholders, Busemeyer and Trampusch (in press) go a step further and explore the dynamic aspects of collective skill formation systems. First, they argue that collective skill formation systems are unstable and constantly face challenges such as economic shocks, technological advances, or ideological shifts. As a result, systems must be able to adapt to and accommodate different supporting coalitions. Second, they posit that the division of labor between firms, governments, and individuals in the financing and provision of skill formation explains, to a great extent, the differences observed in skill formation systems. Third, Busemeyer and Trampusch (in press) find that political struggles among those that provide, pay for, and control skill formation systems determine human capital accumulation policies.

To illustrate their findings, Busemeyer and Trampusch (in press) create a two-dimensional typology of skill formation systems based on the degree of firm/employer involvement in vocational education and the degree of government involvement in the development of a skilled workforce. In "liberal skill formation systems," such as the U.S., there is low commitment by firms and governments to vocational training compared to other advanced industrial democracies. Postsecondary institutions offer generic qualifications complemented by internships and on-the-job training. While there are quality vocational programs, they have limited links to labor markets, and students are responsible for a larger share of the costs of training.

In "segmentalist regimes" such as Japan, there is not only greater emphasis on general education but also high involvement of firms in the skill formation process on the job or in in-house training centers. In "statist skill formations systems," there is significant government commitment to vocational training through the direct provision, funding, and active labor market policies. In contrast to segmentalist regimes, in statist skill formation systems there is much less firm involvement. Sweden and France are salient examples of this regime. Finally, "collective skill formation regimes" such as Germany and Austria are characterized by high commitment by governments and firms to vocational education and the creation of opportunities for individuals to pursue alternatives to higher education due to weak qualifications or individual choice.

Two main points emerge from this literature as important to U.S. VET systems (community colleges and vocational education institutions). First, the organization of the U.S. economy and the division of labor between firms, governments, and individuals negatively affect the production of a skilled workforce and reinforce stratification in labor markets.

> The difference (between LMEs and CMEs) can perhaps be summarized as follows: in the coordinated market economies, the modernization of vocational training is seen as a contributor to innovation in the economy, while in liberal market economies it is seen as a siding into which weaker pupils can conveniently be shunted. (Bosch & Charest, 2010, Section 6, para. 3)

Second, only appropriate coordination between levels of commitment by firms and the public can produce appropriate solutions to the collective action problems common to skills production systems (Hall & Soskice, 2001).

Education Policy and Social, Economic, and Political Outcomes

Given that the main roles of social science research are to help explain our world and to inform policy and practice, it is understandable that the literature on the relationship between educational policies and outcomes is much more developed compared to scholarship focused on explaining why educational policies take the shape that they do. Political scientists and comparative political economists have traditionally focused on the distributional and labor market implications of specific policies (e.g., individual earnings, political participation, well-being indicators). In this context, the theoretical perspectives presented earlier in this chapter as the most commonly seen in the study of community colleges in the U.S.—functionalism and conflict-oriented theories— also dominate. The development of comparable international datasets on student outcomes has also contributed to the expansion of comparative work in this area, but the research is not yet as extensive and empirically sound as what is available in the U.S. (Allmendinger, Ebner, & Nikolai, 2010; Shavit, Arum, & Gamoran, 2007).

The international comparative literature on educational outcomes is rich in rigorous quantitative studies, sophisticated statistical methods, and measurements strategies. However, the literature suffers from the same weaknesses identified in most of its U.S. counterparts. While there is strong evidence of empirical relationships between individual characteristics, educational systems, and general education outcomes (i.e., educational attainment, years of schooling, and cognitive skills), we know little about the interactions between individuals and other institutional factors that lead to socio-political and educational outcomes (Busemeyer & Trampusch, 2011; Hanushek & Woessmann, 2008). There are also limited efforts to incorporate the role of educational institutions themselves and their many internal actors in the larger educational policy processes (Marginson & Rhoades, 2002). Cross-national analyses and comparative work within federal systems such as the U.S. can progress much further to fill this void in our knowledge of the role that educational institutions play in larger political economic processes.

Policy Coordination Challenges

There is empirical evidence to support the claim that individuals in countries with social insurance programs are more likely to invest in vocational education because there are guarantees against the loss of investments in human capital (Bosch & Charest, 2010; Busemeyer & Trampusch, in press). In liberal market economies, vocational education has much lower status than in coordinated market economies. In the U.S., the connections between labor markets and vocational systems are largely informal, and the responsibility for financing skills training is increasingly becoming the responsibility of students (Bailey & Berg, 2010). It is not a surprise, then, that the community college sector does not share the same status as their counterparts in some European countries and that there is a shortage of qualified workers in mid-level occupations (Carnevale, Rose, & Cheah, 2011).

Indeed, recent policy research on the links between postsecondary education, labor markets, and the U.S. economy indicate that coordination (or lack thereof) between skill formation systems and other political-economic institutions matter. For example, middle-skilled jobs will continue to experience robust demand and wage growth, while public educational spending disproportionately favors the four-year sector (Holzer & Lerman, 2009; Wellmann et al., 2009). The emphasis on four-year degrees in combination with deregulated labor markets produces higher wage premiums for college-educated workers but also more income inequality and underproduction of workers with the necessary variety and level of skills (Busemeyer & Trampusch, in press; Carnevale & Rose, 2010; Goldrick-Rab et al., 2009).

Furthermore, challenges for policy-makers tend to increase with the degree of differences in VET systems between and within states. Analyses of community colleges' students, faculty, and organizations continue to be fundamental to our understanding of VET systems as a key player in U.S. economic and socio-political development strategy. Comparative political economists can contribute greatly to our understanding of the coordination challenges presented by the characteristics of U.S. postsecondary education providers, labor market actors, and political-economic institutions. In particular, a lack of coordination mechanisms in the U.S. to link educational programs, labor market needs, and responsibilities for the costs of training the workforce demand from scholars and practitioners much more attention than is presently given to the potential unintended consequences of various policy proposals. For example, recent increases in federal financial aid spending led to a boom in enrollments in the community college sector; however, they were not matched by increased state support for these institutions, reducing even further the amount of resources available per student (Wellman et al., 2009). Potential solutions to the predicted labor market shortages and rising college costs may emerge with the development of specific state, and sometimes industry, strategies to coordinate and incentivize the various collective actors involved.

The literature briefly reviewed here also highlights one important implication of human capital accumulation policies. The interactions between social policy choices and vocational education policy choices under a particular set of institutional constraints lead not only to specific workforce development outcomes but also to a variety of distributive consequences. In other words, while governments seek to promote economic development through their educational investments and regulatory choices, they also aim to promote socially desirable outcomes (e.g., less inequality, lower poverty rates, social mobility) and/or favor particular constituent groups over others. The same distributive preferences are revealed when governments choose to favor more or fewer educational expenditures relative to other social policy mechanisms (Busemeyer & Nikolai, 2010).

In sum, policy coordination challenges that face the U.S. workforce development efforts are pervasive. In spite of growing recognition among various stakeholders that community colleges deliver sizable economic benefits and have the potential to serve as key partners in social policy beyond education (Belfield & Bailey, 2011; Busemeyer & Nikolai, 2010), stratification in the U.S. higher education system continues to grow, with average public spending of $19,000 per postsecondary student, but only $10,000 per community college student in 2008 (Wellman et al., 2009). Scholars in the various disciplines and fields interested in community colleges can benefit from recognizing and incorporating the dynamic characteristics of VET systems discussed here and some of the insights from the comparative work done outside the U.S.

LINKING (MULTI)DISCIPLINARY RESEARCH TO THE STUDY OF VOCATIONAL EDUCATION

Recent scholarship makes a strong case for the adoption of interdisciplinary and cross-national perspectives in the study of skill formation (Mayer & Solga, 2008), and suggests two sets of questions that need to be addressed. The first set of questions concerns the similar challenges created by the (parallel) competitive pressures that face advanced economies and the differentiation in how they share responsibilities for training the workforce including their ability to adjust to changing conditions. The second set has to do with the provision of, access to, and individual and collective returns of education/training.

The call for interdisciplinary, problem-based research is far from new (Strober, 2010). Nonetheless, progress has been slow due to a number of obstacles, including a lack of funding, the academic reward system that penalizes interdisciplinary efforts by scholars, pressures for immediate applicability of research findings, and "hidden" barriers (e.g., disciplinary cultures, organizational dynamics). Strober (2010) explores in depth some of the unspoken or hidden challenges brought on by different disciplinary habits of thought. Strober (2010) argues that interdisciplinarity should be a complement to, not a substitute for, disciplinarity. The complexity and importance of skill formation systems demand a combination of disciplinary and multidisciplinary approaches of inquiry. Enders (2010) makes a similar point by recognizing the legitimacy of ongoing criticisms of the educational sciences as "lacking desirable disciplinary characteristics such as distinct theoretical traditions, relatively codified knowledge and institutionalized channels and styles of communication" (Section 2, para. 4). A potential solution is the pursuit of more disciplinary contributions from social scientists, and political scientists in particular, to the study of education. However, this particular strategy may lead to a lack of research into many "cross-cutting questions" also important to our ability to inform policy and practice (Enders, 2010; Henig, 2011; Hess, 2008). In sum, if we are to find best policies and practices that reflect local, national, and cross-national needs, the advancement of knowledge in the area of vocational education must involve creativity, diversity of ideas, and flexibility.

The complex nature of human capital formation systems requires a combination of approaches to answer questions such as: Given a country's (or state's) socio-economic characteristics and political dynamics, what kind of education is needed, and what kind is possible to obtain? How much should be invested? How should the costs be shared among the many stakeholders? What kinds of public–private partnerships in the provision, financing, and regulation of education produce best results? Which criteria should be used for defining "success" in educational or labor market outcomes?

Comparative political economists have contributed to the identification and explanation of some of the challenges that face contemporary, developed economies. Nevertheless, there continue to be many unanswered questions highlighted in the comparative vocational education literature reviewed here. For example, there is the question of where should vocational education take place? The decentralized nature of vocational education systems in the U.S. creates barriers for coordination between the various partners in the production of a skilled workforce. As a result, inefficiencies are pervasive, such as misaligned funding mechanisms and cost-sharing responsibilities, given federal and state priorities (Wellman et al., 2009) or detrimental competition for public funds within education levels and between education and other social policy areas (Kane, Orszag, & Apostolov, 2005). Moreover, the distinction between vocational and general education is often blurred both in the community college and four-year sectors, making any attempt to identify best practices more difficult (Bailey & Berg, 2010).

Another issue is the changing nature of occupations. Community colleges have become a fundamental piece of the federal government's higher education policy strategy (Goldrick-Rab et al., 2009; Greenblatt, 2010). This shift in focus is the result of realignment in preferences for more cost-effective, timely, and targeted educational options. The main goals of federal policy are to increase the share of the population able to secure jobs and to fulfill the growing need for more skilled labor in the U.S. economy. However, investing in specific professions and skills may be successful in the short term, but this may limit the ability of workers to adapt to the changing nature of professions and to fast-paced technological development (Mayer & Solga, 2008). This mismatch between short-term and long-term workforce needs has a few potential explanations, including the increasing focus on the instrumental goals of education (Levin, 2001), growing vocationalism in U.S. higher education (Grubb & Lazerson, 2005), and historically low investment levels of U.S. firms in vocational training (Busemeyer & Trampusch, in press).

The concern over a perceived decline of the U.S. educational achievement at the postsecondary level compared to other developed economies is ubiquitous in the recent scholarly and policy literatures (Carnevale & Rose, 2010). Empirical projections indicate that the U.S. will underproduce the number of postsecondary graduates needed by the end of this decade, and it is already the case that the U.S. does not produce the right kind of graduates, given labor market needs in each state (Carnevale, Smith, & Strohl, 2010). In this particular situation, scholars of the comparative political economy tradition should emphasize the need to identify strategies that could encourage political and economic support for the private–public partnerships necessary to prevent the aforementioned shortage of workers with postsecondary credentials (Gonzalez, 2010).

CONCLUDING REMARKS

In the U.S., given the magnitude of stress associated with public finances and the polarized nature of the electorate (McCarty, Poole, & Rosenthal, 2006), gathering support and creating partnerships with the private sector are required for the U.S. to be able to fulfill the needs of the labor market and to relieve the pressure in the social welfare safety net. Community colleges are fundamental players in this effort. There should also be a concurrent effort to identify more effective approaches to produce a skilled workforce and to thwart government disinvestment without a clear long-term strategy to counteract current upward income inequality trends (Goldin & Katz, 2008).

Insights from the comparative political economy literature can be directly applied and tested in the study of community colleges in the U.S. The states have great variability in skill production systems and cost-sharing arrangements between the public and private sectors. Comparative state analyses of how different education delivery systems and institutional structures (i.e., regulatory environment, postsecondary institutions' autonomy, and cost-sharing structures) mediate and effect various educational and social outcomes may provide the needed knowledge base and data systems that researchers, policy-makers, and practitioners can use in crafting long-term solutions to the U.S. economic development needs. In particular, rigorous comparative research can also help identify "context-sensitive" solutions that respond to the specific political, economic, and educational characteristics of each state.

Finally, the expansion of the disciplinary and interdisciplinary study of vocational education systems in the U.S. is a promising avenue for scholars and practitioners who seek to contribute to the policy debate and/or implement effective change. By expanding the disciplinary and field boundaries of community college scholarship, researchers can also demonstrate the potential of problem-based research produced by collaboration and the employment of a diverse set of ideas, methods, and perspectives for identifying and solving public problems.

QUESTIONS FOR DISCUSSION

1. How do (or should) community colleges address the mismatch between short-term and long-term economic workforce needs?
2. Are market economies systematically underinvesting in skills?
3. What are the best places to learn training needed for the workplace—the educational system, vocational tracks and vocational schools, the workplace itself, or some combination of each?
4. If empirical projections indicate an underproduction of postsecondary graduates, and the U.S. is producing the wrong kind of graduates, what can be done to improve the outcomes?

REFERENCES

Acemoglu, D., & Pischke, J. (1998) Why do firms train? Theory and evidence. *Quarterly Journal of Economics, 113*(1), 79–118.

Allmendinger, J., Ebner, C., & Nikolai, R. (2010) Education in Europe and the Lisbon Benchmarks. In J. Alber & N. Gilbert (Eds.), *United in diversity? Comparing social models in Europe and America*. Oxford: Oxford University Press.

American Association of Community Colleges. (2011). *2011 community college fast facts*. Washington, DC: Author.

Bailey, T., & Berg, P. (2010). The vocational education and training system in the United States. In G. Bosch & J. Charest (Eds.), *Vocational training: International perspectives*. [Kindle Version.] Retrieved from Amazon.com

Bailey, T., & Morest, V. S. (2006). Introduction: Defending the community college equity agenda. In T. Bailey & V. S. Morest (Eds.), *Defending the community college equity agenda* (pp. 1–27). Baltimore, MD: Johns Hopkins University Press.

Belfield, C., & Bailey, T. (2011). The benefits of attending community college: A review of the evidence. *Community College Review, 39*(1), 46–68.

Biden, J. (2010, April 14). Community colleges: Our work has just begun. *Chronicle of Higher Education*. Retrieved from http://chronicle.com/article/Community-Colleges-Our-Work/65060

Bosch, G., & Charest, J. (2010). Vocational training: International perspectives. In G. Bosch & J. Charest (Eds.), *Vocational training: International perspectives*. [Kindle Version.] Retrieved from Amazon.com

Brown, P., Green, A., & Lauder, H. (Eds.). (2001). *High skills: Globalization, competitiveness, and skill formation*. Oxford: Oxford University Press.

Busemeyer, M. B., & Nikolai, R. (2010). Education. In F. Castles, J. Lewis, H. Obinger, C. Pierson, & S. Leibfried (Eds.), *The Oxford handbook on welfare state policy* (pp. 494–510). New York, NY: Oxford University Press.

Busemeyer, M. B., & Trampusch, C. (2011). Review article: Comparative political science and the study of education. *British Journal of Political Science*, 41(2), 413–443.

Busemeyer, M. B., & Trampusch, C. (Eds.). (In press). *The comparative political economy of collective skill formation*. London: Oxford University Press.

Carnevale, A. P., & Rose, S. J. (2010). *The undereducated American*. Washington, DC: Center on Education and the Workforce, Georgetown University.

Carnevale, A. P., Rose, S. J., & Cheah, B. (2011). *The college payoff: Education, occupations, lifetime earnings*. Washington, DC: Center on Education and the Workforce, Georgetown University.

Carnevale, A. P., Smith, N., & Strohl, J. (2010). *Help wanted: Projections of jobs and education requirements through 2018*. Washington, DC: Center on Education and the Workforce, Georgetown University.

Clark, B. R. (1983). *The higher education system: Academic organization in cross-national perspective*. Berkeley, CA: University of California Press.

Culpepper, P. D., & Thelen, K. (2008). Institutions and collective actors in the provision of training: Historical and cross-national comparisons. In K. U. Mayer & H. Solga (Eds.), *Skill formation: Interdisciplinary and cross-national perspectives*. [Kindle Edition.] Retrieved from Amazon.com

Dougherty, K. J. (2006). Introduction. In B. Townsend & D. Bragg (Eds.), *ASHE reader on community colleges* (3rd ed.). Boston, MA: Pearson Custom Publishing.

Enders, J. (2010). Political science and educational research: Windows of opportunity for a neglected relationship. In A. P. Jakobi, K. Martens, & K. D. Wolf (Eds.), *Education in political science: Discovering a neglected field*. [Kindle Edition.] Retrieved from Amazon.com

Frye, J. (1994). Educational paradigms in the professional literature of the community college. In J. Smart (Ed.), *Higher education: Handbook of theory and research* (Vol. X, pp. 181–224). New York, NY: Agathon Press.

Goldin, C., & Katz, L. F. (2008). *The race between education and technology*. Cambridge, MA: Belknap Press.

Goldrick-Rab, S. (2010). Challenges and opportunities for improving community college student success. *Review of Educational Research*, 80(3), 427–469.

Goldrick-Rab, S., Harris, D. N., Mazzeo, C., & Kienzl, G. (2009). *Transforming America's community colleges: A federal policy proposal to expand opportunity and promote economic prosperity*. Washington, DC: Brookings Institution.

Gonzalez, J. (2010, September 19). *Apprenticeship programs expand with the help of community colleges*. Retrieved from http://chronicle.com/article/Apprenticeship-Programs-Expand/124523

Greenblatt, A. (2010, March 29). *For community colleges, a hard lesson in politics*. Retrieved from http://www.npr.org/templates/story/story.php?storyId=125225059

Grubb, N. W., & Lazerson, M. (2005). Vocationalism in higher education: The triumph of the education gospel. *Journal of Higher Education*, 76(1), 1–25.

Hall, P. A., & Soskice, D. (2001). *Varieties of capitalism: The institutional foundations of comparative advantage*. New York, NY: Oxford University Press.

Hanushek, E. A., & Woessmann, L. (2008). The role of cognitive skills in economic development. *Journal of Economic Literature*, 46(3), 607–668.

Harper, S. R., & Jackson, J. F. L. (Eds.). (2011). *Introduction to American higher education*. New York, NY: Routledge.

Henig, J. (2011, June 2). *How education schools can take back their role in policy*. Retrieved from http://chronicle.com/article/How-Education-Schools-Can-Take/127680/

Hess, F. M. (2008). Introduction. In F. M. Hess (Ed.), *When research matters: How scholarship influences education policy*. Cambridge, MA: Harvard Education Press.

Holzer, H., & Lerman, R. (2009). *The future of middle-skill jobs*. Washington, DC: Brookings Institution.

Kane, T. J., Orszag, P. R., & Apostolov, E. (2005). Higher education appropriations and public universities: Role of medicaid and the business cycle. *Brookings-Wharton Papers on Urban Affairs*, 99–146.

Korpi, W. (2006). Power resources and employer-centered approaches in explanations of welfare states and varieties of capitalism. *World Politics*, 58(2), 167–206.

Levin, J. (2001). *Globalizing the community college: Strategies for change in the twenty-first century.* New York, NY: Palgrave Macmillan.

Linchbach, Mark I. (2003). *Is rational choice theory all of social science?* Ann Arbor, MI: University of Michigan Press.

Marginson, S., & Rhoades, G. (2002). Beyond nation states, markets, and systems of higher education: A glonacal agency heuristic. *Higher Education, 43,* 281–309.

Mayer, K. U., & Solga, H. (2008). *Skill formation: Interdisciplinary and international perspectives.* [Kindle Edition.] Retrieved from Amazon.com

McCarty, N. M., Poole, K. T., & Rosenthal, H. (2006). *Polarized America: The dance of ideology and unequal riches.* Cambridge, MA: MIT Press.

Melguizo, T. (2011). A review of the theories developed to describe the process of college persistence and attainment in higher education. In J. C. Smart & M. B. Paulsen (Eds.),*Handbook of theory and research* (Vol. 26, pp.395–424).The Netherlands: Springer.

Powell, J. J. W., & Solga, H. (2008). Internationalization of vocational and higher education systems—a comparative-institutional approach. *Wissenschaftszentrum Berlin für Sozialforschung* Discussion Paper SP I 2008–501. Berlin: Wissenschaftszentrum Berlin für Sozialforschung.

Shavit, Y., Arum, R., & Gamoran, A. (2007). *Stratification in higher education: A comparative study.* Palo Alto, CA: Stanford University Press.

Shepsle, K. A. (2006). Rational choice institutionalism. In K. A. Shepsle, S. Binder, R. Rhodes, & B. Rockman (Eds.), *The Oxford handbook of political institutions* (pp. 23–38). New York, NY: Oxford University Press.

Stevens, M. L., Armstrong, E. A., & Arum, R. (2008). Sieve, incubator, temple, hub: Empirical and theoretical advances in the sociology of higher education. *Annual Review of Sociology, 34,* 127–151.

Strober, M. (2010). *Interdisciplinary conversations: Challenging habits of thought.* Palo Alto, CA: Stanford University Press.

Thelen, K. (1999). Historical institutionalism in comparative politics. *Annual Review of Political Science, 2,* 369–404.

Thelen, K. (2004). *How institutions evolve: The political economy of skills in Germany, Britain, the United States, and Japan.* New York, NY: Cambridge University Press.

Tilly, C. (1999). *Durable inequality.* Berkeley, CA: University of California Press.

Weingast, B. R., & Wittman D. A. (2006). The reach of political economy. In B. A. Weingast & D. A Wittman (Eds.), *Oxford handbook of political economy* (pp. 3–26). New York, NY: Oxford University Press.

Wellman, J. V., Desrochers, D. M., Lenihan, C. M., Kirschestein, R. J., Hurlburt, S., & Honegger, S. (2009). *Trends in college spending: Where does the money come from? Where does it go?* Washington, DC: Delta Cost Project.

14

COMMUNITY COLLEGE ECONOMIC AND WORKFORCE DEVELOPMENT EDUCATION IN THE NEOLIBERAL AND ACADEMIC CAPITALIST CONTEXTS

MATTHEW M. MARS

INTRODUCTION

U.S. community colleges are complex organizations that are grounded in a broad mission that includes transfer preparation, developmental education, vocational education, workforce training, and community outreach and service (Bragg, 2001; Vaughan, 2006). In some quarters, transfer preparation is often understood to be a primary academic function of community colleges, which is reflected in the historical image of the "junior college" (Frye, 1992; Vaughan, 2006). However, vocational education was present in the mission and function of community colleges beginning in the earliest stages of development (Cohen & Brawer, 2008). In particular, community college pioneers such as Walter Crosby Eells and Leonard Koos advocated early in the development of the community college sector for a broader academic scope that included vocational education as a more central feature (Bragg, 2001; Frye, 1992). Over time, vocational education helped distinguish the role of the community college as more than a preparatory resource for students seeking access to baccalaureate-granting institutions (Koos, 1970). The demand for vocational education increased during the Great Depression when students turned to community colleges for the training required for the few jobs that were available during this dismal economic period (Witt, Wattenbarger, Goolattscheck, & Suppiger, 1994). In the several decades following the Great Depression, soldiers returning from World War II in need of work, and the social and political progress made through the Civil Rights and Women's Movements, significantly increased the demand for higher education (Vaughan, 2006). During this period, the demand for higher education and the open-access mission of community colleges resulted in remarkable enrollment growth and the development of a more diverse student demographic (Vaughan, 1997). The vocational education function of the community college grew largely in response to increased student demand, federal funding initiatives to support workforce development programs, and the lobbying efforts of the American Association of Junior Colleges (Cohen & Brawer, 2008; Townsend, 2001). By the 1970s, community colleges had established the comprehensive community college model of the present, which includes a greater balance between the academic and occupational functions (Cohen & Brawer, 2008; Grubb & Lazerson, 2004; Vaughan, 1997). This chapter evaluates the literature that addresses the theoretical and conceptual underpinnings of a primary aspect of vocational education: economic and workforce development (EWD).

The following exploration of community college EWD education is informed by the community college and broader higher education literatures, and analytically framed within the context of neoliberalism (Harvey, 2005) and what Slaughter and Rhoades (2004) have theoretically categorized and outlined as the academic capitalist learning/ knowledge regime, referred to as "academic capitalism." The chapter is organized into three sections. First, the general themes and trends of community college EWD education are introduced. Second, community college EWD education is explored according to the fundamental principles of neoliberalism and academic capitalism. Third, the growing presence of entrepreneurship education across the community college sector is considered as an emergent innovation in the field of community college EWD education.

COMMUNITY COLLEGE EWD EDUCATION

EWD education is an institutionalized feature of the U.S. community college and is a field that includes a wide range of curricular and programmatic models (Grubb, Badway, Bell, Bragg, & Russman, 1997; Jacobs & Dougherty, 2006). The field "includes all the institutional programs, courses, and activities that prepare students for work. This major institutional function cuts across specific organizational units, and is present in credit and noncredit programs, career and technical areas, and contract training units" (Jacobs & Dougherty, 2006, p. 53). More specifically, community college EWD education models and practices include contracted training arrangements (Dougherty & Bakia, 2000a), specialized training programs that lead to certificates and degrees (Bragg, 2001), career-oriented models designed to increase the employability of low-income students (Grubb, Badway, & Bell, 2003; Prince & Jenkins, 2005), and outreach efforts that support small businesses (Carmichael, 1991) and local and regional economic development (Giloth, 2000; Kasper, 2003). Thus, the models and practices associated with community college EWD education comprise a broad agenda that ranges from supporting and bolstering economic activity within locales and regions to social initiatives intended to provide those on welfare with training in high demand fields.

Community colleges make important contributions to local and regional economic development and the economic competitiveness of the nation (Lowe, Goldstein, & Donegan, 2011; Rosenfeld, 2000). The current macro-economy is global in scope and knowledge based (Powell & Snellman, 2004). Paradoxically, national economic competitiveness has become largely dependent on micro-level activities within local and regional economies (Porter, 2000). The vibrancy of local and regional economies is in part dependent on the existence of highly trained, specialized labor markets (Garmise, 2009). Community colleges are the primary providers of the training needed to create and sustain the specialized workforces that are central to the economic competitiveness of locales and regions (Giloth, 2000). This important institutional role has positioned community college EWD education at the crossroads of private industry and business, local and regional communities, and the various levels of government (Dougherty & Bakia, 2000a; Grubb & Lazerson, 2004, 2005).

This position is not new. The remarkable post-World War II growth of the community college sector was fueled in large part by state and regional legislators, industry leaders, and community college administrators who sought a mechanism by which to develop the specialized national workforce needed to support a U.S. manufacturing economy that ultimately burgeoned and thrived throughout the 1950s and 1960s (Audretsch, 2007; Dougherty, 1994). Building on this momentum, community colleges have continued to develop and improve EWD education models in order to be more responsive to the changing needs and shifting priorities of business and industry within local and regional service areas (Brint & Karabel, 1989; Grubb et al., 1997; Grubb & Lazerson, 2004; Kane & Rouse, 1999). Furthermore, contract education has been identified as a potential source of greater revenue generation for community colleges as business and industry increasingly look to cut operational costs by outsourcing training and continuing education to outside providers (Brumbach, 2005; Dougherty & Bakia, 2000a; Jackson & Glass, 2000; Kisker & Carducci, 2003). Yet, the quantification of revenues and resources gained through EWD education and other market-oriented institutional innovations has gone mostly untracked by community college leadership (Bailey & Morest, 2004). However, data provided by the American Association of Community Colleges (2011) indicate that in 2003 only 1% of public community college revenue came from private gifts, grants, and contracts. This low percentage of total revenues earned through private contracts is unexpected, considering that community colleges are increasingly challenged to pursue new funding opportunities as state budgets continue to become more and more uncertain (Katsinas, 2005; Ryan & Palmer, 2005). Accordingly, the future proportion of institutional revenues raised through EWD education through private contracts warrants the ongoing attention of both scholars and policy-makers.

AN OVERVIEW OF NEOLIBERALISM AND ACADEMIC CAPITALISM

The closely linked conceptual and theoretical positions of neoliberalism (Harvey, 2005) and academic capitalism (Slaughter & Leslie, 1997; Slaughter & Rhoades, 2004) provide a useful context for understanding the current role, function, and position of EWD education in the U.S. community college. Beginning in the 1980s, pervasive shifts in the national and world economy incentivized community colleges to become more focused on vocational training and workforce development activities (Levin, 2005), as well as on meeting the labor demands of local and regional business and industry (Dougherty & Bakia, 2000a, 2000b; Levin, 2001a). The policy environment directing the aforesaid shifts and the economic and political worldwide climate of the present is commonly referred to as "neoliberalism" (Apple, 2001; Harvey, 2005). Neoliberalism emerged in or around 1980 under the leadership of U.S. President Ronald Reagan and U.K. Prime Minister Margaret Thatcher and is a policy environment anchored in the tenants of market fundamentalism (Somers & Block, 2005).

> Neoliberalism is in the first instance a theory of political economic practices that proposes that human well-being can best be advanced by liberating individual entrepreneurial freedoms and skills within an institutional framework characterized by strong private property rights, free markets, and free trade. The role of the state is to create and preserve an institutional framework appropriate to such practices. (Harvey, 2005, p. 2)

In short, neoliberal philosophy argues that society is best served by a policy climate that promotes economic growth through deregulation and free market agency.

The pervasive social and economic effects of neoliberal policy actions have ranged from notable reductions in social welfare programs (Somers & Block, 2005) to the reconstruction of the professional identities of college faculty (Harris, 2005; Levin, Kater, & Wagoner, 2006). More generally, neoliberalism has reshaped the geographical nature and underlying economic infrastructures of society (Harvey, 2005). The global scope of neoliberalism pressures nation-states to become more and more economically competitive within a worldwide marketplace (Porter, 2000). Also, local, regional, and national economic competitiveness within the global marketplace is now based more on intellectual capital and less on physical and human capital, which were the bedrock of the former manufacturing and service economies of the 1950s, 1960s, and 1970s (Audretsch, 2007). Under this condition of rigorous competition, industrial innovation develops quickly with one-time advanced technologies often becoming artifacts within a relatively short period of time (Powell & Snellman, 2004). This rapid pace of innovation and subsequent technological obsolescence ultimately lowers the long-term labor market value of workers with narrow, industry-specific training (Spring, 2008). Thus, neoliberalism and the concurrent emergence of globalization and the knowledge-based economy (Powell & Snellman, 2004) present low- to middle-level workforces with a notable degree of long-term employment uncertainties or at best ongoing workforce training needs.

Before narrowing the discussion to an exclusive focus on community college EWD education in the neoliberal context, a general overview of how the market forces associated with neoliberalism have affected higher education in general is warranted. There is a diverse set of literature that specifically examines the implications of market permeation on the postsecondary academy (Ayers, 2005; Bok, 2003; Geiger, 2004; Lee & Rhoads, 2004; Mars & Metcalfe, 2009; Rhoades, 1998). Academic capitalism is one of the more pervasive conceptual models and theoretical frameworks developed within this robust body of scholarship (Slaughter & Leslie, 1997; Slaughter & Rhoades, 2004). In general, academic capitalism seeks to explain how market permeation (and as such neoliberalism) has altered the organizational structures and academic practices of the academy in ways that favor the market. In introducing the concept of academic capitalism, Slaughter and Leslie (1997) illustrate how globalization and the underlying political economy push academic work closer to the economic marketplace and pull it further away from the traditional, public good domain. These scholars also identify resource dependency as a primary driver of this shift. In general terms, resource dependency occurs when organizations create new organizational models and adapt existing administrative structures in attempts to manage and further maximize exchanges with external organizations (Pfeffer & Salancik, 1978). Slaughter and Rhoades' (2004) elaboration of Slaughter and Leslie's theory of academic capitalism provides a framework for understanding and explaining the implications of market permeation on the organizational structures, academic practices, and institutional identities of colleges and universities. The foundation of academic capitalism is "a cultural system that valorizes higher education's dual economic roles: generating revenue for academic institutions and producing knowledge and wealth to boost the economic competitiveness of corporations" (Rhoades, 2005, p. 38). To clarify, neoliberalism and academic capitalism are interconnected concepts. In fact, during the development of the theory of academic capitalism Slaughter and Rhoades (2000) describe the postsecondary academy as "the neoliberal university" (see also Levin, 2005). From this point forward, neoliberalism will be used to refer to the general economic, political, and social environment, while academic capitalism will be used to refer to market and market-like conditions, organizational structures, and activities within higher education; more specifically community colleges.

The academic capitalism grand narrative has mostly neglected community colleges with its primary focus directed instead at research universities. Of course, community colleges have not been disconnected from or unaffected by the neoliberal policy environment and the market permeation that underpins academic capitalism (Levin, 2001b, 2002; Mars & Metcalfe, 2009; Townsend & Twombly, 2001). In particular, community colleges have responded to the neoliberal climate by restructuring the institution in order to be more businesslike, better aligned with corporate values and agendas, and more capable of responding to the fluid needs and demands of private industry (Levin, 2001a, 2001b). These organizational shifts and modifications to institutional mission are argued to have resulted in community colleges abandoning focus on students as learners and instead directing greater attention to the needs and demands of business and industry (Levin, 2001b). According to this argument, community college students are marginalized, while the agendas of private market actors and interest groups are nurtured. In voicing opposition to the pervasive influence of business and industry on community college curricula and the overall institutional mission, Ayers (2005) declares, "the discourse of economics reconstitutes the meaning of education; the value and legitimacy of knowledge are determined purely by their market value" (p. 545). In other words, the implications of neoliberalism and academic capitalism on the community college setting include devaluing teaching and learning in disciplinary fields that do not match directly the needs and demands of business and industry (Levin, 2006). Thus, curricular programs that are directed at and dependent on the needs and demands of business and industry are increasing in prominence at the expense of more academically oriented fields which are tied to general education and the preparation for student transfer to universities (Dougherty & Kienzel, 2006). The approaches to economic development activities taken by community colleges, which largely center on EWD education, are at the heart of this tension and conflict.

COMMUNITY COLLEGE EWD EDUCATION IN THE CONTEXT OF NEOLIBERALISM AND ACADEMIC CAPITALISM

The goals, structures, and practices of community college EWD education are in many ways symmetrical to the primary premises and overarching structures of neoliberalism and academic capitalism. This symmetry is now discussed according to the three aspects of neoliberalism and academic capitalism: market fundamentalism, globalization, and the knowledge-based economy. More specifically, the following discussion explores the contemporary structures and practices of community college EWD education in the context of external market interfaces, and in doing so extends the otherwise limited coverage of community colleges in the academic capitalism grand narrative (Mars & Metcalfe, 2009).

Market Fundamentalism

The core academic practices of teaching and training are the primary conduits between community colleges and the private marketplace (Bragg, 2001). Consistent with the tenants of neoliberalism, the development and delivery of EWD education is a key mechanism through which community colleges cater to the needs and demands of business and industry (Levin, 2005). Concurrently, the contributions of EWD education to local and regional economic development and growth are often identified as a strategy for meeting the service component of the community college mission (Kasper, 2003). Thus, community college EWD education is a central attribute of market fundamentalism in the community college setting.

A recent curricular trend within the EWD education field, which Grubb (1996) termed "new vocationalism," is particularly useful in illustrating the effects of neoliberal policies and academic capitalism on the community college. The new vocationalism movement emerged in the early to mid-1990s when, in response to the increasing demand for a higher-skilled technical and managerial workforce in the developing knowledge economy, some educational reformers and critics pushed for greater integration of work-related skills into community college curricula (Dougherty & Bakia, 2000b; Grubb, 1996; Grubb & Lazerson, 2004). In response to such pressures, community colleges have refined vocational education to be more aligned with the workforce needs of local and regional businesses (Levin, 2005). Subsequently, community colleges are better able to demonstrate tangible contributions to both economic development initiatives and the betterment of stakeholder communities (Kasper, 2003). New vocationalism involves the departure from the traditional focus of vocational education on entry-level workforce training in favor of more diverse curricular offerings that give greater attention to the enhancement of mid-level technical and managerial skill sets that are highly valued within the knowledge economy (Carnevale, 2000; Jacobs & Dougherty, 2006). In defining this market-induced curricular shift, Bragg (2001) stated that "first and foremost, the new vocationalism emphasizes career clusters or pathways that extend from the entry level to the professional level in career fields integral to the new economy" (p. 6). New vocationalism has also been described as an institutional strategy deployed by community colleges to remain relevant to the demands of business and industry (Jacobs & Dougherty, 2006; Levin, 2000, 2001b). However, this same strategy has been accompanied by the emergence of a "business culture" across the community college sector that encourages institutions to operate "in a less academic way, with decreasing attention to the development of critical, reflective learners" (Levin, 2005, p. 24). Thus, new vocationalism provides community colleges with a curricular link to the needs of business and industry within service areas, but at the expense of the traditional academic identity of the institution and the intellectual capital of students.

The federal government has played an important role in linking community colleges to the private marketplace (Bragg, 2001). Three examples of market-oriented public policies that are indicative of neoliberalism and academic capitalism, and that have influenced community college EWD education and new vocationalism, include the 1990 Tech Prep Education Act, the School-to-Work Act of 1994, and the Workforce Investment Act (WIA) of 1998. The 1990 Tech Prep Education Act prompted the development of vocational curriculum articulation agreements between high schools and community and technical colleges (Bragg, 2000). The articulation agreements helped legitimize the academic identity of vocational education and prompted increases in student demand. Similarly, the School-to-Work Opportunities Act of 1994 called for the creation of career development and certificate programs specific to practical and marketable skill sets and relevant to high-demand industrial fields (Hughes, Bailey, & Mechur, 2001). The WIA of 1998 was a market-oriented policy designed to provide short-term training to unemployed students in areas conducive to the needs of local business and industry (Shaw & Rab, 2003). Importantly, WIA countered the goal of the new vocationalism movement to provide "individuals with skills sets not only for the entry-level occupations but to pursue careers in high-wage, high-skill occupations" (Jacobs, 2001, p. 93). All three of these pieces of federal legislation demonstrate how government policy often works to shape (and reshape) community college EWD education in accordance with the needs and demands of business and industry (Bragg, 2001), and in ways consistent with the principles of market fundamentalism that in part underpin neoliberalism and academic capitalism.

Some EWD education programs that fall under the new vocationalism umbrella provide training to current and prospective employees of organizations that contract out human resource development operations to community colleges (Bragg, 2001). This type of EWD education that involves a single business or organization as the paying customer is commonly referred to as "contract training" (Dougherty, 2003; Dougherty & Bakia, 2000a). Contract training can range from programs that provide narrow, field-specific skills to more advanced technical skills that are required for mid-level technical and managerial positions within and sometimes beyond the sponsoring businesses or organizations (Dougherty & Bakia, 2000b; Palmer, 1990). On the one hand, through contract training community colleges provide increased support to local and regional businesses and industry that are under constant pressure to remain competitive within increasingly rigorous markets (Kisker & Carducci, 2003). In this regard, the contributions to economic development made through EWD education help community colleges fulfill the mission of serving surrounding communities. On the other hand, contract training provides community colleges with expanded opportunities to generate revenues and resources (Dougherty & Bakia, 2000a). Under such arrangements, community college leadership is financially incentivized to create and sustain curricular models that are capable of meeting the needs and demands of business and industry. However, these models often direct students toward specific training programs with narrow vocational applications and away from traditional liberal arts and transfer pathways (Levin, 2005). While the skills gained through contract training may have some transferability beyond a single firm (Grubb et al., 1997; Palmer, 1990), students in such training programs have overall limited long-term flexibility within the job market (Shaw & Rab, 2003).

Globalization

Neoliberalism has blurred national economic borders (Harvey, 2005) and led to the development of an interconnected, fiercely competitive, and knowledge-based global economy (Powell & Snellman, 2004). Paradoxically, the robustness of local and regional economies has become central to the overall economic competitiveness of the nation within global markets (Scott & Storper, 2007). With technology and science as the bedrock of enterprise in the knowledge economy (Powell & Snellman, 2004), the workforces that underlie competitive business and industry must receive regular and often specialized training (Kessels, 2001). Thus, locales and regions are increasingly challenged to develop educational infrastructures that are capable of supporting the specialized workforces that are central to attracting and retaining business and industry (Porter, 2000). Through new vocationalism, community colleges have become central to efforts to meet local and regional economic development needs and goals (Jacobs & Dougherty, 2006; Levin, 2000, 2001b). However, the high fluidity and changing nature of knowledge-based global markets (Powell & Snellman, 2004) place constant pressure on community colleges to develop new programs and revise (or collapse) existing vocational programs in order to meet the shifting labor market needs of surrounding service areas (Jacobs & Dougherty, 2006). Fluidity and flexibility do not equate to stability and predictability for either institutions or students. Thus, the central role of community colleges in supporting local and regional economies within a global context increases resource dependency and heightens the uncertainty of student employability as shifts in global markets continually shape the needs and demands of local and regional labor markets.

The Knowledge Economy

During the neoliberal era, the production and dissemination of knowledge has displaced manufacturing and service as the foundation of the global marketplace (Audretsch, 2007). Powell and Snellman (2004) define the knowledge economy "as production and services based on knowledge-intensive activities that contribute to an accelerated pace of technological and scientific advance as well as equally rapid obsolescence" (p. 201). The rapid pace of innovation and technological obsolescence associated with the knowledge economy necessitates constant change to the operational and workforce aspects of business and industry (Prusak, 1997). Accordingly, businesses competing in the knowledge economy require that technical and managerial workforces have regular access to training specific to the most advanced technologies and innovative procedures (Breu, Hemingway, Strathern, & Bridger, 2001). The demand for ongoing workforce training is often met through community college EWD education programs (Levin, 2005). The constant challenge and threat underlying the rapid pace of innovation and technological obsolescence thus enhance the value of community college EWD education to business and industry.

Community colleges are not the institutional settings where the knowledge that spurs innovation is discovered and advanced. Instead, community colleges are in the role of providing entry- to mid-level technical and managerial workforces with the specialized training that is needed in order to keep businesses and firms competitive within the knowledge economy (Levin, 2005). In other words, community colleges are organizational responders to rather than drivers of innovation in the knowledge economy. One proposition that has emerged from the current analysis of the literature is that the rapid pace of innovation development and technological obsolescence prohibits community college EWD education programs from fully achieving organizational stability and predictability. This proposition is consistent with the established concern that all higher education institutions and disciplinary fields within academic capitalist environments face organizational uncertainty when becoming even partially dependent on resource exchanges with external organizations (Slaughter & Leslie, 1997; Slaughter & Rhoades, 2004). The examination of the merits of this proposition is beyond the scope of this chapter. However, the proposition does warrant further scholarly attention from those researchers interested in the effects of market permeation on the community college sector of higher education.

COMMUNITY COLLEGE ENTREPRENEURSHIP EDUCATION: AN ALTERNATIVE APPROACH TO ECONOMIC DEVELOPMENT ACTIVITIES

The preceding overview and analysis of the position of community college EWD education in the neoliberal and academic capitalist contexts reveal a subtle but important underlying issue of agency. The concept of human agency centers on the capacities of individuals, and more abstractly organizations, to independently determine and act upon opportunities within surrounding environments (Bandura, 2001; Sewell, 1992). Issues of organizational and individual agency that have in the main been overlooked by community college scholars are illuminated by the current review of the literature on and related to community college EWD education. At the organizational level, the agency of community college leadership to develop EWD programs independently is stunted by the need to pursue new revenues through the delivery of curricula that are specific to the external demands of existing business and industry (Levin, 2005). At the individual level, the agency of students to engage community colleges in self-directed ways with the goal of enhancing personal growth and economic prosperity, which is central to the core mission of the community college, risks being compromised by outside agendas and pressures (Shaw & Rab, 2003). Also at the individual level, the agency of community college faculty involved in EWD education to freely create and deliver instruction has been marginalized by the pressures and demands of the businesses and organizations that sponsor curricular programs (Levin et al., 2006). The implications of such losses in organizational and individual agency are in direct conflict with the public good mission of community colleges (Pusser & Levin, 2009). More specifically, the long-established position of community colleges as gateways to higher learning, avenues for individual social and economic advancement, and contributors to the betterment of communities and societies (Cohen & Brawer, 2008) is at risk. Thus, the identification, implementation, and advancement of innovative approaches to community college EWD education that enhance rather than limit the agency and overall well-being of institutions, communities, students, and faculty are needed.

Entrepreneurship education represents one plausible alternate approach to community college EWD education that has the potential to concurrently promote local and regional economic development and preserve, if not enhance, the agency of institutions and institutional actors (i.e., students, faculty, administrators). Fieldwork conducted by Mars and Ginter (2011) provides early evidence that entrepreneurship education is a growing field within the community college sector. Yet, few studies on community college entrepreneurship education have been conducted (see Drury, 1999) and thus further research on this developing trend is needed. Due to this gap in research, the current recommendation is preliminary and based on the application of the robust body of research on university entrepreneurship education (e.g., Honig, 2004; Katz, 2003; Kuratko, 2005; Mars, 2006; Mars & Rios-Aguilar, 2010) to the community college setting. Entrepreneurship education in the university setting is argued to be a field that in certain circumstances provides students with the entrepreneurial agency to access and leverage various forms of institutional capital in support of individual market and market-like pursuits (Mars, Slaughter, & Rhoades, 2008; Mars & Rhoades, in press). Mars and Ginter's (2011) research indicates that the most common goal of community college entrepreneurship education across institutions is to equip students with the skills and knowledge required to create and launch new ventures within local and regional markets. Mars and Ginter (2011) also find that community college entrepreneurship education often provides students with access to institutional capital (faculty expertise, community networks, physical resources) in support of the creation of new enterprises within local and regional markets, a finding consistent with the concept of state-sponsored student entrepreneurship at the university level (Mars et al., 2008). The same study also indicates that the scope and scale of student enterprises created through community college entrepreneurship models are typically modest in size, family-oriented, and based on low technologies that are not dependent on being competitive within the global economy.

The value of community college entrepreneurship should not inherently be measured according to relevancy in the global marketplace and knowledge economy. Instead, the entrepreneurship education trend could be examined in a context that is specific to the community college setting. For instance, the service and student development arms of the institutional mission provide a relevant backdrop for the evaluation of the efficacies of community college entrepreneurship education. In particular, future research that examines entrepreneurship education as an alternative to mainstream EWD that is more aligned with the fundamental community college principles of service and student development would likely prove to be fruitful.

Community college entrepreneurship education promotes the development of local and regional enterprise that is not dependent on established business and industry (Mars & Ginter, 2011). This underlying principle of market autonomy distinguishes entrepreneurship education from conventional EWD models that are anchored in the shifting needs and demands of business and industry, driven by interests that extend beyond local and regional service areas that surround community colleges. In this regard, the modest to moderate size and operational nature of the entrepreneurial ventures of community college students should not be viewed as limitations of community college entrepreneurship education (Mars & Ginter, 2011). In particular, organizational autonomy and individual agency are inherent attributes of the entrepreneurial process regardless of venture size and type (Lumpkin, Cogliser, & Schneider, 2009). Specifically, community college entrepreneurship could be studied further as a potential avenue for providing community colleges with opportunities to contribute to the growth and development of local and regional economies without then becoming more dependent on the shifting needs and demands of business and industry. Similarly, community college entrepreneurship education could be researched further as a potential source of market agency for students based on providing skills and knowledge that promote entrepreneurial behaviors and activities that are self-directed and not dependent on the workforce needs of existing enterprises that fluctuate based on macro-level trends and rapid, short-term innovation cycles.

Community college entrepreneurship education represents only one alternative to mainstream economic development models within the community college setting. This trend is not suggested to be a structural substitute for existing EWD education programs and new vocationalism. Instead, entrepreneurship education is presented as an early example of how community colleges may be able to both engage in and support economic development activities within surrounding communities, while providing students with an educational background that promotes rather than threatens individual agency and long-term professional success and personal satisfaction.

CONCLUSIONS

I began this chapter by providing a theoretical overview of community college EWD education in the context of neoliberalism and academic capitalism. The capacity of community colleges to contribute to the growth and vibrancy of local economies hinges on a tenuous balance between meeting the needs and demands of business and industry and providing students with quality education that prepares them for sustainable, meaningful careers and lifelong learning opportunities. Conventional EWD education falls short of striking such a balance with mainstream models placing heaviest emphasis on satisfying the shifting labor needs and demands within the existing private sector. Consequently, EWD students are trained in narrow skill areas that are directly linked to the labor force's needs of specific industries, if not specific companies. The new vocationalism movement has partially addressed this deficit in EWD education models by enhancing the managerial components of curricula and thereby preparing students for positions above the entry level. However, such curricular innovations leave students dependent on narrow labor markets that are constantly shifting under the pressures of current neoliberal economic environments.

I ended the main body of this chapter with the introduction of community college entrepreneurship education as an alternative to conventional EWD education models. The community college entrepreneurship education example illustrates the potential for both enhancing the overall market agency of students engaged in EWD education and minimizing their dependency on the shifting and uncertain needs and demands of existing enterprises. The value proposition of this approach lies in the potential to satisfy both the economic and student development goals that are common to EWD education and to help build the market agency of students in ways that are not dependent on the needs and demands of existing business and industry.

QUESTIONS FOR DISCUSSION

1. How would you define "neoliberalism" and "academic capitalism?" Can you give examples?
2. What is the role of government policy—federal and state—in shaping community college economic and workforce development programs?
3. What is entrepreneurship education according to Mars?
4. What might be another approach to economic and workforce development programs at community colleges?

REFERENCES

American Association of Community Colleges. (2011). *Public community college revenue by source.* Retrieved from http://www.aacc.nche.edu/AboutCC/Trends/Pages/publiccommunitycollegerevenuebysorce.aspx

Apple, M. (2001). Comparing neoliberal projects and inequality in education. *Comparative Education, 37*(4), 409–423.

Audretsch, D. B. (2007). *The entrepreneurial society.* New York, NY: Oxford University Press.

Ayers, D. F. (2005). Neoliberal ideology in community college mission statements: A critical discourse analysis. *The Review of Higher Education, 28*(4), 527–549.

Bailey, T. R., & Morest, V. S. (2004). *The organizational efficiency of multiple missions for community colleges.* New York, NY: Teachers College, Columbia University.

Bandura, A. (2001). Social cognitive theory: An agentic perspective. *Annual Review of Psychology, 52*, 1–26.

Bok, D. (2003). *Universities in the marketplace: The commercialization of higher education.* Princeton, NJ: Princeton University Press.

Bragg, D. D. (2000). Maximizing the benefits of tech-prep initiatives for high school students.*New Directions for Community Colleges, no. 111* (pp. 23–30). San Francisco, CA: Jossey-Bass.

Bragg, D. D. (2001). Opportunities and challenges for the new vocationalism in American community colleges. *New Directions for Community Colleges, no. 115* (pp. 1–15). San Francisco, CA: Jossey-Bass.

Breu, K., Hemingway, C. J., Strathern, M., & Bridger, D. (2001). Workforce agility: The new employee strategy for the knowledge economy. *Journal of Information Technology, 17,* 21–31.

Brint, S. G., & Karabel, J. B. (1989). *The diverted dream.* New York, NY: Oxford University Press.

Brumbach, M. A. (2005, Winter). Sustaining financial support through workforce development grants and contracts. *New Directions for Community Colleges, no. 132* (pp. 49–58). San Francisco, CA: Jossey-Bass.

Carmichael, J. B. (1991, Fall). Meeting small businesses needs through small business development centers. *New Directions for Community Colleges, no. 75* (pp. 25–30). San Francisco, CA: Jossey-Bass.

Carnevale, A.P. (2000). *Community colleges and career qualifications.* Washington, DC: American Association of Community Colleges.

Cohen, A. M., & Brawer, F. B. (2008). *The American community college* (5th ed.). San Francisco, CA: Jossey-Bass.

Dougherty, K. J. (1994). *The contradictory college.* Albany, NY: State University of New York Press.

Dougherty, K. J. (2003). The uneven distribution of employee training by community colleges: Description and explanation. *The ANNALS of the American Academy of Political and Social Science, 586,* 62–91.

Dougherty, K. J., & Bakia, M. F. (2000a). Community colleges and contract training: Content, origins and impact. *Teachers College Record, 102*(1), 197–243.

Dougherty, K. J., & Bakia, M. F. (2000b). The new economic development role of the community college. *Community College Research Center Brief, 6,* 1–4.

Dougherty, K. J., & Kienzel, G. S. (2006). It's not enough to get through the open door: Inequalities by social background in transfer from community colleges to four-year colleges. *Teachers College Record, 108*(3), 452–487.

Drury, R. L. (1999). *Entrepreneurship education in the Virginia community college system: A doctoral dissertation.* (Unpublished doctoral dissertation.) George Mason University, Washington, DC.

Frye, J. H. (1992). *The vision of the public junior college, 1900–1940: Professional goals and popular aspirations.* New York, NY: Greenwood.

Garmise, S. (2009). Building a workforce development system as an economic development strategy: Lessons from US programs. *Local Economy, 24*(3), 211–223.

Geiger, R. L. (2004). *Knowledge and money: Research universities and the paradox of the marketplace.* Stanford, CA: Stanford University Press.

Giloth, R. P. (2000). Learning from the field: Economic growth and workforce development in the 1990's. *Economic Development Quarterly, 14*(4), 340–359.

Grubb, W. N. (1996). The "new" vocationalism in the United States: Returning to John Dewey. *Educational Philosophy and Theory, 28*(1), 1–23.

Grubb, W. N., Badway, N., & Bell, D. (2003). Community colleges and the equity agenda: The potential of non-credit education. *ANNALS of the American Academy of Social and Political Science, 586,* 218–240.

Grubb, W. N., Badway, N., Bell, D., Bragg, D., & Russman, M. (1997). *Workforce, economic, and community development: The changing landscape of the entrepreneurial community college.* Mission Viejo, CA: League for Innovation in the Community College, National Center for Research in Vocational Education, and National Council on Occupational Education.

Grubb, W. N., & Lazerson, M. (2004). *The educational gospel: The economic power of schooling.* Cambridge, MA: Harvard University Press.

Grubb, W. N., & Lazerson, M. (2005). Vocationalism in higher education: The triumph of the education gospel. *The Journal of Higher Education, 76*(1), 1–25.

Harris, S. (2005). Rethinking academic identities in neo-liberal time. *Teaching in Higher Education, 10*(4), 421–433.

Harvey, D. (2005). *A brief history of neoliberalism.* Oxford: Oxford University Press.

Honig, B. (2004). Entrepreneurship education: Toward a model of contingency-based business planning. *Academy of Management Learning and Education, 3*(3), 258–273.

Hughes, K. L., Bailey, T. R., & Mechur, M. J. (2001). *School-to-work: Making a difference in education: A research report to America.* New York, NY: Columbia University Teachers College Institute on Education and the Economy.

Jackson, K. L., & Glass, J. C., Jr. (2000). Emerging trends and critical issues affecting private fund-raising among community colleges. *Community College Research and Practice, 24*(9), 729–744.

Jacobs, J. (2001). Community colleges and the Workforce Investment Act: Promises and problems of the new vocationalism. *New Directions for Community Colleges, no. 115* (pp. 93–99). San Francisco, CA: Jossey-Bass.

Jacobs, J., & Dougherty, K. J. (2006). The uncertain future of the community college workforce development mission. *New Directions for Community Colleges, no. 136* (pp. 53–62). San Francisco, CA: Jossey-Bass.

Kane, T. J., & Rouse, C. E. (1999). The community college: Educating students at the margin between college and work. *Journal of Economic Perspectives, 13*(1), 63–84.

Kasper, H. T. (2003). The changing role of community colleges. *Occupation Outlook Quarterly, 46*(4), 14–22.

Katsinas, S. G. (2005, Winter). Increased competition for scarce state dollars. *New Directions for Community Colleges, no. 132* (pp. 19–32). San Francisco, CA: Jossey-Bass.

Katz, J. A. (2003). The chronology and intellectual trajectory of American entrepreneurship education: 1876–1999. *Journal of Business Venturing, 18*(2), 283–300.

Kessels, J. W. M. (2001). Learning in organisations: A corporate curriculum for the knowledge economy. *Futures, 33,* 497–506.

Kisker, C. B., & Carducci, R. (2003). UCLA community college review: Community college partnerships with the private sector—organizational contexts and models for successful collaboration. *Community College Review, 31*(3), 55–76.

Koos, L. V. (1970). *The community college student.* Gainesville, FL: University of Florida Press.

Kuratko, D. F. (2005). The emergence of entrepreneurship education: Development, trends, and challenges. *Entrepreneurship Theory and Practice, 29*(5), 577–598.

Lee, J. J., & Rhoads, R. A. (2004). Faculty entrepreneurialism and the challenge to undergraduate education at research universities. *Research in Higher Education, 45*(7), 739–760.

Levin, J. S. (2000). The revised institution: The community college mission at the end of the twentieth century. *Community College Review, 28*(2), 1–25.

Levin, J. S. (2001a). Public policy, community colleges, and the path to globalization. *Higher Education, 42,* 237–262.

Levin, J. S. (2001b). *Globalizing the community college: Strategies for change in the twenty-first century.* New York, NY: Palgrave.

Levin, J. S. (2002). In education and in work: The globalized community college. *The Canadian Journal of Higher Education, 32*(2), 47–78.

Levin, J. S. (2005). The business culture of the community college: Students as consumers; students as commodities. *New Directions for Higher Education, 129,* 11–26.

Levin, J. S. (2006). Faculty work: Tensions between educational and economic values. *The Journal of Higher Education, 77*(1), 62–88.

Levin, J. S., Kater, S., & Wagoner, R. L. (2006). *Community college faculty: At work in the new economy.* New York, NY: Palgrave Macmillan.

Lowe, N., Goldstein, H., & Donegan (2011). Patchwork intermediation: Challenges and opportunities for regionally coordinated workforce development. *Economic Development Quarterly, 25*(2), 158–171.

Lumpkin, G. T., Cogliser, C. C., & Schneider, R. (2009). Understanding and measuring autonomy: An entrepreneurial orientation perspective. *Entrepreneurship Theory and Practice, 33*(1), 47–69.

Lynch, R., Palmer, J. C., & Grubb, W. N. (1991, October). *Community college involvement in contract training and other economic development activities.* Berkeley, CA: National Center for Research in Vocational Education.

Mars, M. M. (2006). *The emerging domains of entrepreneurship education: Students, faculty, and the capitalist academy.* (Unpublished doctoral dissertation.) University of Arizona, Tucson, AZ.

Mars, M. M., & Ginter, M. (2011). *Academic innovation and autonomy: An exploration of entrepreneurship education within American community colleges.* Unpublished paper, University of Arizona.

Mars, M. M., & Metcalfe, A. S. (2009). The entrepreneurial domains of US higher education. *ASHE—Higher Education Report Series, 34*(5). San Francisco, CA: Jossey-Bass.

Mars, M. M., & Rhoades, G. (in press). Socially-oriented student entrepreneurship: A study of student change agency in the academic capitalism context. *The Journal of Higher Education.*

Mars, M. M., & Rios-Aguilar, C. (2010). Academic entrepreneurship (re)defined: Significance and implications for the scholarship of higher education. *Higher Education, 59*(4), 441–460.

Mars, M. M., Slaughter, S., & Rhoades, G. (2008). The state-sponsored student entrepreneur. *The Journal of Higher Education, 79*(6), 638–670.

Palmer, J. C. (1990). *How do community colleges serve business and industry? A review of issues discussed in the literature.* Washington, DC: American Association of Community Colleges.

Pfeffer, J., & Salancik, G. (1978). *The external control of organizations.* New York, NY: Harper & Row.

Porter, M. E. (2000). Location, competition, and economic development: Local clusters in a global economy. *Economic Development Quarterly, 14*(1), 15–34.

Powell, W. W., & Snellman, K. (2004). The knowledge economy. *Annual Review of Sociology, 30,* 199–220.

Prince, D., & Jenkins, D. (2005). *Building pathways to success for low-skill adult students.* New York, NY: Teachers College, Columbia University.

Prusak, L. (1997). *Knowledge in organizations.* Boston, MA: Butterworth-Heinemann.

Pusser, B., & Levin, J. S. (2009). *Re-imagining community colleges in the 21st century.* Washington, DC: Center for American Progress.

Reams, B. D. (1986). *University–industry research partnerships: The major legal issues in research and development agreements.* Westport, CT: Quorum Books.

Rhoades, G. (1998). *Managed professionals: Unionized faculty and restructuring academic labor.* Albany, NY: State University Press.

Rhoades, G. (2005). Capitalism, academic style, and shared governance. *Academe, 91*(3), 38–42.

Rosenfeld, S. A. (2000). Community college/cluster connections: Specialization and competitiveness in the United States and Europe. *Economic Development Quarterly, 14*(1), 51–62.

Ryan, G. J., & Palmer, J. C. (2005, Winter). Leading the fundraising effort. *New Directions for Community Colleges, no. 132* (pp. 43–48). San Francisco, CA: Jossey-Bass.

Scott, A. J., and Storper, M. (2007). Regions, globalization, development. *Regional Studies, 37*(6–7), 579–593.

Sewell, W. H. (1992). A theory of structure: Duality, agency, and transformation. *American Journal of Sociology, 98,* 1–29.

Shaw, K. M., & Rab, S. (2003). Market rhetoric versus reality in policy and practice: The Workforce Investment Act and access to community college education and training. *ANNALS of the American Academy of Political and Social Science, 586,* 172–193.

Slaughter, S., & Leslie, L. (1997). *Academic capitalism: Politics, policies, and the entrepreneurial university.* Baltimore, MD: Johns Hopkins University Press.

Slaughter, S., & Rhoades, G. (2000). The neoliberal university. *New Labor Forum, Spring Summer,* 73–79.

Slaughter, S., & Rhoades, G. (2004). *Academic capitalism and the new economy: Markets, state, and higher education.* Baltimore, MD: Johns Hopkins University Press.

Somers, M. R., & Block, F. (2005). From poverty to perversity: Ideas, markets, and institutions over 200 years of welfare debate. *American Sociological Review, 70,* 260–287.

Spring, J. (2008). Research on globalization and education. *Review of Educational Research, 78*(2), 330–363.

Townsend, B. K. (2001). Redefining the community college transfer mission. *Community College Review, 29*(2), 29–42.

Townsend, B., & Twombly, S. (Eds.). (2001). *Community colleges: Policy in the future context.* Westport, CT: Albex.

Vaughan, G. B. (1997). The community college's mission and milieu: Institutionalizing community-based programming. In E. J. Boone (Ed.), *Community leadership through community-based programming: The role of the community college* (pp. 21–58). Washington, DC: Community College Press.

Vaughan, G. B. (2006). *The community college story* (3rd ed.). Washington, DC: Community College Press.

Witt, A. A., Wattenbarger, J. L., Goolattscheck, J. F., & Suppiger, J. E. (1994). *America's community colleges: The first century.* Washington, DC: Community College Press.

Section IV
THE FUTURE: COMMUNITY COLLEGE RESEARCH AND SCHOLARSHIP

15

UNDERSTANDINGS OF COMMUNITY COLLEGES IN NEED OF RESUSCITATION

The Case of Community College Faculty

JOHN S. LEVIN

The current state of both the literature on the community college and contemporary understandings of the institution suggests a hiatus—research and scholarly literature of the past four decades have run their course. The schools of thought about the community college, whether the institution is indeed "democracy's college" (Diekhoff, 1950), "the contradictory college" (Dougherty, 1994), or "neo-liberal college" (Levin, 2007), have not advanced understanding about behaviors and actions of the institution to the extent that the research literature reflects conceptual thinking and theorizing. That is, the research literature in general does not uphold theoretical or conceptual understandings of the institution and thus is thwarted in breaking new ground.

The research literature on community colleges is not reflective of the behaviors and actions of the contemporary community college, at least those behaviors and actions that are the centerpiece of organizational functioning and development. There is a serious gap between the research literature and actual practice. On the one hand, this parallels the gap identified by Frye (1994) between social scientists and practitioners; on the other hand, it suggests that the social scientists while perhaps scientific are not theoretically based. These gaps can be seen in the understandings of institutional behaviors, including the core processes of education, instruction, and the core operators, the faculty.

The great divide in conceptions and understandings of instruction and faculty can be seen in two rather significant assumptions: first, that faculty can be conceived of as a homogeneous group, instead of as two or more prominent groups—full-time and part-time, majority (or White) and minority—and second, that there is excellence and expertise in instruction, instead of a rather unsystematic approach to and accounting for instruction. The first of these assumptions has been touched upon but only briefly by scholarship (Grubb et al., 1999; Levin, Kater, & Wagoner, 2011), with the exception of minority faculty; the second is challenged by one scholar and his associates (Grubb et al., 1999), not addressed comprehensively in research, and largely ignored in policy.

COMMUNITY COLLEGE FACULTY:
IDENTITY AND INSTRUCTION

Community college faculty constitute a significant occupational group, nationally, comprising 29% of all postsecondary education faculty. There are 373,778 faculty, of which 30% are classified as full-time (U.S. Department of Education, 2011). Little is known, however, about their professional and social identities, and, without knowledge of this body, clear and accurate knowledge about the institution is problematical or even unattainable.

Community college faculty can be understood, at least in part, from their professional or occupation identity and their social identity. As well, they can be understood from their principal function—teaching, which can be conceived of as instructional labor. Together, faculty identity and instruction can serve as windows on the community college as an institution.

PROFESSIONAL IDENTITY

Community college faculty's status as professionals has been raised as a question for decades (Cohen & Outcalt, 2001) but answered unsatisfactorily (Levin, Kater, & Wagoner, 2011). On the one hand, tied to origins as secondary school teachers, community college faculty constitute an occupation, with teaching as their primary activity, suggesting that they are undifferentiated from teachers at all levels. On the other hand, their expertise has been questioned and whether they are content, disciplinary experts or pedagogical experts is debatable. One error in the general higher education literature has been the coupling of community college faculty with four-year college and university faculty. The aggregation of higher education faculty in the U.S. is the default condition of national data sets and national studies (National Center for Educational Statistics, 2002; Schuster & Finkelstein, 2006) that both reflect and characterize faculty in higher education. On quantitative grounds, community college faculty differ from their four-year college and university peers in a number of areas: they are less credentialed at the master's and doctoral levels, they are less associated with national disciplinary bodies, and they have considerably fewer full-time positions relative to part-time than those at the other institutional types. Nonetheless, they are situated in a context where their identity as a labor force is connected to higher education faculty generally.

Academic labor in the U.S. can be construed as a professional community, yet this community is both diverse and complex. Full-time faculty and a component of part-time faculty pass through discrete stages in their employment status; they experience constrained autonomy in their professional work; and they participate as colleagues in a social environment (Levin, Montero-Hernandez, & Yoshikawa, 2011).

Life Cycles of Faculty

Life cycles theory for organizations was adapted to higher education institutions specifically by Cameron and Whetten (1983) in the 1980s. They identified four stages of organizational development. The first stage, "entrepreneurial," the second, "collectivity," the third, "formalization and control," and the fourth and final is "elaboration," characterized by domain expansion and decentralization. These stages paralleled conditions of birth, growth, and maturity for organizations. Mintzberg (1983) worked with a similar conception, but his understanding included the demise or decline of organizations. Similar understandings have been applied to college and university faculty in their employment paths in a more general way, referring to paths to the professoriate (Austin, 2002) and the academic career (Schuster & Finkelstein, 2006). Traditionally, stages for professional positions in the academy are framed by the dividing lines of tenure track and non-tenure track, as differentiations between one form of faculty and another (Levin, Shaker, & Wagoner, 2011). Within tenure track positions and long-term, full-time employment status at community colleges, the employment categories (e.g., assistant professor, associate professor, and professor, or contract faculty, or full-time faculty) signal status, authority, and professional accomplishment. Along with these categories, there are parallels between organizational stages of development and individual professional states of development. That is, part-time faculty, non-tenure track faculty, and assistant professors are those novitiates who are without permanent contracts, untenured, that is without security of employment, and undergoing socialization both into their institutions and their careers as faculty. Relatively new full-time tenured faculty have been accepted into the academy by their peers; they now face advancing along a well-worn or conventional and approved path or choosing a new one. Established full-time faculty have advanced to the senior position within their profession having attained all of the appropriate requisites; they have choices in both the intensity and nature of their work lives.

The community college variation of this pattern is skewed, somewhat, by the preponderance of a part-time labor force, which in some cases serves as the recruitment structure for full-timers; in other cases, as the permanent contingent labor force of community colleges; and, in a proportionately diminishing body, as a pool of specialized, consultant-like experts (Levin, Kater, & Wagoner, 2011). The population of tenured or long-term contracted full-time faculty in the community college is both relatively small (12% of the total according to the *Almanac Issue 2011–12* of the *Chronicle of Higher Education*) and predominantly full-time, White, and non-Hispanic in ethnicity (82.8%), including those in counseling (U.S. Department of Education, 2011), as well as matured or aging, with 52.4% over 50 years of age. Life cycles theory applied to full-time tenured community college faculty suggests that behavioral patterns are well formed and that the future and planning are conditioned by looming career endings (Levin, Montero-Hernandez, & Yoshikawa, 2011).

Collegial Identity

The customary and traditional notion of academic organizations as collegial environments (Baldridge, Curtis, Ecker, & Riley, 2000; Corson, 1960)—a collegium—persists to the present. Such an organization is characterized as directed by peers, with equal authority, and as a collection of experts, what Mintzberg (1983) has termed "meritocracy." While the research literature has not defined the work or labor of a collegial organization, popular views have portrayed academics as working together, with the assumption that collaboration in teaching and research is the norm. Yet, empirical investigations of faculty work (Grubb et al., 1999; Rhoades, 1998; Slaughter & Leslie, 1997) are silent on the matter of teaching collaboration and ignore joint labor on research projects. Goodman's (1962) concept of "community of scholars" may denote a self-governing group, either in practice or imagination, but faculty in U.S. universities and colleges are a collection of individual laborers. Community college faculty do not practice teaching as a community, although there are exceptions (Levin et al., 2009). Faculty do serve on committees—department and institutional—together and may work within these committees collaboratively, but their principal labor is singularly performed.

The process of academic socialization, begun in graduate school (Austin, 2002; Jaeger, Haley, & Levin, 2010), orients graduate students (i.e., future faculty) and faculty to the pursuit of personal accomplishment, individual responsibility, and singularity for the basis of judgment in such matters as tenure. The profession is a career (Schuster & Finkelstein, 2006). The socialization of graduate students to the solitude of research carries over to the faculty career, and choices are made by prospective faculty as to whether they want to continue this research solitude and pressure and secure employment in a research-oriented institution or in a teaching institution (Jaeger et al., 2009).

Community college faculty socialization is much more complex as this workforce is connected to a panoply of disciplines, programs, services, and curricula. Faculty in community colleges combine facets of high school teacher, vocational trainer, adult educator, counselor, and advisor, as well as academic instructor (Levin, Kater, & Wagoner, 2011). Vocational and occupational faculty enter the college from the workforce not graduate school, and thus socialization is considerably different for these faculty than for academic faculty.

Autonomous and Constrained Professionals

One of the primary qualities that faculty rely upon to characterize their professional labor is individual autonomy and freedom of choice in determining work and work schedules. Yet, at the same time, faculty acknowledge other constraints upon their labor. Such constraints include the process of tenure or the acquisition of a permanent contract, obligations to serve on committees for both security of employment and duty, and peer norms within institutions. For community college faculty, tenure is a process of conformity to peer expectations, a process to ensure that faculty will abide by the norms of the institution for faculty work: with emphasis upon what is valued in the institution—teaching and good citizenship at the community college (Levin, Montero-Hernandez, & Yoshikawa, 2011).

Faculty in unionized environments are arguably more managed and thus more constrained than faculty in non-unionized institutions (Rhoades, 1998). These constraints, however, are externally imposed, with some of them acknowledged and adhered to and others not. While faculty in unionized environments will talk about managerial control over behaviors, generally, they do not articulate that such control impedes them personally or professionally. Perceptions about the vitality of academic freedom, nationally, indicate that there is a decline, steepest at research universities, over the past three decades in positive assessments of faculty's freedom of expression in their classes and of administrators' support for academic freedom (Schuster & Finkelstein, 2006). Rhoades (1998) noted a diminution in faculty authority in managing their own affairs, with significant gains in managerial authority captured through collective bargaining. While faculty's autonomy is constrained, faculty themselves value their employment for its "freedom" and "flexibility" in the organization of work for faculty at colleges and universities (Levin, Montero-Hernandez, & Yoshikawa, 2011).

An examination of one community college's full-time faculty illustrates the articulated professional identity of faculty (Levin, Montero-Hernandez, & Yoshikawa, 2011). The professional identity of full-time faculty members at a California community college was expressed as deeply entwined with the faculty members' roles as educators. Full-time faculty members share similar personal attributes (e.g., similar career pathways, strong interests in personal interactions, and constrained-autonomous conditions). In turn, the institutional discourse, which includes institutional policies, expectations, and mission, highlights these shared personal attributes and further socializes faculty as "relational-supportive" professionals. "Relational-supportive" refers to a professional orientation built around fostering meaningful interpersonal relationships through hands-on pedagogy to support both student and local community development. To look beyond the simple characterization of community college faculty as teaching faculty is to begin to unravel a rich and complex identity, an identity carefully negotiated and developed within the context of the community college.

Although community college faculty members came from diverse origins (different cultures, disciplines, and, for some, different countries), almost all recounted a similar story of how they chose their current profession. That is, they began their careers as part-time faculty prior to joining the full-time ranks. For some of these faculty members, their decision to enter the profession was almost accidental: "[B]y chance, I thought, 'Ooo, it'd be interesting to try that.'" However, they also affirmed that the community college was the ideal institutional match for them. In particular, they found that the institutional discourse supported the same personal attributes they valued in themselves: the desire to influence and support the lives of others through direct, interpersonal contact and the agency to fulfill this desire by engaging in activities beyond their required teaching load without institutional pressure or influence.

Faculty members enacted their desire to influence and support others through teaching: "It's like I want to help people. I want to guide people through life. I don't want to just watch them wander around in oblivion not knowing what they're gonna do." Both the reward system and mission at the community college provided an optimal opportunity for this. As their employment contract stipulates, full-time instructional faculty are reviewed based primarily on their teaching competency. Their acknowledgment as a successful teacher resonates deeply with the faculty. They viewed their work with students, although challenging due to the diversity in students' academic ability and social needs, "really rewarding … and the students [are] often very grateful to have the help." They saw the institutional mission in alignment with their professional mission, confirming and reproducing a relational-supportive professional orientation.

The relational-supportive professional orientation was reinforced by faculty members' local self-positioning. While these faculty members belong primarily to the "figured world" (Holland, Lachicotte, Jr., Skinner, & Cain, 1998) of their institution, their identification with the institutional mission and student population extended the boundaries of this world to the local community. In other words, faculty acknowledged a connection with both their institution and their institution's role in the local community. For example, faculty educate students not only to help them succeed occupationally but also to "develop some critical thinking skills" and "become better citizens."

Full-time community college faculty members view themselves as autonomous individuals. This may seem counterintuitive in the context of their relatively heavy teaching load and specific workload requirements outlined in a faculty contract. A 40-hour work week involves "fifteen hours in the classroom teaching, fifteen hours for preparation, and for the grading … five hours a week for institutional service … and then it's five office hours." Yet, these faculty note a condition of freedom in their work because of the high level of specificity of their bargaining contracts. Many chose to work at this community college to avoid the competitive pressures faculty face at comprehensive and research universities, having to invest "a whole lot of work for very little payback." Without the requirements to publish, secure grants, and support graduate students, these faculty use the structure of their teaching requirements to provide a more predictable work week, allowing them to allocate free time to activities of their choice (e.g., formal or informal research projects and collaborations, community projects, overload teaching, professional development, or their personal lives). Nonetheless, full-time faculty experience a form of constrained autonomy. First, they conform to the norms of a "practitioner's culture" (McGrath & Spear, 1991), which entails experience with students as the basis of professional knowledge and consensus as the operating principle with peer interactions. Second, their activities are constrained by their contracted teaching requirements, even though they have autonomy in the availability and use of their extra time.

While the decades have passed since Earl Seidman's bleak portrayal of community college faculty (Seidman, 1985), those sentiments provided scholars with a watermark (low or high depending upon personal taste) that can be followed to the present. Significant change including institutional development (e.g., emphasis upon workforce and career-technical education), employee demographics (e.g., part-time faculty as a dominant labor force), and state actions (e.g., funding diminution) can be seen to affect faculty and faculty perceptions. As well, satisfaction surveys, such as the National Study of Postsecondary Faculty (NSOPF), indicate a high level of satisfaction, in considerable distinction from Seidman's sample, for community college faculty. Seidman's (1985) faculty were full-time, largely liberal arts and sciences faculty, and male. Most expressed aspirations for a university career. Contemporary community college faculty are considerably different from this sample. Not only are faculty more heterogeneous in their backgrounds than Seidman's sample but also the main labor force has become a contingent one.

Part-time Labor and Professional Identity of Faculty

As the institution developed through the 1980s and 1990s, expansion of educational and training services was achieved through additional labor. Without increases in state funding, community colleges were obliged to rely upon lower cost faculty (Levin, Kater, & Wagoner, 2011). By 2011, close to 70% of the faculty labor force could be designated as part-time. Scholars have not explored this condition, with few exceptions including effects upon student academic attainment (Jaeger & Eagan, 2010). Far from determined are the effects of this condition of a dominant contingent labor force upon the professional status and identity of community college faculty.

Culture theory or, more specifically, cultural identity theory (Holland et al., 1998) is one framework for viewing the condition of a predominantly part-time labor force. Full-time faculty express considerable uniformity in their occupational identities, in the context of life cycles, collegiality, and autonomy discussed above. They align themselves—what Holland et al. (1998) call "figured worlds"—with both their programs or departments and their institution; they portray themselves as actors or players within the institution; they construct their working lives as engaged with students; and, they express a high degree of autonomy or choice in their current work patterns (Levin, Montero-Hernandez, & Yoshikawa, 2011).

Part-time faculty in specific program areas where they teach, not as an ancillary activity to their other employment but as the main form of their occupational labor, express a distinctly different view from full-time faculty. They align themselves with the teaching area of a particular department or program, not with the institution; they portray themselves as invisible workers within the institution; they construct their working lives as fragmented and confined within their colleges to classrooms or course sites for online learning; and, they express little autonomy or choice in their work patterns (Levin, Kater, & Wagoner, 2011; Levin, Montero-Hernandez, & Yoshikawa, 2011). In this, part-time community college faculty share occupational perceptions with other contingent faculty in other institutions (Levin, Montero-Hernandez, & Yoskikawa, 2011).

A female part-time biology instructor at several Southern California colleges and universities noted that generally part-time teaching relieves the individual of responsibilities toward both department and college, which, although "positive" in her view, is "negative" in that "you don't have much of a say in terms of the department and the college" (Levin, Montero-Hernandez, & Yoshikawa, 2011). As for interactions with faculty or students, this instructor noted its absence.

> I didn't really interact with anyone … My classes were not in the department's building. It was somewhere else on campus. So I just would get to campus. I'd have my office hours near—because they don't have a standard office for adjuncts … I would just have my office hours near the classroom; then I'd teach; then I'd go home … I didn't hear much from the department that much … until it was time for my evaluation.

Furthermore, her relationship to the department was in the form of an outsider: "I didn't know the direction the department was heading in, or I didn't know what major focus the department was, like what they were assigning concern." While she pursues a Ph.D., she contemplates an academic career, and a predominantly teaching institution is her goal for full-time employment. Part-time teaching is "nerve-wracking" she claims, because "the hardest thing about adjuncting … is being semester to semester and not having guaranteed work."

This division between part-time/contingent labor and full-time faculty suggests two classes of faculty, two workforces, and two occupations. It suggests a fractured or incomplete professional body. Departments and programs comprising two full-time faculty and five or ten times as many part-time faculty stretch the boundary definitions of what constitutes a professional organization. Mintzberg, in his conceptualization of a professional bureaucracy (Mintzberg, 1991)—his label for universities—did not give a passing notation to a condition where the core operators would be part-time labor.

Not only are there two major classes of community college faculty, essentially two main occupations that characterize the institution, but also within one group—full-time faculty—there are particular kinds of professionals who have "relational-supportive" orientation that differentiates them from other higher education faculty.

SOCIAL IDENTITY

There has been much written that addresses minority faculty at four-year institutions; this cannot be said of underrepresented faculty at community colleges. The proportion of community college faculty who are categorized as minority is 22% (National Center for Education Statistics, 2008). "[T]he overall picture of community college faculty does not reflect an image of diversity" (Eagan, 2007, p. 6). Recent research stresses the importance of minority faculty to the academic community and the resultant quality of education offered at colleges and universities. Minority faculty often have perspectives or utilize approaches to practice that raise new questions and alternate solutions that can challenge traditional epistemologies and explore new frontiers in research (Bernal & Villalpando, 2002). In an analysis of faculty surveys collected from 134 higher education institutions, Umbach (2006) found that faculty of color were more likely than White faculty to use active and collaborative teaching techniques; African American and Native American faculty interacted with students more often than other faculty; with the exception of Native American faculty, faculty of color engaged students in higher order cognitive activities; and with the exception of Asian Pacific American faculty, faculty of color engaged students in more diversity-related activities than White faculty. The assumption here is that exposure to such educational experiences and diversity-related activities benefits all students, not just those with diverse backgrounds themselves, as White students gain familiarity with new ways of thinking and cultures, and students of color receive an education that legitimates their presence in higher education.

Research directed to community colleges offers a similar discourse regarding the value of diversity in the faculty. Hagedorn, Chi, Cepeda, and McLain (2007) studied faculty in the Los Angeles Community College District and found that a "critical mass" of Latino faculty increased Latino student retention. They argue that a greater representation of Latinos among community college faculty increases "the availability of role models for students and fosters a sense of belonging and social integration among students" (p. 89). This sense of belonging, in turn, increases Latino student academic achievement and educational aspirations. In addition to fostering increased connectivity between minority students and community colleges, minority faculty play crucial roles in developing community college cultures that value diversity (Harvey, 1994; Owens, Reis, & Hall, 1994). Although minority faculty can be powerful advocates for institutional change and are pivotal figures in a community college's commitment to diversity, faculty of color are underrepresented in the professoriate.

While higher education research highlights significant differences in status between White faculty and faculty of color, the variation is more complex than color. In general, White and Asian/Pacific Islander faculty have higher rank, tenure, and earnings than Black/African American faculty. Hispanic faculty appear to be situated in between those groups as their attainment fluctuates depending on the variable measured (Bradburn & Sikora, 2002; Nettles, Perna, & Bradburn, 2000). Menges and Exum (1983) argued that women and minority faculty experienced similar difficulties in the academy as they are both overrepresented at less prestigious four-year colleges and community colleges and more susceptible to layoffs, given that these were predominantly unionized environments (Rhoades, 1998). Additionally, faculty with lower status—often the combination of low-status disciplines where faculty of color more generally reside—have larger teaching loads than higher status faculty and are thus able to commit less time to conducting research. At institutions that reward research more than teaching, these faculty of color are less successful at gaining promotions than their White counterparts. However, with the added variable of gender, being a woman has a negative effect on attainment between different racial/ethnic groups. Women generally earn less money, have more difficulties with promotion, and are as a group therefore less tenured than their male counterparts (Bradburn & Sikora, 2002; Toutkoushian, Bellas, & Moore, 2007).

Demographic research has also identified important disciplinary and institutional differences in the distribution of faculty along racial/ethnic lines. NSOPF indicates that White and Asian/Pacific Islander faculty are more concentrated in the natural sciences, engineering, and business disciplines, while Hispanic and African American faculty are more concentrated in the social science, education, and humanities disciplines. Institutionally, the NSOPF data illustrate that White and Asian faculty are more likely to teach at doctoral institutions than Hispanic and African American faculty (Bradburn & Sikora, 2002; Cataldi, Fahimi, & Bradburn, 2005). Furthermore, within the African American group, men are more likely to be in the sciences or business disciplines and more likely to be in more advanced institutions than their female counterparts (Agathangelou & Ling, 2002; Gregory, 2001).

While community colleges employ the largest group of minority faculty, there are nonetheless many more White faculty than underrepresented faculty at the community college level (Carter, 1994). Nicholas and Oliver (1994) argue that in spite of growing sensitivity to faculty diversity since the 1960s, culminating in affirmative action policies and institutional quotas for minority faculty during the 1970s and 1980s, the community colleges of the 1990s had not attained a diverse faculty (Harvey, 1994). In over a decade and a half since Nicholas and Oliver (1994), little has changed in community colleges. Even in states as diverse as California, community college faculty are overwhelmingly White and underrepresented faculty are overrepresented in the counseling, education, social science, and humanities disciplines. Sixty percent of all California community college faculty are categorized as White; 14.95% as Hispanic; 10% as Black; 5.79 % as Asian American; and 0.79% as Native American (Chancellor's Office California Community Colleges, 2011).

To address racial as well as gender disparities, researchers have turned to a variety of critical perspectives that provide insight into the cultural or organizational climate issues in colleges and universities that create barriers to faculty diversity, thus impinging upon social identity of faculty. Whether from feminist, post-colonial perspectives (Agathangelou & Ling, 2002) or more explicitly racial perspectives (Brayboy, 2003; Diggs, Garrison-Wade, Estrada, & Galindo, 2009; Fenelon, 2003), this body of literature assumes and asserts that the dominant academic cultures at colleges and universities favor White male faculty.

One of the most common of these perspectives is critical race theory (CRT). CRT holds that racism persists in everyday interactions, but since it is ingrained in the dominant culture, racism does not manifest itself to those of the dominant culture (Diggs et al., 2009). Fenelon (2003) situates this perspective within the dominant research culture's underlying assumptions about objectivity or neutrality.

> [R]esearch ... has important political manifestations, including the justification for racial inequalities that are replicated within the student and alumni bodies of institutions that may formally state that they value diversity even as all of their internal mechanisms reproduce exclusionary dominance for some racial groups. (p. 91)

To criticize dominant cultural assumptions and actions, CRT emphasizes the importance of storytelling to give voice to those outside of the dominant culture. Thus, CRT offers a critical perspective for the analysis of the dominant culture's role in creating racial and ethnic inequalities as well as all attempts to decrease those inequalities (Diggs et al., 2009). It stresses that efforts to decrease inequality that are constructed within the dominant culture's framework may do little to decrease inequality.

Studies that rely upon CRT identify cultural barriers to faculty diversity in higher education. These barriers include issues of cultural identity conflict, a "double bind" (Brayboy, 2003), devaluation of work, tokenism, isolation, and lack of mentoring (Turner, Myers, Jr., & Creswell, 1999). These issues are particular to women and minority faculty, giving dominant, White male faculty an advantage in the higher education workplace.

Identity conflict may occur between a minority faculty's self-articulated identity and the identity imposed on him or her by the college or university. For example, Stanley (2006) found, in interviewing 27 faculty of color at primarily White institutions, that faculty struggled to assert their own nuanced perspectives of their identities in the face of institutionally imposed identities that often highlighted race, based on physical characteristics. Even the term "faculty of color," she explains, indicates an assumption about the association of physical traits and cultural heritage. Instead, identity is often complicated and layered. Turner (2002) investigated identity along racial/ethnic and gender lines. While male minority faculty at least have the advantage of being male, female minority faculty experience "multiple marginality" where both racial/ethnic and gender characteristics position them as minorities.

Another theoretical perspective that offers useful insight into the cultural aspects of higher education is acculturation theory. Acculturation theory describes "the process by which individuals adapt their socialized world views to function in a culture different than their primary one" (Sadao, 1995, p. 31). This adaptation may occur in several ways: through assimilation, when an individual sacrifices their cultural beliefs in favor of the dominant culture; through integration, when the dominant culture incorporates some aspects of the individual's culture; through separation, when an individual retains their original cultural beliefs and remains an outsider; and through marginalization, when a minority is torn between their original culture and the dominant culture, ultimately losing both.

From this perspective, minority faculty are often placed in a tenuous situation. Turner (2003) argues that while assimilation offers the promise of progress for individuals, it offers nothing to change the reward structures that favor White male faculty over others. However, minority faculty endeavor to avoid separation or marginalization because to remain an outsider or to become culture-less offers them little hope for their advancement. Aguirre, Martinez, and Hernandez (1993) also discuss this insoluble situation, suggesting: "the segmented position minority faculty hold within the organizational structure of the postsecondary education institution may be instrumental in reinforcing their perception that they are peripheral participants in academe" (p. 381). As a result, faculty of color concerned about racial/ethnic inequalities often face what Brayboy (2003) refers to as a "double bind," a conflict between assimilation and separation.

Further isolation and marginalization experienced by minority faculty include the lack of professional role models at these institutions (Turner et al., 1999). Without adequate professional networks, faculty of color are separated from academe and have fewer tools for advancement and professional success than White faculty, who have greater access to mentors and networks. Stanley (2006) and Diggs et al. (2009) both identify mentoring relationships as significant factors that positively influence the experiences of faculty of color, even when the mentor is of a different race/ethnicity or gender. Scholarship on community colleges supports this finding, as Harvey (1994) indicates that African American faculty in community colleges who lack an adequate professional network are significantly debilitated. This condition is acknowledged by Opp and Smith (1994). Without a strong minority faculty presence, underrepresented minority community college faculty have limited power in the institution and little influence on minority students. Nevertheless, while they are more abundant than professional mentors of color, unofficial mentors of color receive few, if any, institutional rewards for their work. The lack of professional mentors and limited or no reward for unofficial mentoring constitute another example of Brayboy's (2003) "double bind" concept.

In some distinction to a process of acculturation that has negative results, Sadao (1995, 2003) identifies another acculturation possibility, which she calls "biculturalism," where minorities embrace aspects of their original culture as well as the dominant culture. Similarly, Diggs et al. (2009) indicate that some faculty are able to practice "code-switching" between these different cultures depending on their situation. This practice enables them to navigate institutions that are not their own, while also maintaining their original cultural identities.

CRT theory is less sanguine about results of acculturation. CRT-guided research highlights the presence of tokenism, where colleges and universities use women and faculty of color to "represent diversity not to practice it" (Turner, 2003, p. 122). For example, women or minority faculty (and sometimes both) may receive promotions to fulfill some implicit or explicit quota for minority faculty at a given institution (Turner, 2002). Tokenism devalues the efforts and achievements of minority faculty, reducing them to a symbol for diversity: because of their symbolic presence they might satisfy administration and the community, but their presence as tokenism reduces the opportunities available to these faculty members to increase diversity and cultural equality.

CRT and other critical perspectives provide a lens through which to evaluate the influence of institutional norms and policies and their interactions with women and minority faculty. These perspectives recognize the power of the dominant culture and its ability to define norms, a power not granted to minority cultures. As such, inequalities between racial/ethnic groups are difficult to identify when the measurements used reflect the norms, policies, and values of the dominant culture.

Research that addresses community colleges, specifically, suggests that minority faculty experience similar cultural or climate barriers to those experienced at four-year institutions (Bowers, 2002; Harvey, 1994; Opp & Gosetti, 2002; Opp & Smith, 1994). Bowers (2002) interviewed African American and Latino women faculty at two Florida community colleges and found that these faculty experienced discrimination from other faculty, staff, administration, and some of their students. This finding highlights the importance of institutional culture (or climate) to the experiences of minority faculty at community colleges. Other research on community colleges resonates with the general higher education literature regarding the importance of minorities on boards of trustees, administration, faculty, and other staff positions to the relative comfort levels of minorities in the institutions (Harvey, 1994; Opp & Gosetti, 2002; Opp & Smith, 1994). The greater the network opportunities for minority faculty with other minorities the more likely those faculty will experience comfort, satisfaction, and efficacy in the community college. It appears, then, that the idea of a "critical mass" of faculty has value to other faculty as well as to students (Hagedorn et al., 2007). Recent research on community college faculty of color confirms this observation (Levin, Montero-Hernandez, & Yoshikawa, 2011).

Faculty in community colleges are not a homogeneous group, but rather are separated by professional and social identities. Not only are their identities diverse and complex but also their primary institutional role—teaching—is far more variable than portrayed in the literature. No doubt, teaching is the locus of confusion about the professional status of community college faculty.

INSTRUCTION

In previous scholarship (Levin, 2008), I noted that the behaviors of faculty do revolve around community college students and the teaching of students in spite of Grubb et al.'s (1999) claim that the teaching focus of community colleges is neither rationalized nor validated. Community college faculty adopt and internalize the student-focused mission of their institution, and function in an environment of internal consistency, organizational consensus, and the denial of ambiguity. Faculty membership in the organization dictates conformity to the expectations and norms of the institution (Burton, 2007). This environment, what McGrath and Spear refer to as a "practitioner's culture" (1991), arises from an institutional emphasis on teaching a wide range of students with varying levels of academic preparation and abilities. In order to succeed and indeed survive, faculty fit their teaching philosophies and styles to this population. Thus faculty are connected to the students and the courses and programs where students are found. This means that faculty teaching is distinctive by program area—from university transfer to career-technical to basic skills—and these areas constitute subcultures within the institution.

In scholarly history, teaching at community colleges is viewed as a singular process, a form of knowledge application, without attention to program area. Grubb et al. (1999) conducted one of the few national investigations of instruction: they noted that the primary and predominant approach of community college faculty is void of interaction with students. With the exception of a handful of classrooms, participatory student engagement was found wanting. While their work predates the rise of online instruction and distributed learning, Grubb et al. indicate that instruction is largely a stimulus-response process. Yet, they do acknowledge that in the more practical fields there are differences, even though their work did not emphasize program differentiation or sample proportionately equal areas, such as career technical, basic skills, and university transfer. They make one of the first attempts to indicate that not all instruction in community colleges is identical but they stop short of asserting that instructional differentiation is conditional upon student characteristics. In the main, they opt for one kind of optimal method of instruction and those faculty who avoid this method are both the majority and duly criticized and those who adopt it are praised.

This is not to say that community college instruction is without merit and without effective outcomes. Yet few have documented the general effects of instruction, that is, the extent to which instruction matters. Levin (2007) and Levin and Montero-Hernandez (2009) investigated outcomes for students including student identity development and student performance and achievement broadly. Rather than relying upon grades or course taking patterns or other quantitative measures of student performance, they investigated the larger concept of college's affects upon students. For non-traditional students, the majority of community college students, they noted that the construction of learner identity takes place during the college experience. In almost all cases of the dozens of students observed at 10 community colleges nationally, they noted the instructional efficacy of faculty and staff, including counselors and advisors, as well as administrative personnel. Learning was not always about problem-solving but also about gaining knowledge of academic culture and developing organizational skills and career goals and plans. Additionally, these students demonstrated high levels of motivation and considerable resilience. According to faculty and administrative personnel, these qualities not only led to but were also necessary for achievement for this population. Scholarship, with some exceptions, ignores both these learning outcomes and fails to connect motivation and resilience to student performance and achievement. Moreover, scholarship ignores the critical role of faculty.

Community college faculty themselves, contrary to early scholarship (Grubb et al., 1999; Kempner, 1990), and to omissions in empirical research (Roueche, Roueche, & Milliron, 1995; Valadez & Antony, 2001), have become sensitized to students' needs and the characteristics of student demographics. A recent examination of community college faculty in one California community college (Levin, Montero-Hernandez, & Yoshikawa, 2011) reflects this more active, student-focused approach. A sociology full-time assistant professor exemplifies this approach: "I do a lot of small group work ... and it's easier for me then to connect with each student individually ... I make a real concerted effort to make that connection with each student." A biology professor expresses not only her attraction to teaching a diverse population but also her satisfaction in connecting students to science.

> I just fell in love with just the mixture of people [at this college]. Everything from your 17 year old who knows nothing ... through to people in their 60s who've lived, and then everybody in between ... [I am] always trying to seduce people with science ... seeing the light in somebody's eyes when they get it, and then seeing people struggle and make it through.

Faculty make a difference in student achievement. Indeed, under the right conditions, faculty have the major effect upon how college affects community college students. These conditions include an educational environment where faculty, collectively and by program area, are both responsible for educational outcomes and work in concert, even though loosely coupled, to develop student potential (Levin et al., 2009). This is to suggest that while faculty in community colleges can be construed as independent workers, their effects upon students are enhanced when they function in tandem: their collective approach is a central feature of effective instructional practice. This may indicate that a professional identity in community college is collective.

THE INSTITUTION–FACULTY CONNECTION

The question of professional identity may also be tied to institutional association and thus, because the community college is deemed to be a problematical institution (Pusser & Levin, 2009), faculty professionalism is also questionable. Community college faculty are absent a coherent identity as experts. They have no claim to specialized knowledge and no formal designation or reputation as pedagogical gurus. Yet, their institution is characterized and differentiated from other higher education institutions by its teaching mission (Cohen & Brawer, 2008; Grubb et al., 1999). Recent research offers new insights, however, indicating that full-time community college faculty define themselves through their students (Levin, Montero-Hernandez, & Yoshikawa, 2011). Faculty justify their labor and their self-efficacy by noting the students that they have motivated, developed, and rescued, as well as those who have advanced beyond the institution to employment or further education.

The faculty labor force for community colleges both reflects and shapes institutional identity. Faculty as an incomplete professional body reflect an institution that has a problematical identity (Pusser & Levin, 2009). This problematic identity can be seen in the multipurpose and consistently changing function of the community college; in the low status of the community college relative to universities and four-year colleges; in its inability to turn public support into financial support; and in its use as a policy vehicle for legislatures to solve economic and social problems, such as welfare. This labor force shapes institutional behaviors both in permitting enrollment expansion without ensuring student outcomes, especially persistence (Vaughan, 2002), and in enabling a more managerial culture and a less engaged faculty in institutional governance (Kater & Levin, 2005). Additionally, a smaller percentage of faculty are entitled—provided the same benefits, rights, and responsibilities—to the extent they were in the past as a result of the expansion of part-time labor.

The case of community college faculty, then, is instructive: there is no clear professional identity for this body in that they are not a coherent occupational class and their labor, while generally referred to as "teaching," incorporates those who teach and those who develop students, those who interact with students face-to-face and those who interact online, those who show up once a week for several hours in a classroom and those who reside all week long on a campus, is too diverse to pigeon-hole. Understanding faculty, then, is a heuristic for understanding the community college. The heterogeneous labor force, their uncertain professional status, and the divided condition (in employment categorization and what that entails) parallels the institution—without a coherent and unified identity. Community college faculty labor conceived as teaching needs to be systematically examined and theorized, not unlike what is needed for the institution itself.

THE STATE OF KNOWLEDGE ABOUT COMMUNITY COLLEGES AS INSTITUTIONS

In order to improve conceptual understanding of community colleges, to create the organizational saga of the community college, which is lacking, what is missing generally is an in-depth understanding of the institution, through its members and students. This lack of understanding can be seen in both the numerous misunderstandings and oppositional understandings of the institution. Pusser and Levin (2009) explain the misunderstanding as one based upon perspective.

> Community colleges find themselves facing both praise and criticism on so many dimensions that it is difficult to make an overall assessment of their legitimacy in the broader U.S. political economy. The diversity of inputs and outputs in these institutions defies easy categorization. The identity of the colleges in the media,

in the policy community, and in the institutions themselves varies depending on standpoint and context. They are at times characterized by their students—demographics, academic background—by their curricula and programs—academic, vocational, remedial, continuing education—by their utility for communities, states, and in meeting national goals—economic development and workforce preparation—and more recently by their own effectiveness. (p. 8)

The identity of the institution is muddled, unclear, and highly dependent upon who is talking about the institution and their context. Student outcomes at community colleges result in contentious and polarized views of the performance of the institution. While those who question the worth of the institution point out that large percentages of students fail to persist or complete programs—for example, only 50% of credit students persist beyond eight months of college—others point out that the institution has increased access to postsecondary education, particularly for low socio-economic status populations. Similarly with financing the institution: some analysts note that costs are reasonable at community colleges and this justifies outcomes; others suggest that the outcomes, particularly in economic terms, are not worth the costs (Pusser & Levin, 2009).

Pusser and Levin (2009) attempt to locate a cause for the diversity of perspectives. They propose three origins. The first entails the missions of the community college and thus the ensuing interpretations and understandings of scholars and policy-makers. The second is the purpose of the institution for constituents, such as the community college as development center, as community education center, and as transit center to further education or employment. These various missions and purposes lead to a third origin for the diversity of perspectives.

Perhaps most important, community colleges' many purposes lead to multiple identities, both within the institutions and for those observing from outside. Many of those identities are likely to be poorly understood by external actors at any given time given the complex and conflicting demands on the institutions. (p. 8)

Yet, what Pusser and Levin fail to acknowledge and then reflect in their analytical report is the view from inside, from the institutional members, including faculty, staff, administration, and students. The ways in which these parties experience the institution and institutional daily life are largely obscured from understandings of the institution; yet, these experiences and thus institutional realities can inform understandings of the institution. Feelings, experiences, and morale—what Watson (2009) and others refer to as levels of happiness and unhappiness—shape institutional life and institutional identity. Scholars of community colleges have neglected to analyze and make sense of the discourse of community colleges. Watson argues that in universities "academic discourse is especially prone to paradox and plain inconsistency" (2009, p. 3). Pusser and Levin (2009) relay the ways in which others—those outside—view the community college, and thus formulate an institutional identity, but there are little or no articulations about the ways in which those inside view their institution. Of course there have been some exceptions: Seidman (1985); McGrath and Spear (1991); Cooper and Kempner (1993); Herideen (1998); and Shaw, Rhoads, and Valadez (1999). Until there is more attention to the views and experiences of those inside the institution, there will be little understanding of what is going on in the community college.

The view of the community college as an institution, subject to and shaped by its participants, has been dimmed over the past decades, replaced by an emphasis upon highly specific components of particular behaviors (or outcomes) of students and responses by institutional officials. That is, there are specialized efforts to quantify and then analyze student behaviors in the area of persistence, academic attainment, and mobility (i.e., how long students remain in the community college, what grades and credentials they gain, and where they go after community college—for example, university or employment) and then determination of institutional interventions that have, or may have, salient effects upon these particular student behaviors. In the majority of cases, students are portrayed as underperforming (Bailey, Jenkins, & Leinbach, 2005) and the community college as falling far short of expectations (Brint, 2003), with both combined (Bailey et al., 2005). These efforts to find the cause of both student inadequacies and institutional underperformance have been muted periodically by those who endeavor to offer a larger picture (Adelman, 2005) or a less specialized view (Cohen & Brawer, 2008).

The influences of policy-makers and legislators (and perhaps the researchers who influence these parties) have directed attention from the institution as a social and cultural entity to an economic and political one. The focus upon student outcomes is tied to economics: to the costs of education and to the economic benefits of education. Whereas the community college is deemed a less expensive vehicle for the education and training of youth than four-year colleges and universities, its efficiency in leading students to baccalaureate degrees more so than four-year colleges and universities is questionable. It may cost all parties more to use the community college as a baccalaureate pathway than a four-year college or university (Santos & Melguizo, 2007). The same can be said for employability and earnings. Not all community college education and training has a financial benefit or significant gain for all student groups (Grubb, 1996). Yet, policy-makers and legislators emphasize the economic value of the community college, and the federal government through the American Graduation Initiative has set in motion an initiative to raise degree and credential attainment levels that far exceed reasonable predictions, yet take main stage in community college policy (Pusser & Levin, 2009).

The political aspect is tied to the economic as the community college is seen as a panacea for a number of problems—educating large numbers efficiently and developing a trained workforce, as the more palatable purpose, and removing large numbers of youth from un- and underemployment and retraining an obsolete workforce, undone by technology, as the less savory rationale. Every political persuasion and ideology can use the community college, including those who characterize the community colleges as the "green light" or Statue of Liberty of U.S. education (Vaughan, 2000) and those who see the reflection of U.S. society through student behaviors (Adelman, 1992). At the national level, community colleges have become centerpieces in fixing the nation's educational and productivity ills, and the American Association of Community Colleges has launched a commission, with a general agenda, to guide leaders of community colleges into a new era, and presumably more favorable conditions (Times, 2011).

Institutional behaviors including governance behaviors, instructional behaviors, managerial behaviors, and indeed student development behaviors are fading from the focus of those who study community colleges, replaced by these economic and political concerns. Research scholars have not adopted the theoretical orientations that would help in an explanation of institutional behaviors. They come close from time to time with reliance upon human capital theory or even organizational theory (Shaw & Rab, 2003; Twombly & Townsend, 2008), but these efforts are not substantial and generally speak to the era of the 1980s and earlier. After the early 1990s, few attempted sophisticated analysis of community colleges using neo-institutionalism. After the late 1990s, few turned to culture theory, and certainly not social identity theory, to explain behaviors and conditions within community colleges.

UNDERSTANDING COMMUNITY COLLEGES

It is conceivable that the community college of the past decades—from the 1960s to the present—has altered its structures and behaviors to the extent that understanding in the present and future should focus not on deinstitutionalization, as Scott (2005) might propose for these institutions, but on postmodern institutionalism. Such a concept was touched on by Bergquist (1992) and explored in greater detail by Tierney (1993), whose work emphasized pluralism in institutional functioning. Some of Tierney's recommendations for practice align well with community colleges and their practices for the past 30 years. Neither Bergquist nor Tierney had little evidence for what has transpired for the community college, specifically, in these decades: fragmentation of the faculty labor force, the multiple cultural and ethnic backgrounds of the student body, the rise and prevalence of distributed learning and hybrid methods of instruction combining face-to-face and screen time, and the elaboration of mission, including the community college baccalaureate degree, welfare-to-work programming, reverse transfer and swirling (e.g., students returning from baccalaureate institutions to gain employment skills and students moving from one institution to another) and English as a second language, as well as growth of 44% in credit enrollment in community colleges from the early 1990s to the end of the first decade of the 2000s (U.S. Department of Education, 2011).

The community college as an institution has changed. Theoretical frameworks, such as new institutionalism, social and cultural identity theory, globalization theory, critical theories, and sustainability or eco-theories, are necessary to help us understand the new organization. Yet, the focus needs to be broadened, beyond functional concerns for the institution's well-being or progress to the broad development of students, local communities, states, the nation, and other countries and their people. More than maintaining a narrow focus upon the U.S., scholars and policy-makers should consider an international context and as well gain new knowledge from the examination of other countries' postsecondary, postcompulsory sectors that parallel in some ways the U.S. community college. Canada, of course, is one obvious jurisdiction, given its institutions' historical parallels with those in the U.S. Australia, the U.K., and South Africa are other jurisdictions that have gained considerable experience over the past few decades in providing postsecondary education to highly diverse populations. New efforts in both China and India should also be followed as these countries move economically and socially in competition with the U.S. and endeavor to undergird this movement with further education of the masses. Although the community college in the U.S. is without question a local institution, its international appeal is obvious and its international parallels provide an opportunity for U.S. scholars and practitioners to adopt a global perspective and both study and learn from others' practices.

The community college is both an expanding institution and one that is fragment-ing to the extent that its parts are not bounded by a greater whole. In contrast to Scott's (2005) assumptions on institutions, which included critical phases of their existence—beginning, middle, and end—I propose that the postmodern community college has no discernible, rational timeline, aside from one assumed and believed by scholars who take a modern perspective that understands the institution from a periodization per-spective (Ratcliff, 1994) or even a developmental perspective (Cohen & Brawer, 2008).

As the institution expands, both in size and in mission, it becomes less of its bounded former self (e.g., two-year institution) and more deeply an elaboration of its histori-cal purposes and values (e.g., community and personal development). There may be an imagined beginning, but there is no scripted ending. The call, then, is for the next gen-eration of scholars to inform practitioners and policy-makers about the actual behaviors and conditions of community colleges. To examine diverse effects of community college attendance for students, career-technical program potentials for developing not only workforces but also individual students, and consider new perspectives on financing, managing, and governing community colleges, as the authors of this book have done, is to set off in the right direction.

QUESTIONS FOR DISCUSSION

1. In what ways are faculty in community colleges categorized or conceptualized?
2. What would constitute appropriate ways to determine the quality of teaching in a community college?
3. In what ways do large proportions of part-time faculty at community college affect the learning experiences and outcomes of students?
4. Are community college faculty professionals?

REFERENCES

Adelman, C. (1992). *The way we are: The American community college as thermometer.* Washington, DC: U.S. Department of Education.

Adelman, C. (2005). *Moving into town—and moving on: The community college in the lives of traditional age students.* Washington, DC: U.S. Department of Education.

Agathangelou, A. M., & Ling, L. H. M. (2002). An unten(ur)able position: The politics of teaching for women of color in the US. *International Feminist Journal of Politics, 4*(3): 368–398.

Aguirre, A., Jr., Martinez, R. O., & Hernandez, A. (1993). Majority and minority faculty perceptions in academe. *Research in Higher Education, 34*(3), 371–385.

Austin, A. E. (2002). Preparing the next generation of faculty: Graduate school as socialization to the academic career. *Journal of Higher Education, 73*(1), 94–122.

Bailey, T., Jenkins, D., & Leinbach, T. (2005). *Is student success labelled institutional failure? Student goals and graduation rates in the accountability debate at community colleges.* New York, NY: Teachers College, Colum-bia University.

Baldridge, J. V., Curtis, D. V., Ecker, G. P., & Riley, G. (2000). Alternative models of governance in higher educa-tion. In M. C. Brown (Ed.), *Organization and governance in higher education* (5th ed., pp. 128–142). Boston, MA: Pearson Custom Publishing.

Bergquist, W. (1992). *The four cultures of the academy.* San Francisco, CA: Jossey-Bass.

Bernal, D. D., & Villalpando, O. (2002). An apartheid of knowledge in academia: The struggle over the "legiti-mate" knowledge of faculty of color. *Equity & Excellence in Education, 35*(2), 169–180.

Bowers, B. L. (2002). Campus life for faculty of color: Still strangers after all these years? *New Directions for Community Colleges, no. 118* (pp. 79–88). San Francisco, CA: Jossey-Bass.

Bradburn, E. M., & Sikora, A. C. (2002). *Gender and racial/ethnic differences in salary and other characteristics of postsecondary faculty: Fall 1998* (NCES 2002–170). Washington, DC: National Center for Education Statistics.

Brayboy, B. M. J. (2003). The implementation of diversity in predominantly white colleges and universities. *Journal of Black Studies, 34*(1), 72–86.

Brint, S. (2003). Few remaining dreams: Community colleges since 1985. *The Annals of the American Academy of Political and Social Sciences* (March), 16–37.

Burton, C. (2007). *An ethnography of faculty in a community college and a public, regional, comprehensive university.* (Unpublished doctoral dissertation.) North Carolina State University, Raleigh, NC.

Cameron, K. S., & Whetten, D. A. (1983). *Organizational effectiveness: A comparison of multiple models.* New York, NY: Academic Press.

Carter, D. J. (1994). The status of faculty in community colleges: What do we know? *New Directions for Community Colleges, no. 87* (pp. 3–18). San Francisco, CA: Jossey-Bass.

Cataldi, E. F., Fahimi, M., & Bradburn, E. M. (2005). *2004 national study of postsecondary faculty (NSOPF:04): Report on faculty and instructional staff in fall 2003 (NCES 2005–172).* Washington, DC: National Center for Education Statistics.

Chancellor's Office California Community Colleges. (2011). Data mart. Retrieved from http://employeedata. cccco.edu/gender_ethnicity_10.pdf, accessed August 23, 2011.

Chronicle of Higher Education. (2011). *Almanac Issue 2011–12.* LVIII (1), August 26.

Cohen, A. M., & Brawer, F. B. (2008). *The American community college* (5th ed.). San Francisco, CA: Jossey-Bass.

Cohen, A. M., & Outcalt, C. (2001). A profile of the community college professoriate. A report submitted to the small research grant program of the Spencer Foundation. Center for the study of community colleges, Los Angeles, June.

Cooper, J., & Kempner, K. (1993). Lord of the flies community college: A case study of organizational disintegration. *The Review of Higher Education* (Summer), 419–437.

Corson, J. (1960). *Governance of colleges and universities.* New York, NY: McGraw Hill.

Diekhoff, J. (1950). *Democracy's college: Higher education in the local community.* New York, NY: Harper and Brother Publishers.

Diggs, G. A., Garrison-Wade, D. F., Estrada, D., & Galindo, R. (2009). Smiling faces and colored spaces: The experiences of faculty of color pursing tenure in the academy. *Urban Review, 41*, 312–333.

Dougherty, K. (1994). *The contradictory college.* Albany, NY: State University of New York Press.

Eagan, K. (2007). A national picture of part-time community college faculty: Changing trends in demographics and employment characteristics. *New Directions for Community Colleges, no. 140* (pp. 5–14). San Francisco, CA: Jossey-Bass.

Fenelon, J. (2003). Race, research, and tenure: Institutional credibility and the incorporation of African, Latino, and American Indian faculty. *Journal of Black Studies, 34*(1), 87–100.

Frye, J. (1994). Educational paradigms in the professional literature of the community college. In J. Smart (Ed.), *Higher education: Handbook of theory and research* (Vol. X, pp. 181–224). New York, NY: Agathon Press.

Goodman, P. (1962). *The community of scholars.* New York, NY: Random House.

Gregory, S. T. (2001). Black faculty women in the academy: History, status, and future. *The Journal of Negro Education, 70*(3), 124–138.

Grubb, W. N. (1996). *Working in the middle: Strengthening education and training for the mid-skilled labor force.* San Francisco, CA: Jossey-Bass.

Grubb, W. N., Worthen, H., Byrd, B., Webb, E., Badway, N., Case, C., et al. (1999). *Honored but invisible: An inside look at teaching in community colleges.* New York, NY: Routledge.

Hagedorn, L. S., Chi, W., Cepeda, R. M., & McLain, M. (2007). An investigation of critical mass: The role of Latino representation in the success of urban community college students. *Research in Higher Education, 48*(1), 73–91.

Harvey, W. B. (1994). African American faculty in community colleges: Why they aren't there. *New Directions for Community Colleges, 87* (pp. 19–25). San Francisco, CA: Jossey-Bass.

Herideen, P. E. (1998). *Policy, pedagogy and social inequality: Community college student realities in post-industrial America.* Westport, CT: Bergin & Garvey.

Holland, D., Lachiotte, Jr., W., Skinner, D., & Cain, C. (1998). *Identity and agency in cultural worlds.* Cambridge, MA: Harvard University Press.

Jaeger, A., Austin, A., Levin, J., Haley, K., Cox, E., & Ampaw, F. (2009). *A mysterious and sometimes perilous path to the professoriate: Graduate students of color in the research university.* Paper presented at the Association for the Study of Higher Education, Vancouver, BC.

Jaeger, A. J., & Eagan, M. K. (2010). Examining retention and contingent faculty use in a state system of public higher education. *Educational Policy, 24*(4), 1–31.

Jaeger, A., Haley, K., & Levin, J. (2010). *Not all going in the same direction: The effects of social identity on graduate student career choices.* Paper presentation for the annual meeting of the American Educational Research Association, Denver, CO, April.

Kater, S., & Levin, J. (2005). Shared governance in community colleges in the global economy. *Community College Journal of Research and Practice, 29*(1), 1–24.

Kempner, K. (1990). Faculty culture in the community college: Facilitating or hindering learning. *The Review of Higher Education, 13*(2), 215–235.

Levey, T. (2005, November). *Reexamining community college effects: New techniques, new outcomes.* Paper presented at the Association for the Study of Higher Education, Philadelphia.

Levin, J. S. (2007). Faculty work: Tensions between educational and economic values. *The Journal of Higher Education, 77*(1), 62–88.

Levin, J. S. (2008). Community college teaching. In T. Good (Ed.), *21st century education: A reference handbook* (pp. 455–463). Thousand Oaks, CA: Sage Publications.

Levin, J. S., Cox, E., Kisker, C., Cerven, C., Haberler, Z., Smith, M., et al. (2009). *Promising practices: California's community colleges.* Riverside, CA: California Community College Collaborative (C4), University of California, Riverside.

Levin, J. S., Kater, S., & Wagoner, R. (2011). *Community college faculty: At work in the new economy* (2nd ed.). New York, NY: Palgrave Macmillan.

Levin, J. S., & Montero-Hernandez, V. (2009). *Community colleges and their students: Co-construction and organizational identity.* New York, NY: Palgrave Macmillan.

Levin, J. S., Montero-Hernandez, V., & Yoshikawa, S. (2011). *A multi-site case study: The context and production of the academic identity of faculty members in the three-tiered higher education structure in California.* Riverside, CA : University of California.

Levin, J. S., & Shaker, G. (2012). Arrested development, undervalued teaching, and personal satisfaction: The hybrid identity of full-time nontenure-track faculty in U.S. universities. *American Behavioral Scientist.*

Levin, J. S., Shaker, G., & Wagoner, R. (2011). Post neoliberalism: The professional identity of faculty off the tenure-track. In B. Pusser, K. Kempner, S. Marginson, & I. Ordorika (Eds.), *Universities and the public sphere: Knowledge creation and state building in the era of globalization* (pp. 197–217). New York: Routledge.

McGrath, D., & Spear, M. (1991). *The academic crisis of the community college.* Albany, NY: State University of New York Press.

Menges, R. J., & Exum, W. H. (1983). Barriers to the progress of women and minority faculty. *The Journal of Higher Education, 54*(2), 123–144.

Mintzberg, H. (1983). *Power in and around organizations.* Englewood Cliffs, NJ: Prentice Hall.

Mintzberg, H. (1991). The professional bureaucracy. In M. Peterson (Ed.), *Organization and governance in higher education.* Needham Heights, MA: Simon & Schuster.

National Center for Educational Statistics (NCES). (2002). *The condition of education 2002.* Washington, DC: U.S. Department of Education.

National Center for Educational Statistics (NCES). (2008). *The condition of education 2008.* Washington, DC: U.S. Department of Education.

Nettles, M. T., Perna, L. W., & Bradburn, E. M. (2000). *Salary, promotion, and tenure status of minority and women faculty in U.S. colleges and universities, NCES 2000–173.* Washington, DC: U.S. Department of Education. National Center for Education–Statistics.

Nicholas, F. W., Sr., & Oliver, A. R. (1994). Achieving diversity among community college faculty. *New Directions for Community Colleges, no. 87* (pp. 35–42). San Francisco, CA: Jossey-Bass.

Opp, R. D., & Gosetti, P. P. (2002). Women full-time faculty of color in 2-year colleges: A trend and predictive analysis. *Community College Journal of Research and Practice, 26*(7), 609–627.

Opp, R. D., & Smith, A. B. (1994). Effective strategies for enhancing minority faculty recruitment and retention. *New Directions for Community Colleges, no. 87* (pp. 43–55). San Francisco, CA: Jossey-Bass.

Owens, J. S., Reis, F. W., & Hall, K. M. (1994). Bridging the gap: Recruitment and retention of minority faculty members. *New Directions for Community Colleges, no. 87* (pp. 57–64). San Francisco, CA: Jossey-Bass.

Pusser, B., & Levin, J. (2009). *Re-imagining the role of community colleges in the 21st century.* Washington, DC: Center for American Progress.

Ratcliff, J. (1994). Seven streams in the historical development of the modern community college. In G. Baker (Ed.), *A handbook on the community college in America* (pp. 3–16). Westport, CT: Greenwood Press.

Rhoades, G. (1998). *Managed professionals: Unionized faculty and restructuring academic labor.* Albany, NY: State University of New York Press.

Roueche, J., Roueche, S., & Milliron, M. (1995). *Strangers in their own land: Part-time faculty in American community colleges*. Washington, DC: Community College Press.

Sadao, K. C. (1995). *Variables influencing academic career choice and success of ethnic and racial minority faculty at a state research university*. (Unpublished doctoral dissertation.) University of Hawaii, Honolulu, HI.

Sadao, K. C. (2003). Living in two worlds: Success and bicultural faculty of color. *Review of Higher Education, 26*, 397–418.

Santos, J. L., & Melguizo, T. (2007). Increasing baccalaureate attainment rates using California community college transfers: An exploration of cost-effectiveness. *California Community College Collaborative (C4) ejournal, 1*(1).

Schuster, J. K., & Finkelstein, M. J. (2006). *The American faculty: The restructuring of academic work and careers*. Baltimore, MD: Johns Hopkins University Press.

Scott, W. R. (2005). Institutional theory: Contributing to a theoretical research program. In K. G. Smith & M. A. Hirt (Eds.), *Great minds in management: The process of theory development* (pp. 460–484). New York, NY: Oxford University Press.

Seidman, E. (1985). *In the words of the faculty*. San Francisco, CA: Jossey-Bass.

Shaw, K., & Rab, S. (2003). Market rhetoric versus reality in policy and practice: The Workforce Investment Act and access to community college education and training. *The Annals of the American Academy of Political and Social Science* (March), 172–193.

Shaw, K., Rhoads, R., & Valadez, J. (Eds.). (1999). *Community colleges as cultural texts*. Albany, NY: State University of New York Press.

Slaughter, S., & Leslie, L. (1997). *Academic capitalism, politics, policies, and the entrepreneurial university*. Baltimore, MD: The Johns Hopkins University Press.

Stanley, C. A. (2006). Coloring the academic landscape: Faculty of color breaking the silence in predominantly white colleges and universities. *American Educational Research Journal, 43*(4), 701–736.

Tierney, W. (1993). *Building communities of difference: Higher education in the 21st century*. Westport, CT: Bergin and Garvey.

Times, Staff. (2011, June 29). AACC announces members of 21st-Century Commission. Community College Times. Retrieved from communitycollegetimes.com/Pages/Campus-Issues/AACC-announces-members-of-21st-Century-Commission.aspx, accessed July 1, 2011.

Toutkoushian, R. K., Bellas, M. L., & Moore, J. V. (2007). The interaction effects of gender, race, and marital status on faculty salaries. *Journal of Higher Education, 78*(5), 572–601.

Turner, C. S. V. (2002). Women of color in academe: Living with multiple marginality. *Journal of Higher Education, 73*(1), 74–93.

Turner, C. S. V. (2003). Incorporation and marginalization in the academy: From border toward center for faculty of color? *Journal of Black Studies, 34*(1), 112–125.

Turner, C. S. V., Myers, S. L., Jr., & Creswell, J. W. (1999). Exploring underrepresentation: The case of faculty of color in the midwest. *Journal of Higher Education, 70*(1), 27–59.

Twombly, S., & Townsend, B. K. (2008). Community college faculty: What we know and need to know. *Community College Review, 36*(1), 5–24.

Umbach, P. D. (2006). The contribution of faculty of color to undergraduate education. *Research in Higher Education, 47*(3), 317–345.

U.S. Department of Education. (2011). *Digest of educational statistics*. Washington, DC: National Center for Educational Statistics.

Valadez, J. R., & Antony, J. S. (2001). Job satisfaction and commitment of two-year college part-time faculty. *Community College Journal of Research and Practice, 25*, 97–108.

Vaughan, G. (2000). *The community college story*. Washington, DC: American Association of Community Colleges.

Vaughan, G. (2002, March 24). The big squeeze at community colleges. *The News & Observer*.

Watson, D. (2009). *The question of morale: Managing happiness and unhappiness in university life*. New York, NY: Open University Press.

LIST OF CONTRIBUTORS

Marilyn J. Amey is Professor of Higher and Adult Education and Chair of the Department of Educational Administration at Michigan State University. She was previously on the faculty at the University of Kansas and worked in student affairs administration for many years at universities in Ohio. Her research focuses primarily on leadership and postsecondary governance, leadership, organizational change, and faculty issues that fall within that broad rubric. Amey has collaborated on research with the American Association of Community Colleges, serving as principal investigator studying leadership development programs, community college administrative leadership and career development, and the institutional context of community college administration. For the last decade, Amey has examined organizational collaborations within and across educational sectors, interdisciplinary faculty work, and issues associated with leading strategic academic partnerships domestically and internationally.

David F. Ayers is Associate Professor of Higher Education at the University of North Carolina at Greensboro. His research interests include cultural studies, critical discourse analysis, and organization studies in higher education. He holds graduate degrees from Appalachian State University and NC State University and has pursued additional studies at Lancaster University and University of North Carolina, Chapel Hill. Prior to his current appointment, he taught Spanish in North Carolina community colleges and North Carolina public schools.

Michael V. Ayers is a proud graduate of Surry Community College in Dobson, North Carolina, keenly aware of the importance of community colleges. Michael graduated from Surry in 1987 and transferred to Appalachian State University where he earned both a bachelor's degree and a master's degree in biology. Michael has dedicated his 21-year career to the community college. He has served as both biology instructor and science division chairman. Currently, he is Dean of Math, Science, and Technologies at Forsyth Technical Community College in Winston-Salem, North Carolina.

Debra D. Bragg is a professor in the Department of Education Organization, Policy, and Leadership at the University of Illinois and Director of the Office of Community College Research and

Leadership. Her research focuses on P-20 education policy, with a special interest in the transition of youth and adults to college and careers. She has led research funded by federal, state, and foundation sponsors, including examining the participation of underserved students in college transition and career pathways. Recent studies include evaluations of bridge and career pathway programs funded by the Joyce Foundation and the U.S. Department of Education and applied baccalaureate programs funded by Lumina Foundation for Education. Dr. Bragg holds a Ph.D. and master's degree from the Ohio State University, and a bachelor's degree from the University of Illinois. She is the recipient of the career teaching and distinguished research awards from the College of Education at the University of Illinois, and the senior scholar award from the Council for the Study of Community Colleges.

Christine Cerven is currently a postdoctoral Fellow in the Education Studies Department at the University of California, San Diego, co-managing a study that examines the educational pathways of low-income youth in a community college district. This specific study is part of a broader five-year project composed of a set of mixed methods studies that focus on maximizing opportunities for low-income youth to earn higher education credentials. Specifically, her work examines how women students witness an evolving sense of self that includes the development of new epistemological perspectives (i.e., ways of knowing), self-meanings, self-esteem, and expectations for the future as they navigate the community college terrain. She obtained her Ph.D. in Sociology specializing in Social Psychology and Gender Studies at the University of California, Riverside and is dedicated to the interdisciplinary examination of the interplay between identity processes, psychological well-being, and the pursuit of higher education.

Luciana Dar is an assistant professor at the Graduate School of Education at the University of California, Riverside. Her research interests fall into three interconnected areas of inquiry: comparative political economy of higher education, the relationship between higher education and social inequality, and the politics of higher education. She approaches each of these areas with a combination of theoretical and methodological tools from the positive political economy, comparative politics, and public finance literatures in close connection with insights from the public policy and higher education fields. Dr. Dar's recent work seeks to explain why public support for higher education has decreased while the public demand and value of a college education has increased and why states' priorities for higher education are frequently misaligned with states' economic needs. Luciana holds a Ph.D. in Political Science from University of California, Los Angeles and an M.A. in Economics from the Federal University of Rio de Janeiro.

Pamela L. Eddy is an associate professor of higher education in the area of Educational Policy, Planning, and Leadership at the College of William and Mary. Her research interests include community colleges, leadership development, gender roles in higher education, and faculty development. She is author of *Community College Leadership: A Multidimensional Model for Leading Change* (2010) and *Partnerships and Collaborations in Higher Education* (2010). Eddy served as president of the Council for the Study of Community Colleges (2011–2012) and was a recipient of the Council for the Study of Community Colleges 2006 emerging scholar award. She was a 2009 Fulbright Scholar at Dublin Institute of Technology and in 2011 received the Plumeri Award for Faculty of Excellence at the College of William and Mary in recognition of her scholarship.

Tara E. Frank is a doctoral candidate in the Higher Education Administration Program at Virginia Tech. She earned her B.A. and M.S. at Shippensburg University of Pennsylvania. She served as a student services administrator, predominantly in student activities and leadership, at universities in New Jersey, Georgia, and Pennsylvania prior to enrolling in doctoral studies. Her research interests include European higher education, the legal relationship between institution and student, and student services professionals' satisfaction. Her dissertation research focuses on student services professionals and why they depart from the profession.

Linda Serra Hagedorn is Associate Dean of the College of Human Sciences and Professor in the Department of Educational Leadership and Policy Studies at Iowa State University. Hagedorn's research focuses on community college student success, retention, and transfer. She is also a researcher in the area of international students. Prior to joining the faculty at Iowa State University, she directed the Institute of Higher Education at the University of Florida. She was also Director of the Transfer and Retention of Urban Community College Students Project (TRUCCS), a longitudinal study of over 5,000 students enrolled in the Los Angeles Community College District. Although Dr. Hagedorn performs both quantitative and qualitative research, she is especially known for developing techniques to analyze enrollment and other college files. She has created new rubrics and designs for the longitudinal analyses of transcript data (transcript analysis).

Joan B. Hirt is Professor of Higher Education Administration at Virginia Tech. She earned her B.A. at Bucknell University (PA), her M.A.Ed. at the University of Maryland, and her Ph.D. at the University of Arizona. Prior to assuming her faculty role, she served as an administrator at universities in Maryland, California, and Arizona. Her past research focused on the nature of administrative life at different types of institutions and that catalyzed her current interest in administration at universities outside the U.S. She has received numerous professional, teaching, and advising awards from Virginia Tech, the University of Maryland, the American College Personnel Association, the National Association of Student Personnel Administrators, the Association of Fraternity Advisors, and the Association of College and University Housing Officers International.

Susan T. Kater is Director of Institutional Planning, Research, and Effectiveness at GateWay Community College, one of the Maricopa Community Colleges in Phoenix, Arizona. Sue has held a variety of administration positions during her tenure at GateWay, including serving as the acting Executive Director of the Maricopa Skill Center, the vocational skill training arm of the college. Sue has a Ph.D. in Higher Education from the University of Arizona and her research interests and publications center on governance in community colleges, but include faculty issues, student assessment, and student persistence. Having had the privilege of being a doctoral student of both Ed. St. John and John Levin, in addition to this current volume Sue has had the opportunity to collaborate with John Levin on a number of projects, including a review of community college faculty work with Richard Wagoner—*Community College Faculty: At Work in the New Economy* (Palgrave Macmillan, 2006, 2011).

Carrie B. Kisker is an education research and policy consultant in Los Angeles, California, and a director of the Center for the Study of Community Colleges (www.centerforcommunity colleges.org). She engages in relevant and applicable research pertaining to community college policy and practice, and has managed several large projects working to improve community college transfer, governance, coordination, effectiveness, and student success in California and Arizona. Dr. Kisker holds a B.A. in Psychology and Education from Dartmouth College, and an M.A. and Ph.D. in Higher Education from the University of California, Los Angeles. She is co-author, with Arthur M. Cohen, of *The Shaping of American Higher Education: Emergence and Growth of the Contemporary System* (Jossey-Bass, 2nd ed., 2010).

John S. Levin is the Bank of America Professor of Education Leadership and Director and Principal Investigator of the California Community College Collaborative (C4), University of California, Riverside. He is a widely published scholar in the U.S. and an acknowledged expert on community colleges in both the U.S. and Canada. His books in the 2000s include *Globalizing the Community College* (Palgrave, 2001), *Non-Traditional Students and Community Colleges: The Conflict of Justice and Neo-Liberalism* (Palgrave Macmillan, 2007), *Community Colleges and Their Students: Co-Construction and Institutional Identity* (Palgrave Macmillan, 2009), with Virginia Montero Hernandez, and *Community College Faculty: At Work in the New Economy* (Palgrave Macmillan, 2006, 2011), with Susan Kater and Richard Wagoner. His most recent research addresses faculty work, including nontenure track faculty in universities, faculty and institutional practices in Mexican state universities, faculty identity in colleges and universities, and graduate students' career paths to faculty roles.

Lindsey E. Malcom is an assistant professor of higher education administration in the Graduate School of Education and Human Development at the George Washington University. Her research focuses on the relationship between higher education policy and broadening participation in the sciences, engineering, and related (STEM) fields. She is also particularly interested in the role of community colleges and minority-serving institutions in facilitating access and success in STEM for historically underrepresented populations. Malcom received her bachelor's degree from the Massachusetts Institute of Technology, her master's degree from the California Institute of Technology, and her doctorate from the University of Southern California.

Matthew M. Mars is a lecturer and researcher-in-residence in the McGuire Center for Entrepreneurship in the Eller College of Management at the University of Arizona. He teaches courses on topics that include innovation, entrepreneurship, and organizational theory and change. Dr. Mars earned a doctor of philosophy through the Center for the Study of Higher Education at the University of Arizona. Dr. Mars has extensively studied innovation, entrepreneurship, and organizational change within college and university settings and environments. The primary conceptual and theoretical basis of his work includes academic capitalism, neo-institutional theory, and most recently human ecology. His scholarship has appeared in publications such as the *Community College Review, Higher Education, Journal of Management Inquiry, Journal of Change Management,* and *The Journal of Higher Education.*

Ken Meier is an alumnus of Mt. San Antonio Community College. He possesses a B.A. in History from University of California, Los Angeles, an M.A. in European Intellectual History from UC, Irvine, and a Ph.D. in Higher Education Theory and History from the University of Arizona. In 2009 he was awarded the national dissertation of the year award by the Council for the Study of Community Colleges for his work on the history of the community college mission debate in the 20th century. Meier taught history at Yavapai College in Prescott, Arizona where he also served as interim executive dean of instruction and student services. In 2001, he assumed the position of vice president for student learning at Bakersfield College. From 2006 to

2011 he served as vice president for student learning at Butte College in Oroville, California. He is currently vice president of student learning for College of Marin.

Virginia Montero-Hernandez is a graduate from the University of California, Riverside and an assistant professor at the Autonomous University at the State of Morelos, Mexico. Her research analyzes the ways in which university actors, faculty members, and students engage in learning experiences to construct their identity and define personal and professional goals. Dr. Montero-Hernandez has worked with Mexican and U.S. scholars to examine critical issues in the life and work of academics in higher education institutions in both countries. As part of her international collaborative endeavors, Dr. Montero-Hernandez explores the ways in which institutional factors influence the definition of academic practices and curricular structures in universities.

Jim Palmer is a professor of higher education at Illinois State University (ISU). Prior to joining the ISU faculty in 1992, he served as acting director of the Center for Community College Education at George Mason University, vice president for communications at the American Association for Community Colleges, and assistant director of the ERIC Clearinghouse for Community Colleges at the University of California, Los Angeles. At ISU, Palmer teaches courses on the American community college, adult and continuing education, and the history of American higher education. He currently serves as editor of the *Community College Review* as well as editor of the *Grapevine* compilation of state fiscal support for higher education (http://grapevine.illinoisstate.edu).

Dolores Perin is a professor of psychology and education in the Health and Behavior Studies Department, and Senior Research Associate at the Community College Research Center at Teachers College, Columbia University. She coordinates the Applied Educational Psychology Reading Specialist M.A. Program, which prepares students for certification as K-12 reading teachers. Her research interests are in pedagogy, curriculum, teacher preparation, and professional development. She has studied the contextualization of basic academic skills, academic-occupational integration, instructional approaches in developmental education and adult literacy programs, preparation of secondary science and social studies teachers for adolescent literacy, school-to-work transition of moderately handicapped adults, workplace literacy, and adult learning disabilities. She has published in a wide variety of journals including *Community College Review*, *Journal of Developmental Education*, and the *Community College Journal of Research and Practice*, and is a licensed psychologist who has expertise in working with children, adolescents, and adults with learning difficulties.

Yi (Leaf) Zhang, born and raised in Central China, is a postdoctoral fellow in the Department of Educational Leadership and Policy Studies, Iowa State University (ISU). She received her Ph.D. in Educational Leadership from the same department. She is also serving as an assistant to the Associate Dean of the College of Human Sciences at ISU. Her research focuses on community colleges and international education. She serves as a committee member of international education in the College of Human Sciences and on the Council for the Study of Community Colleges (CSCC). With educational and professional experiences in both cultures, her career goal is to strengthen educational exchanges between the U.S. and China.

INDEX